MANY MAPS

The Charles and Joy Staples South West Region Publications Fund was established in 1984 on the basis of a generous donation to The University of Western Australia by Charles and Joy Staples.

The purpose of the Fund is to highlight all aspects of the South West region of Western Australia, a geographical area much loved by Charles and Joy Staples, so as to assist the people of the South West region and those in government and private organisations concerned with South West projects to appreciate the needs and possibilities of the region in the widest possible historical perspective. The fund is administered by a committee whose aims are to make possible the publication by UWA Publishing of research and writing in any discipline relevant to the South West region.

Charles and Joy Staples South West Region Publications Fund titles

1987
A Tribute to the Group Settlers
Philip E. M. Blond

1992
For Their Own Good: Aborigines and Government in the Southwest of Western Australia, 1900–1940
Anna Haebich

1993
Portraits of the South West
B. K. de Garis

A Guide to Sources for the History of South Western Australia
Compiled by Ronald Richards

1994
Jardee: The Mill That Cheated Time
Doreen Owens

1995
Dearest Isabella: Life and Letters of Isabella Ferguson, 1819–1910
Prue Joske

Blacklegs: The Scottish Colliery Strike of 1911 Bill Latter

1997
Barefoot in the Creek: A Group Settlement Childhood in Margaret River L. C. Burton

Ritualist on a Tricycle: Frederick Goldsmith, Church, Nationalism and Society in Western Australia
Colin Holden

Western Australia as it is Today, 1906 Leopoldo Zunini, Royal Consul of Italy, edited and translated by Richard Bosworth and Margot Melia

2002
The South West from Dawn till Dusk Rob Olver

2003
Contested Country: A History of the Northcliffe Area, Western Australia
Patricia Crawford and Ian Crawford

2004
Orchard and Mill: The Story of Bill Lee, South-West Pioneer
Lyn Adams

2005
Richard Spencer: Napoleonic War Naval Hero and Australian Pioneer
Gwen Chessell

2006
A Story to Tell (reprinted 2012)
Laurel Nannup

2008
Alexander Collie: Colonial Surgeon, Naturalist and Explorer
Gwen Chessell

The Zealous Conservator: A Life of Charles Lane Poole
John Dargavel

2009
"It's Still in My Heart, This is My Country": The Single Noongar Claim History South West Aboriginal Land and Sea Council, John Host with Chris Owen

Shaking Hands on the Fringe: Negotiating the Aboriginal World at King George's Sound
Tiffany Shellam

2011
Noongar Mambara Bakitj and *Mamang*
Kim Scott and Wirlomin Noongar Language and Stories Project

Guy Grey-Smith: Life Force
Andrew Gaynor

2013
Dwoort Baal Kaat and *Yira Boornak Nyininy*
Kim Scott and Wirlomin Noongar Language and Stories Project

2014
A Boy's Short Life: The Story of Warren Braedon/Louis Johnson
Anna Haebich and Steve Mickler

Plant Life on the Sandplains: A Global Biodiversity Hotspot
Hans Lambers

Fire and Hearth (revised facsimile edition) Sylvia Hallam

2015
Running Out? Water in Western Australia Ruth Morgan

A Journey Travelled: Aboriginal–European Relations at Albany and Surrounding Regions from First Colonial Contact to 1926
Murray Arnold

The Southwest: Australia's Biodiversity Hotspot
Victoria Laurie

Invisible Country: South-West Australia: Understanding a Landscape Bill Bunbury

2016
Noongar Bush Medicine: Medicinal Plants of the South-West of Western Australia
Vivienne Hansen and John Horsfall

2017
Never Again: Reflections on Environmental Responsibility After Roe 8
Edited by Andrea Gaynor, Peter Newman and Philip Jennings

Ngaawily Nop and *Noorn*
Kim Scott and Wirlomin Noongar Language and Stories Project

2018
Dancing in Shadows: Histories of Nyungar Performance
Anna Haebich

2019
Refuge Richard Rossiter

That Was My Home: Voices from the Noongar Camps in Fremantle and the Western Suburbs
Denise Cook

MANY MAPS

CHARTING TWO CULTURES FIRST NATIONS AND EUROPEANS IN WESTERN AUSTRALIA

BILL AND JENNY BUNBURY

UWAP
UWA PUBLISHING

First published in 2020 by
UWA Publishing
Crawley, Western Australia 6009
www.uwap.uwa.edu.au

UWAP is an imprint of UWA Publishing
a division of The University of Western Australia

THE UNIVERSITY OF
WESTERN
AUSTRALIA

This book is copyright. Apart from any fair dealing for the purpose of private study, research, criticism or review, as permitted under the *Copyright Act 1968*, no part may be reproduced by any process without written permission. Enquiries should be made to the publisher.

Copyright © Bill and Jenny Bunbury 2020

The moral right of the authors have been asserted.

ISBN: 978-1-76080-002-4

NATIONAL LIBRARY OF AUSTRALIA

A catalogue record for this book is available from the National Library of Australia

WESTERN
AUSTRALIAN
HISTORY
FOUNDATION

Cover image by Bill Bunbury
Cover design by Upside Creative
Typeset in Bembo by Lasertype
Printed by Lightning Source

CONTENTS

Contents	v
Introduction	vii
Acknowledgements	xi

1 When Do Ships Die?	1
2 'A Little Bit Occupied by Natives'	35
3 A Moral Wilderness?	91
4 The End of the Beginning or the Beginning of the End?	135
5 Snapped Shut the Lawbook	189
6 The Past Is Still Part of Us	243
Afterthoughts	305

Uluru Statement from the Heart	308
Notes	311
People Mentioned in Text Interviewed by Bill Bunbury 1983–2019	347
Bibliography	349
Photographic credits	365
Index	367

INTRODUCTION

From Bill

For almost four decades, I have been interviewing people both about their lives and their views. Some are or were leaders and/or academics in their field. Others are ordinary Australians (although I have not yet met an ordinary person).

Most of these interviews, or conversations, were undertaken for the ABC's Social History Unit or more recently commissioned by Community Arts Network (WA). In any event, I wanted to ensure these voices would continue to be heard, at least in print. Additional interviews were undertaken specifically for this book (a list of all interviewees is on page 347).

My wife, Jenny, studied history at university while I studied literature, with a predilection for narrative. We had previously written a regional history together and we made an early decision to collaborate again. Jenny has done much of the research and the final editing and writing.

From Bill and Jenny

The idea for this book came from many experiences of listening to and learning from First Nations people, whose long tenure of an island continent has enabled them to develop and nourish a distinct culture and spiritual beliefs, closely and inextricably linked with the country that gave them sustenance and defined their identity.

Bill's book *Invisible Country*, published by UWA Publishing in 2015, chronicles a case study of European adaptation to an unfamiliar

INTRODUCTION

landscape. It describes how in the nineteenth century most new settlers, confident in their own culture, technology and religious certainty, often ignored the earlier 'tenants' or failed to enquire how best to understand the ecology of an unfamiliar landscape. There were notable exceptions but many newcomers neglected to ask the locals. For our First Nations, engagement with this land was governed by spiritual beliefs, codes of conduct and innate understanding of an animate world and was not dictated by Western agricultural practice. Europeans, when they arrived on the Australian continent, were guided by a different map, one which emphasised the economic benefit that the land could provide. But for First Nations people, land was governed by a different benefit; seeing country as an intrinsic part of their identity, their sustenance, their sense of being and the way they mapped their world.

Maps can mean different things to different cultures and the word itself has many applications. A map can chart, record, represent, plot or plan. It is possible to map a path through life, find a way through a forest or traverse a desert, chart a sense of self and guide one's relationship to the natural world.

Many Maps is an attempt to chart understandings and misunderstandings between two cultures over two centuries of European occupation of Australia. We trace two very different ways of looking at the continent we all now inhabit. This enquiry, while confined mainly to Western Australia, a third of the entire continent, is also broadly culturally and physically representative of the rest of Australia in terms of gaps in understanding.

The first chapter, 'When Do Ships Die?', explores reciprocal curiosity in the early nineteenth century when the original occupants met strange newcomers who made attempts to understand a culture based on reverence for nature and a different interpretation of human existence.

Chapter 2, '"A Little Bit Occupied by Natives"', reminds us that prior occupation of the country 'wasn't in the brochures' when the first European settlers came to Western Australia. Australia's First Nations people were soon declared to be 'British subjects' but then deprived of the right to own their own land.

Chapter 3, 'A Moral Wilderness?', takes us into the early nineteenth-century evangelical era, when missionaries came to a landscape lacking temples or churches, with the firm intention of converting 'the natives'

INTRODUCTION

to Christianity, while rarely enquiring whether their potential converts had spiritual beliefs of their own.

Towards the end of the nineteenth century, Aboriginal people in Western Australia began to ask themselves, 'Is this the end of the beginning or the beginning of the end?', a question that provides the title for Chapter 4. The expansion of European settlement inland and particularly to the north of Western Australia was bringing profound change to Aboriginal society, altering the landscape and largely eliminating the traditional Aboriginal sharing economy. The First Nations of this continent could, increasingly, only survive as part of another culture's workforce.

As with religion, European Australians came with their own legal system and remained largely ignorant of Aboriginal law and culture. In Chapter 5, 'Snapped Shut the Lawbook', we hear from Aboriginal people who, for most or all of their lives, were subject to the infamous *Aborigines Act 1905*. The effects of this legislation, including the breakdown of family structures and the separation of children from their parents, created destructive impacts on traditional life.

Chapter 6, 'The Past Is Still Part of Us', explores the fact that in Western Australia, as elsewhere in this country, Aboriginal culture and society had been changed irrevocably by dispersal and adjustment to a white world. However, despite two centuries of dispossession which has included loss of land, non-acceptance and dependence on European institutions, the First Nations people of Western Australia have proved resilient. They have reasserted their cultural identity and have much to share with us, if we are willing to listen.

A number of people Bill interviewed, either for this book or in earlier years, made perceptive comments which we have included in Afterthoughts. These statements are mainly messages of hope for the future. Furthermore, as Fred Chaney emphasises, the Uluru Statement from the Heart is integral to a way forward for Australia's future. We hope that this book, in a small way, also allows Aboriginal and non-Aboriginal people to hear and listen to each other's stories.

Apart from the inclusion of interviews recorded for ABC radio documentaries and Community Arts Network, this book does not claim to be solely the product of original research. We have accessed secondary written sources and relied on academic historians and anthropologists for insights. *Many Maps* could not have been written

INTRODUCTION

without their painstaking and often detailed research. We aimed to summarise and interweave the story of evolving relationships, both positive and negative, between the First Australians and European settlers.

We acknowledge that this is not a comprehensive history of interactions between the two cultures within Western Australia. No account could ever cover that ground or tell all the stories. We have concentrated particularly on events and geographical areas where we had interview material available to highlight what we see as important issues in understanding and misunderstanding over almost two centuries of interaction between the late arrivals and First Nations people.

We have had to make some decisions about spelling, especially of words which have alternative spellings. In general, we have attempted to standardise on one spelling, for example Noongar, except in citing an original reference. Aside from this, wherever possible we have left letters and other original material as written, although this has sometimes involved use of non-standard English.

ACKNOWLEDGEMENTS

This book would never have seen the light of print without the generous help of many people and organisations.

Financial assistance to enable us to travel for research and interviews to regional Western Australia and to purchase essential material was received from the Western Australian History Foundation (secretary Lenore Layman).

Community Arts Network (CAN) has been a strong partner in this enterprise and commissioned many of the interviews from which we have drawn. Monica Kane and June Moorhouse have supported this project throughout and helped to ensure that we contacted all the people quoted in the Yagan and Central Eastern Wheatbelt audio documentary programs. CAN made it possible for Yolande Ward to travel to the Wheatbelt and make the important and necessary connections with Barladong people. Yolande was also instrumental in helping us obtain the agreement of some of the original interviewees to include their contributions. Ivy Penny, also formerly with CAN, has also been a valued colleague, identifying contributors and providing wise advice.

Local historians Bevan and Jennie Carter read the first draft and provided invaluable additional information. We very much appreciate their support and enthusiasm for this project. Our good friend Judith O'Keeffe (Murphy) read the second draft and saved us from some previously undetected pitfalls.

The Undalup Association Inc. (Busselton) has been a great support throughout the latter stages of this project. Wadandi Cultural and Traditional Custodian Wayne Webb and Toni Webb kindly read and

ACKNOWLEDGEMENTS

commented on our second draft. We are very grateful for their support and endorsement of this book. Undalup Vice-Chairperson Rachelle Cousins smoothed our path and provided wise advice in ensuring that we observed correct protocols in writing about Noongar people and culture, including the Wadandi (the Saltwater People of the Busselton and Cape to Cape region). Craig McVee, chairperson of the Kojonup Aboriginal Association, kindly allowed us to use a depiction of the original Kodj Place mural in Kojonup while Iszaac Webb gave us a Wadandi map of the Capes region of south-west Australia.

Special thanks to Claire Hadley, Claire Preston and all the staff at the Margaret River branch of the Augusta–Margaret River Library who ordered and patiently re-ordered books for us from Inter-library loans over a lengthy period, while Janice Bowra (Flying Fingers) prepared accurate transcripts of oral history interviews, often with very short deadlines.

Grateful thanks also to the following who lent books and provided information and advice, photographs and/or documents, sometimes in addition to their helpful interviews: Dr Murray Arnold, Peter Bindon, Carol Bolton, Grant Boxer, Keith Bradby, Fred Chaney, Dr Cathie Clement, Dr Denise Cook, Steve Hawke, Peter Hocking, Dr Jackie Huggins, Professor John Kinder, Steve Kinnane, Kim Lofts, Dr Neville Marchant, Patrick Richardson-Bunbury, Margaret Robertson, Professor Bruce Scates, Dr Tiffany Shellam, Dr Rowan Strong, Wendy Thorn, Emeritus Professor Robert Tonkinson and Myra Tonkinson, Professor Sandy Toussaint, Malcolm Traill and the Albany Museum, Ruth and Dr David Watson, and Ann Williams, Archivist at the Ravensthorpe Historical Society.

We would also like to acknowledge the help we have received from other organisations and individuals. Dr Chris Owen and other dedicated librarians at the State Library of WA went out of their way to ensure that source books were available exactly when we needed them. We are also indebted to a number of other local libraries for finding books at short notice for us. We received help from staff of the WA Museum (including Moya Smith), the Department of Mines, Industry Regulation and Safety (including Sarah Roberts) and *The Record* (published by the Catholic Diocese of Perth). ABC Kimberley (Vanessa Mills and Sam Tomlin), Shire of Halls Creek (Natasha Niven), Kimberley Web Design (Amanda McInerney), and Jill Harrison and

ACKNOWLEDGEMENTS

the Ravensthorpe Historical Society (Ann Williams), all searched out photographs for us. Bob Symons of the ACE Camera Club kindly took some additional photographs around Albany for us

We would also like to record our appreciation of the support and encouragement which Terri-ann White, Kate Pickard, our editor Kelly Somers and all the staff at UWA Publishing have shown us over several years.

Bill and Jenny Bunbury, May 2020
Margaret River, Western Australia

Chapter 1

When Do Ships Die?

It's a question Mokare, a Menang man, asks his friend, Englishman Collet Barker, commandant of the occupying force at King George Sound (present-day Albany), in 1830 during one of their many conversations.[1]

The Menang, a group or clan of Noongar Aboriginal people, had inhabited this area from time immemorial. Their vantage points were high above the Sound, on the hills that we now know as Mount Clarence and Mount Melville, as Menang Elder Vernice Gillies explains.

> *I imagine that the people of long ago would have used the hills around here to actually climb and to observe, particularly Mount Clarence – Corndarup, we call it – and Mount Melville, which is Kardarup. They would have used that as their lookout. You can see way, way out into the distance from those hills. So, they would have used the height around here to actually look out there to see where the fires were and where the camps were, who was coming, who wasn't coming, and I think from that they were also able to look at the country and mind-map it.*[2]

Looking out from Mount Clarence. Photo by Bob Symons.

Although a coastal people, the Menang were not seafarers. Thus, traditionally, ships would not have featured in their 'mind-map'. But after Albany's natural harbour was charted by English explorer, Captain Vancouver, in 1791, they had become used to European ships visiting the natural harbour, now named by the British for King George III, the reigning monarch. Within his lifetime, Mokare would have seen several of these unfamiliar 'beings'. In his discussion with Collet Barker, Mokare was showing obvious interest in the enormous and unfamiliar structures the newcomers were bringing to their shores. But his question is as interesting as any conceivable answer.

On the one hand Mokare's curiosity might suggest a technical interest in the construction of such vessels. In this sense it is a perfectly understandable enquiry. How long do these structures last? After all, ships do rot, sink or wear out and get broken up. Collet Barker's account of this conversation suggests that he saw Mokare's curiosity as technical.

Enquired the age of Ships, how long they would last before they broke up, or <u>died</u>, as he called it. How it was managed to build them on the water & in what way the carpenters continued to make a beginning, which seemed to puzzle him not a little.[3]

But Mokare's application of the word 'died' might equally suggest something intrinsic to the culture and understanding of his world, a world with a different perception of what was 'animate' or 'inanimate'. Wadandi Cultural Custodian Iszaac Webb describes that understanding.

> *For us as first people, First Nations people, I guess we always look out to the ocean and so, as saltwater people, we see the ocean and the sky meet together and that place is what we call Koranup and that is like a resting place or a stopover where your spirit will go back to, before it journeys back. And the old people sing you back and you are reborn or rebirthed into the country, so you will become a tree or an animal, an object whether it is animate or inanimate. So whether it is a dolphin swimming in the water or just the rock that sits beside the river or in the ocean, they cannot be disconnected from either one. I guess that's the connectivity.*[4]

Historian Tiffany Shellam, author of *Shaking Hands on the Fringe*, mentions Mokare's understandable enquiry in her account of conversations between the Menang and members of a garrison sent from Britain in late 1826.[5] She agrees that Mokare's question is probably metaphysical.

> *And I say that now with more confidence than when I wrote* Shaking Hands on the Fringe *because I've been reading other exploration accounts. They included one where Migeo, a Whadjuk Noongar who travelled as an intermediary aboard* The Beagle, *described to the ship's chronicler, Assistant Surveyor Lieutenant John Lort Stokes, his sense of the ship as a 'being'.*[6]

> *His description of the ship's sailing and anchoring were most amusing to Stokes: Migeo would say, 'Ship walk – walk – all night – hard walk – then by and by, anchor tumble down'.*[7]

Shellam adds:

> *There are clear suggestions that ships could be live beings and I've heard volumes about Aboriginal connection to land and water and animal life. You can see this in terms of their totems and their strong connection to animals and a lot of their Dreaming or Creation stories are about these beings having this metaphysical characteristic.*[8]

As a historian, Shellam is highly conscious of the interpretation of words spoken or written in another, different time frame, words which often carry distinct and varied cultural meanings, a point she acknowledges in a chapter of *Shaking Hands on the Fringe* entitled 'Finding My Own Vocabulary for Encounters'.[9] This approach seems helpful in unpicking understanding and misunderstanding between two very different cultures. An examination of the exchange of knowledge between the original inhabitants of the King George Sound region and the British garrison after 1826 offers valuable and thought-provoking insight into the way two cultures tried to discover and understand each other. The Menang were well aware of the presence of strange vessels. They seem to have had a way in which they could read ships. Different kinds of ships meant different kinds of trading encounters and there are records of that knowledge in early accounts.[10]

The European ships did not die. They kept coming and would bring more people to 'a new world' and, in the process, change both the lifestyle of the original inhabitants and the local landscape. Noongar Elder Lynette Knapp is a Menang descendant and closely understands the country around Albany and the way it has changed. She is concerned about what she now sees in her local area.

> *These waterways are created by the serpent, the Wagyl. It's not something on the surface of the soil, it's also underneath as well. All our swamps and waterways all connect. So, when I see houses and country being cleared, and a lot of rubbish then filling a waterhole, that's a waterhole our serpents can't come up and breathe through. All our swamps and waterways are our serpents' breath ways. And if you build houses there you break that.*[11]

Waterway created by the Wagyl. Photo by Bob Symons.

Commandant Collet Barker and his predecessors, Major Lockyer and Captain Joseph Wakefield, were by no means the first Europeans to explore the area, nor were they the earliest white men to observe Australian First Nations people and their way of life at close quarters. Other white visitors had 'called in' to what had become known to Europeans, as far back as the seventeenth century, as 'New Holland', but their accounts of contact contain few helpful observations about Aboriginal society.

The Dutch East India Company, the VOC (Verenigde Oost-Indische Compagnie), had benefitted from Hendrik Brouwer's discovery in 1611 of a faster way to reach their Asian trade empire. By sailing directly east from the Cape of Good Hope and turning north parallel to the west coast of Australia, sailors could avoid the becalming doldrums of the Indian Ocean and rapidly reach Batavia (now Jakarta) in the then Dutch East Indies. But the *Brouwersroute* could be dangerous. Without accurate longitude measurements, ships could, and did, drift too close to land and collide with the continent's reef-strewn western shores.

Shipwrecks aside, New Holland seemed to have little to offer spice traders, and planned visits were rare.

Occasionally sailors deliberately made landfall. On 29 December 1696, Dutch captain Willem de Vlamingh landed on Rottnest Island, which he named for the native animals he thought to be rats, in fact quokkas. Overall, as his journal attests, Vlamingh liked what he saw.

> I had great pleasure in admiring this island, which is very attractive, and where it seems to me that nature has denied nothing to make it pleasurable beyond all islands I have ever seen, being very well provided for man's well-being, with timber, stone, and lime for building him houses, only lacking ploughmen to fill these fine plains. There is plentiful salt and the coast is full of fish. Birds make themselves heard with pleasant song in these scented groves.
>
> So, I believe that of the many people who seek to make themselves happy, there are many who would scorn the fortunes of our country for the choice of this one here, which would seem a paradise on earth.[12]

Vlamingh was correct in assuming that no one inhabited this paradise, known to the Noongar people as Wadjemup, which means 'place across the water where the spirits are'.[13] The island does not appear to have been inhabited by Aboriginal people after it was cut off from the mainland during the last ice age some 7,000 years ago.[14]

Vlamingh was unsuccessful in meeting any of the inhabitants of the mainland but he sailed a long way up the Swan River. Beyond the present site of Perth, he observed numerous black swans and also many signs of human habitation, huts and smoke from fires.[15] Despite trying, he failed to meet any of the local people. But they would have been observing these strangers, unseen. In the words of Noongar scholar Len Collard:

> Imagine what Nyungar [man] must have thought. Here they were having watched the very conspicuous djanga [spirits] come ashore

and prepare to explore their boodjar or land. Without doubt Nyungar would have had enough warning to make themselves scarce and likely would have hidden and observed these strange people. Nyungar families would come to say many times over, they would have given each other instructions to:

> Balayi, barl, koorliny nidja. Nguny koorliny djinang baal unna.
> *Look out, here they come. We'll go and hide in the bush and watch them eh?*[16]

William Dampier – English buccaneer, sometimes labelled pirate, but also explorer and author – wrote very informatively about many of the places he visited in his voyages of discovery. But he was not impressed by the western coast of New Holland or its inhabitants when he landed there in 1697 and again in 1699. Dampier did meet with Aboriginal people on numerous occasions and even tried, without success, to use them as water carriers. He reported unfavourably on their physical appearance and concluded that, in addition to the northern coastal shores being 'barren and unproductive', its inhabitants were 'the miserablest people in the world for they have no houses', appeared not to 'worship anything' and failed to till the soil or pasture livestock. Moreover, they did not possess 'iron or any other sort of metal'.[17] Furthermore, Dampier noted that 'unlike the great variety of savages' he had encountered, the Australian Aborigines had 'no houses and skin garments, sheep, poultry and fruits of the earth'.[18]

As linguist John Kinder has noted, Dampier was the first Englishman to use the term 'savage' in this context. Kinder suggests why Dampier regarded these people as miserable.

> *Firstly, because they are different, and secondly because they are savages living in forests. Now the opposite of 'savage' in the vocabulary of European philosophy of the time, is 'civilised'. So, to an educated man of that time it is very clear what 'savage' meant. Selvaticus in Latin is a neutral, scientific, descriptive term meaning a person who lives in a forest, as opposed to a city-dweller* [19]

So, does the term 'savage' or 'sauvage' mean wild or barbaric?

> *The word 'wild' has, for us, acquired the connotation of 'out of control' etcetera. I think it meant 'barbaric' later. When Captain Cook, Flinders and others came, they had instructions from the King to treat the 'natives' with respect. But before Cook, in the earlier eighteenth century, the English always talked about the 'savage'.*[20]

Dampier's bleak assessment of the 'miserablest people' significantly influenced the expectations of later British and French visitors as eighteenth-century exploration led to increasing contact with the inhabitants of the 'Great South Land'.

British naval officer and maritime explorer George Vancouver was the first known European to traverse the south coast of 'New Holland'. He named the harbour he 'discovered' in 1791 'King George the Third's Sound'. Vancouver called in to get fresh water and to cut wood for ship repairs. He also mapped some of the country. He did not meet any Aboriginal people, although he saw huts and left beads, knives, looking glasses and

Vancouver 'discovered' King George Sound.

other trinkets in recompense for wood he had taken. As Shellam notes, 'encounters may happen even when actual meetings do not. The local inhabitants were presumably watching, studying and discussing the strangers.'[21] Commenting on an Aboriginal bough shelter, Vancouver appears to echo William Dampier, describing it as, 'The most miserable human habitation my eyes ever beheld'.[22] In short, Vancouver was not impressed by what he saw of human existence at the Sound. He was more taken with the potential for commercial exploitation of the seals and whales that he observed as he sailed into the harbour.

It is likely that in the twenty-five years following Vancouver's visit the Menang had reasonably regular contact with European visitors. As historian Murray Arnold has pointed out, once King George Sound had been charted, whaling ships frequently called in and took advantage of the safe harbour.[23]

The next official British visitor was Matthew Flinders, on his mission to complete the mapping of the Australian coastline. One of his instructions from the British was to determine whether New Holland was part of the same landmass as New South Wales. Flinders had an Aboriginal man from Port Jackson on board and arrived at the Sound in December 1801 when the Menang were at the coast, taking advantage of seasonal food. He made a number of contacts with them and, on 30 December, Flinders engaged his soldiers in an exhibition of military drill, a display the Menang apparently imitated later as a dance.[24]

Other French and British sailors made landfall between 1801 and 1826. The late eighteenth century was still the 'Age of Enlightenment' in Europe and scientific curiosity exercised the minds of explorers and astronomers alike. The Enlightenment also encouraged investigation of indigenous cultures, and the French, in particular, took a keen interest in the concept of 'the noble savage'. Australian Aboriginal people appeared in many ways to match that description.

This curiosity is particularly evident from French explorer Nicolas Baudin's detailed anthropological encounters with the original Tasmanians. Baudin also visited King George Sound in 1801 and his men camped along the Kalgan River, where they observed the ingenious fish traps created by original inhabitants in Oyster Harbour. Vernice Gillies is a descendant of the people who built these constructions.

> *The age is anywhere between six-and-a-half and ten thousand years old, so they're ancient fish traps. They were used by the Menang people a long, long time ago, obviously, and they were very, very clever about farming the fish. They were built in such a way that there were little holes between the stone arrangements, so that when the tide started to drop, the fingerlings would escape. The larger fish would, of course, be trapped behind.*[25]

Baudin's first encounter with Noongar people had been at Geographe Bay, where they shied away from gifts offered and fled without making contact. Later Baudin's party met a group of men armed with spears. At this point, the French chose to retreat and avoid bloodshed.[26] However, according to historians Konishi

Oyster Harbour fish traps.

and Nugent, the French remained relatively open to making contact as they continued their exploration of the continent.[27]

In October 1826, two months before Major Edmund Lockyer brought the brig *Amity* into King George Sound and claimed the territory for Britain, another French expedition under the command of Jules Dumont D'Urville, sailed into the same harbour. He was there partly to repair damage to his ship, the *Astrolabe*, but probably also to look at possibilities for settlement.

French interest in the native people continued. They rowed into Oyster Harbour in their whaleboat and the sailors made for the shore when they saw native fires. Here they encountered a man of about forty years of age with a long beard. The French recorded that he had straight black hair, a long beard and a pierced membrane between his nostrils. Eventually he got into the whaleboat and spent the night on the *Astrolabe*. Apparently, everyone aboard made friends with him and he was delighted to receive many presents from the French. Dumont D'Urville records that, among others, there was one native called Maukorrai, almost certainly Collet Barker's friend, Mokare.[28]

The ship's artist, Louis Auguste de Sainson, drew Maukorrai and captured meetings between the Europeans and the Menang. He also described them in print.

> Their bright expressive eyes observed us with curiosity and roved all over us. Their thin hard hands alternately touching our clothing and our skin and every word we uttered amazed them and provoked laughter. One of the natural ways to start a conversation with them was to tell them our names and learn theirs. A lot of repetition was necessary before they managed to articulate words for which their vocal cords seemed inadequate. This custom that travellers have found to be widespread among the archipelagos of the Southern Ocean certainly amazed us among these human beings who seemed to us so little endowed with intelligence. The exchange of names took place to their great satisfaction.[29]

Clearly the French were still not sure what to make of their new acquaintances, given that being 'so little endowed with intelligence' appeared to be at odds with the friendly and inquisitive reception they received.

What do these early encounters by Europeans tell us about their perceptions of the Aboriginal people they met? Tiffany Shellam suggests that:

> *The French were disappointed, as they often were, when the Aboriginal people didn't take up their presents. And they saw that as a lack of curiosity, whereas actually that mightn't have been the case. But the French and the Menang spent nights together, camping side by side, so even at that stage there was quite a welcome and an intimacy between the Menang and these visitors.*[30]

While intimacy might have been the order of the day, the way most Europeans viewed 'native' people at this time was based on assumptions of their primitiveness, their savageness. That theme is also present in other accounts. Phillip Parker King, a British naval officer and hydrographer, who made several visits to King George Sound between 1818 and 1821, was disgusted that the native people would eat the putrefied flesh of a whale that was dying on the beach.[31]

However, King did comment on the quality and diversity of spear-making at Oyster Harbour and he was well aware that when it came to trading with the Europeans, the Menang deliberately made some weapons for what was in effect 'a tourist trade'. These spears were not made with the same care and were not of the same quality as the weapons made for hunting.[32]

In addition to learning quickly how to trade with their European visitors, the local people diversified their language skills in order to communicate more effectively and extend contact. When King arrived in 1818 and again in 1821, they spoke to him using the Port Jackson (NSW) word for water, Badu Badu. 'Water' was often the first request and understandably a common word for thirsty seafarers. According to Shellam, there was an

Replica of *Amity*, arrived December 1826.

expectation among the Menang that these Europeans had come from another place and thus would have picked up words from a different Aboriginal language (the Port Jackson vocabulary) before coming to King George Sound.[33]

More continuous interaction between these two distinctly different cultures came with the arrival of Major Edmund Lockyer on Christmas Day 1826. He brought with him twenty-three convicts and a small detachment of soldiers.[34] Lockyer's orders were to claim 'New Holland' for Britain in order to forestall any similar claim by the French, who held a long-term interest in Australia, despite it being for them *La Terre Sauvage* or *La Terre Inconnu* – a wild and unknown country. The term *sauvage*, savages or forest dwellers, also applied to the inhabitants, as John Kinder has shown.

Kinder has pointed out that the British dropped the term 'savage' in favour of 'native' as the latter term better suited recognition of the need to negotiate with the original inhabitants.

I think when England decided to take possession of a place like Australia, they knew full well that there were people living here. The question was, what were the legalities of ownership? Accordingly, they dropped the word 'savage' in favour of 'native' which means a person born in that place because the English had to negotiate some kind of legal compromise about ownership of the country.[35]

The legal compromise meant that, although the English invaders also introduced the concept of *terra nullius* (unoccupied land), their intention was that the natives would become British subjects and that British law and justice would apply to both native and newcomer.

These legal niceties would not have been at the forefront of Lockyer's mind in 1826. First, he had to ensure the stability of his venture through careful handling of conflicts both within his own small party and with the local people. An early test of understanding came with the spearing by the Menang of one of Lockyer's men, Dennis Dineen, seemingly in retaliation for the killing of one of their own people. White sealers, not British

Michaelmas Island. Photo by Bob Symons.

soldiers, had abducted and kidnapped Menang men and women and marooned them on nearby Michaelmas Island. Dineen had perhaps been mistaken for one of the abductors.

Lockyer and his crew had noticed a fire on the island. It appeared to indicate distress. Boats were sent to investigate and returned with some of the abducted Aboriginal people. At this point, Dineen was unexpectedly speared. Tiffany Shellam describes how Lockyer defused a volatile situation, while, as he saw it, upholding British law.

> *It's not a fatal spearing, none of the spears were aimed at vital organs, but, as I read it, Lockyer used this moment to show the local people what British law was about and how to serve justice. He's very keen to show that he's a fair man. His aim is to bring the sealers to account for murder, not to retaliate against the spearing of Dineen. For him it's a matter of the majesty of British law and conflict resolution.*[36]

This approach was almost certainly lost on the Menang. Similarly, it would not have occurred to Lockyer that, with the act of spearing, the Menang had served justice on *their* own terms. Retaliatory spearing for them was, most importantly, about putting their social world back in order. Three spears in Dineen and honour was satisfied.[37]

Whatever the understandings or misunderstandings that arose from this incident, a unique relationship then evolved between Europeans and the Menang people, an association which, as Shellam has shown, was built on previous encounters with European visitors.

> *By the time Lockyer arrived, there had been about three decades of meetings with British and French explorers and with American sealers who were very active around that southern coast. The Europeans recorded the local language and made a lot of scientific observations as well. Their enquiries were genuine and influenced by the spirit of the Enlightenment. I think there was a curiosity on both sides, particularly deriving from Phillip Parker King's earlier encounters, and on the British side there was a lot of interest in the Menang people.*[38]

Isaac Scott Nind, the first medical officer at the garrison, was one newcomer who showed particular interest in the people living around King George Sound. He arrived with Lockyer in 1826 and stayed for three years. Nind compiled a vocabulary of the local language and seems to have found relief from a sense of isolation in a strange land through friendship with the Menang. He mentions Mokare, who he calls 'Mawcarri, a native black who has now resided with me many months'.[39] Shellam suggests that Nind was 'on the edge of his own sanity' at King George Sound and very unwell. At the same time, however, he was a keen observer of Menang life and documented important observations. 'So Nind must have been close enough and intimate with them to have done that…He's a keen ethnographer, really observing what's going on.'[40]

In the spirit of the Enlightenment, Scott Nind observed and recorded, in great detail, aspects of the lives and behaviour of the Menang.

> Painting the body, with the natives of this part of the country, is not, as in New South Wales, a sign of war. It is considered by them merely as an ornament and is never neglected at their dances, or when they visit neighbouring tribes. It is a very general practice at those seasons of the year when they can procure fat from fish or animals; but there are some individuals we have remarked who very seldom use it.[41]

Nind provides us with a very clear picture of some aspects of Menang life. However, we have to thank the last commandant of the garrison, Collet Barker, for a richer knowledge of the relationship between the British and the local people. Barker was at King George Sound for just over a year (1830–31) and wrote a diary or journal of his life and work there. This included detailed records of his friendship with the Menang, and in particular with Mokare. We are also strongly indebted to teacher and historian Neville Green, who first realised the value of Barker's diaries – documents which had lain undeciphered for almost 150 years.

In the 1970s Green began to transcribe Barker's almost illegible handwriting.

> *Being a school teacher and feeling I could read anything that anyone had ever written, I decided to get microfilms from the Sydney Mitchell Library of Barker's manuscript. They turned out to constitute two hundred pages of very tight, small, difficult to read writing. I wrestled with it for a while and found the only way I could handle it was to put it into an old Aldis school projector, project the writing onto the wall and sit there with a tape recorder night after night trying to work out the words.*[42]

Green's diligence has given us a picture of a relationship between two people who were genuinely curious about each other's culture.

> *Barker and many of his predecessors had found that the Aboriginal people were interesting and interested in them. Barker would invite them into his house and there are many beautiful vignettes of Aboriginal men sitting round his kitchen, sharing jokes, laughing, sometimes letting Barker into stories where Mokare, who had some command of English, is explaining the stories to him. At other times they're having a grand old time with tea and biscuits with Collet Barker.*[43]

Despite this recognisable image of a conversation over tea and biscuits, the past is still often a foreign country and so are its people. As a twenty-first century Australian, Shellam sensed that the mindsets of early nineteenth-century British soldiers and their Menang counterparts were equally unfamiliar to her. To understand these protagonists, she had to learn about their backgrounds.

> *When I first started reading the accounts from Major Lockyer and his successors, including Captain Collet Barker, I realised how foreign they were to me, as foreign as the Indigenous people of that time, and I thought I could not assume that I could relate to what they were experiencing. I had to make them strangers before I could really understand them. Collet Barker had brought his background in the Napoleonic wars with him.*

> *It influenced how he understood Indigenous violence, judged it, policed it and asked himself questions about how to handle it.*[44]

As a military man, Collet Barker fully understood, and had been involved in, violence on European battlefields. But on the south coast of another continent and another hemisphere, he had to come to terms with different manifestations of aggression. One aspect of violence was the continual tension between the Menang and a powerful clan to their north, the Wills people, considered to be physically superior. These people were large individuals, who engaged in warfare and were politically dominant in terms of controlling both country and resources. Shellam comments that internal violence within Menang society was another disturbing aspect of the relationship between the garrison and the long-term inhabitants.

> *There's a lot of commentary in Barker's journal about Indigenous violence and its causes, and part of the cause is women and marriages. Barker doesn't see much of this himself but these stories come to him.*[45]

Stories about violence emphasise different cultural perspectives, notably, for example, the concept of single spearing in retaliation for an injury or insult. It was a practice that illustrated the potential for misunderstanding between the two societies.

> *Mokare is trying to explain to Barker 'A spear for a spear'. There is a sense that Mokare also wants this practice to stop; there is a concern that this is not right. He talks about different encounters way back in the past and about violence changing over time. There is an understanding about violence but the different commanders, Lockyer, Wakefield and Barker, understand violence in different ways and they police it in different ways. This is relevant because it becomes a conundrum for the soon-to-be settlers in the Swan River Colony.*[46]

What do they do about this violence and are these people now potentially British subjects? Do they police them under their laws? Or is it 'out of sight, out of mind'? Where are the loopholes and what does Barker do about them? As commandant he has several tasks: watching out for the French and looking after his staff, while at the same time sustaining a friendly relationship with his 'hosts', the Menang. Shellam sees this third task, while aided by his friendship with Mokare, as nonetheless one of control.

> *I am not sure whether he singles out Mokare as his friend for tactical reasons. But he certainly uses tea, biscuits and food as a way of controlling people. Bribing and handshakes are a key part of that as well, and these strategies develop together but perhaps that sense of military order is always there. That's the entire backdrop for this settlement period: violence going on in the north and a background that Barker is painfully trying to understand and control, but knows that he can't.*[47]

As Barker himself understands, the power balance at King George Sound is crucial.

> In our present weak state it is desirable to interfere by acts as little as possible with their customs, however much one may wish some of them abolished. By a contrary proceeding we might draw down their enmity to us without producing any good. As we have not power to rule them we must at present be content with endeavouring to reform them by persuasion.[48]

It is also possible that the Menang saw the British as protectors and, in political terms, as useful allies in taking retaliatory action against the Wills people to their north. Barker, on the other hand, had very limited military resources and no inclination to become involved in tribal warfare.

Clan conflict aside, personal relationships were important for both parties. Barker maintained his journal for most of the time he was stationed at King George Sound. Almost every day he mentions local Menang men turning up at his house while, as with Isaac Scott Nind, his relationship with Mokare was special. On at least one occasion Barker put off an exploration journey because Mokare was too ill to travel:

> 1 February 1830…Mokare still very unwell and we must put off our expedition as I would not go without him, after promising he should accompany us.[49]

Tiffany Shellam points out that Mokare was ideally placed in Menang society as an intermediary with the newcomers, although he was not the senior person there. His older brother Nakinah was, as the British called him, the 'king' of the tribe. Mokare was a single man who had the freedom to live with the soldiers in the settlement. And he, in turn, found a richness in being able to engage with these Europeans.[50]

Neville Green comments that there is no doubt that Barker enjoyed Mokare's companionship and we know from many entries in Barker's journal that their relationship extended to conversations about Aboriginal beliefs and understandings. For example, on 3 June 1831, he wrote:

> Passed a pleasant evening enough, Mokare entertaining me with his knowledge of the stars & the seasons. Pointed out by them & by some *fabulous* histories told him by his father, but which he seemed to have a kind of belief in.[51]

From an interview in *Talking History*, Green comments:

> *Barker is so involved, and so connected in friendship with Mokare and his relatives, that he cries when one of Mokare's brothers dies. Taragon had been bitten on the hand by a snake. The garrison doctor and the soldiers went out to the Aboriginal community. They constructed a hut for Taragon to rest in and brought him soup. He seemed to be recovering but when Barker arrived, he found the young man had just died. The community was expressing deep grief.*[52]

He describes the moment:

> To show my sympathy with them I sat down at the foot of the corpse opposite Nakinah and, while mingling my tears with theirs, for I felt sincerely for Taragon who was of a most amiable character. I could not help observing that his brothers showed

their sorrow in a less violent way than most of the others. It was deep however, but they were not absorbed in it but they, two or three times, seized my hand in a very natural and feeling way, as grateful for my sympathy.[53]

Barker also records that he returned to Taragon's grave to shake hands with Nakinah. Shaking hands, or failing to do so, was an important ritual at King George Sound. Handshakes perhaps suggested a gesture, physical recognition and goodwill where interests coincided. As Shellam read about life at King George Sound, she became aware that:

> *the first thing that happens are these handshakes. And I questioned whether this was simply a European gesture or whether this was an Indigenous gesture as well. I tried to unpack the idea of open hands and shaking hands as important in understanding the idea of friendship and peace.*[54]

Withdrawing a hand could also be used as a tactic to punish people. Alternatively, Mokare used hand shaking with the Wills people to denote that they were no longer at war. On another occasion Barker records that when two of the Menang would not come into the settlement, Mokare said that he would go the next day and shake hands with these men.[55]

Whether or not handshakes were a new departure for the Menang or a practice introduced by Europeans, there is no doubt that increased contact with white men began to alter the behaviour of the First Australians in various ways. Isaac Scott Nind recorded that they began to include shellfish, formerly a forbidden food, in their diet, after they saw the British eat these with no ill effects.[56] The Menang also donned kangaroo skins when dancing as they became aware that the British did not approve of people appearing naked in public.[57]

Trading with the British also brought changes. Some of the soldiers wanted to keep parrots as pets so these became a tradeable item. This in turn modified Menang practices of bird hunting.[58] Spears were often an item of trade. On one occasion Mokare reported that they had no spears left with which to fight the Wills men as they had given them all to the British.[59]

The fact that the garrison was in effect a 'holding station' is important in this story. King George Sound was not, initially, a permanent settlement. Four years of dialogue progressed in a relatively calm atmosphere. Shellam sees conversations and companionship as very important in this time.

> *Mokare's very interested in Barker's own collection of plants and natural specimens. And he had questions about where England was and the countries around it and you can see that Mokare was trying to conceptualise this man and his country.*[60]

There is also a sense that the Menang people wanted to share knowledge of their own country and to tell Barker about the distant lands to the west of the Sound and around Mount Manypeaks to the east.

Barker records stories from Mokare that describe a spiritual geography and he relates these to his own Christian beliefs. For example, when Mokare describes the creation of Oyster Harbour

Mt Manypeaks.

and the waterways, Barker wonders if this is an account of the Deluge, the Great Flood described in Genesis. Shellam is not sure whether Barker completely gets the Indigenous sense of animate land and water. 'But he understands how the country is filled with stories and he sees this rich connection through those stories.'[61]

Historians John Host and Chris Owen have also looked closely at Barker's writings. They acknowledge his affection for Mokare and his ability to relate to the people of King George Sound. However, in their view, Barker had difficulty in understanding the Menang because he was trying to make sense of a world that was not susceptible to Western logic. Land ownership is a case in point. For Europeans, individual land ownership is a proprietary right under which land is an asset that can be bought or sold; in contrast, under traditional Noongar lore, territory is inalienable. In fact, the very concept of alienation in the Western sense was incomprehensible to Noongar people, including the Menang.[62]

In his evocative historical novel *That Deadman Dance*, Kim Scott, a writer with strong connections to the Albany region and to its original owners, takes up the theme of land and ownership. Researching the story of the King George Sound garrison era, he noted that British documents of the time had described the traditional owners, the Menang, as landlords. Conventionally, the word 'landlord' conjures up the image of a rent collector. Scott explained that that was exactly why the word 'landlord' was appropriate:

> *They [the whitefellas] talk about feeding their Noongar hosts with flour and biscuits, and I think they saw that as a sort of rent they were paying. 'And they outnumber us so we have to keep on the good side of them.' There's a strong awareness of power relationships and the local inhabitants are not sure whether the new people are staying or not.*[63]

One of the really interesting aspects of this story, and apparent in Scott's novel, is the sustained confidence, generosity and accommodation of the Aboriginal hosts. This can be seen, he says, as 'a unique manifestation of the spirit of place'.[64]

While the Menang are the landlords or, as they saw themselves, custodians of the land, their white visitors are exiles, temporary campers on a small portion of territory. Shellam sees this as a key aspect of the King George Sound situation.

> *I think it is distinctive. While, say, settlements at Port Jackson, Sydney, and Port Phillip, Melbourne, are very different from each other, they are still about land. In Melbourne rapid settlement with a vast number of people coming in immediately dispossesses large numbers of people.*[65]

However, there was soon potential for conflict over land use, especially in the hinterland of King George Sound. In December 1829, a mapping expedition travelled over what is now known as the Mount Barker district (named for Collet Barker), inland to the north west of the harbour. The expedition leader, Surgeon Superintendent and keen botanist Thomas Braidwood Wilson, noted the potential for a pastoral industry in the country at Rivetts Creek.

> *We observed that its banks were covered with luxuriant grass, sprinkled with yellow buttercups, which put us in mind of home…The alluvial soil, however, extends no great distance; but gently swelling lightly wooded adjacent hills are well adapted for sheep-walks.*[66]

The 'lightly wooded' nature of this area was almost certainly the result of Aboriginal fire-stick farming, designed to create clearings where kangaroos could easily be hunted. For Europeans, it seemed perfect pasture for sheep to 'safely graze'.

Kojonup, 100 kilometres north of Mount Barker, was one of the earliest districts in the region to be settled by Europeans. Farmer Robert Sexton's grandfather described a similarly cleared landscape very well suited to sheep farming.

> *He told me the bush was very open when he was a young man in the 1880s. They could drive a two-wheeled buggy through the bush and easily ride a horse at a good strong canter, whereas in my time the bush was so*

thick, you rode with difficulty – you certainly couldn't ride a pushbike through it. So, the landscape had changed very dramatically even in his lifetime. He said 'You would shoot a kangaroo with a rifle' in his time and when I started it was with a shotgun because the sight distance was less.[67]

Sexton says that the original inhabitants definitely farmed the land. However, the European notion of something like 'sheep walks' appears to have caused concern among the Menang, especially after explorer Thomas Bannister reported favourably in 1831 that:

> A very great proportion of this tract was land of the first description, fit for the plough, sheep or cattle…I cannot but think that the Colony must possess a considerable quantity of fertile land in this part of the territory.[68]

Bannister had reached King George Sound from the Swan River settlement, established in 1829. His arrival caused anxiety among the Menang about their future, a concern they raised with Collet Barker.

> Numbers of natives in, anxious to know if they would be employed & fed by the settlers. Mokare again told me again in

Bannister saw fertile land.

the evening that they talked of coming to stop constantly about King George Sound. I desired him to say they must not come in numbers at first, with the expectation of plenty, that it was probable few settlers would arrive & even if many did, their food would be limited as it would be some time before they could grow much. If the blacks, however, would work & make themselves useful, they would be employed & fed.[69]

For Neville Green, this is one of several passages in Barker's journal that captures the concerns of a particular group of Aboriginal people at a very critical point of contact with the new arrivals.

> *This was a time before their culture was changed but at a period when the Menang were showing great curiosity about this alien culture and asking questions. They were beginning to see that these visitors were not returning spirits, but real people. When they hear that more European people are coming, they are asking: 'What will happen to us? What will we be expected to do?'*[70]

Barker was summoned to Sydney in April 1831 and left the Sound, accompanied by both soldiers and convicts. Tragically, he was to die on the way. Exploring the mouth of the Murray River in South Australia, he was speared, apparently by mistake, by local Aboriginal people. Mokare died only a few months later in June that year, possibly a victim of disease brought unknowingly by Europeans.

King George Sound now came under the jurisdiction of Governor Stirling and the Swan River Colony. Barker's replacement was a British 'government resident' responsible to Stirling. King George Sound was renamed as the settlement of Albany.

The first government resident was medical officer Alexander Collie, who moved into the commandant's residence. For the short time left to Mokare, he and Collie seem to have enjoyed a warm relationship. Collie himself died at Albany in 1835, probably of tuberculosis. He asked to be buried with Mokare, who he had nursed and cared for during the latter's final illness in June 1831. Biographer Gwen Chessell has suggested that perhaps Collie's most important bequest to nineteenth-century Western Australian European history is the story of his friendship with Mokare and the people of King George Sound.[71] Mokare and his brother Nakinah stayed in Collie's house whenever they were in the settlement. Collie describes them not as visitors to the settlement but 'as our hosts, as we had certainly come into their country and had set ourselves down at, if not in, their homes and upon their territories'.[72]

The Menang might have been 'hosts' to the British, but Collie, as his writings show, was still a man of his time. Chessell notes that both he and Barker were convinced that, as 'civilised' Europeans, they could bring benefits to an unfortunate people.[73] The tone in which Collie wrote about the Menang was that of a paternalistic protector, often exasperated and irritated by behaviour that seemed inappropriate to a nineteenth-century Englishman.

Collie's long-term aim was for the original inhabitants of the colony to model themselves on their new masters. In 1832, he wrote a report to Governor Stirling advocating this policy but he had no illusions about how long it would take 'to raise the native people from their primitive and nomad life to become cultivators of the soil and to remain permanently in a place of fixed abode'.[74] Collie's report suggested that an 'intelligent member of the tribe' should be appointed as an advisor to the governor and 'reside at the chief seat of authority'. That person should be the medium for dispensing punishments and rewards and also a guide and interpreter.[75] Perhaps he was thinking of his late friend, Mokare.

When, in later times, 'protectors of Aborigines' were appointed, the person chosen was often a European with little understanding of Aboriginal culture and people. Future policies in relation to such appointments diverged markedly from Collie's proposals.

> Happy to give my strongest recommendation to the general principal [sic] so successfully pursued by the late and much-lamented Captain Collet Barker; a principle never to be lost sight of in the intercourse between the foreigners and the natives, this was to observe a uniformly kind and steady demeanour towards the latter with occasional and well-timed gratuities of provisions and other articles of essential benefit to them.[76]

Collie's advice was to fall on deaf ears. Under Stirling's watch, land was being opened up for European-style cultivation and, although settlement was slow within Menang territory, it began to encroach on their hunting grounds. An inevitable clash between black and white had begun.[77]

After eighteen months in Albany as Stirling's representative, Collie returned to Perth to become colonial surgeon and in 1833, Sir Richard Spencer, a retired English naval officer and Napoleonic war hero, was appointed as government resident. Spencer had not previously visited the colony but he hoped it would make him a landed gentleman of substantial means. He must have been disappointed on arrival in Albany to find only six settler families and none of them engaged in agriculture.[78]

Murray Arnold sees Spencer's tenure as marking a change in relationships with the Menang. There was now no interpreter and mediator to match Mokare. Spencer moved his headquarters from Mount Melville, where there had been regular interaction with the local people, to what had previously been the government farm. Renamed Strawberry Hill, this also became his home. Arnold comments that although Spencer showed sympathy for the original inhabitants of his new domain, the degree of intimacy between the leaders of the two communities was now lost. The friendship that had been a marked and unique feature of the first British settlement in Western Australia had faded. But while the relationship altered in ways that adversely affected the original inhabitants, traces of goodwill remained.[79]

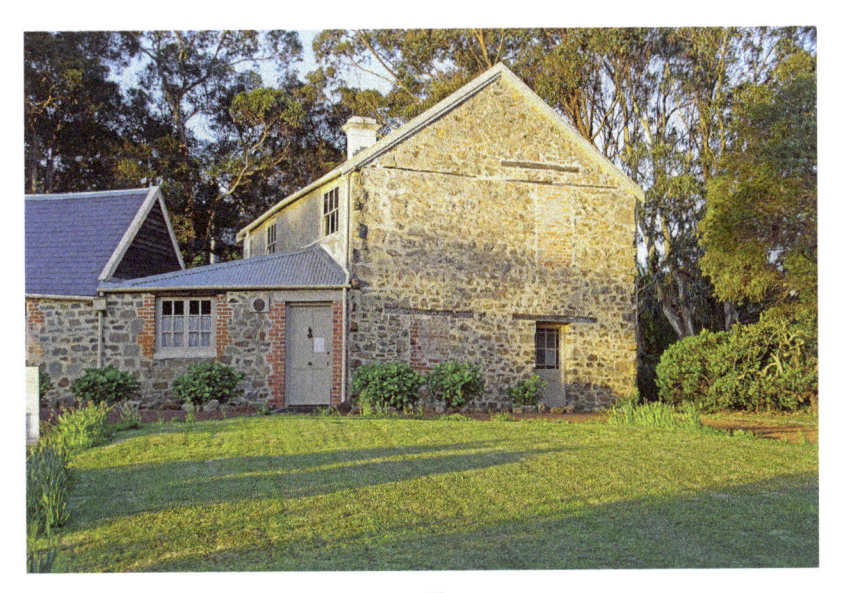

Sir Richard Spencer's home, Strawberry Hill.

Spencer seems to have been well disposed towards the Menang, and his wife, Ann, was interested in their welfare. In keeping with the moral standards of her time, she was particularly concerned about the nakedness of the Aboriginal women and children. In 1834, she asked friends in England for material to make clothes for the native people. Some three years later, she received five bales of red flannel for this purpose.[80]

Like Collie, Spencer believed that if the local people were to desist from what he saw as unpredictable violence, they needed to be 'Christianised' and 'civilised'.[81] His son, Hugh Spencer, recorded that some of the Menang did join in aspects of the Spencer family's daily routine, including attendance at daily prayers and church services.[82] Such behaviour must have heightened the settlers' expectations that the 'heathens' could be recast in the European mould. There was some violence, probably caused by the encroachment of white people (wadjelas) onto Noongar land. The settlers always had to be alert to the risk of conflict but, in general, during Spencer's stewardship, cooperation prevailed over confrontation.

On the other hand, as Barker had found, the threat of serious aggression sometimes persisted between the local tribes. In December 1833, Spencer wrote to the colonial secretary in London detailing an incident that occurred soon after his arrival.

> Last week a numerous body of natives of the Wiel [Wills] Man and Cockatoo tribes, about 90 stout men assembled here with a hostile intention towards the King George Tribe. All our native men and women came crying to me for protection and the men assembled, armed and went forward to meet them, where after a long parley, peace was made and they all returned together...[83]

The Menang might have needed Spencer's protection but he also needed them. There was a serious shortage of labour in the colony and particularly at Albany. Spencer lost no time in employing the locals. Within a few months of arrival, he recorded having engaged:

> Six or eight natives daily the last fortnight as Agricultural labourers, cutting down trees, clearing the land and paying them 1lb. of flour and two ounces of suet for a forenoon's work or a job equal to that for which we are all very grateful.[84]

Spencer also employed local people to clear the road between Strawberry Hill Farm and Middleton Beach in 1836. On this occasion, they were paid money rather than food.[85] As Arnold notes, this was a more formal pattern of employment than the system which had operated under Barker. Under the former arrangement, the Menang had carried out occasional tasks for the soldiers, such as catching swans, in return for 'biscuit'. In modern parlance, they probably would have been termed 'temporary subcontractors' rather than employees.

Increasingly, having the original inhabitants work for the settlers as domestics or labourers was regarded as an essential aspect of 'civilising the natives'. While this would have been seen as 'progress' by the Europeans, it became a major factor in the disruption of the traditional Menang way of life. Lynette Knapp's forebears would have suffered this dislocation.

> *If you can imagine all this beautiful country, all this boodja [land] that they lived off, they survived — it wasn't a case of catching this and catching that, it was a matter of survival. Everything they did was survival. And then all of a sudden, their walk paths had got fences which they had to walk around. If they went through the fences they'd get shot.*[86]

One of the casualties in this breakdown in their way of life was that the Menang no longer carried out their traditional burning practices.

> *I think when everything had been stripped from them, that broke a tradition of burning country because it didn't belong to them anymore. All the Aboriginal families here had strips that they burnt. My father said it was like a parkland, going out to Israelite Bay. When you re-burn, we say, the land is reborn. Indigenous plants have a cycle that has been shaped by smoke and fire. It replenishes the earth, and if you get young plant regrowth you get plenty of animals. And you learn to farm them as well. There was a way of burning and a certain time of burning. And all the families burnt their strips at more or less the same time.*[87]

Wadandi Cultural Custodian Iszaac Webb describes that burning regime.

> *During djeran [April/May], this is when we would put karlar, fire, through the country, because the first few rains have come, they've dampened the country and it's going to reduce intensity of that and then it sits within the cycles of how the plants are seeding themselves, how the animals are moving and how they are breeding.*[88]

But the old ways did not die out altogether or immediately. Local Elder Vernice Gillies describes how these traditional burning arrangements had been practised by her father.

> *My Dad was a bushman from way back. He was born out the other side of the Stirlings in the bush and he always talked about burning methods,*

Stirling Ranges.

> *mosaic burning, soft burns, trying to burn up a hill rather than down a hill because a fire can get away so very easily. But burning gently and burning often kept that load under control...Start your burning in July or August. If we all did that then we wouldn't have such huge bushfires which destroy lives, homes, all those little animals that actually live in that bush.*[89]

Vernice described how the Menang were increasingly affected by the white settlers' push for land.

> *The big change was that with the settlers, of course, they pushed the Menang people further and further out and in doing that, it pushed them closer to the edges of areas that belonged to other Aboriginal groups. That caused friction. They also severed the walking, the song and the dance lines, because all of a sudden, there were these big squares of fencing that were put up to put these odd, smelly animals behind, and when the Menang people pulled the fences down, because they happened to be across a walking trail or a songline or a dance line, they, of course, were in trouble. So, relationships between the first white settlers and the Menang people became a little bit frayed.*[90]

And, as Vernice added:

> *It would have been terrible times for them to see their country changing, the patterns of the seasons changing, the food cycles changing. But we are very adaptable people and despite many, many efforts, we are still here.*[91]

Swan River settler and lawyer, George Fletcher Moore, visited Albany with the colony's deputy governor, Frederick Irwin, in 1833. He describes an incident which shows clearly how the British now regarded their new subjects. A settler, John Morley, was asked to address an assembly of natives on behalf of Irwin. He spoke in pidgin but his words were translated by Moore as follows:

> Now attend, the Governor desires me to tell the black man if the black man spear the white man the white men will shoot them. If a black man steal it is not good. If a black man spear a black man it is not good. If the black man be friendly with the black man, if the black man do not steal, if the black man give the white man wallabees, bring wood and bring water, white man will befriend the black man and give him plenty of biscuits, plenty to eat, and give him blankets, rice, tomahawk. Now the Governor desires me to give each black man one knife.[92]

Arnold comments that Moore found the speech amusing but that Barker and Collie might have found it tragic.[93] A people who had subsisted successfully on their land for thousands of years were reduced to life as compliant servants, working for and dependent on the 'white man' for all forms of sustenance.

Mokare and his relatives had been right to express their concerns to Barker about the future of their people as they unwittingly became British citizens. The relationship which had developed between the British soldiers and the original inhabitants at King George Sound was probably unparalleled in the history of Australia. It was a partnership that would not endure or be repeated elsewhere.

MANY MAPS

Albany – land and sea. Photo by Bob Symons.

Chapter 2

'A Little Bit Occupied by Natives'

In the early 1990s, a theatre group which included actor Geoff Kelso, wrote and performed *Bindjareb Pinjarra,* a play about events that occurred in 1834. This was some five years after the founding of the Swan River Colony. The Bindjareb Noongar people are the original inhabitants of the area around the Murray River, and the event is known, depending on who tells the story, as the Battle or Massacre of Pinjarra. Governor James Stirling led the troops and white settlers at that 'encounter'. In the play, Western Australia's first governor is introduced by Geoff Kelso:

> James Stirling, after the Napoleonic Wars, was an ambitious British naval officer on half pay who seized on a brilliant real estate opportunity at the Swan River – after he had 'discovered' it – a beautiful place but unfortunately a little bit occupied by 'natives'.[1]

Murray River – Bindjareb Noongar country.

The land was much more than 'a little bit occupied' as Stirling was well aware. Bevan Carter has researched and written about Noongar land tenure and ownership prior to European settlement:

> Not only did many British colonists know that the land was previously owned; by the mid-1830s, the local officials had lists of the names of Aboriginal owners, as well as property names and boundaries.[2]

Francis Armstrong arrived in the Swan River Colony from Scotland as a teenager, in the year of settlement, 1829. He learned the local language and later became both interpreter and advocate for the original occupants. Armstrong formed the view that the land was not only occupied but that it was held by particular Aboriginal families, asserting that 'land is beyond doubt, an inheritable property among them'.[3] Armstrong was one of a number of early European arrivals who identified the Aboriginal owners and the boundaries of their country. However, it was, understandably, difficult for the newcomers to possess the same clarity on 'land ownership' as the people who had been the custodians of that country for thousands of years.[4]

Unlike the military garrison at King George Sound, Britain's new Swan River Colony was unashamedly a land-based settlement. This made future conflict between the traditional owners and the newcomers predictable and almost certainly inevitable. Even before settlement began the local people showed that they did not want intrusions into their country from people who were unknown to them and who obviously did not understand Aboriginal protocol in relation to entering 'foreign' country.

Captain Fremantle, under instructions from the British Admiralty Lords, landed at the Swan River, which had previously been explored by Captain Stirling in 1827, and claimed the western coast of the continent for the British. On 2 May 1827 he recorded in his diary for that day that his presence was apparently unwelcome.

> We rowed up the river a considerable distance & saw & heard natives on both sides, who halloa'd to us very loud & appeared to cry out 'Warra, warra', which I supposed to be 'go away'. I took no notice but proceeded up the river where Captain Stirling has marked as having established a garden...[5]

The explorers were not deterred by their seemingly unfriendly welcome and in June 1829 the British came to stay. This new settlement was intended to offer a fresh economic start for, among others, former military men and their families. After the defeat of Napoleon at Waterloo in 1815, peace reigned in Europe. Armies were stood down and discharged officers on half pay sought to re-establish themselves as 'land-owning gentry'. They had little likelihood of attaining this status in Britain and thus were willing to try their luck with a land grant in an unknown territory. Historian Tom Stannage described their hopes.

> *If we go back in Western Australia's history to the foundation of European settlement, here we have a second-rank English gentry intent on creating a*

sort of Arcadia, something lost in England, lost, they thought, sometime in the eighteenth century, at the beginning of the Industrial Revolution.[6]

The man appointed as governor, Captain James Stirling, was himself among the many land claimants. But Stirling knew that the land did not belong to the British and that he was occupying a country that was already inhabited. Later, in 1837, when he gave a speech to the local Legislative Council about treatment of the local population, he used the term 'invading the country' to describe the actions of the British in settling this new colony. As Bevan Carter has commented:

> *Stirling was well aware when he arrived in the Swan River Colony in June 1829 that he was seeking to take, and allocate to others, land that was already occupied. Indeed, perhaps fearing trouble from the existing inhabitants, this may have been why he set up his first house on Garden Island, rather than on the mainland. Perhaps he was concerned for the safety and well-being of his family?*[7]

Biographer Pamela Statham-Drew cites Stirling's views.

> In referring to 'their territory', Stirling acknowledged that the land belonged to others, and it is pertinent that he later used the word 'invasion' even for his exploring party. But his experience in South America had taught him that invasion led to ownership and that ownership by Britain was an enviable position. This he never queried.[8]

As Statham-Drew implies, from Stirling's perspective, 'ownership by Britain' was something to be sought by the existing inhabitants, and of which to be proud. However, the local people did not appear to appreciate the benefits the British thought they were bestowing on them.

Within a few months of Stirling allocating land along the Swan River to himself and others, communication between the local residents and the European settlers began to differ markedly from the amicable exchanges at King George Sound. Anger and interrogation on both sides frequently replaced curiosity and friendliness. It became apparent to the people of the Swan River Plain that they would soon be outnumbered. The pace of British settlement did not make for peaceful acceptance. Over six hundred British settlers arrived in 1829 and many more in 1830.

By May 1830, only eight months after Stirling had begun to assign land holdings, it had become clear that the new arrivals were here to stay and Noongar people living around the Swan River made a stand. For the first time, there was collective and organised opposition to the settlers. This event became known (or perhaps more accurately, largely forgotten) as the Battle of Perth.

The following is taken from an account published almost a century later in the *Western Mail*.

> Early on the morning of May 3, 1830, the natives visited the cantonment of the military in Perth. The body which was accompanied by a large number of women and children formed only one portion of the visitors as another and still larger body was found to be following the bank of the Swan River towards Mt Eliza. Both parties were strongly armed in the native fashion and the whole displayed a truculent disposition never before exhibited.[9]

Captain (later Major and Lieutenant Colonel) Frederick Irwin was in charge of the colony's troops. He indicated that shots should only be fired in self-defence but also stated in his report to the governor, who had been absent from Perth inspecting land further south, that:

> This daring and hostile Conduct of the Natives induced me to seize the Opportunity to make them sensible of our Superiority. By shewing how severely we could retaliate their Aggression, but that we had no Wish to injure them.[10]

At first it seemed that the situation had been successfully defused. But as the day progressed reports were received that the locals were spearing poultry at one settler's property, while other newcomers claimed that there were incursions into 'their' land. Ensign Dale was speared and at least one other soldier injured. The *Western Mail* article suggests that events now began to resemble a serious battle as:

> the combined forces of the settlers and the military, for every man who possessed arms had turned out, were divided into two parties. One party was placed under the command of Mr Dale whose wounds were not so severe as to incapacitate him from further action and Major Irwin retained command of the other portion.[11]

A number of Noongars were killed or wounded in the resulting 'engagement'. Irwin's official report is imprecise on this point but hostilities apparently ceased for the time being. Irwin concluded his report to Governor Stirling in terms which indicated his satisfaction with the outcome.

> Some Days after several Natives came into the Cantonment and pointed out their Women and Children passing along the Outskirts, evidently to make a Show of Confidence in us. I desired that they should be received in the usual friendly Way but ordered a Sergeant and a File of the Guard with their Muskets to watch their Motions. At seeing the Arms, they looked alarmed and made Signs to put them away. The Effect of this Precaution was apparent for on their moving to the Western Extremity, the Serjeant kept out of their View till he saw a considerable number had collected round Paton's House (which they had before rifled), trying to push open the Doors and Windows. On this he made his Appearance when the Natives all ran off to the Rear. Since that time, they have not visited the Cantonment and I am happy to learn that they have committed no Act of Aggression against the Settler in any Part of the Country.[12]

The Battle of Perth (or for Perth) was over, but the war over land ownership was only just beginning. This would continue to be a case of 'might over right' while the settlers continued to believe that the original inhabitants should be grateful for the

British presence. Even in 1914, the writer of the *Western Mail* article lamented the absolute effrontery of the local people in invading the settlers' huts and suggested that 'one of the gravest difficulties of pioneering was the adverse and militant attitude of the existent Aboriginal population'.[13]

New settler George Fletcher Moore arrived in the colony in October 1830, a few months after the Battle of Perth, to take up land on the Upper Swan. Moore was a lawyer and a diarist who recorded his Swan River experiences, including interactions with the local people. At first, relationships appeared to be harmonious. In March 1831, he wrote:

> The natives are not so despicable a race as was at first supposed. They are active, bold, and shrewd, expert in thieving, as many, (and myself among the number) have experienced; they are courageous when attacked; however, they are not very numerous, and we are on good terms with them. I walk occasionally to and from Perth through the woods alone and unarmed; so, you may perceive from this circumstance, we are not in much dread of them.[14]

When Moore participated in an early expedition beyond the new settlement, he found himself:

> at land much dug by the natives, several of whom we heard, but they in general kept out of view...Two natives, immediately succeeded by others, joined us in a friendly way...These people appeared to have painted themselves fresh for the visit; and if we could judge from their anxiously pointing in a particular direction, they invited us to take lunch at their village; however, we went in a line precisely opposite. Soon afterwards, finding ourselves perplexed in the mazes of a swamp, we began to think that we should have taken their advice and that the exclamation of 'Bogh' was kindly meant to indicate some bridge or stream higher up.[15]

But within another year, Moore was less enthusiastic about his new acquaintances, writing in his diary on 16 June 1832:

> All my pigs are missing. I greatly fear that the natives who killed sixteen of them in my neighbourhood, have taken away or killed mine also. To add to my probable loss, one of my lambs has been so much torn by a native dog, that I have been obliged to kill it.[16]

Three years after the founding of the Swan River Colony, such episodes had led Governor Stirling to express his concerns in a letter to the colonial secretary in faraway London.

> I have endeavoured to open up amicable communication with the tribes in this district, but hitherto with little success. I would wish to persuade them that it is safer and better to obtain those things they desire by free gift on our part, than to take them by force, but I am still unsuccessful in this endeavour. At King George's Sound where I found a good understanding established, I have caused it to be preserved and cultivated, and there the natives confide in, and in fact live very much with the Europeans. In the Swan River District, they sometimes meet us in amity and perhaps on the following day they commit a robbery or a murder.[17]

Stirling's complaint about native robberies reveals his lack of understanding of the Aboriginal concept of land ownership or, as Aboriginal people themselves saw it, connection to, and caring for, land. At the same time, George Grey, a British explorer and administrator in Western Australia in the 1830s, was one of the first Europeans to understand and appreciate the Noongar view of 'country'.

> They themselves never having an idea of quitting their own land, cannot imagine others doing it; and- thus, when they see white people suddenly appearing in their country, and setting themselves down in particular spots, they imagine that they must have formed an attachment for this land in some other state of existence; and hence conclude the settlers were at one period black men, and their own relations.[18]

Dorothy Winmar's ancestors were among Noongar people who believed that the new arrivals were returning spirits.

> When the Wedjelas (wadjelas/white people) first came here the Nyungars lived on top of Kings Park and they saw the ships coming in. Grandmother said they thought it was the spirit of their people coming back and they were scared of what was coming back, that they were ghosts. But then they learnt that they were another sort of people, white people.[19]

Lynette Knapp, a Noongar Elder living on the south coast of Western Australia, illustrates the connection between the ocean and returning white spirits.

> *We believe that when people die, their spirits go and sit in the Christmas tree, the one with all the orange flowers. And they'll wait for a while to see if someone's coming behind them before they take their journey to the land they see between the sky and the sea. And we believe that when the spirits come back from there to visit, they come back in vessels and they turn white.*[20]

Land, sea and sky.

For Australia's First Nations the most common explanation for the arrival of white people was that they were returning spirits. As George Grey had concluded, connection to land was so strong that they could not imagine human beings would want to leave their country of birth and sail across the sea. As Swan River man Albert Corunna asserted:

> We always maintained that we were waiting for them to go to their own land. We couldn't understand that people could come to another land and abandon their own country because we didn't want to abandon ours and go and live somewhere else.[21]

Wadandi Cultural Custodian Iszaac Webb describes this belief system in more detail:

> When our people first saw non-Indigenous people, European people, we were very welcoming, because the old people saw them as being spirits of some of their children who may have passed away, and by coming back on country, the old people said that 'they've been on a spirit journey, and they forgot their country', their boodjara. So, our people would take them to gnamma [waterholes] and the country places, saying 'Remember this is where we used to sit. Remember this.'[22]

The concept of welcoming and hosting outsiders was traditionally well understood. Many Noongars frequently visited other people's country. Land was controlled by respecting a group's protocols at seasonal festivals and at ceremonies with visitors sometimes travelling hundreds of kilometres. But for Albert Corunna's people, land clearing and the erection of fences was an unwelcome change. It was both offensive and unacceptable.

> Then our people started to see a lot of land clearing, and the landscape changing. Fences started to be erected cutting us off from fresh water and, as human beings, we need water. There was a lot of exclusion by fences and things being put up. It did start to cause a lot of conflict.[23]

Fences started to be erected.

Jesse Hammond, born in 1856, grew up in the south-west. The son of a European settler, he wrote, sympathetically, in 1933 about what he saw as the destruction of Aboriginal society.

> Very few white people are alive today who have heard from the natives who took part in the conflict of the pioneering days, what they thought in their own minds about the white people. They have told me that many times, years before the permanent settlement took place, they had seen ships on different parts of the coast and white men had landed and then gone away again after a short stay. When the settlers first came, they thought the same thing was going to happen again. Then they saw the houses being built and this caused a great deal of worry to them.[24]

It is unlikely that Stannage's 'second-rank English gentry', who arrived after 1829, knew much about the people who already lived along the Swan River, their lifestyle or the land on which they lived. Playwright Phil Thomson suspects that:

> *They weren't mentioned in any of the brochures. They assumed there were only a few hundred. And it was only when the payback killings*

started, when settlers shot people for stealing flour or spearing sheep that they realised how many people were living here.[25]

Not only did the white people, the wadjelas, underestimate the size of the existing population, they also failed to understand the nature of this very structured society and the capacity of its people to live in balance with their environment. Swan River Noongar man Ted Wilkes describes how the technology of fire-stick farming was disrupted.

Our people used to hunt kangaroo by burning the bush and leaving certain green parts and the animals would have to go and live in these green parts and we could go there and hunt the kangaroo for the next season and once that resource diminished, they could move to another section and burn that. But once you weren't able to burn the bushes because fire-stick farming requires burning, you then come into conflict and of course if you're burning and there are sheep in the paddock, the sheep get burnt. This causes conflict and that means people are being harmed and killed.[26]

After the Battle of Perth conflict soon returned. Yagan, whose family inhabited the area south of the Swan River, known as Beeliar country, became a notable leader of the resistance to British settlement. For Noongar man Peter Wilkes, Yagan is still close to his family (moort).

We always talk about him and his father Midgegooroo and we always feel we are connected, especially through the Swan River, being from the Whadjuk people, through what was handed down to me by my brothers and sisters, my mother and father.[27]

George Fletcher Moore was often sympathetic to the original inhabitants, despite his complaint about pig stealing, and he was very aware of, and recorded, events that led to Yagan's death. On 27 May 1833 Moore came across Yagan, and they had a 'long, angry and wholly unexpected but spirited conversation'. Yagan made his case in pidgin language and Moore conjectured from the tone and manner that his message was:

'You came to our country; You have driven us from our haunts, and disturbed us in our occupations: as we walk in our own country, we are fired upon by the white men. Why should the white men treat us so?'[28]

To some extent the level of conflict depended on the attitudes and behaviour of the settlers themselves, as this 1837 letter from Robert Stewart, living in the Armadale district, suggests. Writing to his brother James, in response to a question from another brother, John, asking 'whether the natives were troublesome', Robert says:

I must say the natives are troublesome in some parts of the country and dangerous at times too. They speared four of the white people, wounded two or three more since our arrival but whether the fault of the quarrel was on the part of the whites or blacks, I have never been able to ascertain. I never found them anything troublesome.[29]

The Hall family, who arrived in the colony and held property south of Armadale and in the Mandurah area, also had good relations with the local inhabitants. When their six-year-old son, Anderton, disappeared from a beach near Mandurah one evening, two Noongars, Migo and Mollydobin, tracked him for over 10 hours and travelled 20 miles looking for him. They found and rescued the boy the next day, just in time to save him from drowning.[30]

While the newcomers varied in their attitudes and behaviour towards the existing occupants of the land, their impact on the lifestyle of the original inhabitants cannot be denied. Ted Wilkes, former head of the Derbal Yerrigan Health Service, has described what happened when the new arrivals brought with them their own European farming practices.

People were now coming from an agricultural population in England. They'd been practising farming for six thousand years or more and they were bringing it to the south-west of Western Australia. They wouldn't have been able to move into the desert region or the more arid areas of Australia because they were wheat growers, they were sheep growers and they needed regular rain. So, the southern places were where they started

> *to populate. But once the sheep were fenced in and people started to mark off property and as more whitefellers came in, this land was absolutely ideal for growing sheep and wheat and other domestic forms of farming. Noongar people farmed the kangaroo and lived off the native bush.*[31]

Tension between two very different societies was about more than land use. As had been the case at King George Sound, the Aboriginal sense of appropriate retaliation and the British concept of punishment for crimes committed, were in conflict from the outset. A misunderstanding between an Aboriginal woman and Captain T. Ellis, commander of the Native Police, illustrates the contrasting notions of appropriate punishment.

In 1834, Ellis banished a woman, known as Benillo, from his property because she allowed her dog to worry his chickens. Banishment from land, in Noongar culture, was a major punishment imposed only for very serious crimes. Accordingly, Benillo asked Ellis to allow her to return but to exact punishment instead by spearing her in the leg. This suggestion obviously horrified the captain, who, feeling sympathy for her, contented himself with a scolding as sufficient punishment. Lois Tilbrook, who recounted this tale, suggests that Benillo, 'in turn, must have wondered how Ellis could change from his extreme position to take such a mild stand in what must have seemed to her to be a very inconsistent and unpredictable manner'.[32]

As Tiffany Shellam and Murray Arnold point out in their discussion of the King George Sound settlement (see Chapter 1), if you judge only from the context of your own time, it is easy to misunderstand the actions of people in past eras. One can dismiss really important motivations and their reasoning. This is not to excuse behaviour, but to understand it.

The diaries and letters of men like George Fletcher Moore and the scholarly Robert Menli Lyon, who arrived in 1829, assist our comprehension of life at that time and place. Moore and Lyon were not only very interested in colonial life, but were also well aware of the tensions it produced. They examined their circumstances critically and wrote about their experiences in detail. For both men it was important to learn the local language so that meaningful dialogue could take place.

Moore, like Isaac Scott Nind at King George Sound, developed a 'vocabulary' of words used by the people living around the Swan River. One use of this document was, he argued, 'to enable actual settlers to communicate more freely with the natives and thus to acquire and extend an influence among them'.[33] By 'influence' Moore means that his vocabulary could be used to educate Aboriginal people in the ways of Europeans.

> There are few situations more unpleasant than when two individuals are suddenly and unexpectedly brought into collision, neither of whom is acquainted with one word of the language of the other…But when it happens that one of the individuals is in a state of a mere savage nature knowing nothing of the habits and usages of civilised life, and perhaps never having heard of people other than his own, the situation of both becomes critical and embarrassing. It was this predicament that the early settlers of Western Australia found themselves in on first taking possession of lands in this colony.[34]

At the same time, Moore considers the situation from what, he assumes, would be the Aboriginal viewpoint:

> ignorant alike of the nature, the power and the intentions of this new people, and possessed of some vague idea of their being spirits or reappearances of the dead, the natives were restrained, possibly by superstitious awe alone, from attempting to repel the colonists at once by direct or open hostility.[35]

While Moore's intention is not altogether altruistic, since he sees information as 'extending influence among them', it still contrasts with later suppression of Indigenous languages by the dominant wadjelas.

Robert Lyon saw language as the key to better relations with the Noongar people and pointed to the relative success achieved at King George Sound. He suggested that if Yagan, the 'rebel' leader, could meet with the Menang and learn of their apparent rapport with the British, relationships at the Swan might improve.

In May 1832, Yagan had been imprisoned for spearing a settler at the Canning River, and Lyon, at his own request, became Yagan's gaoler on Carnac Island, a few kilometres off the coast south of Fremantle. After Yagan's daring escape by boat, Lyon arranged for two well-regarded Menang men, Manyat and Gyallipert, to travel by ship from Albany to the Swan. The Menang representatives probably did not see these meetings in the same light as the colonists. It is likely that they saw an opportunity to travel and that meeting Whadjuk strangers provided them with diplomatic and strategic advantages.[36]

Whatever their motivations, the two intermediaries reached Fremantle on 18 January 1833 and were taken by their British 'hosts' to meet the local Aboriginals at Lake Monger (known to the First Nations as Galup).[37] The *Perth Gazette* reported on these meetings, first with a prominent figure from the north of the

Lake Monger (Galup) today.

Swan, Yellalonga, and later with Yagan. As Shellam notes, the newspaper's account of the meetings was filled with presumptions about native behaviour and reported a successful outcome for the colonists, whereas for Yagan and his group and also for Gyallipert and Manyat, expectations of the meeting might have been quite different and there is no evidence that the gathering led to an improvement in cross-cultural relationships. In fact, they would get worse.[38]

For their part, the colonists had held high hopes of achieving a better understanding from the Lake Monger and subsequent meetings. The emissaries stayed for a month, apparently exhorting, in the words of the *Perth Gazette*, Yagan and his followers 'to conduct themselves in a peaceable and kindly manner to their white neighbours'.[39] On their return southwards, Manyat and Gyallipert were accompanied by three prominent colonists – Stirling's deputy, Captain Frederick Irwin, the explorer Ensign Dale and George Fletcher Moore. This was the occasion when Moore listened with amusement to the speech given in pidgin to the Menang people at King George Sound (described in Chapter 1). The Europeans were evidently keen to witness the effect of the intermediary mission on the Menang. Irwin reported to his superiors that Manyat and Gyallipert were 'hailed by their Tribe with great satisfaction and increased confidence in our good faith and friendship'.[40]

The settlers thought they had demonstrated their own good intentions to both the Menang and to the Whadjuk people. However, Shellam reminds us that:

> Rather than being the focus or purpose of the Aboriginal journeys, the colonists were being used strategically by these men. A colonial vessel took the Aboriginal men to a distant place, the newcomers were used as 'guides' and 'mediators' for the Aboriginal interactions, and they acted as hosts to Manyat and Gyallipert, the celebrated visitors. But the newcomers remained on the edges of the Aboriginal world...[41]

After the departure of the Menang, hostilities again increased along the Swan. Yagan vowed revenge for the death of his brother, Domjum, during an Aboriginal raid to steal flour from a Fremantle shop on 29 April 1833. Later, at Bull Creek, a large group of Noongars met a party of settlers who were loading carts with provisions, killing two settlers, Tom and John Velvick, who had themselves recently been released from prison for assaulting Aboriginal people on Christmas Day.[42] The Noongars would have seen their own actions as exercising their traditional law obligations by taking appropriate reprisals.

Captain Irwin, then acting governor, declared Yagan and his father, Elder Midgegooroo, who was also the traditional youlin (councillor) for the Beeliar people, outlaws in their own Swan River country. On 17 May 1833, Midgegooroo was captured and his spears broken. On 20 May, Moore wrote in his diary:

> Heard from Irwin that Midgegooroo, one of the proclaimed natives has been taken and there is a great puzzle to know what to do with him. The populace cry loudly for his blood but it is a hard thing to shoot him in cold blood. There is a strong intention of sending him into perpetual banishment. In some out of the way place.[43]

This was seemingly Irwin's preferred 'solution'. However, the demand of the populace prevailed and Irwin ordered Midgegooroo's execution by firing squad. On 25 May 1833, the *Perth Gazette* reported the following under the heading, EXECUTION:

> The death warrant was read aloud to the persons assembled, by the Resident, who immediately afterwards went inside the Jail, with the Constables and the necessary attendants, to prepare the Prisoner for his fate. Midgegooroo, on seeing that preparations were making to punish him, yelled and struggled most violently to escape. These efforts availed him little, in less than five minutes he was pinioned and blindfolded, and bound to the outer door of

the Jail...they then fired – and Midgegooroo fell. – The whole arrangement and execution after the death did not occupy half an hour.[44]

Local people, including Noongar descendant Albert Corunna, still recall and mourn Midgegooroo's death.

> *Midgegooroo didn't know he was a hunted man and we don't think he did anything wrong. We think he was taken and executed by a firing squad and then they hanged him up on a tree to display what they had done, no matter how evil it was. Then they cut him down and they still wouldn't give his body back to my tribe, so that they could give him a tribal burial by our customs. They deliberately denied him that.*[45]

Yagan, too, met his death shortly after the argument recorded by George Fletcher Moore. On 11 July 1833 he was ambushed and shot by two teenage youths, William and James Keates.

After the deaths of Yagan and Midgegooroo, Moore made a diary entry which showed that, like Armstrong and others, he understood the local people had a system of land tenure that provided for particular families to have rights over, and responsibilities for, specific land or country.

> The country formerly of Midgegooroo, then of his son Yagan, belongs now of rights to two young lads (brothers) and a son of Yagan. Some trespassers went upon this ground, lighted their fires and chased the wallabies, this was resented by the young lads...[46]

Noongar people today, like Gwen Corunna, still revere Yagan as their earliest and most important champion for confronting European settlement on Whadjuk land and for his inspirational leadership, including negotiating for justice and advocating respect for, and understanding of, his people and their culture.

> *He signified our struggle more so than anyone else. And I guess all of us today carry that same yoke that Yagan carried, in still seeking justice for our people and giving us equal rights, which we've never had, even though we're here in our own country and our own land.*[47]

Yagan remembered: *Wirin* (spirit), Yagan Square, created by Tjyllyungoo (Lance Chadd) and sculpted in collaboration with the art services from Trish Robinson and Stuart Green (Big Spoon Art Service).

Yagan's head, or 'kart', was cut from his body, preserved and, as Moore conjectured, 'possibly it may yet figure in some museum at home'.[48] It soon did, when the explorer Robert Dale took the skull to England in 1834. There, phrenologist Thomas Pettigrew described Yagan's head as 'an anthropological curiosity'. Dale's description of Yagan was of a man 'strong and active, perfectly fearless, and the best spearsman of his tribe – but passionate, implacable and sullen; in short, a most complete and untameable savage'.[49] With or without the benefit of Dale's description, Pettigrew's understanding of phrenology, a popular pseudo-science at the time, led him to a scarcely proven conclusion.

> His natural disposition would incline to cruelty, cunning, malevolence and revenge, and from the deficiency of those faculties proper to man, and which especially constitute his humanity, it is likely the animal propensities would be in danger of uncontrollable action if not of brutalising sway.[50]

Part of the problem in understanding the role of a semi-mythical figure like Yagan arises from the perspective of the chronicler. It depends on who is writing the story and at what point in time. Bob Reece draws our attention to Alexandra Hasluck's 1961 article on Yagan in which she suggests that:

> Yagan was not...a patriot in the true meaning of the word. I doubt very much whether he consciously thought of the white men as invaders, as people who wanted his land; on the evidence it seems more as if he thought of them as people who had something he wanted – food.[51]

Hasluck's argument was based on documented accounts of food-store raids by Aboriginal people who stole the settlers' scanty stocks of flour and sugar and killed their domesticated animals. However, her assertion that this occurred 'while the indigenous kangaroo, duck, swan and fish flourished abundantly'[52] is not supported by the complaints of Aboriginal people. It would appear that those same traditional food sources, kangaroo and other animals, were no longer abundant after 1829, but in sharp decline due to the settlers' preference for fresh meat rather than 'salty pork and weevilly flour'.[53]

Traditional food sources were by no means limited to meat and fish, as anthropologist Sylvia Hallam demonstrated in her 1991 paper, 'Aboriginal women as providers: the 1830s on the Swan'. Hallam explained that plants of all kinds, gathered by Noongar women in areas such as the swampy land in East Perth and around what is now the main Perth train station, were important sources of nutrition.[54]

All native foods had to be stretched further with the arrival of the Europeans. Occupation of Aboriginal traditional land also meant occupation of their kitchen garden.[55] Competition between Noongars and the newcomers for food soon became fierce, as a letter written by Jane Dodds, who settled in Guildford with her husband in 1830, reveals.

> Celery and eringo root grow abundantly, also the sow thistle. I was advised to eat plentifully of each, therefore it became a daily task for the little ones to collect it. The eringo root was boiled as potatoes, and the thistle cut up in vinegar as salad, and so eagerly were these ingredients sought by every class of persons that our supply failed long before vegetables were produced in reality...[56]

Yams were also a major source of food for the Swan River people. The Upper Swan area, one of the first areas claimed by white settlers, was particularly suited to yam growing. Moore himself, in his 'Descriptive vocabulary', is explicit about the important role of yams in the Aboriginal diet.

> Warran – one of the Dioscoreae. A species of yam, the root of which grows generally to about the thickness of a man's thumb; and to the depth of sometimes four to six feet in loamy soils. It is sought chiefly at the commencement of the rains when it is ripe and when the earth is most easily dug; and it forms the principal article of food for the natives at that season. It is found in this part

The Upper Swan, settled by Europeans from 1829 onwards.

of Australia, from a short distance south of the Murray, nearly as far north as Gantheaume Bay [Kalbarri, north of Geraldton].[57]

Yam cultivation and the availability of this important food source was very quickly affected by the arrival of the European settlers, as Hallam explained:

> Yams, however, were very important to Aboriginal subsistence and settlement patterns because they occurred in concentrated localised patches, mainly on rich alluvial soils. Indeed, the Europeans used them as an indicator of good arable land, with devastating consequences for their Aboriginal owners. Where European settlers took over fertile, yam-growing soils, there is a chance for the survival of evidence about fluctuations in the numbers of Aborigines frequenting those areas, and the seasonality, periodicity and lengths of time involved. Obviously however, the pre-European situation will almost immediately be altered by the effects of European cultivation and stock, and the assertion of European property rights.[58]

As a result of increased competition for limited resources, both original inhabitants and recent settlers were experiencing food shortages. Moore commented in March 1833 that he had shot and been forced to eat crow: 'Birds are very scarce now'.[59]

Soon after 1829, some colonial settlers were as much in conflict with their new environment as with the First Australians. The locals knew how to 'live off their land', as descendant Gary Wilkes tells it.

> *We knew where to go to, where the most food was or was going to be. We knew when the weather patterns were changing. We knew when the tides were coming in and how the rivers were running and we'd cordon off certain parts of the river and do our fishing once the tide went back out and there'd be little pools of fish to catch and that's our technology.*[60]

But for the new arrivals, the land itself could and did confront them. In one account, 'A genuine portrait', possibly around

March 1830, an anonymous writer describes the situation of a settler described as Captain H but identified as Thomas Hester, an army officer who had come to the Swan River with his wife and six children. Hester was struggling to farm on his 2,000 acre block on the Canning River.

> I am now, says he, completely ruined – my money is all gone, there are no fish in the river, for the water is dried up…'I have sown seeds, but such is the heat and the drought that scarcely any vegetate, and if by chance, a blade appears it is immediately devoured by the flies and the ants. The natives are constantly hovering around us – they seem less friendly than when we first arrived – they appear more shy and our interviews are less frequent, and as a husband and a father, I dread the possibility of the slightest misunderstanding – my land is of no value, it is all sand – I have not 20 acres capable of cultivation – my store of flour of beef and of pork is daily diminishing and God alone knows, how when exhausted it is to be replenished. Oh! My wife, Oh my children! I cannot now remove from the place where I am situated – if I had the will I have not the means – my misery is complete – my destruction is certain'.[61]

The fact that both groups were going hungry would have strongly influenced Captain H's fear of 'misunderstandings' between the Swan River settlers and long-term locals, and the situation continued to deteriorate as the 1830s wore on. The settlers introduced sheep and cattle and put up fences to keep their animals from straying, measures that kept out Aboriginal people but also kept out kangaroos and other animals. These barriers reduced the land available to the Noongars for hunting and foraging and provoked retaliation – the capturing and killing of the settlers' livestock.

Aboriginal people would not have seen their actions as 'retaliation'. If an area was fenced and kangaroos could not be hunted there, why not take sheep? They are also sources of food.

In this context, in his history of the Wandering district, local historian Albert Schorer reminds us that Aboriginal people:

> firmly believed that the bush and all its contents were the general property of mankind; private property being only what is carried in the bag. At the close of the day those who had been successful divided with those who had not. Nor was any gift considered as a favour but a right brought to the needy.[62]

Many settlers, assuming that the Aboriginal people were nomadic and wandered in the bush at random, thought that they did not appreciate or care for the land in which they lived. Nigel Wilkes corrects this assumption.

> *The more you gathered, the more you could share with your people but not only that, we didn't gather that much because we were nomadic, in the sense of 'carry light stuff' but resourcefulness was our greatest gift, I think.*[63]

Some settlers, like Robert Menli Lyon, did understand that country was important to the Aboriginal people.

> What though the grass be their couch, and the tree of their forest their only shelter, their blue mountains and the country where they first beheld the sun, the moon and the starry heavens, are as dear to them as your native land with all its natural and artificial beauties, its gilded towers and magnificent spires, is to you.[64]

Peter Wilkes affirms Lyon's understanding of country.

> *Whadjuk people, we've lived in the land, not on the land and we look after the land and the land looks after us. We took what we needed and basically that was to survive. We took bushes for shelter, kangaroos that lived on the land and lizards to eat to survive. We lived with the rivers, with the trees, with nature. The earth will always be mother and my mother.*[65]

Len Collard expands on what is, and has always been, the relationship between Indigenous people and their land.

> Noongar are literally related to country. We talk with it, walk with it, feed it and get nourished by it. Country reveals things to us. Let me explain some more. Before you and I were born we dwelt within country as spirits. When we pass away, we head back to this form. Each tree, animal, rock and piece of vegetation are moort [family]. We have brothers and sisters that are certain trees, rocks that are my grandparents, animals that are my parents.[66]

Noongar Elder Lynette Knapp, a descendant of the Menang people, puts this relationship very simply.

> *We're totemic people. Every black person in Australia has got an animal and a plant, belonging to their totems. And we don't own the land. We're an integral part of an ecological system.*[67]

This strong relationship between a people and their natural world was not obvious to newcomers like Canning River settler John Okey Davis. Writing to a cousin in January 1832, he was clearly puzzled by his local neighbours.

Trees and rocks are moort – family.

> Now for the natives, here we have nature in its pure unadorned state…They are probably the furthest removed from civilisation of any human creatures on the globe, for they have neither religion, laws or government, houses nor clothing none worthy of the name, and yet they do not appear stupid.[68]

Not surprisingly, Davis defined 'civilisation' in terms of his own understanding, which, in effect, is partly a 'non-understanding' of Aboriginal people's appreciation of law, spiritual reality and a lifestyle that enabled them to survive. His last 'and yet' is possibly a perplexed concession. Ted Wilkes has his own thoughts about what constitutes 'civilisation'.

> *The cultural conflict came about between hunters and gatherers and Anglo-Saxons who brought here a Western lifestyle which they called the civilising of the planet. But some of the things that happened in the recent history of Australia don't extol the virtues of civilisation. To me they say other things.*[69]

Civilisation for the white man was also stratified, with degrees of acceptability. Aboriginal (black) people existed at one level but within the European (white) world, they were at the bottom of many layered hierarchies. James Stirling complained to Sir George Murray in 1830 about some of the less desirable people who had been brought out to the colony as servants.

> Among the heads of families, there is a great majority of highly respectable and independent persons, in the working class there is a great variety; some masters have been careful in the selection of their servants and workmen, but the greater part have either engaged the outcasts of parishes, or have brought out men without reference to character; and the consequence is great inconvenience to such masters and endless trouble to the authorities established here.[70]

At the Swan River, the sense of a social hierarchy was alive and well. While settlers recognised the plight of the people they were displacing from the land, their own cultural stance worked against any compensatory action. The process of depriving the traditional owners of their land was gradual but inexorable.

The Noongars began to look for a solution to their plight, and a few white men, including Lyon, also called for the establishment of a peaceful agreement with the local inhabitants.[71] By 1832, he was openly advocating for a treaty to be negotiated between the settlers and the Swan River people, who, Lyon believed, were ever ready to agree to the sale of some of their land.[72] He thought that there might be a chance of persuading the government to agree to this proposition. Stirling was leaving for England but his deputy, Frederick Irwin, appeared more amenable to this idea.

In the end the suggestion lapsed when both Irwin and Lyon left the colony in 1834. Nevertheless, when Irwin published his book on the colony (*The State and Position of Western Australia*) in 1835, he suggested that treaties should be negotiated with Aboriginal people. In his view, responsibility for such agreements should not lie with the settlers, but with the Colonial Office in London.[73] George Fletcher Moore, who classed himself as a 'poor struggling settler', endorsed Irwin's views about the need for providing recompense to Aboriginal people but he, too, believed that the British government should foot the bill. In a diary entry for 17 September 1836, Moore wrote:

> There are great discussions here about the propriety of *purchasing* from them their interest in the land. I consider it a matter of justice that some recompense should be made to the natives or some consideration given, but I consider it is the part and duty of the British Gov't to do this as a national measure on account of the large territory which has been acquired & added to England, whether it be by conquest or by mere occupancy.[74]

When Moore wrote these words, the Noongars, concerned that fences erected by the colonists prevented access to their land and water, had already taken their complaint to Francis Armstrong, who, like Lyon, was sympathetic to their plight. He had first translated for the Aboriginal community during the earlier unsuccessful negotiations with Irwin. Armstrong was now the official government interpreter and the Noongars came to him with a proposition which he passed on to Stirling. On 13 September 1836, the governor informed the Executive Council that:

> Some time back the native interpreter had been applied to by certain of the leading natives of their district, on the subject of their lands which had to a considerable extent been taken from them in consequence of the settlements effected by the whites, and expressive of a wish to dispose of the same to the Government for a small consideration provided they were allowed free access to such parts as were not enclosed.[75]

By this time several settlers had, like Moore, recognised that Aboriginal people had proprietorial interests in land. Armstrong, on the basis of his own investigations, was able to report that:

> The right to property is well recognised among them both as to land and as to moveable effects. The land appears to be apportioned to different families, and is not held in common by the tribe…These co-proprietors appear equally interested in their respective districts, and are equally ready to revenge any trespass, which may be committed, not only by unauthorised hunting but by taking Swans' nests etc…Land is beyond doubt an inheritable property among them and they boast of having received it from their fathers' fathers etc, to an unknown period back. All the sons appear to succeed equally to their fathers' lands.[76]

Noongar woman Bella Bropho supports this view of the relationship between particular groups of Aboriginal people and land.

> *Certain people had boundaries of country and were responsible for looking out for your clan. And clan comes with your land. My father was always telling me land was Mother Earth and we're supposed to*

> be there protecting her. It's the boodja [country] of who we are and they tried to protect it until the settlement came and disrupted everything of our life.[77]

While Stirling would probably not have understood the Noongar claim that they were 'protecting' their land, he initially indicated that he favoured some agreement with the Aboriginal people to ensure their 'good conduct'. However, the colony's Executive Council, over which he presided, eventually rejected the Noongar proposal in the following terms:

> After some conversation, it seemed more advisable to advise the natives that it was not the wish of the government to deprive them of any part of their land beyond that which is or maybe required by the white inhabitants of the territory, and upon which they are not to trespass or commit any theft on pain of forfeiting the good will shown, and the protection.[78]

Commenting on this decision, law lecturer Ann Hunter has noted that, 'Armstrong was told verbally and in writing about the outcome. Aboriginal people were instead given flour and the question of the recognition of their land rights was avoided altogether.'[79]

Two months later, Stirling was deliberating on ways of dealing with Aboriginal theft and 'trespass on private property'. In effect, the original Australians were being warned not to trespass on their own land. As a result, many Aboriginal people were later prosecuted in the Court of Quarter Sessions as British subjects, under criminal law. Those convicted were transported to and imprisoned on Garden and Rottnest islands.[80]

For his pains, and his attempts to broker an agreement between the settlers and the local people, Armstrong was abandoned by both sides. Alan Thompson, who has researched Armstrong's part in attempting to conciliate between white and black, wrote that: 'By 1837 there were periods when he was completely alone, isolated from both the Europeans and Noongar. He complained with some bitterness that, "the natives never come to converse with me now, on any subject".[81]

Despite the new laws, Stirling was also still bound by instructions from the Colonial Office as to the 'rights of the natives'. At the same Executive Council meeting where the suggestion of a treaty was finally rejected, he ordered the following minutes to be published in the *Perth Gazette*.

> It is the determination of the Govt. to visit every act of injustice or violence on the Natives with the utmost severity...You will make it imperative on the officers of the police never to allow any injustice or insult re the Natives, to pass by unnoticed, as being of too trifling a character, and they should be charged to report to you with punctuality every instance of aggression or misconduct...[82]

And in that proclamation, Stirling reminds the settlers that:

> Colonists in their dealings with the Natives will sometimes have to encounter conduct which in a civilised society would be looked on as highly offensive; but it will be the duty of the settler to practise forbearance & moderation &...set an example of justice and good faith.[83]

Stirling and his Executive Council might have exhorted 'moderation' and wished for peaceful coexistence, but even before they dismissed the concept of a treaty or agreement, there had been plenty more bloodshed. The 1830 Battle of Perth proved to be a beginning, not an end. Matters came to a head in 1834 in what is still called by British settlers the Battle of Pinjarra, and by First Nations people, the Pinjarra Massacre.

In July 1834, Hugh Nisbett, a soldier and servant to an army officer, Lieutenant Armstrong, was murdered after he and a colleague had been assisted by seemingly friendly Aboriginal people to recover a stray horse. The horse's owner, Thomas Peel, had a large landholding in the area. As Statham-Drew notes, Peel would have been mystified by this killing. He would not have recognised that it was a clear warning from the local Aboriginal community for white men to stay off tribal land and to leave their women alone.[84]

In October that year Stirling, who had long intended to make a tour of this area to evaluate its suitability for further settlement, decided to ride south, in part to assess the 'native situation'. His account of what then transpired, later sent to the Colonial Office, indicated that his action against the local Aboriginal people was not premeditated. The sole intention had been to consider the region's settlement potential. Stirling was accompanied by his surveyor-general, John Septimus Roe, whose function was to advise on land allocation. This lends credence to Stirling's claim. Moreover, Roe remained unarmed.

The surveyor-general's own written recollection of what ensued accords reasonably closely with the governor's account. Roe states that Stirling and his party, which included armed troopers, unexpectedly met a group of natives at a river crossing. The meeting point was on the Murray River, close to what is now the town of Pinjarra, and the group was quickly identified as 'the obnoxious tribe', the perpetrators of the Nisbett murder and other attacks on settlers.

> So soon, however, as it was ascertained that they were the obnoxious tribe, the firing commenced at full charge in which the chief, Capt. Ellis was wounded in the temple and knocked off his horse by a spear thrown at 4 or 5 yards distance. The same native wounded one of the police (Heffron) in the right arm so as to completely disable him. The native was, however, almost immediately shot dead.[85]

Roe added that four or five Aboriginal people were killed in this 'unplanned' encounter. While obviously there are no written accounts from an Aboriginal perspective, most Noongars have always believed that this was a planned ambush and that the majority of the warriors were not present that morning. They are certain that well over fifty, possibly hundreds of Noongar people, mainly women, children and old men, were killed.[86]

While Aboriginal accounts of this event have been passed down in oral tradition, later generations have not always recognised the significance of the stories they were told, as Winnie McHenry recalled in 2010:

> My grandmother used to tell us this and I used to think 'What's this old woman talking about?' She used to tell me that her mother talked about the time when she was a baby and the troopers came in at Pinjarra and the massacre there, she used to tell me about this massacre and I didn't understand what she was saying because nothing was taught to us in school. My grandmother's mother had told her: 'When the troopers came in and thought they'd shot them all, the last of them laid upon this baby and pretended they were shot. Then they took off through the hills up to Kalamunda and there was a big tree up there. And from there they watched the tall ships coming in.'
>
> I went back to Curtin University and did my fourth-year studies. We had to read a book on Aboriginal history and I read about the Pinjarra story. That really opened my eyes. I didn't know about this, and I was in my forties.[87]

Jesse Hammond would have learned about what happened at Pinjarra from his grandfather, William Leeder, a settler friend of James Stirling. Despite the fact that local tribes had killed members of his own family, Hammond, in his later life, had great sympathy for his Aboriginal friends.

> The unfortunate thing for the natives of the South-West is that it is many years since there was one of them alive who could tell their side of the story; and so they are usually looked on as being in the wrong. But there are always two sides to a story and, although we are of a different colour, we should try to be fair and just.[88]

The Pinjarra location is significant. This area, like Success Hill at Bassendean and Kings Park in Perth, was neutral or common ground between land looked after by particular Aboriginal families. They were places where large numbers of Noongar people gathered during festive seasons. Here also Europeans would take reprisals for 'crimes' such as sheep stealing.[89] In September 1832, Guildford settler Jane Dodds reported on one such action.

> *in almost every instance, the settlers have been the aggressors...A party of natives drove off several of Mr Browne's sheep in sight of the shepherd, calling 'Kangaroo, kangaroo', which was a plain way of saying, 'you have killed our kangaroo, now we must have yours', but the sequel is dreadful to contemplate; they were followed, and the soldiers and others fell in with them about midnight (it was supposed their number exceeded two hundred men, women and children) seated round several large fires, at which were roasting about ten sheep; the followers all fired into the midst of the thickest groups, killing some, and wounding many; however the others fled in the greatest confusion, leaving all they possessed behind them, and among the rest the spears in question.*[90]

The story handed down to Winnie McHenry through her grandmother and great-grandmother suggests that the soldiers at Pinjarra had also fired indiscriminately.

In 1998, Natalie Contos, in conjunction with Noongar man Theo Kearing, prepared a comprehensive report on events at Pinjarra for the Murray Districts Aboriginal Association. She examined contemporary reports and evidence, and concluded that the main victims probably were, as Winnie McHenry now believes, women and children.[91] The encounter with Stirling's men, Contos says, took place near the women's ceremonial area where they were camped, protected by a small number of male guardians and older men. The warrior men were camped elsewhere at a site between Herron Point and Pinjarra on the Peel Inlet and were not present when Stirling's party arrived.[92]

The local Bindjareb men, Contos explains, were known by both Noongars and wadjelas to be the fiercest and best fighting men in the south-west. If they had been present, Stirling would almost certainly have experienced more casualties, whereas only two of his men were injured.

Contos supports her claim with a detailed description of the relative efficiency and efficacy of British rifles and muskets compared with that of Noongar spears or gidgis. Competent soldiers took over a minute to reload their rifles and these had a range of about 200 metres. Muskets with an accurate range of, at the most, about 35 metres could fire an absolute maximum of four shots a minute in the hands of well-trained soldiers. On the other hand, before an anticipated battle, Bindjareb Noongars would have made sure that they had hundreds of gidgis. They could reportedly throw twenty to thirty spears a minute and pick up new spears with their feet while continuing to throw. On the basis of this information, Contos contends that usually exchanges between Noongars and wadjelas were less one-sided than is often recorded in the history books.[93] But there is no dispute that, at Pinjarra, the Bindjareb Noongars experienced by far the larger number of casualties.

In summary, the evidence suggests that the main Bindjareb warrior group was not present and that this was a premeditated attack on a defenceless group of Aboriginal people, the majority of whom were women and children. Stirling's account suggests otherwise, however. Part of his report to the Colonial Office reads as follows:

> The women were kept until after our company had been collected around the two wounded men; they were then informed that this punishment had been inflicted because of the misconduct of the tribe, that the white men never forgot to punish murder; that on this occasion, the women and children had been spared, but if any other person should be killed by them, no one would be allowed to remain alive on this side of the mountains[94]

Stirling certainly attempted to portray events at Pinjarra in as favourable a light for himself as possible. He would not have wished to be accused of offending against the Colonial Office policy of 'moderation' towards the 'natives'. On the other hand, he did not deny that the Europeans had exacted retribution for a murder of one of their own.

The plaque on a rock in the Pinjarra Memorial Park recognises that there were two sides to the story. It refers to the deaths of Bindjareb Noongar people as well as to the death of a colonial officer as part of a 'confrontation'. However, some Noongar people would like recognition that, in their eyes, this was a massacre.[95]

Not surprisingly, Stirling found it difficult to act in a consistent manner towards the 'native people'. On the one hand, he was under instructions from officials in London to deal fairly and perhaps leniently with them. On the other hand, he was under pressure from the settlers to protect them against what they saw as the local marauding tribes. Some, like Lieutenant H. W. Bunbury, a young professional soldier who served in Western Australia during 1836 and 1837, complained about Stirling's vacillations. Bunbury was also impatient with what he saw as appeasement on Stirling's part.

Rock and plaque at Pinjarra Memorial Park.

Not the slightest reliance is to be placed on the Governor's word: he changes his mind and his measures ten times a day and it is notorious in the colony that except in writing no promise of his is worth anything…personally I like him but his public character is in many respects open to censure and his weak, vacillating conduct has done much harm to the colony.[96]

Lieutenant Bunbury clearly found dealing with 'the natives' very frustrating and difficult, particularly because Stirling gave apparently contradictory orders. He himself made comments indicating that he was conflicted. Bunbury complained that government policy was paying too little attention to the safety of the settlers: 'The measures of the Home Govt lead one to suppose that they consider the life of a Christian settler as of less value than that of a savage'.

On the other hand, Bunbury, like Stirling, considered that settlers should not take matters into their own hands, continuing:

> Far am I from sanctioning & supporting any violence against the ignorant benighted wretches. I certainly object to the white settler ever taking the law into his own hands or taking away the life of a Native except absolutely in his own defence, when he would be equally justified in killing a white man.[97]

This statement stands at odds with Bunbury's entry dated Tuesday 10 July 1836, when he wrote:

> My duty is very fatiguing and disagreeable, as my men are stationed at the different farms on the Avon…a district nearly 50 miles in length…I have no fixed residence or quarters…and in the middle of winter with a pleasing alternation of rain and frost I do not find the life very pleasant. I hope, however, it will not last very long as the Natives seem inclined to be quiet since I shot a few of them one night.[98]

Cameron and Barnes, who have edited Bunbury's letters and other documents relating to his three years (1834–37) in Australia, suggest that these words when writing to his father, who had also been a soldier, were simply a case of youthful boasting (or perhaps an attempt at a bad joke). To support this interpretation, they cite the fact that the then government interpreter, Francis Armstrong, reported only two deaths of Aboriginal people around York and that these occurred on 15 June that year. Yet the *Perth Gazette* for 9 July did report a rumoured incident in the previous week in which a group of York Aborigines had been attacked at night, several being wounded and one woman killed. It is not clear whether this incident is the one to which Bunbury was referring or, indeed, whether he was involved.[99]

Lieutenant Bunbury's contradictory statements illustrate the lack of understanding that could occur between the two cultures. He claims to have been in daily contact with Aboriginal people and, having observed them, concluded that:

> In some respects, however they appear to respect private property and are honest towards each other whatever they may be towards us. They will steal nothing from each other except women and in love all is reckoned fair even among more polished nations.[100]

At the same time, these First Nations people who were fighting to retain possession of their own land, appeared to Bunbury as 'treacherous and not to be trusted'.[101]

Bunbury's account of this time in Western Australia (March 1836 to November 1837) reflects the reality that disputes over land and justice were increasingly leading to greater tensions within the settler community and harsher attitudes from the military who were there to keep the peace.

Major conflict arose partly when newly arrived farmers sought to grow crops and graze animals much as they had done in their own country. The limited river-bordering land was prime hunting ground as well as suitable for yam growing and the source of nutritious plants for Noongar communities. Stories about some of these food resources have been handed down to Ted Wilkes:

Swan River – a rich source of food.

> There were lots and lots of resources along the river…Also, on the outskirts of the Swan River there are many bush plants which we need to rekindle our interest in. But certainly, the turtle, the fishing, the swamp eggs, the bush tucker including the quandong, the berries that are associated with the forest around the river, the gum leaf and the health qualities that you can get from a eucalypt leaf, these are all things that our people knew about.[102]

Given the apparent land shortage at the Swan, the extreme south-west of the continent, with its cooler climate and higher rainfall, seemed to offer better prospects for would-be migrant farmers. With few readily available land grants remaining in the Perth region, Governor Stirling, who had appropriated a considerable amount of this land for himself, now advised new arrivals to look elsewhere. He recommended the area near Cape Leeuwin and in May 1830, prospective settlers, including the Turner, Molloy and Bussell families, arrived at Flinders Bay, where the Blackwood River meets the Southern Ocean, at a site Stirling named Augusta.

Flinders Bay, Augusta – landing place, 2 May 1830.

The Wadandi people, who know this area as Talanup, watched the arrival of the white men. Their oral tradition says that:

> years ago, there was a big bird that lived down around the southern part of the country. It was a huge white bird. One day the bird flew away and went across the *wardan* or sea. Nyungar didn't know where it went. But when they saw the white people's ships coming in with the big sails up, they thought it was the bird coming back. So they all went down to greet the bird that was coming back. As they were waiting, they realised that it was the djanga, white people who were about to land on the shore.[103]

The white people were here to stay and their settlement expanded in time to include land around Undalup, initially known to the newcomers as Vasse but soon renamed Busselton. As at King George Sound and the Swan River, these new Australians would have to come to an understanding with both the local people and the land they intended to cultivate.

John Garrett Bussell captures something of a European, perhaps a distinctly English, apprehension of unfamiliar surroundings. In a letter to a friend, written in July 1831, he suggests appreciation of his surroundings and, at the same time, unease with respect to the local people.

> The place is beautifully picturesque, but so wild, so savage…But man alas! is more uncultivated than all, living on the rind of nuts, the interior of which is poisonous, fish, which they catch with an ill constructed spear, and the kangaroo. Sometimes they content themselves with fern roots and grubs which they display, great, I was going to say, instinct in finding about the grass tree.
>
> They are here at present very peaceful and yet there is something which makes one shudder when he crosses, unawares in his path, the naked lord of the forest.[104]

Paths did cross at Augusta. Settler and early European botanist Georgiana Molloy was able to write, on 20 November 1833, that in comparison with the Swan, relations with the local people were harmonious.

> The natives are very fond of all the settlers at Augusta and we live on the most peaceful terms. But at The Swan, from the indiscretion of several persons and particularly their servants, they are hostile.[105]

Initially, the 'beautifully picturesque' landscape of Augusta posed more of a problem for the newcomers than establishing relations with the long-term residents. As John Bussell reported in a letter to his mother in August 1830:

> The grand difficulty is clearing away trees of stupendous magnitude and great hardness. Horticulture is all we attempt at present. The potatoes from the box you so nicely packed we have just dug. Owing, however, to the season when we were obliged to put them in, and the weakness of the sets, from the length of shoots they had put forth, we have a crop of marbles rather than potatoes.[106]

This settler group had little or no farming knowledge. They had taken up land in densely forested country and could only clear and farm small acreages. By 1834, there had been crop failures at Augusta and the Bussells had lost their second homestead, the Adelphi, further up the Blackwood River, to fire.

It was time to find more fertile and accessible soil and most of the Augusta settlers relocated to the coastal plain around Geographe Bay. Bussell gives an account of an early meeting with the locals on the banks of the river Vasse.

> We were hailed by three natives who were wading over from the opposite side, fearful probably that we were likely to interfere with some snares they had constructed for fish, near the spot where we were. They carried spears, but approached withal in such friendly guise and courtly seeming that I did not hesitate to advance to meet them alone and unarmed…I obtained some words of their language. It seemed much the same as that used at Augusta…I enter into these particulars because I infer that, as a judicious treatment of the natives at Augusta has procured in them towards the settlers a peaceful disposition, it will be satisfactory to learn that the population about to flow towards the Vasse has grounds for expecting that friendly reception which a previous knowledge of the habits of Europeans, or a favourable report circulated amongst the tribes, and a consequent predisposition to amity, may seem to promise.[107]

Bussell was anticipating a harmonious relationship with the original occupants. He also hoped that the lighter tree density, together with flat and well-watered land, would offer better prospects for farming.

These 'park-like' features of the landscape were probably the result of long-term activity by the Wadandi. As historian Bill Gammage has shown, 'parks chequered Australia' and were the result of burning every two to four years, promoting perennial grassland. As he suggests, it might have seemed a small jump to think of these 'parks' as human-made, as in Europe, but in fact:

the leap was so vast that almost no-one made it. Almost all thought no land in Australia private and parks natural. To think otherwise required them to see Aborigines as gentry, not shiftless wanderers. That seemed preposterous.[108]

Settlements sprouted along the Vasse River as they had along the Swan, Canning and Murray rivers. Bussell reported favourably on this country:

> The country as we advanced improved rapidly; the ground on which we trod was a vivid green, unsullied with burnt sticks and blackened grass trees. Not that it was covered with a decided turf, but the vegetation seemed more succulent than woody, and the plants, growing to about the same height presented to the eye a smooth surface…Though the flowers were perhaps not precisely the same that characterise an English meadow, they were not the less beautiful in appearance, varied in form and brilliant in colour. Grass was in plenty…[109]

Grass for cattle and sheep, as the newcomers saw it, and easy meals for Iszaac Webb's Wadandi people.

> *Later on, the settlers started to have livestock in there as well and then our old people thought, 'Oh, this is great, fenced-in cows, fenced-in sheep. You don't have to run a kangaroo down or an emu or climb a tree to get a possum.' So, it was easy to get meat. But obviously they didn't realise that then by spearing that the repercussions were going to be either hung or sent to prison up at Wadjemup [Rottnest Island].*[110]

The same land issues now arose as those that had already emerged on the Swan. New arrivals had to find a sustainable relationship with the original owners.

The Bussells were a large family of siblings. Historian Marian Aveling has described their situation and social position as, in some ways, similar to other settlers at the Vasse as well as at the Swan.

> *They were the adult children of a clergyman who had died fairly young and left very little money. What he'd left was family position and when*

the children were in their teens and older, Mrs Bussell decided they'd be better off in Western Australia, that they should gather together the last remnants of their fortune and cross the seas so that they could achieve in Western Australia the kind of social position they deserved, but would never get in England because they didn't have enough cash. So, she sent them out, in several relays, boys first and then girls, and they became farmers effectively.[111]

Within this large family there were different reactions to the people who had lived in this area from time immemorial; diverse attitudes that would re-emerge among other nineteenth-century settlers and writers.

John Garrett Bussell, the eldest brother and head of the family, had originally intended to take holy orders in the Anglican church and was 'an avowed humanitarian'.[112] His description of 'the natives', however, was not flattering:

> The countenances of two of them were certainly ugly and brutal enough; but the third had a sprightly air and good-humoured

Cattle Chosen – the Bussell homestead, built 1834–36 (drawing by Stan Dilkes).

expression unaccompanied with that revolting laugh which is so general with these savages.[113]

Edward Shann, writing within fifty years of Bussell's death, tells us that while John Bussell never clearly articulated his own view of the settlers' duty and policy towards these 'savages', 'Certain facts indicate however, that he recognised the white man's duty to provide for the black, out of the surplus his better use of the land would provide'.[114] Shann recorded that when Bussell was present, 'Relations with the natives were almost uniformly peaceful. Rations were given to those round "Cattle Chosen" [the Bussell homestead], and a tradition of kindness still clings to the name "Mowen" by which they called him'.[115] Shann's source for a 'tradition of kindness' is not clear as, according to the Wadandi, Bussell is remembered more for his role in events that followed the 1841 killing of George Layman at Wonnerup, north of Busselton, than for distributing largesse to the local people.[116]

Historian Malcolm Allbrook sees John Garrett Bussell as eventually conflicted in the context of nineteenth-century Aboriginal–European contacts in south-western Australia.

> John Garrett Bussell was an avowed humanitarian who largely supported the colonial government's policies of non-violence and benevolence towards the local Aboriginal people. Yet his primary purpose as a coloniser was clear. His family sought to own land and to carve out an estate exclusively for its own benefit.[117]

Colonial government policies, which Stirling, as governor, was expected to support, were designed to avoid undue severity when dealing with Aboriginal communities. For John's brothers Charles and Lenox, family protection was the first priority.

The Bussells not only needed to keep on good terms with the Wadandi people; they also depended on them for local knowledge, such as where to find water. Importantly, all these would-be gentry needed labour on the land and in the home. Like other families, they had arrived in the colony with their retainers. In this new country, however, servants began to take up land in their own right rather than continue to work for the 'gentry'. As Marian Aveling comments:

> *They thought they'd have lots of servants and they'd be able to reproduce English society there and then. But they found themselves working with their hands and labouring in the fields themselves and in the dairy and the household for the women.*[118]

All the settler families at the Vasse had to rely on Aboriginal labour. The latter were now often short of food because of the white man's practice of enclosing land. Thus, from time to time, the Wadandi were obliged to work for the settlers in return for flour and other supplies. But these original Australians were not the kind of dutiful servants to which some English families were accustomed. In 1837, Bessie Bussell, John's sister, wrote in her diary about her problems with the 'native servants'.

> The natives really completely beset us. They nearly drive me out of my mind. I am obliged to stand about and watch them, and when I am obliged to return to my lawful labours, I find myself thoroughly tired, and then evening comes when we used to enjoy ourselves. The noise they make puts conversation out of the question. They throw the tea all over the tables that have been taken all possible pains with in the morning and wilga [stain with red pigment mixed with grease] all they come near. To me now, it seems sacrilege to breathe the name of 'native' in an hour of rest, it is so fraught with fatigue, fear and anxiety.[119]

For the Bussells in the 1830s, relationships with the local Aboriginal people became more than a 'servant problem'. In their letters and diaries, along with other Vasse settlers, they expressed concern and frustration about raids on their newly built homes, broken windows, and the stealing of tools and flour. Bessie Bussell described the situation as living in a 'council of war' and writes about the retaliatory measures taken by the soldiers and settlers.

> Eleven days later, on Sunday, 30th July [1837], natives were heard shouting on the estuary. Everyone immediately armed themselves, and in a little while we heard the firing of guns. After two hours' absence, they returned amidst crowds of natives. I fear more women were slain than men. All our little party returned safely. All was intended to be right, so I hope this skirmish will turn out for the best. Three women, one man, one boy are known to be dead, but more are supposed to be dying.[120]

Brothers Alfred and Vernon Bussell seem to have had something of a bad conscience about what had occurred. Bessie records that three days later they:

> went down to the estuary, and saw that the natives had been afraid to return and bury their dead. So they left their cows and came home for spades to perform this last office for them. They were joined by many others who participated in their feelings, and when they had dug the graves, they spread grass at the bottom, lowered the bodies down, and sprinkled grass over them. They threw in the dirt and laid the sods carefully over like an English grave.[121]

Like an English grave? Or was this green camouflage to ensure no further investigation of these events? In any event, relationships with First Nations people were now at their lowest ebb. As European farming changed the landscape the Wadandi were losing their own food sources. Noongar historian Len Collard suggests that it is not clear when his people realised that they were losing control of their land, its resources and their own lives and lifestyle. But inexorably this was happening. As Collard comments, the wadjelas needed the summer waterholes to see their stock through the dry months of the year and were unwilling to share this resource with the traditional owners. Furthermore:

> The Noongar summer burning of the land, which was the principal means of gaining kangaroo at that time, and which had

produced the open pasture land so attractive to the Europeans, now threatened the pastures the settler needed for his sheep and cattle.[122]

By the 1840s it had become illegal for the Noongar to burn the bush and the contrast in approach to land management became a critical fault line in the relationship between settlers and the Wadandi. In addition, with the settlers often themselves on short rations, there was competition for the native fauna, as Lenox Bussell reported in July 1834.

> We have been here for three months and have been living on kangaroos which is as good as beef. We have caught twenty-two during that time. We never go out without catching one and sometimes two…[123]

An additional incentive for 'pilfering', as Europeans described it, was the Aboriginal awareness that these strangers had ready-made food, including flour and biscuits, at their disposal. Hunger inevitably influenced the conflict.

The Vasse River at Busselton.

Any events that reduced the likelihood of conflict were welcomed by the settlers at the Vasse. Charles Bussell expressed relief that what he called the 'Field of Pinjarra' had resulted in the defeat of the Bindjareb, the Aboriginal people living around the Murray River.

> The most powerful and most successfully insolent tribe in the then peopled settlement, received a shock which never has and will never be erased from their memory! They have kissed the rod by which they have been scourged and the white man is permitted to walk unarmed and unharmed through scenes which have witnessed repeated murders of his unfortunate countrymen.[124]

In an effort to create a more judicial approach, within what Edward Shann has described as 'Western Australia's first group settlement', Captain John Molloy had been made magistrate for the Vasse district, with authority over the military, while John Garrett Bussell had been appointed a justice of the peace. During the latter's absence in England in 1837, his brother Lenox temporarily took over the position. In June that year Lenox had to deal with an accusation by the Chapman family that a heifer had been stolen, killed and eaten by Aboriginal people. A warrant was issued for the arrest of several men and a conflict near the Sabina River in the Vasse district resulted in the deaths of three suspects. Others thought to be involved got away. Lenox then wrote to Molloy, asking him to make soldiers available because the inhabitants were 'in a totally unprotected state'. Molloy replied that he could offer no more assistance than the two men he was despatching. The situation was made more tense by the settlers' knowledge that Stirling intended to replace soldiers with a police-based protection system. Bussell's response sheds light on settlers' fears.

> Steps, prompt and decisive were called for and were absolutely necessary to prevent the occurrence of the same act again and again, until the whole herd and the prospects, perhaps the lives of

a thriving settlement have fallen a sacrifice to savages incapable of discriminating between clemency and cowardice.[125]

Lenox said that he was not motivated by undue severity and that he was aware of the importance of maintaining friendly relations. But he stated that the 'natives' were inferior beings who would in time come to appreciate, and gratefully accept, the benefits of civilisation if sufficient force was used against them.[126]

As Busselton historian Rodger Jennings observed,

> Lenox's opinion that severity would breed respect was no more successful then, than at any other time in the history of man. One action led to another. Blacks and whites polarised. The black people were treated abominably, being killed or maimed for reasons beyond their understanding. The white people in their turn suffered from acute nervous tension, alarm and even panic, at the possibility of sudden and violent death.[127]

At the end of the 1830s, conflict between black and white at the Vasse still threatened. A crisis arose in early 1841 with the killing of settler George Layman by Gayware, a Wadandi Elder. To some extent Layman had invited his fate by challenging Gayware over a minor disagreement which involved (depending on which version of the story is accepted) either theft of damper or the return of Gayware's wife, then working in the Layman home at Wonnerup. Layman apparently seized Gayware by his beard and shook him.[128] This was a cultural offence for the Noongars, an unpardonable affront to the Wadandi, who still believe that Layman knew this to be an insult. Gayware then immediately speared Layman, who died almost instantly.

The death of a white man was seen by the entire Bussell family, including John Garrett, as an appalling deed and they and others were determined to retaliate. An avenging party was led by magistrate Captain John Molloy. It included three Bussell brothers, John, Charles and Alfred, who hunted down Gayware and shot him dead.[129] Wadandi custodian Iszaac Webb has been told that not only did the Bussells kill his ancestor, but they also 'chopped our grandfather's head off, smoked it in a hollow log and sent his sons to Rottnest'.[130]

Settler retribution did not stop there. As with events at Pinjarra in 1834, there are differing views of what happened at and around Wonnerup after Layman's death. As Noongar historian Len Collard asserts:

> In the 13 day period, many innocent Nyungars were to die in the battle for Wonnerup and the invader way of life. There is likely to be a Nyungar bias in the account of the Layman affair or Nyungar killings, murders or massacres as this view is a part of the overall Wonnerup Homestead story. The Nyungar version must be compared with the Wedjela version as both appear to tell the same story that a massacre did occur, but have differing emphasis.[131]

In their account to the colonial secretary, Bussell and Molloy stated that 'four men and one woman, in spite of every effort, were killed'.[132] Collard, however, knows of two accounts of this event handed down to the descendants of Wadandi families. One informant stated that:

> Our great great grandmother who saw this happening said Gayware went to get his women back from the Laymans who was [sic] working in their house. The massacre took place after she saw her mother and two stepbrothers shot before her own eyes. Her mother and brothers were full-bloods of the tribe of Wonnerup. She was part white. Her father was Elijah Dawson.[133]

The same eyewitness's oral testimony covers the next phase of the story.

> The river was red with blood where they used to keep alive...the white men's guns were too many so some of the Aboriginals got away, but they were rounded up and shot, north of the Capel River (Mollakup). Now what I call the killing fields...that's where men...if you can call them men, but I say they were murderers

and killers to wipe out a whole tribe of people, women and children.[134]

The death of Layman and its aftermath was reported in the *Perth Gazette* on 13 March 1841. The newspaper dismissed the deaths of innocent Aboriginal victims as 'irrelevant' and pointed out that:

> As our conduct has been, with acts of kindness, and consideration for their situation, as contrasted with us of civilised life – the benefits we have conferred upon them far outweigh any loss they may have experienced from our occupation of their lands.[135]

The pendulum of history has swung away from this characterisation of events and we might now well debate the meaning of terms like 'civilised life' and what then constituted 'kindness and consideration'. But the arguments continue, including the role of John Molloy as the leader of the settler party who first pursued Gayware and his associates.

According to William Lines, Molloy tricked three of the remaining Aboriginal men by asking the captain of an American whaler ship which they visited regularly to lure them aboard his ship and seize them. Molloy wrote to Captain Blaskett:

> I take the liberty of the service of humanity and your actual love of justice to beg you would interest yourself in the apprehension of [the] three natives...Any movement from this quarter would lead to their immediate flight. But as they suppose you are ignorant of their crimes they will not suspect you.[136]

These 'natives' were duly captured as a result of this subterfuge and Blaskett asked for, and received, 25 pounds for his pains.[137]

The settlers were determined to take further action to avenge Layman's death. In his 1897 history of Western Australia, American John Kimberly wrote that:

> The white men throughout Wonnerup, Capel, Vasse and Blackwood banded together to take a dire revenge...Colonel (captain) Molloy ordered his men to prepare to march, and he

took command of them and the chief settlers in the south western districts. He gave special instructions that no woman or child should be killed, but that no mercy should be offered the men. A strong and final lesson must be taught the blacks...All were well-armed.[138]

Kimberly recorded that several Aboriginal people were killed but that the settlers and soldiers were not satisfied. They then traced 'the terrified fugitives' to Lake Minninup (South Bunbury) and, according to Kimberly's narrative:

> Native after native was shot...The white men had no mercy. The black men were killed by dozens, and their corpses lined the route of march of the avengers. Then the latter went back satisfied... On the sand patch near Mininup, skeletons and skulls of natives reported to have been killed in 1841 are still to be found. Mixed with them are the bones of dogs shot on the same day.[139]

A graphic oral account of this pursuit and killing of the Wadandi mob at both Mollakup (near the Capel River) and Lake Minninup comes from a Noongar descendant, who, as a young boy, reported that he had found skulls at the site.

> They (the Nyungars) left in the middle of the night. That same night and the next morning, the whitefellas went after them on horseback, see. They (Nyungars) stuck to the hills along the river close to the coast, coz they knew that if they went out on the flat country, they soon be chased down, on horses. The first mob was caught, was just the other side of the Capel River (Mollakup). When I was a little boy, we found some skulls up there. One of them had a bullet in it, it had gone through the forehead and was just sticking out the back. There was quite a few with holes knocked in them in the skulls, and the next mob they caught was at Muddy Lake (Minninup) that's this side of Bunbury and then they chased the others right through Australind somewhere around Australind area they caught up they killed some more there and the rest got away. That's about all I can tell you that's all dad told me.[140]

Even at the time, some white settlers considered the extent of the reprisals to be unjustified, as the following handed-down memory suggests.

> (my) Father condemned the massacres. As I've said before he didn't condone the massacres…he said [the Nyungars] were gentle people and they didn't deserve it [the massacres] and they (the white people) could get around if they negotiated.[141]

While later historians have disputed or discounted Captain Molloy's role in these events, writer Jessica White has suggested that there have been deliberate attempts to play down his involvement.

> As I pieced together these documents and attended to their language, I realised that the massacre had been depicted in such a way as to obfuscate John Molloy's role. I also came to understand that this role had been covered, uncovered and contested over the ensuing years.[142]

A changed landscape.

White asserts that accounts written by colonists constructed a particular view of the massacre, while denying a substantial voice to Wadandi people. There seems little doubt that the reprisals for the killing of George Layman were extensive and that many Wadandi people were killed.

Interpretations of events in the first three British establishments in Western Australia — King George Sound, the Swan River Colony and Augusta–Vasse — continue to differ. One undisputed fact is that in south-west Western Australia, within the space of little more than twenty years, the world of the original Australians had been disrupted and altered almost out of recognition. More changes were to follow in every corner of what would become the State of Western Australia.

Chapter 3

A Moral Wilderness?

British settlers had taken possession of a large slice of a new continent in the 1820s and, while aware that the land was already occupied, they justified their presence with an assumed cultural superiority, viewing the original inhabitants as primitive and uncivilised. They were also certain that they could provide the First Nations people with material and cultural benefits.

Yet a few of the newcomers publicly recognised that Aboriginal people owned this land. One who did, Robert Menli Lyon (born Robert Milne), came in the first year of European settlement.[1] In a public speech, he said:

> Reflect. You have seized upon a land that is not yours. Beware, and do not...add to the guilt of dipping your hands in the blood of those whom you have spoiled of their country.[2]

But Lyon still had no doubt that the locals would be better off if brought into the Christian fold.

> The adoption of the English character and the use of a common alphabet, will not only afford a facility of communication between those who engage in the great work of evangelizing the aboriginal inhabitants, but may tend to assimilate the different dialects so that millions of this vast continent, may yet communicate with one another in one tongue, and sing the praises of the Redeemer of men in the same language.[3]

Unlike many Europeans, however, Lyon appreciated that the Noongar people did 'seem to have an idea of the existence of a supreme being'.[4]

Another observer, George Fletcher Moore, was intrigued but perplexed by what looked like sun worship. On an expedition in the bush, he recorded that his party:

> Examined a singular cavern which had been discovered the year before…At the extreme end of it on the rock there was a rudely marked round figure which was supposed to represent the sun (but I do not know why) and in different places near this round figure

All Saints Upper Swan, first settler church.

were the impressions of open hands. It appeared as if the rock had been covered with some reddish pigment & these impressions formed by rubbing a stone against the rock like this...This cave has been supposed to be a place of worship. I know not on what grounds. We know not that they have any veneration for any thing. Is this to represent the sun? Why so, more than any other round thing? Have they any veneration for the sun?[5]

Moore's perplexity about the role of the sun illustrates the problem of cultural adjustment for early nineteenth-century colonists. Unlike Lyon, he seemed uncertain about where veneration could be directed.

Almost two centuries later, it is perhaps easier to appreciate Aboriginal acknowledgement of the sun as part of a belief system, a system based on the generosity of nature, dependence on the sun for light and growth, and the close relationships between all living things. The moon also comes into this understanding, from a very practical perspective.

Astronomer Ray Norris found that the Yolngu fishermen in Arnhem Land had used their powers of observation to gain a clear understanding of the relationship between the moon and the tides on our planet.

> *People saw the moon and they saw its phases and they tried to understand how those phases are linked to the tides. When you get a full moon, you get a very high tide. When you get a quarter moon the tide isn't so extreme. And so, they evolved a notion of the moon coming up through the ocean and it fills and empties water. And so, the phase of the moon is related to the tides.*
>
> *Now that isn't the mechanism we talk about in science. We talk about the gravitational pull of the sun and the moon. But actually, it is very closely linked to observation. And what I find very interesting is that a few hundred years ago, Galileo dismissed any link between the moon and the tides. He called it superstitious nonsense. The Yolngu got it right and it's that process of linking your model to the world through observation.[6]*

For men like Moore it was difficult to understand that Aboriginal people had their own distinctive way of interpreting the world and applying relevant technology, based on a highly developed observational culture. But he was impressed by one early encounter with his new neighbours.

> There were three strangers today, whom I had not seen before: a brother & an uncle of Weeip & a smart youth called *'Blackman'*. Him I saw for the first time throwing a crooked stick which describes a course in the air which I could not have believed possible had I not seen it. Standing in this attitude and catching it by one end, he flung it in the air rather towards the left. The weapon whirls round & round, performing horizontal revolutions & gradually rising in a large circular direction from left to right when it seems to get an impulse in a new direction and to return in a sort of descending half circle…How in the name of wonder could they invent such a shape of a weapon? How can they make it describe such an extraordinary course? Verily, it is a puzzle to me at present.[7]

Moore's puzzlement at first seeing 'Blackman' flying a boomerang is understandable. Leonardo da Vinci's fifteenth-century sketches had suggested the potential for air travel. But by 1833 Western technology had made no further advances in this sphere except for ballooning. It was a revelation to Moore that an observant people could understand and apply the dynamics of flight within their hunter-gatherer culture. Menang Elder Vernice Gillies suggests that:

> *They obviously had studied birds flying and I think they probably practised on different shapes of wood. I think they probably took a long time to get to the point where they would be able to use a boomerang based around the wings of a bird. We see the same shape on planes of today. Their wings are the same shape as the wings of a bird and it goes all the way back to nature.*[8]

Despite being impressed with Aboriginal inventiveness, Moore, like Lyon, was certain that the locals would still benefit from acquiring European culture and religion. He was not alone. The

A MORAL WILDERNESS?

Did birds in flight inspire the boomerang?

Reverend John Wollaston, in effect an Anglican missionary, who made Australia his home, would come to describe his new abode as 'a moral wilderness'.[9] But whose wilderness and whose morality?

Evangelical Christians in Australia had come face to face with a distinctly different culture and a highly spiritual apprehension of life and its meaning. For this ancient race there was no 'wilderness', only 'country', with all its associations. Anthropologist Deborah Bird Rose reminds us that:

> Country in Aboriginal English is not only a common noun but also a proper noun. People talk about country in the same way that they would talk about a person: they speak to country, sing to country, visit country, worry about country, feel for country, and long for the country. Country is not a generalised or undifferentiated type of place, such as one might indicate with terms like 'spending a day in the country' or 'going up country'. Rather, country is a living entity with a yesterday, today and tomorrow, with a consciousness and a will toward life. Because of

this richness, country is home and peace; nourishment for body, mind and spirit; heart's ease.[10]

Robert Lyon recognised that Aboriginal people related primarily to the natural world.

> Think not, then, that the Aboriginal inhabitants of Australia, offspring of the same great parent with yourselves, and partakers of all the kindred feelings of a common humanity, can resign the mountains and seas, the rivers and lakes, the plains and the wilds of their uncradled infancy, and the habitation of their fathers for generations immemorial to a common foe, without the bitterness of grief.[11]

Lyon was concerned as much with ethics as with religious observance. He questioned the assumption that while Indigenous resistance was seen and punished as a crime, Aboriginal people were not allowed to act in self-defence.

> They may stand to be slaughtered; but they must not throw a spear in their own defence, or attempt to bring their enemies to a sense of justice by the only means in their power, – that of returning like for like. If they do – if they dare to be guilty of an act which in other nations would be eulogised as the noblest of a patriot's deeds – they are outlawed; a reward is set upon their heads; and they are ordered to be shot, as if they were so many mad dogs! Thus, in the barbarous manner, ye practice what in them ye condemn, the law of retaliation.[12]

Lyon went on to make a prediction: 'Choose for yourselves. If ye determine upon a war of extermination, civilized nations will be mute with astonishment at the madness of a policy so uncalled for, so demoniacal.'[13]

For most of his fellow settlers, Lyon was now an unwelcome eccentric with unpopular views. Early in 1835 he left the Swan River for Mauritius, only to return some years later to New South Wales, where he continued his condemnation of the treatment meted out to First Nations people.

Within a year, another critic arrived in Western Australia. Dr Louis Giustiniani had been appointed by the newly established Western Australian Missionary Society to 'establish a Christian mission (in conformity with the principles of the Church of England) to the Aborigines and to the more destitute of the settlers'.[14] Fluent in several languages, including English, Giustiniani has been described by Henry Reynolds as 'an exotic, a sophisticated Italian convert to Anglicanism who was denounced for daring to criticise British policies and manners'.[15] Like Lyon, Giustiniani saw an ethical conflict between British law and Noongar law and practice.

In contrast to the colonial chaplain, John Wittenoom, who was described by John Wollaston as 'Old High Church Tory Party, argumentative, somewhat stiff and unyielding in matters of secondary importance',[16] Giustiniani was an evangelical Christian and a passionate crusader for the principles in which he believed. He might have been a foreigner in a British colony but the movement he represented came from 'the mother country'. In Britain, as in other parts of Europe, the eighteenth-century Enlightenment or Age of Reason, with its notion of the 'noble savage', was now confronted by a revival of stricter Christian precepts. These resonated strongly among Evangelicals. The firm intent was to civilise and save souls.

Evangelism also challenged a perceived spiritual laziness within the Church of England, whose guidelines were seen by sterner Christians as based on political and social allegiances rather than on spiritual conviction. Historian Tom Stannage has described this as an arrangement where 'the Anglican church served the State and the State served the Anglican church'.[17] Evangelical thinking also associated itself with anti-slavery campaigns. In the early 1820s, the Exeter Hall Movement, based in London, had begun to push for the abolition of slavery in the British Empire. The *Slavery Abolition Act* came into effect in 1833. Protestant evangelism contended that if slaves were to be freed, their souls must be saved and their cultures transformed wherever the British landed and hoisted the flag. Moreover, the settler churches, both Catholic and Protestant, were at the forefront of discussions about the morality of empire in a wide range of debates about slavery, convict transportation and the impact of colonisation on the Aboriginal population.[18]

Giustiniani understood his 'mission' within this context. When, early in 1837, the *Perth Gazette* suggested that 'forcible measures' would be required to subdue the original inhabitants of the York district and that 'a second Pinjarra' was called for,[19] Giustiniani was quick to respond to this apparent 'call to arms' Perhaps mindful of Lyon's warning that 'a war of extermination would ensue', he argued in the opposing newspaper, the *Swan River Guardian*, that the *Perth Gazette* was 'nourishing thoughts of total extermination'. Significantly, Giustiniani reminded settlers of the principles laid down in 1836 by the British colonial secretary, Lord Glenelg, for dealing with conflict. These precepts stated that, irrespective of the enemy, 'the gratuitous aggravation of the horrors of war, on the plea of vengeance or retribution, or on any similar ground, is alike indefensible'.[20]

Glenelg was both a humanitarian and a committed member of the evangelical Church Missionary Society. He had been largely responsible for amending legislation in the British Parliament to protect workers in the West Indies after the abolition of slavery.[21] During his brief time in the Swan River Colony, Giustiniani addressed no fewer than nine letters directly to the colonial secretary seeking his intervention to prevent the unjust imprisonment and killing of Aboriginal Australians.

The editor of the *Swan River Guardian*, William Nairn Clark, supported Giustiniani, calling him a 'true friend of the people'. Clark also had a low opinion of the colony's decision-makers, describing them in June 1837 as, 'A certain class here who at home were bankrupts...and glad to leave the mother country in order like bloated frogs to swell into a little importance at Swan River'.[22]

Again, in response to killings of Aboriginal people at York, Giustiniani asked more uncomfortable questions in the *Swan River Guardian*.

> Are they (the Aborigines) British subjects or are they not? Yes, thanks be to God they are and have the same rights as Mr Mackie, the Judge and Captain Stirling, the Governor! My Lord, unlawfulness is arrived at the summit, the evil to a crisis. The British Constitution is trampled upon. The death of Jones and Chidlow has caused the death of eighteen innocent victims (that is the complaint of the Aboriginal British subjects).[23]

A correspondent to the *Perth Gazette* who called himself 'John Bull the Younger' hit back, stating that, 'The missionary's affront to the settlers might have been acceptable if he were a Briton'.[24]

In his support for displaced traditional owners, who were unfamiliar with British law, Giustiniani involved himself in their legal defence. In the Quarter Sessions of October 1837, a Noongar man (Neu-anung) was charged with stealing two bushels of wheat. The only evidence against the accused was that, two months after the theft, he was wearing an empty wheat sack. The jury returned a verdict of guilty and sentenced Neu-anung to six months imprisonment. Two other natives were found guilty of similar crimes and each sentenced to seven years transportation. Giustiniani argued that these people had been deprived of their traditional sources of food, had no parish to go to for sustenance, had not been taught any form of work and had no understanding of British law.[25] His arguments cut little ice with the settlers and animosity against him increased. Rumours included the unfounded accusation that he was in the habit of beating his wife,[26] while a York settler wrote in the *Perth Gazette*,

> Under the sacred garb of a missionary, he attempts to poison the mind of Lord Glenelg and a sensitive British public – he attempts to raise the hue and cry of the English press against us, by such barefaced falsehoods under the guise of humanity and Christian feeling.[27]

No immediate support from Lord Glenelg or the 'sensitive British public' was forthcoming and Giustiniani could not continue the fight. He was dismissed by the Missionary Society and in January 1838 a small notice in the *Swan River Guardian* announced that Giustiniani was leaving the colony. That newspaper ceased publication in March 1838 and in its final edition railed against the 'diabolical inveteracy of the Swan River Clique, who never rested until they had hunted him away…they will rue the hour when they persecuted the Missionary and embittered his life by their assassin-like conduct'.[28]

Giustiniani had also not enjoyed support from fellow clergymen. Historian Lesley Borowitzka describes a then complacent community.

> We see an insular colony with an elite of mostly middle-class Britons, who had come to the colony to better their prospects with ambition to become gentry. The Anglican elite were comfortably embedded as leaders in colonial society with an investment in maintaining the status quo.[29]

The Anglican elite might have supported the status quo, but the evangelical movement continued to exert pressure about the treatment of black people in this outpost of empire. In Australia the original inhabitants were not classified as slaves in the legal sense, but were consistently seen as being at the bottom of the social pyramid and, by members of the evangelical movement, as oppressed. In 1838, following Giustiniani's allegations, a subcommittee of the Aborigines Protection Society in Britain was set up to investigate reports of settlers and soldiers ill-treating Aboriginal people in the Swan River Colony. This committee eventually concluded 'that a major cause of the problems had been a lack of systematic policy to guide colonists in their conduct with the indigenes'. A copy was provided to Lord Glenelg, who approved the appointment of two 'protectors' of the Western Australian 'natives'. These protectors eventually arrived in Australia in 1840.[30]

James Stirling's term as governor ended in 1839. His final years in the colony were characterised, as the Giustiniani affair had shown, by a deterioration in relations between settlers and the original inhabitants; gone were thoughts of a treaty. Australia's First Nations people had become troublesome rebels to be punished harshly for acts of robbery and retaliation against the settlers.

The new governor, John Hutt, himself an evangelical Christian, was a member of the Exeter Hall Movement and adopted a more benevolent, if paternalistic, approach to the indigenous peoples of the British Empire.[31] Hutt was also instructed by Glenelg to investigate Giustiniani's allegations and he duly wrote letters to the relevant parties. However, there were delays and avoidance tactics in settler responses. In the end, time and distance precluded an effective resolution of these issues, and, as Ann Hunter notes, 'with the trail now cold, no further action was taken'.[32]

Hutt's instructions from the British government included a commitment to:

> promote religion and education among the native inhabitants and especially take care to protect them in their persons, and in the free enjoyment of their possessions, and by all lawful means prevent and restrain all violence and injustice which may be practised or attempted against them, and take such measures as may appear to you to be necessary for their conversion to the Christian faith and for their advancement and civilisation.[33]

Hutt attempted to live up to the intent of these instructions. He adopted more conciliatory tactics, aiming to build bridges between the two societies. He showed interest in local language and culture as well as respect for Indigenous spiritual beliefs. Hutt also considered how Aboriginal laws and culture might be included within a dominant British authority. Aware of the importance of ending violent racial conflict, he felt that Aboriginal people should be left to follow their own laws where these did not clash with imperial priorities. However, the need to protect European property led him to conclude that British law had to be modified to suit the situation and what he saw as very large cultural differences between the two races.[34]

Evangelicals regarded education and training for Aboriginal children as important. Hutt concurred, financially supporting the foundation of schools and other institutions operated by different religious denominations.[35] The evangelicals hoped that commitment to schooling would be accompanied by conversion to Christianity, an expectation not confined to Protestant sects. Catholics were equally dedicated to education, setting up schools in Western Australia during the 1840s.

However, if instruction could render Aboriginal children literate and numerate, it would also require them to accept and adopt a 'superior' European culture. The empire-builders assumed that the Almighty smiled upon those who progressed from 'savagery to civilisation'. For all his moderation, Hutt was a man of his time, a committed Christian, who saw the role of missionaries as important in providing both religion and 'civilisation'. In our own time we might question the view that Christianity and 'civilisation' are always interrelated. However, as Murray Arnold reminds us, the English historian Kitson Clark, writing about this era, saw Christianity and the Bible as supplying, 'the only comprehensive system of thought of which many people were aware. They supplied the only philosophy or ethics easily available, the only cosmology or ancient history.'[36]

For the first time in the colony's short history, Hutt's government apportioned a percentage of the budget to Aboriginal welfare, including schooling.[37] Like other evangelical Christians, he hoped that basic education would assist Aboriginal children to acquire skills and obtain employment to further their acceptance by white society. Soon after his arrival, the new governor formed a close working relationship with interpreter and advocate for Aboriginal people, Francis Armstrong. Between them, Hutt and Armstrong established a 'native mission school' at the foot of Mount Eliza. The mission came under the aegis of the Wesleyan Methodist Church and its newly arrived missionary, John

Smithies. The school's explicit aim was the long-term assimilation of the Aboriginal people through employment-related training of their children.[38] Armstrong and his wife were responsible not only for teaching their pupils but also for feeding, clothing and housing them.[39]

Some colonists found it impossible to recognise Aboriginal pupils as members of the human family, despite the Christian faith requiring all people to be seen in that light.[40] Settler apathy and Aboriginal reluctance to send their children to the Mount Eliza institution ensured that the venture was unsuccessful.

In 1843, Smithies relocated the school to a rural block in the Wanneroo district, near what is now Lake Goollelal, where Noongar people could learn European agriculture. Armstrong departed to manage a store in Guildford, presumably a less frustrating enterprise.

Smithies continued pastoral work and became a key figure within the colony's Wesleyan Methodist mission. Uniting Church pastor Richard Roy has re-examined Smithies' ministry and

Lake Goollelal, site of Smithies' mission

contends that the latter saw his work with Aboriginal people as both secular and spiritual, setting out to instil Christian values in his students while protecting them from 'moral danger'. He also taught the English language and agricultural self-reliance.[41]

> 'For some two years past we have been endeavouring to obtain a few acres (say 4 or 5) of land for native purposes, to teach them to cultivate land, grow produce, and especially in connection with school operations, the means of grace and the blessing of God, to socialize them and bring before their attention the advantages belonging to civilized and Christian life'.[42]

Smithies' plan was that Aboriginal children living at the farm should marry young and remain there as a family in one small community. His long-term aim was for these settlements to become self-supporting Indigenous Christian communities.[43] The Wanneroo venture was unsuccessful. Aboriginal people had been accustomed to living from the land, but only where and when it could provide for them. When the crops failed at Wanneroo, they saw no reason to stay around.

In the early 1850s, the Wesleyans made a third attempt to establish a farm-based Indigenous community, this time at York. The pupils were Whadjuk people from the Fremantle and Perth districts. This was not their own country and Smithies reported that 'one after another left York, men, women and boys 'til there were three left. They returned to their own areas...we were soon minus Natives.'[44]

Smithies and his fellow missionaries generally attributed their failure to bring the Christian message to a 'heathen people' to shortage of finance and lack of personnel. But the main 'stumbling block' was a failure to understand that different cultures were involved. In time, Smithies himself began to recognise something of Aboriginal people's attachment to land. In his report for 1852, he wrote, 'a native is never at rest out of his own locality',[45] a concept foreign to Europeans who often moved and lived in two hemispheres.

Barladong man Tom Hayden would agree with Smithies' assessment of 'locality'. When he walks through his 'backyard', the bush of the central wheatbelt in Western Australia:

> *It doesn't matter how far you go away from here, there's always something pulling you back. I think it's to do with the old Noongar spirits. And once you get on the trail where your ancestors were, there's this feeling that they're there with you. It's beautiful. You walk out into the bush and you can hear its sounds. You can hear the ants breathing.*[46]

More than a century earlier, Englishwoman Janet Millett had lived in York, which is Barladong country. She wrote that:

> The feelings of the natives are very strong with respect to ownership in the soil, and some of them will still point to certain spots as theirs which have long been cleared and occupied by Englishmen.[47]

Land is an integral and essential part of the Aboriginal spiritual world right across this continent. Yawuru man Pat Dodson, from Broome, speaks for his Kimberley country:

> *In their local countryside Indigenous people already see the transcendence of the spiritual world. They're part of that spiritual world. They don't have to remind themselves of it. It's part of their being.*[48]

On the southern coast of Western Australia, Elder Vernice Gillies also describes the relationship between religion and land, citing her mother's conflict in embracing a 'foreign' religion.

> *I think our religion is based around our culture. Our religion really is our land, our boodja, because that's what provides for us, and so to have someone else's religion foisted on you, whether you wanted to have that religion, understand that and be a part of that religion, you didn't have any choice. My mum always talked about having to go to church every Sunday and prayers just before meals and bedtime, and how that was kind of foreign to her in the beginning, and yet when we were kids, she insisted that we all go to Sunday School every Sunday, which we did.*[49]

Lynette Knapp, also a Noongar Menang Elder, expresses a similar view.

> *I believe there's a higher Being. But I also believe that when we pass on, we go back to our spiritual place, and all our people who have passed on before are there as well. But I think that the Bible and Jesus belong elsewhere.*[50]

Aboriginal belief systems, with their sense of an animate world, have sometimes been seen as a form of animism. Pat Dodson, himself a former Catholic priest, emphasises their very human perspective.

> *It's a form of belief that the land is more than just your mother. It's your whole essence. You return there. Your spiritual assistance comes from the land and your spirit returns to the land, and not just in the Christian sense of man returning to dust. You return as a being to your land. And that being is capable of maintaining an influence and a presence.*[51]

When Tom Hayden and Pat Dodson speak about their connection to country, they describe an acceptance of a spirit-assisted world. Their 'religion' was built around their understanding and acceptance of that spirit world. Anthropologist Kingsley Palmer has studied the accounts of writers like Daisy Bates, Jesse Hammond and Ethel Hassell, who all recorded recollections handed down by Noongar people before such knowledge became fragmented or sometimes lost.

> The accounts of early writers present a picture of South West Aboriginal society that was deeply informed by reference to spirits, death and the afterlife of the departed. This typifies a society that made of the spirit world a preoccupation that informed much belief, action, opinion and emotion. Several consequences flowed from this. First, there existed in parallel with the physical world of people and things, a spirit world that had to be accommodated, placated and negotiated. This meant that certain things could not

be done, particularly travel at night and to certain places known to be the resort of spiritual entities. Certain things also had to be done, typified by the lighting of fires or the provision of grave goods. The known world was resonant with spiritual presences, many of which were at best ambiguous, and [at] most dangerous. Activity in country needed to accommodate the eventualities of the spirit world, and people had to be on guard to ensure their safety.[52]

Janet Millett, an Anglican parson's wife found that, for the Barladong people, her husband, Edward, while still very much alive, was actually a deceased relative who had returned to them. She described their rationale:

> In some of the newcomers such strong personal resemblance to deceased native individuals was thought to be detected, that the surviving relations gave the strangers the names of the departed, and would even assert that upon their bodies would still be found the mark of the spear wounds which had caused the deaths of their prototypes.[53]

Janet Millett was prepared accept the validity of their belief.

> As these ideas still prevailed to a certain extent, my husband came in for his share of metempsychosis and was known amongst the older natives by the name of an Aboriginal gentleman who had been speared in the back at some bygone battle.[54]

For most Protestant missionaries, such suppositions were, at best, misguided beliefs which must be eradicated if Christianity was to take root.

Perhaps for this reason, the Reverend John Smithies failed to connect with Aboriginal spirituality. But Smithies himself accepted dreams as useful in Wesleyan church practice, and Richard Roy suggests that Wesleyan missionaries might have been more successful had they attempted to understand Indigenous spirituality in the light of practices already accepted by

Holy Trinity York, the Milletts' church built 1854.

Christians,[55] particularly in relation to religious experience. He quotes Aboriginal leader and pastor Ron Williams:

> I get more excited looking at [life] from an Aboriginal culture than the European culture I've grown up with…When I see it from an Aboriginal point of view, I can easily go back into the dreamtime and eternity more quickly than having to question God [through an abstract rational Greek world view].[56]

Smithies was not alone in failing to recognise Aboriginal belief systems with their strong connection to country. Those colonists who had petitioned for the service of a missionary had also assumed that the original Australians had:

> Not the least distant Idea of any Supreme Being…and before the arrival of the White people, it is a matter of Doubt whether they had any Idea of existence after Death in any state whatever.[57]

But for Wadandi Cultural Custodian Iszaac Webb, there is no 'after death':

> *We say when this vessel breaks down, it will become the dust of the country. It will become the mother again. But our spirits are always going to be interconnected and we get a reincarnation so when we look at all the trees, and the animals and the rocks, and animate and inanimate objects, we see them as our granddads, they are our grandmothers, our sisters, our brothers, our sons and daughters, they're our mothers and fathers. They're all our demmanger [people from before]. And that's why we will show respect, and why, when we break off the branches of a tree or kill a kangaroo, we use every part and we sing to it.[58]*

This explanation parallels the Buddhist belief in reincarnation, a concept possibly not familiar at that time to British missionaries like John Smithies. After working in the colony for a year and attempting to reach Aboriginal people, he wrote that:

> They are now receiving ideas of God, of his presence, goodness and justice; it is remarkable that this people (perhaps the only people) have no God, no idols, no temples, no worship, no priests and it is this fact which makes it so difficult to give them moral or spiritual ideas or knowledge and if we consider the paucity of their language that they have no word for faith, prayer worship, devotion, faith, prayer or praise, at once see the difficulty of religious instruction among them.[59]

Sheila Barley, in her analysis of the early Protestant missions in Western Australia, suggests that Governor Hutt came to understand that Aboriginal people viewed the world very differently. Under his watch, a school for Aboriginal students was set up in Albany in 1843, although it attracted few pupils and appears to have closed after 1845.[60] Hutt then wrote that:

> The Aborigine clings to his ancient ways, frequently, tenaciously, as his rights because they are opposed to the will and customs of the stranger who has intruded upon him...They are so diametrically opposed in most points...that it seems as though the very being of a man must be changed before he can forsake the one and take to the other.[61]

Smithies, like Governor Hutt, was steeped in the evangelical tradition and saw himself as someone who had Aboriginal interests at heart, in contrast to the indifferent and brutal attitude of many settlers. He also wanted to protect Aboriginal children from what he saw as European evils. For example, he forbade his students to attend Foundation Day on 1 June 1841, seeing the festivities as likely to corrupt his charges.[62]

Wesleyan Methodists were concerned to 'protect' Indigenous people from some aspects of secular white culture, which they saw as often immoral and 'unchristian'. They thought that the more they converted and consequently transformed individuals, the more the nation would be improved from a moral perspective and that 'scriptural holiness would spread across the land', thus achieving moral and spiritual reform.[63]

The Church of England in Australia was also dedicated to saving souls for Christianity but, as the 'established church', it was committed to maintaining the social order with its hierarchical view of society.

Even church seating arrangements made clear distinctions between the socially and economically influential and their underlings, be they soldiers, convicts or the poor.[64] The Reverend, later Archdeacon, John Wollaston left his English parish in East Anglia in November 1840 and arrived in the Swan River Colony in April 1841. Cambridge educated, Wollaston was a product of a culture and society where established church clergy had long considered themselves to be guardians and promoters of a distinct social hierarchy. Wollaston's religious views mirrored the social and racial order of his era. Church historian Rowan Strong relates that when a Mrs Grey breastfed her baby in the front pew of the church, Wollaston commented that she showed 'as much exhibition as a native woman'.[65] As Strong points out, distaste for such behaviour corresponded closely with Wollaston's view of the lower orders of his own society. He believed that colonial society should aim to be a microcosm of English culture.

Strong also notes that, in 'all his life in England, Wollaston had lived within the cultural confines of the rural Anglican clergy'.[66] He had also lived entirely within the confines of the 'green and pleasant' English countryside. In his new country he bought land in what he hoped would become the equally verdant pastures of south-west Western Australia. With what historian Geoffrey Bolton has called 'enterprise remarkable in a newly arrived clergyman, no longer young, and not by temperament readily adaptable to the change from English life to a pioneering society', Wollaston began to build a chapel on his new property at Picton, now a semi-industrial suburb on the outskirts of the City of Bunbury.[67] Dislocated from his own ordered English landscape, his first impressions of south-west Australia in 1841 suggest disappointment. Wollaston confesses that:

> I have been almost tempted to shed tears at the desolateness of the Scene, had I not called to mind the ubiquity of the God of Nature, who can make 'a wilderness like Eden & a desert like the Garden of the Lord' – Can cause 'joy and gladness to be found

Wollaston's church at Picton.

therein, thanksgiving, & the voice of melody'. Before, however, this happy time can come, the moral wilderness of the world must be broken up and cultivated.[68]

For Wollaston, a migrant from long-cultivated farming country, this new country was both unfamiliar and hostile. He appears not to have asked how Aboriginal people had lived successfully in this unique environment from time immemorial. While they had not starved, Wollaston seems to have come fairly close to doing so:

> Tuesday 11 April 1843. There is an American whaler in the bay but we have nothing to sell him; a schooner also from Java laden with rice. We have eaten all the potatoes we had not previously disposed of. We must grow more. We were forced to have them for breakfast, dinner and supper. We have bought some seed for which the boys went to Vasse last week. For fear these should be devoured also, by general consent, they are kept strictly under lock and key.[69]

Despite intermittent hunger, Wollaston thought that the land would in time resemble what he and his fellow immigrants saw as 'civilisation'. Similarly, he believed that the Aboriginal inhabitants could also be trained to become both 'civilised' and Christian. Wollaston held an ambivalent view of Aboriginal people, seeing them as inevitably victims of displacement. Although they appeared to be without religion, he was convinced that 'they seem to have a belief in a sort of transmigration of souls imagining that white men were formerly blacks and they themselves when they die will go to white man's country'.[70]

Wollaston hoped to connect this belief to Christian views of heaven and thus achieve conversions.[71] Efforts to convert the heathen were an obligation placed on all who called themselves Christian.

> Notwithstanding the natives are often troublesome, the only feeling in the breast of a really humane and religious settler on viewing their condition is one of pity; a feeling painfully increased when

he reflects that God has given their lands to Christian Englishmen in possession with the imperative duty annexed to the gift that they should, both by precept and example, teach them "the good and right way".[72]

Historian Anne O'Brien describes this view of Christianity as a mobile faith: 'Its all-powerful, all-knowing God was a personal companion who accompanied his people on trips of exploration and guided their acquisition of new lands'.[73] And in the minds of Anglicans like Wollaston, God had given the lands of the Aboriginal people to the British explicitly in order to bring them to Christ. It was the duty of the colonisers to spread the Christian Gospel, a belief far removed from the First Nations spiritual immersion in their own land.[74]

Failure to strive for the conversion of the 'native people' was to ignore the divine purpose for which God had given the British an empire that included Australia. John Smithies and his fellow Methodists shared this view, although as Wesleyans they would not have seen the Church of England as God's only agent! Furthermore, there was an implication that God might confiscate the empire. This was based on the belief that the British only held it on divine condition that the gospel was proclaimed and the heathen converted.

Rowan Strong suggests that there is also a sense of desperation in Wollaston's efforts to enlighten the original inhabitants, particularly the adults. Commenting on the failure of the Reverend John Smithies' mission at York, Wollaston stated that:

> adults could not be retained at such mission farms because 'no kindness will ever wean them from their bush habits and wild licence. Children must be trained from infancy in habits of civilization and industry or they will never be fixed anywhere.'[75]

In Wollaston's view, in order for such training to succeed, Aboriginal children needed exposure to 'a white dominated environment' and to be removed from their traditional 'nomadic' lifestyle. Inevitably, this involved separating them from their 'black dominated' upbringing, in effect from their family. Wollaston justified his proposals for separating children from their parents, stating that:

> Of course, the children must be, as in primitive times, voluntarily given up by their parents, which would readily be done, for there is no stronger tie among these poor savages than that between an animal and its offspring. The infants I would have baptized forthwith...& not allowing them ever to return, after their adoption, to their heathen relatives.[76]

Accordingly, Wollaston suggested setting up a Native Institution on Rottnest Island, where Aboriginal children would acquire white culture and white religion. Parents would have no say in their children's upbringing and family contact would be prohibited. Here, according to Strong, Wollaston was applying contemporary European understanding that children had no rights and could not determine their own futures.[77] He might have added that in this instance parents were also deprived of their right to raise their own children.

Rottnest remained an Aboriginal prison and his proposal did not take root. However, Wollaston did become involved in the establishment of an institution managed by an English couple, Henry and Anne Camfield. Both had been strongly influenced by the evangelical movement. In Perth Anne had been governess to the children of the Reverend William Mitchell, who had replaced Anglican missionary Louis Giustiniani. Mitchell's wife ran a school for 'native' children which eventually closed due to increasing Aboriginal resistance to European ways and education.[78]

Another Anglican mission commenced in Fremantle in 1842 with the arrival of the Society for the Propagation of the Gospel missionary Reverend George King, who was expected to devote his time both to the needs of white settlers and to the conversion of the Aborigines. King also opened a school for 'native' children.

He felt that although, in his view, their spiritual needs came second to those of the white settlers, the Aborigines were 'but still, members of the human family, and as such fit subjects of that gospel which Christ came to be preached to every Nation and to all people'.[79] King also commented perceptively on the problems then facing Aboriginal people as well as the difficulty delivering to them the Christian message.

> The scarcity of human food in the bush now that the European Colonists have taken possession of their hunting grounds, renders the habits of the Natives so extremely erratic, that the same tribe, or the same individual will seldom come within the reach of a European for more than one or two days at a time, and to follow them through the bush, even if the teacher were exclusively devoted to the bush mission, would be impracticable.[80]

The Camfields would have been familiar with the work of both Mitchell and King and also with that of Archdeacon Matthew Hale in South Australia. After visiting the ill-fated Wanneroo Wesleyan mission, Hale had established a similar, but initially more successful, 'native institution' at Poonindie in South Australia. He firmly believed in Aboriginal humanity, stating that:

> [S]uccess…is *possible*, no one who believes the scriptures can doubt; being *men* it cannot be *impossible* that these natives should come to the knowledge of the truth, and obtain eternal life…to say that the individual men, women, and children of any given race are *absolutely and essentially incapable* of attaining to everlasting life, would be a position which I trust no one would venture to advance…how shall we dare to stay our efforts, or say that we are weary of the work, until we shall have exhausted every means which God shall put it into our power to attempt?[81]

Anne Camfield endorsed Hale's sentiments. Her husband, Henry, had been one of the earliest settlers on the Swan, arriving in 1829, but he had also travelled widely within Australia. His attitude to the 'native people' differed from that of many other Swan River settlers. He refused to carry arms and wrote to his sister: 'From first to last, I have been friendly with them. I would never hurt them, only in the most extreme case would I now, for the same Almighty God made black and white'.[82]

In 1847, the Camfields left Perth for Albany, where Henry had been appointed resident magistrate. The following year John Wollaston was assigned to the parish of St John the Evangelist in Albany. These three Europeans had an opportunity to observe how the Menang people were now faring in what remained an outpost of an impoverished colony. An observer of the day wrote to the Perth newspaper, *The Inquirer*, that 'Albany was struggling with its unfavourable position, the impolitic high price of land and, as is reported, a revenue altogether disproportionate to its expenditure'.[83] Albany was a town of only fifty houses occupied by less than 250 people.[84] According to Joan Groves, who has studied the Camfields' work, the gaol was home to those Aboriginal people 'who had not yet learnt that they had lost sovereignty to their land'.[85] Although the hinterland was then being developed for pastoral leases, poor soil limited agriculture around the vicinity of the townsite.

Mokare, Collet Barker's Aboriginal companion and friend, had anticipated in 1830 and 1831 that things would change. They did. By the early 1850s the population of native animals, a source of food for both settlers and natives, was diminishing. The Menang relied increasingly on European handouts. Alcohol, together with equally addictive tobacco, was commonly used to pay local labourers and Aboriginal people. This inevitably aggravated social and health problems.[86] The Menang people's early curiosity and willingness to share useful knowledge with the garrison settlement had given way to a realisation that not all the British were their friends.

The continued presence of American and other sealer and whaler fleets in King George Sound also made life worse for the Menang. Murray Arnold cites a comment from Patrick Taylor, a settler in Kalgan, describing the effects of their presence. Not only did the sailors spread venereal disease in their contacts with Menang women, but the local people also gathered:

> in the hope of obtaining money, biscuits, tobacco and ardent spirits from the seamen who they may encounter…In this way they are more and more corrupted; acquiring the vicious habits of the most abandoned seamen; encouraged by idleness; and tempted when disappointed in their expectations to commit crime in order to satisfy their cravings of nature.[87]

The sealers, in particular, had been partly responsible for the breakdown of culture within Aboriginal society. The men sought, and often sexually exploited, Menang and other Aboriginal women, leading to pregnancies and an increase in the Aboriginal population. As Lynette Knapp recalls:

> *There were bad stories about sealers in particular because it wasn't just the women they hunted. It was young girls as well. Round here, as we heard from our father's stories, they were locked up on islands. Aboriginal people were afraid of the open ocean, because of its spiritual significance. But the sealers also brought in Tasmanian women and there were a lot of families here with that Tasmanian Aboriginal blood.*[88]

The plight of Aboriginal people in Albany could not be blamed entirely on the sealers. There were other factors.

> *I think they lost their independence and their culture and they expected non-Indigenous people to give them their food, rather than go out and hunt for it. And the settlers might have been giving them food so that they could get the land. And because these new people were coming in and claiming the land and clearing it, their hunting grounds, and rules and laws which governed that hunting on their home ground, were gone. There was a sense of not belonging there anymore.*[89]

It was in this social and economic climate that, in 1852, the Camfields, with strong support from the Reverend John Wollaston, began their efforts to house and educate Aboriginal children at the Albany Native Institution. Of all the Protestant enterprises established in the wake of the evangelical movement, Annesfield, as it became known, would have the longest history of such institutions. For some twenty years the Camfields looked after their charges, with support from the Anglican church and the colonial government.

Some children taken in by the Camfields were orphans as a result of increasing ill-health among the local tribes. Others, with official support, were simply removed from Aboriginal families. A number of children were described as 'half caste', foreshadowing the plight of the twentieth century's Stolen Generations. In her Annesfield Report in 1868, Anne Camfield defended the practice.

> The objection many people make, that it is cruel to take their children from them, is not a solid one; because the children, left to the parents' management, or non-management, soon cast off all submission, and all care or love for the parents, so that when the latter become old and helpless, they are almost wholly neglected.[90]

The Camfields' house, Serpentine Road, Albany.

Anne Camfield has been described as kind and motherly. Childless herself, she took in young people and provided both care and education. She argues here that she is doing the parents a favour because their children, if left with them, will neglect their parents in their old age! Today we still hear and read many accounts of distress in Aboriginal families resulting from the loss of children to institutional life and it seems likely that these nineteenth-century families were similarly affected.

However, in the late 1840s, many parents were reduced to poverty and hunger, and therefore willing for white couples, like the Camfields, to feed and care for their children. Camfield also wrote that parents saw their children 'whenever they like and their children are taught to treat them with kindness and consideration'.[91] Her approach contrasted with Wollaston's view of how such institutions should operate, and even more with twentieth-century experience, where many Aboriginal children were denied contact with their parents and sometimes never regained it.

The Camfields were working in a changing social climate and, in time, their efforts became subject to criticism. Society's social conscience had further dimmed. Darwin had published his *On the Origin of Species* in 1859 and the theory of survival of the fittest became prominent, together with the notion of a hierarchy within the human species. Skin colour had always been an issue and, for white settlers, Aboriginal people were on the bottom rung of a social ladder, if they were on it at all. While earlier, men like explorer George Grey had tried to understand a unique culture, this approach was now rejected. Aboriginal people were now seen only as useful cheap labour. Florence Nightingale, who professed interest in the health of indigenous peoples within the empire, believed 'that very few of the human race are lower in the scale of civilisation than these poor people' and considered that education for such a race was inappropriate. Her advice was: 'Show him his duty to God. And teach him how to plough.'[92]

Annesfield survived until the Camfields became old and ill. At the same time, it became clear that the colonial government no longer wished to support this nominally religious enterprise. For a short time in 1870, Matthew Hale, who had become Perth's first Church of England bishop, considered retiring to Albany and taking over the reins. Explaining his intentions, he wrote:

> I have no hesitation in saying that a European population, disregarding the welfare of the natives, whom it has displaced from their country, will not ensure God's blessing, and therefore I do hope that the public generally will support the Mission at Albany.[93]

Instead Hale became Bishop of Brisbane and moved to Queensland. He arranged for the remaining Annesfield children to be taken to Perth in March 1871.[94] They were eventually housed in Middle Swan near Guildford at Bishop Hale's Institution for Native and Half-Caste Children.

Janet Millett, living at York between 1864 and 1869, admired the Camfields' work.

> The institution is on the model of an industrial one at home, all the housework and cookery being performed by the pupils, in addition to which they receive such an education as is usually imparted in National Schools in England. None of the inmates of Mrs. Camfield's home have ever run away from it, the secret of her art in retaining them being that she really loves the natives, and treats their children in all respects like those of white persons as to their clothing, diet, and lodging.[95]

Millett spent only five years in Western Australia, owing to her husband's ill health, but she was a thoughtful observer of European-Aboriginal interaction and its effect on land and culture. Later, back in her home country, she wrote an account of her years in the colony, revealing a sensitive understanding of Aboriginal culture and society.

Millett refers to York by its Aboriginal name, Barladong (often spelled Balladong today). Inland from Perth, it was one of the first agricultural areas settled by Europeans. Her use of the original name reflects her understanding that the land on which they lived had belonged to the Noongar Barladong people. She describes what happened when the people she called the 'proprietors' realised that white people were not their ancestors returning as spirits, but settlers, here to stay.

> The original proprietors became 'very troublesome,' as the phrase goes for native behaviour under such circumstances. They continued to oppose the appropriation of the land until cowed into submission, and seemed disposed to treat the invaders with as little hospitality as our own ancestors showed towards Julius Caesar, for whose ill reception by their forefathers modern Britons are not in the habit of expressing much remorse.[96]

Later in England, Millett was often asked 'whether the Australian native is not the lowest member of the human family – its shabbiest and least creditable relation'. She comments that, 'her questioners generally seemed to have made up their minds beforehand that such was certainly the case'.[97]

Janet Millett's writing reveals a sympathetic, if not completely accurate, understanding of Barladong culture.

> Even the quickness of the poor native's senses is often brought forward against him, as though he were something less than a man, because his acuteness of observation and keenness of sight reach a perfection that we are accustomed to consider as the birthright of the inferior animals alone. Born, however, in a country that is devoid of Indigenous fruits or grains fit for man's use, the native's existence has depended not on the cultivation of the soil, but on that of his five senses; and that he should see like a hawk and track like a bloodhound, or should resemble the bee in his power of steering a direct course through pathless forests, are the natural results of that cultivation, just as the excessive delicacy of touch possessed by the hands of blind persons results from the constant exercise of their sense of feeling. But granting that the lowest condition of mankind is to be found on the great island-continent, I can yet assure Europeans that they have no

reason to feel ashamed of owning affinity with the savages of Australia West, either in respect of mental qualities or that of manly appearance.[98]

We now know, thanks to Bruce Pascoe, author of *Dark Emu*, that this country was not devoid of Indigenous fruits or grains.

> Records of the land's cultivated appearance are common in the early records and are spread across the continent...Areas beyond the high rainfall zones of the coastal regions favoured grain as the staple crop whereas in wetter areas, yam production took over.[99]

The problem, and the misunderstanding, was, as Iszaac Webb points out, that European settlers did not see anything that they recognised:

> *We weren't conventionally farming the land in the Western wet practice. We were farming in an arid country. We didn't have hooved animals, we didn't have cows, we didn't have these things. So, the perception from the settlers was that we were Neanderthal; we were savages. Because we weren't doing what they were doing, in their eyes, we weren't doing anything.*[100]

Janet Millett did not see the First Nations people in that light. Although the Milletts came to Western Australia to preach the gospel, she differed from many Christians of her era in reconciling her own theology with that of another culture. She links her description of Noongar laws about the sharing of goods with early Christian church practices. These comments suggest that Millett did not see ethical behaviour as solely a Christian prerogative.

> It is scarcely possible to imagine a stronger exemplification of that community of goods which distinguished the early Christian church, when 'neither said any of them that aught of the things which he possessed was his own' than exists amongst these savages, only with this difference, that the self-abnegation instead of being voluntary is produced by compulsion...This law is especially

> binding with respect to strangers of another tribe, with whom, if friendliness is to be maintained, a native is bound to make an exchange of property however greatly to his own disadvantage.[101]

Millett was aware of Reverend John Smithies' failed attempt to found a mission in the Barladong area in the early 1850s, although this endeavour had almost faded from public memory when she and her husband came to York.

> The school broke down, and had come to an end about ten years before we went to live in Barladong. A friend of ours once met a native woman who said that she had been one of the runaways, and held up her fingers eagerly to count upon them the number of children who had died. 'Black fellow die – black fellow die'… This was all that we ever learned of the Barladong Wesleyan Mission, and we were never able to find any printed account of it…[102]

However, Millett did detect remnants of Christian teaching among the local people. Taking in a Noongar girl, Binnahan, at the request of the child's dying mother, Janet was struck by the fusion of Christianity with traditional beliefs.

> The natives of Western Australia are extremely impressionable to religious instruction, but Binnahan's unquestioning faith did not prevent her from occasionally making very quaint observations on what she was taught.[103]

Binnahan once asked what angels had to eat in heaven, and being told that they eat nothing, the child said: '"Then are they always gorbel mooràt?" (i.e. stomach-full)'. On another occasion, Janet says she enquired, 'If her dead brothers and sisters were gone to heaven, and being told that all innocent children would be there, she remarked, "Little kangaroo do no harm – little kangaroo go too"'.[104] It's a remark that any child might make, but is equally suggestive of the persistent survival of the Indigenous animate and all-embracing view of creation.

Janet Millett did write extensively about the one mission that appeared to be working successfully with the Aboriginal population. Spanish Benedictine monk Rosendo Salvado came to Western Australia in January 1846 after a distinguished career as a priest and as a talented musician. He was accompanied by fellow Benedictine Joseph Benedict Serra. In March that year, they established a mission at a place they called New Norcia and set about bringing Roman Catholic Christianity to the rural Aboriginal community. Though Protestant herself, Millett admired Salvado and his work.

> I must now proceed to give some account of the Roman Catholic Mission where, in the words of our shipmate, 'the bishop lived with the natives in the bush.' No biographies are said to be so perfect as those that betray the author's affection for his subject, and the bishop's pen runs *con amore* in discussing the topic of his beloved savages, and speaking of their docility and intelligence.[105]

As Millett's reference to 'his beloved savages' suggests, Salvado brought a markedly different approach to missionary work but, as he admits, this was initially 'flying blind'.

> We had not the slightest idea, nor could we find anyone who would enlighten us, as to the life and customs of the Australian aborigines. Having landed in Australia we immediately found out that the opinions about them were very much at variance among European settlers. I myself soon came to the conclusion that the best way of realizing our aims was to land ourselves in the midst of them in the bush, where the evils of our European civilization had not penetrated.[106]

A former abbot at New Norcia, Father Bernard Rooney, saw the first abbot as a sensitive learner,

> born of a determination to respect and understand the culture of the Aboriginal people...Bishop Salvado believed the Catholic faith should be built on the cultural conditions and understandings of the Indigenous people themselves.[107]

Father Bernard reflected on the influence of Darwinian evolutionary theory on missionary perspectives and policies within the Catholic church:

> This perspective underpinned the words addressed by Pope Gregory XVI to Doms Salvado and Serra on the eve of their embarkation for Western Australia on 5 June, 1845.
>
> 'Civilise and Christianise' was the directive issued by His Holiness. But...how was this to be interpreted? Should Indigenous cultures be set aside and replaced by the Christian cultures of England and Europe? In many missions such policies had proven disastrous?[108]

Linguist John Kinder sheds light on what Pope Gregory probably meant by 'civilise'.

> *The Italian word is* civilizzato, *which Salvado would have known came from the Latin word* civile, *from which is derived* civitas, *which means a city. In this context, it means human beings who have left the forest and have moved into a state where they are governed by human laws as in a city, and not by natural law...So, when Pope Gregory says to Salvado, 'You've got to go and civilise the natives', what he means, I think, is 'You've got to help them make the same progress that we have made'.*[109]

In the mid-nineteenth century, archaeologists believed that all humanity was climbing the same evolutionary ladder but that Aboriginals were still on the lowest rung; that is, at the point where Europeans had been about ten thousand years ago. In material terms, Aboriginal people were well below nineteenth-century Spaniards or Britons.[110] For Salvado, the task seemed to be to gradually bring his 'beloved savages' up to the state of civilisation which Europeans had now attained and the word 'gradually' is significant here. Salvado acknowledged that this task had to be undertaken slowly and over time.

> We look at them with European eyes, consider them as Europeans, and try to train them as such; but in doing so we delude ourselves. Their case is quite another, quite different from ours, and we

ought to bring them to our case and high position, not at once, but by the same way we came to it, by degrees.[111]

At the same time, as Kinder emphasises, Salvado clearly understood that civilisation is not just a matter of material progress.

> *He had great understanding of the spirituality of the Noongar. He writes about it in his memoirs. I think he saw that Noongar cosmology is a long way from the Christian revelation of the Incarnation. But it is united to our Christian understanding in its recognition of a supreme being, of a continuity of being, between, we would say, heaven and earth, but we might say between a transcendental dimension and the present dimension.*
>
> *I think that what we call the Dreamtime or the Dreaming is not another moment in time, it's another dimension of the present time. So, our present contingent reality is simply one manifestation of an eternal ground of being. There's no evidence that Salvado thought he was working with pagans. He was working with a spiritual people who had a relationship to that other dimension of being.*[112]

Salvado also seems to have instinctively understood an important protocol in Aboriginal discourse, 'wait time'. This means 'not rushing in' but waiting to be asked why you are here and what is your business. As Kinder points out, he got it right.

> *When Salvado and his companion, Father Serra, first set up their first camp before they moved to the present site, New Norcia, they didn't attempt to speak to the Noongar. They made their camp nearby and waited. And it was the Noongar who came towards them. It's an interesting dynamic. It's not 'white to black', it's 'white' positioning themselves on 'black' land and the Noongars allowing it.*[113]

The mission Salvado established in Western Australia took a different approach from other religious bodies. For him, conversion of the Aboriginal people to the Christian faith and 'civilisation' needed to begin within their cultural community, not simply as a system of belief and practice imposed from the outside.[114] As Kinder sees it:

A MORAL WILDERNESS?

New Norcia country.

> *His vision was the creation of a self-sufficient village, consisting of monks in their cloister and the Noongar in their houses. The two communities lived together. The Noongar who worked on the land, the Noongar who learnt to shear sheep, and those who became blacksmiths, were always paid.*
>
> *But I think for him, agriculture was the basis for civilised living. He wants to take people from the forest to the city but the economic foundation of 'the city' is agriculture, not industry.*[115]

Farming, Salvado hoped, would ensure continuing vitality among the Noongar. Early in the mission he noted distinct differences between European and Aboriginal approaches to health and survival. Salvado cited a case where an Aboriginal man became sick and received treatment in a hospital:

> Nothing is wanting, nevertheless the native grows worse every day and after a short time his life is despaired of. An European, in the same case, would have recovered his health by that time, but the unfortunate native is dying, there is no remedy for him. His disease has baffled the Doctor's skill and care, and, as the last resource, the native is consigned to his relatives or friends, by whom he is brought to the woods and there by them taken care of in their own way.[116]

Salvado goes on to say that, returned to his country, the man quickly recovered.

The failure of his 'beloved savages' to thrive outside their own country led to correspondence with English nurse reformer Florence Nightingale, an exchange which proved instructive and led them both to interesting conclusions. Her interest in Indigenous people's education and survival had been stirred by an encounter in 1859 with the explorer George Grey, an early observer of Australia's First Nations. Nightingale became convinced that statistical information was necessary to understand why Aboriginal people were not thriving under British rule.[117]

In April 1860, Nightingale, with the help of British sanitation and public health experts and advice from Grey, began a survey of colonial schools. When this enquiry reached Salvado, he had already been collecting the type of information requested by Nightingale for several years. His return for the period February 1857 to October 1860 included information about thirty-five boys. None of them had contracted any diseases and none had died. He then reiterated his view that civilisation of these 'savages' was a matter to be undertaken slowly and that the system adopted at New Norcia had prevented the destructive effects of too rapid a transition: 'On the whole it will be found that the idea of bringing savages from their wild state, at once to an advanced civilization serves no other purpose than that of murdering them'.[118]

Like Nightingale, Salvado believed that Aboriginal ill-health had identifiable origins which, once recognised, could be successfully addressed. One measure seemed to offer a clue.

> As a further precaution against illness from too much confinement or little exercise, every Thursday and occasionally some other days, all the native boys and girls separately go out through the forest around this Mission, hunting the timid kangaroos...and sometimes the grown-up natives go on shooting the graceful emu...they enjoy very much such excursions, and whenever they

return home after having such a recreation, evidently they appear to have improved their health.[119]

At the same time, Salvado became aware that when strong and healthy young natives had been at the mission for some time, some of them appeared to become 'depressed'. Salvado explained what happened to such a boy.

> He takes his meals as regular as ever, he has no fever, yet he daily and almost at sight loses his flesh, strength, and health. What is the technical name of such a disease? Perhaps consumption, perhaps liver complaint. Let it be so; but is there no remedy for such diseases? Are there no preventions of their causes? Yes, there are; but nevertheless, that native died shortly after.[120]

Salvado described this 'fatal melancholy' to doctors in Europe. They all concluded that the sickness was 'nostalgia', what the English would call 'homesickness', eventually identified as a real disease. Both Salvado and Nightingale agreed that the only cure for Aboriginal people separated from their country was to treat them similarly to depressed soldiers in military camps who had suffered from 'nostalgia' while serving in foreign countries. Nightingale based her diagnosis on experience of sickness among British troops in the 1850s Crimean war. The patient must return home, receive physical exercise and live in good conditions.[121]

Nightingale began to support this solution to a medical problem, showing sensitivity to Aboriginal well-being. As Tiffany Shellam adds in her careful and detailed analysis of the diagnostic work undertaken by Nightingale and Salvado,

> The historical and present-day record is littered with comments about Aboriginal people being 'heartsick' or 'homesick' for country. More important, for my argument: while Salvado and Nightingale suggested this physical and mental vulnerability was peculiar to native peoples, they believed that a considered regime of management could deal with it. They were not fatalistic.[122]

In Salvado's view, Aboriginal people needed to be provided with a healthy and independent life, away from large cities. Like Wesleyan John Smithies some twenty years earlier, Salvado saw the potential for establishing small Christian communities 'who would become acquainted with the various branches and different works of a farm'.[123] The members of the community would then marry within it and have children who would be further down the path to 'civilisation'. Salvado saw his employment system at New Norcia as a prototype for similar institutions.

> The crop of his field is respected as his property, but it is also well understood that whatsoever money that crop will produce to him, that money shall be employed in buying tools and utensils of agriculture…Of the money he receives as wages for the work he does at the establishment, he may dispose at his pleasure, although he is often advised to employ it usefully.[124]

Salvado regarded this kind of enterprise as a way to help Aboriginal people gradually 'reach the high state of civilisation achieved by Europeans'. At the same time, he was aware that many colonists would have thought him unduly optimistic.

> It seems impossible to some people to believe a native of Australia capable of working or doing any real material good for himself… Surely, if the aborigines are left to themselves, they cannot but follow their forefathers' traditions and customs, but if properly and timely trained, I, for one, do not see the impossibility of their being truly civilised.[125]

In a letter to the colonial government Salvado acknowledged the financial assistance he had received from the colonial government. Frederick Aloysius Weld had arrived as governor in 1869 and showed sympathy for Aboriginal people. Salvado took advantage of the new governor's wish that they should not suffer from violence at the hands of settlers. For his concern and pains, Weld was called a 'nigger coddler' by sections of the colony's population, but until he left Australia in 1874, Weld and Salvado were able to work together.[126]

It seemed that in many ways, Salvado's enlightened approach was workable and the mission continued, encouraging Aboriginal people to become farmers. However, after Salvado died in 1900, New Norcia changed direction. Father Fulgentius Torres arrived from Spain in April 1901 with eleven monastic recruits. He became the second abbot and initiated a new monastic mission in the Kimberley.

Torres placed a greater emphasis on education of the wider community. He also set about rebuilding New Norcia, changing what had been a rustic bush mission into a grand European-style monastery and bringing with him a very different understanding of the Benedictine monastic mission. This involved a substantial reduction in their local landholdings and farming activities, a central feature of Salvado's fifty years labour.[127]

According to Father Bernard Rooney, not everyone favoured these new policies and directions, as they led to a substantial

New Norcia became a grand European-style monastery.

change in New Norcia's missionary profile. Aboriginal residents were now encouraged to move away and find work with local farmers while leaving their children to be educated in the mission's orphanages. Most Aboriginal people left willingly, tempted by farmers' offers of higher wages, but also confident that New Norcia would always be their home and that they could always return, as Salvado had told them. Yet it was soon evident that their attachment to a home which had by now become their 'country' meant little to New Norcia's new regime. Torres discouraged visits to the monastery and curtailed parental access to the children. Families who insisted on taking their offspring away to the bush were told: 'Do not return these children to the mission'.[128]

A promising approach to what was becoming characterised as the colony's 'Aboriginal problem' had been abandoned. But even during Salvado's lifetime, other factors had affected the mortality and survival of the First Australians.

> At the latter end of 1860, the measles, introduced about that time in this colony, reached here, and since then several of our native boys died, their death being attributed to that plague and to its effects.[129]

The introduction of European diseases was just one of many problems now facing the original Australians. Janet Millett was saddened by the recognition that:

> The gradually decreasing numbers of the natives suggest sadly yet surely that they are not destined to share any exemption from that fate, which has already fallen to many aboriginal races of dying out wherever the white man erects his dwelling among them.[130]

Millett was writing in the context of a much-changed Aboriginal culture. Extensive European occupation of First Nations 'property' had changed their status and their economy from a life based on communal cooperation. 'Sharing' had begun to give way to labouring for the now firmly entrenched occupiers, and Millett observed that:

> All the better class of colonists in the bush have their favourite natives, who, in return for old clothes and food, which principally consists of flour, will consent to act as cleaners of pots and pans, as well as hewers of wood and drawers of water.[131]

The transportation of convicts to Western Australia between 1850 and 1868, as Millett also noted, further limited the likelihood of a successful Christian mission to the Aboriginal people.

> It was plain to us that any endeavours of ours to teach the natives must end in failure, situated as we were near a town where about nine out of ten men were of the convict class, and where the character of the hotel tap-rooms was such as might be expected in consequence.[132]

Convicts also took labouring jobs which might otherwise have been available to Aboriginal people. With their traditional hunting grounds now appropriated for European-type agriculture, some local communities were further reduced to poverty.

At New Norcia, by the first decade of the new century, there had been an exodus of former residents. Like Noongar communities elsewhere in the south-west of Western Australia, they were now forced to live in permanent camps on the fringes of towns. Some found work or a home on the outskirts of the Perth metropolitan area. But, as with other Aboriginal and part-Aboriginal men and women, they were the target of social discrimination. Unemployment and poverty remained the most serious problems for this 'underclass' of people.[133]

The Wesleyans, following the lead of their founder John Wesley, had held a practical concern for assisting the poor. When the Reverend John Smithies arrived in 1840, he reported that:

> Here we have literally no poor, the few paupers which are here and supported by Local Government are such from intemperance and dissolute habits and lives. After the first Sacramental collection here I enquired for the poor to distribute it as at home, but to my surprise they told me that there were none...We,

however, find great demand for all such surplus means amongst the natives.[134]

Smithies had identified a problem which would persist. A displaced people were now 'the new poor'. Their situation would well outlast the evangelical missions of the nineteenth century. Australia's First Nations peoples had, from time immemorial, enjoyed a common wealth and a sharing economy. Now they were regarded by most Europeans as, at best, a labouring class at the bottom of the social scale. However, they and some of their culture had survived as Whadjuk man Gary Wilkes reminds us:

> *We still try to hold on to our Aboriginal history, even though so much of it is gone, we still believe it. We still talk the language. We still practise our laws, our hunting skills.*[135]

You can hear the ants breathing.

Chapter 4

The End of the Beginning or the Beginning of the End?

That's how Barladong Elder Tom Hayden sees the economic, social and environmental changes white settlers brought to Aboriginal life as they ventured into the Western Australian hinterland and changed both his land and his culture.[1]

Jesse Hammond, author of *Winjan's People*, identified some of those changes in a conversation with an elderly man who had 'learned to count and read and write' at New Norcia.[2] Hammond, born in 1856, had learned the local Noongar dialect as a young man and asked if they could converse in the native tongue. The response was disappointing.

> I forget all black-fellow language now. It would be no good to me now. I do all my business with the white fellow and have to talk to him in white-fellow talk. Plenty other country blackfellow here now. All talk different. This-country blackfellow can't talk to them. Better we talk white-fellow talk. We have to wear the same clothes, eat the same food. We are now all the same white men.[3]

This expression of cultural loss was also relevant to the dispersal of Aboriginal people from their own particular country. Hammond could remember a time when Aboriginal people had their own culture and way of living that had spanned the millennia.

> And so, these natives went on, age after age. They had their food of many kinds; they had their freedom; they had their amusements; they had good health; they had their laws and, for them, they were good laws and worked well; they had their friends of their own colour. All this the natives of the South-West lost when civilisation came among them.[4]

In the first years of colonial settlement, Sir George Grey, like other early explorers of Western Australia, had acknowledged the quality of the Aboriginal diet and their health and vigour.

> Generally speaking, the natives live well; in some districts there may at particular seasons of the year be a deficiency of food, but if such is the case, these tracts are, at those times, deserted. It is however, utterly impossible for a traveller or even for a strange native to judge whether a district affords an abundance of food, or the contrary...But in his own district a native is very differently situated; he knows exactly what it produces, the proper times at which the several articles are in season and the readiest means of procuring them.[5]

Above all, it was this capacity to live in harmony with the land, taking from it only what they needed, that the Noongar people had largely lost by the end of the nineteenth century. George Grey had predicted just such an outcome when he wrote in his journals, published in 1841:

> The first great fault committed was, that no distinct rules and regulations were drawn up for the protection of the Aborigines. Their land is taken from them, and the only benefit given in return is that they are made British subjects – that is, having a right to

the protection of British Laws, and at the same time becoming amenable to them.[6]

The protection of British laws meant little when the British themselves alienated more and more land for their farms. In many places this was the country of a specific family group. Menang Elder Vernice Gillies describes what happened to her ancestors in the Albany region.

> *We tend to stick to our own country and within the Menang area, we had lots and lots of family groups who would move around but always had to ask permission to cross over into someone else's country, and with white settlement happening here, of course the Menang people were pushed further and further and further out. So, it created an isolation for them from their own lands, but it also caused a little bit of frustration because they were beginning to cross onto country that wasn't theirs. That's not traditionally acceptable unless you ask permission.*[7]

Menang country (Albany). Photo by Bob Symons.

Initially the settlers assumed that the alienation of land would not pose a major problem. Both the local administration and the colonial government in London concluded that sheep grazing on unfenced land, rather than labour-intensive agriculture, seemed a better option for making money from poor soils.[8]

But European expansion into previously open country further tested the government's ability to respond to settler demands for protection from Aboriginal reprisals. In London, the Colonial Office attempted initially to live up to its proclamation that Aboriginal people would be protected under British law, and the Imperial *Waste Lands Act 1846* gave 'Australian natives' the right to hunt, or wander in search of subsistence, but not on cultivated or fenced-in land.[9] However, as settler expansion continued, this provision was generally ignored. For example, by 1851, the colonial government in Western Australia had failed to bring any York settlers to court, clearing the way for the dispossession of tribal groups.[10]

As flocks increased and pastoralists extended their sheep runs south and east in their new colony, contact and conflict with outlying tribal groups intensified. Traditional Noongar food harvest areas were surveyed, fenced and became 'forbidden zones' into which Aboriginal people could not venture without risking death or arrest.[11]

English settler and Perth lawyer E. W. Landor arrived in the colony in 1841. Although a landowner himself, he voiced concern in words reminiscent of Robert Lyon, a decade earlier, about the effect of legislation intended to protect Aboriginal rights, but evidently still flouted.

> Nothing could be more anomalous and perplexing than the position of the Aborigines as British subjects. Our brave and conscientious Britons, whilst taking possession of the territory, have been most careful and anxious to make it universally known that Australia is not a conquered country; and successive Secretaries of State... have repeatedly commanded that it must never be forgotten that

'possession of this territory is based on right of occupancy'! A 'right of occupancy! Amicable sophistry! Why not say boldly at once, the right of power? We have seized upon the country and shot down the inhabitants, until the survivors have found it convenient to submit to our rule. We have acted exactly as Julius Caesar did when he took possession of Britain. But Caesar was not so hypocritical as to pretend any moral right to possession.[12]

For the Noongars, the newcomers' notion of occupancy exposed a completely different way of looking at land. As Vernice Gillies explains, her people could not understand:

Why people were putting up fences. We don't operate that way. We have our sites all over the place. They're not one spot. So, it was very difficult to understand the 'not sharing'. Aboriginal people right across this country have always shared with each other and all of a sudden it became, 'No, you can't go there because that's mine'. The people who lived here were not used to that. They were used to being free to go wherever they wanted to go, and very suddenly that whole thing changed. So, yes, we had to adapt to that.[13]

For many Aboriginal people, adaptation meant working for the whitefellas. Noongar historian Len Collard sums up their immense contribution to the development of what would become the State of Western Australia.

From the earliest contact, Noongar offered practical expertise and mastery to non-Aboriginal people trying to establish economic enterprises in the infant Swan River Colony. Almost immediately Noongar took up this challenge and became expert horsemen and women, skilled shepherds, and adept at using European agricultural technology and firearms. As well as acting as guides, Noongar took on work, chopping wood, fetching water, clearing land and discovering and mining mineral deposits, undertaking domestic chores such as scrubbing floors, preparing food, and looking after children.[14]

The mail got through too. Brian Pope's study of early postal services in Western Australia has shown that in the 1840s and 1850s, Noongars performed an essential service: the carriage of mail to new settlements in the Avon Valley and to the southwest. Pope comments that, without the Aboriginal mail carriers, Bunbury would not have had its weekly service. Even earlier letters and packages had been carried by local people. In 1838, the *Perth Gazette* had carried a report stating that:

> The arrival of three natives from King George's Sound overland in fourteen days with dispatches from His Excellency Sir James Stirling, and a few letters for private individuals has afforded another instance of the facility of communication and the utility of employing the Aborigines in this manner.[15]

However, as Jennie and Bevan Carter have noted, there was a major problem in keeping this service running. These mailmen would inevitably cross into territories that belonged to different communities, which could make them vulnerable to attack by other Aboriginal groups.[16]

In any case Noongar people were often asked by settlers to venture beyond their own country. This was especially true in their role in guiding explorers such as John Forrest and his brother Alexander. When not naming landmarks after English patrons or politicians (such as with Mount Singleton in the Mid-West), the Forrests and others were often influenced by Aboriginal names, though these were sometimes not the local name, as Yamaji man and Badamia custodian Ashley Bell explained:

> *Because the Europeans came here with Noongar guides, they thought that Ninghan was the original name. We call Mount Singleton, Kundawa, pronounced Koondawa, which is our word for echidna.*[17]

Indigenous Australians often became co-explorers with white men and contributed strongly to geographical knowledge of the vastness of Western Australia. Speaking to the Legislative Council in 1883 about Aboriginal people, John Forrest claimed

Mt Singleton, also known as Ninghan and Kundawa.

to be 'not without some experience of their nature'.[18] He had also acknowledged the contribution of his Noongar guide, Tommy Windich, by paying for a monument to be erected over Windich's grave. However, the view that Forrest genuinely cared about Aboriginal people has been questioned by some historians, including Goddard and Stannage.

> On no occasion in Parliament after 1888 did he attribute the Aborigines with being major instrumentalities in the development of the colony. In the Federal Parliament from 1901 to 1918 he uttered scarcely a word on behalf of the Aborigines. And throughout all these years his pastoral investments flourished, for he, like Harper and other friends, were locked into and promoted an ideology of development, which had racism at its heart.[19]

While the history of colonial exploration has been told largely from the perspective of men like John and Alexander Forrest, Collard and Palmer have examined both 'Noongar accounts and settler diaries, journals and other historical documents which demonstrate many explorers had a deep reliance on Noongar hospitality, knowledge and labour'.[20] And they note that:

> As soon as colonists started exploring country it became apparent that Noongar, (particularly the young and fit) possessed very sophisticated knowledge of immense value. Noongar presence in an area became a sign that food, water and other valuable resources and knowledgeable men and women were close to hand.[21]

The Forrest brothers and others surveyed the northern districts for settlement but initially the pastoral industry expanded in the south of the colony, offering some opportunities for Indigenous employment. From the 1840s until the convict era, which began in 1850, there was a severe labour shortage and thus a demand for Indigenous workers. Noongars were employed in the early settled districts of York and Toodyay. Inevitably, those working for white men grew more familiar with European ways and, like Jesse Hammond's 'elderly man', they began to forget their culture and language.

In his 1981 history of Narrogin, where graziers took up land in the 1850s, shire historian O. Pustkuchen observed a growing reliance on Aboriginal labour: 'With the shortage of labour, some of these people became attached to the white families, and though not a reliable source of manpower, the farmer became more and more dependent upon it'.[22] However, as settlers moved eastwards from the Swan Valley to land beyond the Darling Range, antipathy to Aboriginal people increased. Historian Don Garden records that at Northam, some 170 kilometres north of Narrogin, use of fire became a point of contention.

> As flocks grew during the 1840s and the pressure upon pasture became greater, the fires also multiplied in frequency and destructiveness, partly because hungry Aborigines were resorting more often to fires, their traditional summer method of trapping game...The Aborigines were probably blamed for many fires which were not theirs, for all too frequently it was a European

who caused the fires either because he was careless with sparks...
left a campfire burning...dropped broken glass...[23]

There was some 'give and take' in the relationship. Garden notes that the settlers rewarded the local tribes for not burning the bush by providing sheep and flour for a corroboree.[24] It seemed that:

> Most settlers genuinely desired to live in amity with the natives. They saw a country only very sparsely populated, and believed it right and proper that they should occupy it and make it productive, expecting the Aborigines to either move aside and share the land, or better still, benefit by learning about European civilisation and religion and becoming a useful part of the colonial workforce.[25]

The problem, as settlers saw it, was that Aboriginal people sometimes failed to conform to this expectation and were then thought by Europeans to be dirty, lazy and savage. Respect and goodwill were largely replaced by distaste and even hatred.[26] Misunderstandings between the two cultures ran so deep that, as Garden observed:

> Even the best motivated of the Europeans failed to see resistance by the Aborigines to invasion of their tribal land as anything more than treachery. So, fear, distrust and revenge were the usual products of black and white relations.[27]

Misunderstanding only deepened as the century wore on. Pustkuchen notes that, while many of the local Noongars around Narrogin became trusted shepherds and later farm workers, newer settlers 'mostly established an antipathy to what they termed "lazy and useless black bastards"'. From then on, it would seem, 'all chances of assimilation vanished and not even education was granted to the vast majority, who were forced into a nomad existence'.[28]

Nevertheless, historian Henry Reynolds suggests that despite 'distaste and hatred', Aboriginal people were not always seen as victims.

By the middle of the nineteenth century many settlers had concluded that the Aborigines would never adopt European civilization, that they were incapable of 'improvement' and were indeed a doomed race. Yet a minority of whites appreciated that black behaviour manifested faith in their own culture, that it betokened strength not weakness, affirmation not failure. The problem they realized was not the incapacity of tribesmen but their 'intractableness', their martial spirit.[29]

Many Europeans thought that the roving life was important to Aboriginal people yet most failed to understand the importance of living 'on country' and that its inhabitants defined 'country' territorially. Others felt that they did understand the 'native people'. Theodora Sanders, daughter of a pioneer family in the Bunbury region, expressed appreciation of some of their attributes and skills:

> The Aborigines have been described as being very primitive people, but they had many skills of their own. They had very little mathematical calculation but they had smoke signals before Marconi invented wireless. They had a very keen sense of touch, smell, direction, and eyesight and were marvellous trackers. The Aborigines had no religion or a God, but believed in a life hereafter and all their lives were surrounded by good and bad spirits and, with secrets of their own, never became over-populated.[30]

Sanders also recorded that her family employed a number of Aboriginal workers and noted with some satisfaction that:

> Towards the end of the 19th century, some of the natives had settled in nicely with the farmers of the district. Some had attended school and could read and write, others were trained in the households as domestics. One of our doctors owned a farm and orchard. He employed a manager and among other workers, Joe and Nelly. Joe was very handy in the orchard, he made fruit cases, fed stock, milked cows and was quite a good worker. However, he tired if the same work went on too long...He was

a good cricketer and played in the local team…Nellie…did the washing and was a very good washerwoman.[31]

For the Sanders family, it seemed that the 'native problem' had been solved and that the original inhabitants had been assimilated into white culture, living useful lives as servants. However, when Theodora published her memoir in 1975, she was saddened but also puzzled by a changed relationship.

> The Aborigines are today a great problem and many of us wish to do something for them, but it is difficult to know where to begin. There have always been some with good intelligence, these should be the ones to be trained and educated to help their own people, for they would have a better understanding of the needs of their own race. The earliest settlers, were I think, the kindest to them, and today it's kindness they need most of all.[32]

The perceptive Jesse Hammond, writing in 1933, was already aware of the apparent disappearance of Noongar culture.

> The advance of settlement in the South-West dating from the early 60s of the last [nineteenth] century has brought about the gradual contamination and almost the complete extinction of the pure-blooded black…
>
> Then, after the 'eighties [1880s], the organisation of the tribes in the South-West began to break up. The number of half-castes was growing, blacks from other parts of the State were coming in; and the blacks were beginning to drop their own ways and their own language…after that date unless one could challenge them in their own language and keep a close watch on their answers, it would be impossible to get any certain information from them about themselves.[33]

Hammond's observation that 'blacks' from other parts of the state 'were coming in' identifies an important issue. The expansion of 'whitefella' farming not only displaced people; it scattered them. As more farmers and later pastoralists ventured into new territory, they often took Aboriginal people with them into country inhabited by different people with less familiar languages.

Lynette Knapp's family history illustrates the effects of this dispersal and also the growth of a part-Aboriginal population. Her great-grandmother, a Menang woman from Albany met a former convict, ticket-of-leave man William or Thomas Egan. He was an Irishman from Kilkenny who had been held in Albany's convict gaol. Lynette's great-grandparents eventually moved north to New Norcia, where their children married into Noongar families from the Avon Valley and further north. Much later, Lynette's mother was sent back to 'her own country', to the native settlement at Carrolup, north of Albany, where she met her future husband from the south coast.[34]

Only male convicts were sent to Western Australia between 1850 and 1868, increasing the gender imbalance. As former convicts obtained their release, competition for brides increased. Few white female settlers wanted to marry a convict, even if he was a freed man.[35] Thus, sometimes long-term liaisons and marriages formed between Aboriginal women and convict men. Murray Arnold notes that many Aboriginal families living in Albany

Albany convict gaol (now museum). Photo by Bob Symons.

today can trace their descent from such consensual unions.[36] The colonial government even established a scheme where 10 acres of land would be given to such couples. Arnold reports that at least four such grants were issued in the Albany area.[37]

Vernice Gillies's family also experienced the dispersal process and the inevitable cultural confusion.

> *My mother was a Yamaji woman from Carnarvon, taken away, and through sheer luck met my dad and they were married in 1937 and, as a dutiful wife, she followed him back to his country, the south coast, where she learned to speak our language quite fluently. She had to, so that she would fit in. She was from the north-west and was viewed quite often with a lot of suspicion, but she learned, because of her own background. We spoke the forbidden language and my grandmother told us stories, and we've kept those stories.*[38]

Disease, as well as dispersal, had by now severely affected the viability of the Aboriginal population. Jesse Hammond saw first-hand the effect of European introduced diseases on First Nations people.

> The sicknesses that broke them up were not those which they had known among themselves before the white men came. The measles epidemic of the 'eighties killed them off in scores. The other curse was the venereal disease introduced by the whites. It ravaged them terribly. In the 'nineties, in the tribal territory to the north of Perth, I have seen miserable wretches of women, visibly affected to an extreme extent. Not a moment of medical attention was being given to them.[39]

The effects of these epidemics were still within living memory in the 1920s and 1930s. Paul Hasluck, later politician and governor general of Australia, was then a journalist with *The West Australian* newspaper. Using Pitman's shorthand, Hasluck captured many oral history accounts of later nineteenth-century life, including European memories of Aboriginal mortality. In September 1931, he recorded an interview with Ralph Ashworth at his home in York.

> As a boy once, when I was coming down from Daliak [a settlement a few kilometres outside York] I remember seeing fifteen or sixteen blacks lying dead and their mates too weak to bury them. That was when there was an epidemic of measles. There were hundreds of blacks about before then but that started the end of them.[40]

A sad observation in itself, but also expressive of the then widely held 'dying pillow' assumption that Aboriginal people were doomed to extinction.

Hasluck also talked with Mrs Blechynden, born in 1860 at Boyerine (formerly Boyadine), a small settlement in the Great Southern, south of Wagin. She too recalled the effect on an unprepared population of an early measles outbreak.

> The measles broke out the year I was born. I know that because my mother told me that when I was a month old, they travelled by horse and cart to get me baptised because they thought I might die in the epidemic. The natives outback died in great numbers at that time...The natives were very numerous before the first breaking out of the measles. I believe that they died terribly in that first epidemic. It was beyond their experience. They believed that the white people had given them that punishment and it gave them a dread of the white people. That is what I was told by my people.[41]

Mrs Blechynden also had personal recollections of the original inhabitants of this country.

> The natives used to do a bit of hut robbing but there was no particular crime and I never knew anything worse than taking a bit of food and knocking over a sheep occasionally. They were very useful people. Where they made friends, they stood true.[42]

While few settlers wrote about the Aboriginal people in their midst, for country-dwellers, like Mrs Blechynden, they were part of the landscape and 'useful people'.

THE END OF THE BEGINNING OR THE BEGINNING OF THE END?

Jesse Hammond gives us a glimpse of the ability of First Nations people to adapt to the 'new normal'.

> Natives were sometimes employed, and made much better shepherds than the white men for several reasons. The first was that a native never lost any sheep. If any were missing, he could soon track them up. He also had his gin [woman] with him and that meant another pair of eyes for the work. A second reason was that native shepherds never knocked the sheep about or hurt them in any way. When they were given charge of a flock, they soon got to like the sheep and had their pets among them.[43]

Interestingly, back in the 1830s, Commandant Collet Barker had once asked his Menang friend, Mokare, whether he thought Aboriginal people would make good shepherds, like Nathan, one of the convicts at King George Sound.

> On asking M if his people would make good shepherds like Nathan, he said 'yes, that just at first they might not, but in a little time, it would be Nathan middling, black fellow very good'.[44]

In the south, pastoralism was a mainstay of the economy.

For much of the nineteenth century, smaller scale pastoralism in the south remained a mainstay of Western Australia's economy and sheep farmers had a source of inexpensive but useful 'black fellow' labour. The Hassell family developed a large estate centred on Kendenup and Jerramungup, north of Albany. In 1878, Ethel Clifton married Albert Hassell and went from Albany to live at what was then Jerramungup pastoral station. Ethel immediately became curious about the people camped on her husband's land. Although he warned her 'never to trust a native', she made friends with local women who told her their creation stories and taught her how to track wildlife.

> If I wanted to explore any distant part, I could always get some of the women to go with me…I often look back on the really interesting walks and talks, for a native is observant — it is part of their life to watch and notice. I soon learnt to track, and the women used to derive great amusement at my blindness in not taking notice of small things which is really the true art of tracking.[45]

Ethel Hassell recorded her memories of that time in *My Dusky Friends*. Introducing Ethel's recollections, Sara Meagher suggests that without this account, we would have no real knowledge of the original inhabitants of the Jerramungup area.[46] The writer herself recognised the value of her recollections.

> I have looked over my notes and trust the public will find some interest in the manners, legends and customs of a fast disappearing race. Most interesting because of their great antiquity and the obscurity of their origin, their legends are few and hard to trace. Those I have written were told me before the whites had much religious influence, indeed I doubt if any of the natives had ever heard anything of our religion, for their early acquaintance with the white man was not the missionary but the whaler and sealer, and the treatment they received at their hands was cruel in the extreme.[47]

THE END OF THE BEGINNING OR THE BEGINNING OF THE END?

Ethel gave detailed descriptions of Aboriginal life, customs and legends. But one account of a challenging incident is vividly illustrative of differing cultural priorities.

> The women the day before had all been sent to collect and drive some sheep across the river and on their way had found a honey tree...What were sheep in comparison to a find like this? So they were left to their fate, while all the women set to work to burn the tree down and smoke the bees out...so the sheep wandered off where their own sweet wills dictated...Meanwhile at the homestead my husband was getting more impatient and worried at the non-arrival of the sheep...a native on horseback was despatched to see what could be the matter. He arrived just as the tree was about to fall, of course he had to assist them, when it was down, examine it, see the size of the hive and taste the honey. Then bark had to be found and stripped from the trees bent into shape to hold the honey comb on to carry back to the camp. What were sheep compared to such an interesting and unexpected find?

Back at the homestead:

> It was getting near sunset, and nothing had turned up, the women had been sent before midday...At last my brother mounted his horse and rode off. About a mile from the homestead he met some of the wanderers laden with honey in bark baskets. But where were the sheep? 'The sheep, oh, we lose em,' was the chorus 'but look, master, what lovely honey, taste some it is very good.'
>
> My brother could not help laughing though he was so annoyed. It was far too late to try and get the sheep, so he rode back to the station and explained the situation.[48]

For Ethel's husband, the missing sheep were still the main issue.

> Bye and bye the women and children straggled in sticky from head to foot, carrying baskets with honey in all stages, new and old comb, perfectly happy, utterly unconscious of any wrong, delighted with their find and anxious to share honey with all

Old Hassell homestead, Jerramungup.

on the station, utterly astonished when they were scolded and told there would be no food for their camp until the sheep were found and brought to the homestead. A great wail rose up... What were they to do? They were sternly told they could feed on honey. Apparently, they had about enough honey and wanted something substantial but my husband was adamant...The sheep had wandered far and half the homestead had been out since daylight collecting them and they were not all in yet, so there was very little prospect of supper at the camp that night. They all knew perfectly well that once the order went forth, it would be carried out, for the only way to deal with natives is to treat them like children. Whatever you promise, do, whether it is gift or punishment, but a native, like a child, has a keen sense of justice. If they think they are not justly treated they quietly early one morning walk off.[49]

From then on, Ethel Hassell tells us, if a tree laden with honey fell right across their path the women would walk away from it!

This account of life at Jerramungup is valuable because nineteenth-century settlers wrote very little about the original inhabitants. Aboriginal people, however, told the newcomers about the localities where they lived and Western Australia has a wealth of relevant place names as a result. Jerramungup, for example, means 'place of upstanding Yate trees'.[50] Collard and Palmer conclude that more than sixty per cent of place names in the south-west are of Noongar origin and tell us stories about the land and its history.

> One example is the place name Manjoordoordap which is the old name for the modern place we know as Mandurah. According to claims made by historians, Mandurah means a place of trade and festivities. By speaking out this word and listening to how it sounds, its meaning has come to me, *Manda* is the word for gathering to exchange, *Djoorkoord* is a wife or female lover. *Ap*, *up* or *p* is the location of a place. Taken together and spoken out loud a much richer meaning revealed itself to us. In this way Manjoordoordap speaks to us as a source of its own history, outlining the importance of the area as a place for romantic interludes during times of trade and exchange and cultural festivities.[51]

Place names excepted, Rhoda Glover, in her history of the Shire of Plantagenet (Mount Barker), describes the Aboriginal inhabitants as 'shadowy figures that emerge briefly from the yellowed pages of explorers' journals and other official documents, then vanish again into the mists of history'.[52]

The people that Ethel Hassell wrote about lived not far from Mount Barker and were by no means 'shadowy figures'. The lack of other accounts is not evidence that the Aboriginal people disappeared or that their culture vanished. John Host in his report for the South West Aboriginal Land and Sea Council on the Single Noongar Claim refers to the development of regional Aboriginal organisations and contends that:

the corporations themselves and the cultural and social initiatives that they have developed reflect, in my opinion, 'the living matrix of traditional law and custom that underlies and sustains Noongar existence'.[53]

In the nineteenth century, disease and dispersal of First Nations people from their original lands were not the only threats to their traditional society. A now mixed-race population was subject to controls imposed by the newcomers. These 'controls' included, in some instances, the killing of large numbers of people.

Aboriginal Elder Lynette Knapp has a handed-down memory of a massacre of the local people which occurred near what became the town of Ravensthorpe, between Albany and Esperance.

> *My father, when he was a child, he said he could remember coming through Ravensthorpe, into one area where all the ground was swept black. it must have been one of the old corroboree grounds. And there were skeletons of babies on the ground, that they'd hit with sticks and been killed. They had to get rid of the children because they wanted the Aboriginal women because they [the settlers] needed women to keep them going, because, as often as not, it was the women who did the cooking for them, especially for those men without wives.*[54]

Lynette's account probably refers to the notorious event known as the Cocanarup (Kukenarup) massacre. In the 1880s, local pastoralist John Dunn was speared by an Aboriginal man in retaliation for the rape and attack of a young Aboriginal girl. After a trial in which the Aboriginal man was acquitted, the Dunn family rounded up and slaughtered around thirty or more Aboriginal men, women and children.[55] Novelist Kim Scott has written a fictional account of this event in his novel *Benang*. He has also recorded the account given to him by his Aboriginal aunt, Hazel Brown, of her parents' visit to the site of the massacre.

> *After Mum and Dad got married in Carrolup, Dad took Mum down to Esperance to meet some of the family, and on the way*

THE END OF THE BEGINNING OR THE BEGINNING OF THE END?

he wanted to take her and show her where his mother's family were massacred.

[...] Just before they got to the actual site, Mummy said she wanted to go bush, you know. Go to the toilet.

She went behind a bush and while she was squatting, she noticed a singlet there. She thought it was a singlet. After she got up, she went and got a stick. She scraped the leaves away...and it all come to pieces.

It wasn't a singlet, it was like a tunic. You know, the old khaki clothes the troopers wore years ago, woolly ones. It was the buttons, the brass buttons. They picked up about eight or nine brass buttons, so the person that they killed there must've been wearing an old soldier's tunic or something.

[...] There were bones too. There was no legs, only the torso and the hip bones and that. The foot part and everything was all gone. The arms and head were gone. But there was these buttons laying around.

[...] They would have been the first to go there for a long time, apart from old *Dongup* [Grandfather], and different old ones. There weren't many Noongars anyway, to go there. It was taboo.[56]

In 2015, the ABC reported the unveiling of a memorial to this event outside Ravensthorpe.

More than a century after a horrific massacre, a memorial has been unveiled on Western Australia's south coast, prompting reconciliation between farming and Indigenous communities.

[...] Noongar Elder Carol Petterson said it was one of the first memorials of its kind in Australia, acknowledging the past and reconciling the future for both the local Indigenous people and agricultural industry.

'It's important because it's a hallmark of the reconciliation process. Reconciliation is an action, not a word, and that's what's happened here today'.[57]

Remembering Kukenarup. (Courtesy Ravensthorpe Historical Society)

Both this memorial and Kim Scott's writings have brought the events at Kukenarup into history's spotlight. While most settlers regarded Aboriginal people as a 'dying race', decimated by disease, we do not know to what extent the supposed population decline was hastened by events such as this massacre.

Yet we do know, as Jesse Hammond correctly noted, that in the nineteenth century there was a substantial growth of a part-Aboriginal population. Historian Michael Howard has outlined, from a dispassionate European perspective, how this occurred.

> Miscegenation occurred in the south-west virtually from the time of the arrival of the first Europeans. On the south coast it appears to have been initiated by whalers and sealers. During the 1840s, pastoralists in the Victoria Plains frequently availed themselves of Aboriginal women. As the country became more established and as more non-Aboriginal women became available during

the latter part of the nineteenth century, however, such practices became less frequent and more covert – many whites seeking to hide previous and now embarrassing relations with Aborigines.[58]

Wadandi Cultural Custodian Iszaac Webb illustrates what happened in his own country: a situation which has led to further misunderstandings and hurt.

> *There were fifteen or so settler men and one settler woman. The other men didn't have any wives and our women were walking around balak, naked. Remember, this was a time when the Europeans were wearing petticoats and dress after dress and it was all this conservative sort of thing. That's where a lot of times, they would have half-caste children or children of mixed blood. They would be off to the side where there was an Aboriginal woman, and she was still the housekeeper, but had these children and it was never questioned why those children were lighter and she was the housekeeper.*[59]

Michael Howard estimated that:

> There were about 600 part-Aborigines in the south-west by 1890 – not many, but enough to be noticeable at a time when most Whites had begun to think that they were soon to see the last of that 'dying race'. Because of the growing numbers of part-Aborigines, changing attitudes on the part of White West Australians and a deteriorating economic condition, the situation of part-Aborigines in the south-west began worsening rapidly towards the end of the century.[60]

As more and more southern farmers began to clear the bush to grow wheat and other crops, pastoralism moved north.[61] When settlers began to establish large sheep runs in the Gascoyne, the Pilbara and, finally, the Kimberley regions, they encountered societies which had experienced far less contact with Europeans. Not surprisingly, Aboriginal groups resisted territorial encroachment and there was further misunderstanding between white settlers and the original inhabitants.

A meeting in the early nineteenth century had suggested potential for future conflict. Historian Cathie Clement recounts an encounter on 7 August 1821 between the local people and 'visitors' on a British naval ship, the *Bathurst*, exploring the north-west coast.[62] The ship was commanded by Lieutenant Phillip Parker King, who also visited King George Sound on several occasions.

> *The encounter at Hanover Bay was on top of a rocky shore. The Aboriginal men had stayed to meet King. He had taken fish as a gift. The men in turn gave a gift to King and his Aboriginal companion. The encounter was proceeding quite well until that point, in the sense of there being no animosity.*
>
> *The ship's surgeon, Montgomery, then came up the rocks, bringing a fish but also carrying a gun under his coat. King himself was not armed. When the Aboriginal people declined to take the fish from Montgomery, he flung it at their feet. This changed the tenor of the interaction to one of hostility. King tried to retrieve the situation by taking his gift, which had been a clasp knife, back from the Aboriginal people and again demonstrating to them how the mechanism worked.*
>
> *This action only increased Aboriginal hostility and King decided to return to his boat. But when he turned his back on the Aboriginal men, they flung spears after them and Montgomery was hit in the back. Initially King saw to providing first aid to Montgomery.*
>
> *But when he went back to his ship, he organised a reprisal against the Aborigines and that reprisal fitted the White man's view that Aborigines must respect Europeans and must be taught that they cannot act in a hostile manner against Europeans without being punished.*

And the message from that exchange?

> *I think what you are looking at there is cultural difference and failure to appreciate that both sides have their own codes of behaviour and their own expectations about how they should be treated by another group.*[63]

Cultural differences surfaced again in the Gascoyne in the 1880s, when pastoralists needed an Aboriginal workforce because, as historian Howard Pedersen explained,

> *It was difficult to bring up white shepherds from the south so the dependence on Aboriginal labour was enormous. They needed a lot of workers and they wanted a servile force.*[64]

That 'servile force' was gradually losing its traditional sources of sustenance and spearing of pastoralists' sheep became inevitable.

> *So, the pastoralists were saying to the Government, 'look we are losing a lot of sheep through spearings and we're in danger of our own lives'. And they threatened to abandon the region.*[65]

As Pedersen suggests, this situation gave pastoralists an excuse to demand government protection, including a police force, to bring Aboriginal people 'into line'. Their expectations were largely met since the colonial government in Perth encouraged territorial expansion and because many of the parliamentarians held pastoral leases themselves. Prominent among these individuals was Alexander Forrest, who had amalgamated his properties with those of the Emmanuel family to become the largest pastoral landholders in the West Kimberley.[66] In November 1888, Forrest moved in the Legislative Council that:

> 'Protection must be taken to protect the settlers in the Kimberley from the treacherous hostility of the Aborigines' and that the 'most humane way' to deal with Aboriginal groups was to engage groups of special constables to assist the police to use force 'and leave a lasting impression upon the minds of these aborigines… to make it plain to them that an attitude of hostility towards the settlers will not be permitted'.[67]

Employing Aboriginal people on pastoral stations or pressganging them to work on pearling boats meant catching them first. Henry Reynolds describes this acquisition of 'free labour':

> They were frequently recruited at the point of a gun, were ruled by fear, flogged, underfed and unpaid. Aboriginal women were universally taken by white men either for casual sex or for longer relationships in which they provided sexual comfort and

unrewarded labour. Critics who questioned the system threatened not only the self-esteem and moral standing of frontier settlers but their economic survival as well.[68]

Nevertheless, two critics were prepared to bear witness to the way in which north-west Aboriginal people were forcibly enslaved. One was a former but pardoned convict, David Carley, the other an Anglican priest, John Gribble.

Carley had arrived in the Pilbara in 1872. Despite his own convict background, he believed that if the truth were known about events in northern Australia, English justice would prevail.[69] In order to bring this situation to public notice he documented the kidnapping and ill-treatment of Aboriginal men, women and children.

> In September, 1878, I was inside my house at Cossack, when I heard a native woman call out to me to save her boy from a man who was kidnapping him, I went out and saw the woman struggling with a white man for her boy. I did not interfere, as it was useless, knowing that the man's brother was a J.P., who I had seen sign away numbers of kidnapped natives. The man tore the boy away from his mother, and took him to a store close by and got him assigned. The next day the boy was put on a cutter in spite of the screams and struggles of his poor mother. I drew the attention of a constable to the case, and he said he could not interfere. I have seen hundreds of children brought into Cossack who have been torn away from their mothers, and yet it is said that where the British flag flies, slavery cannot exist.[70]

The Reverend John Brown Gribble had come from Victoria in 1885 to a base at Carnarvon. He travelled throughout the Murchison and Gascoyne regions. Howard Pedersen comments that:

> *Gribble was absolutely horrified at what he saw and particularly at the notion of enslavement. The attacks on Aboriginal women and the atrocious situation of the police rounding up Aboriginal people. Carting them for often several hundred miles led round the neck by chains, marched over hot*

> desert regions all the way to Carnarvon or Geraldton to be transported to the prison on Rottnest Island where Aboriginal people were chained up for days on end and given little water.[71]

Gribble was not to be silenced. Within six months, he had caused a furore. *Dark Deeds in a Sunny Land, or Black and White in North-West Australia* was published in late June 1886 by the *Inquirer* newspaper.[72] In this pamphlet, Gribble alleged that a system of slavery existed in the north.[73] 'The Gribble Affair', as historian Neville Green recalls, became the sensation of Western Australia in the later 1880s.

> He brought it to the notice of the people in the city that the pastoralists were imposing a form of slavery on Aborigines in the Gascoyne. When the people in Perth wouldn't listen to him, he took his story to Melbourne and to anyone who would listen.[74]

Gribble had met David Carley for the first time on 4 March 1886 and publicised Carley's observations of his time in the Pilbara.[75] In a Melbourne *Daily Telegraph* article on 9 July 1886, Gribble quoted Carley:

> It is very well known by all old hands who knock about Nickol Bay [modern day Karratha] and the 'Flying Foam' passage, that in one day there were quite sixty natives, men, women and children, shot dead. The natives themselves have shown me the skulls of fifteen who were shot. Three of the skulls were those of children, and two of these small skulls had bullet holes through them. I have seen many natives shot in the back for no other cause than that of running away from their cruel slave masters.[76]

Gribble contended that laws supposedly covering Aboriginal workers were openly flouted in the Gascoyne.

> Most certainly that in some cases at any rate, the natives are not consulted in the matter of engagement, but are by compulsion made the bondservants of the whites…and not free laborers…The wife of a certain settler told me that her husband said 'he could

> keep his natives as long as he liked'…I know that there are worthy exceptions…but these exceptional persons are laughed at for their honesty in the treatment of their natives, as one of them told me himself.[77]

Gribble's pastoral work took him long distances across his wide brown parish. He recalled one of his first impressions of Gascoyne station life.

> I drew attention to the neglected appearance of certain of the natives, and that if the blacks were unkindly treated, they would certainly run away. I was told in reply that the treatment was quite good enough for the 'niggers', and that it was absurd to think that they should have tea, sugar etc.[78]

While his comments attracted some support, John Gribble's observations appeared to threaten the social and clerical community. In Neville Green's words:

> *He not only antagonised the pastoralists, he antagonised the Governor, he antagonised the Legislative Council and he antagonised his own Bishop.*[79]

Henry Reynolds suggests that Gribble had probably also offended the governor's wife, Lady Broome, by 'belittling her pet project, the construction of Perth's new Anglican cathedral'.[80] Apparently, Gribble had suggested that human lives should have a higher priority than bricks and mortar. Forty years later, Gribble's son, Ernest, was told by the retired editor of Perth's *Daily News*: 'Your father was sacrificed to build the Cathedral. We were raising money for it at the time.'[81]

Gribble's Bishop, Henry Parry, who had initially supported his missionary work, now turned on him. He attempted to censor any publication of Gribble's north-west findings in the daily newspapers and expressed concern about Gribble's intent to write to the Aborigines Protection Society in England. As historian Su-Jane Hunt observed:

St George's Cathedral, Perth.

Despite pleas by the Perth press to bury 'misunderstandings and grievances in the fathomless depths of charitable oblivion', the tensions continued. At a public meeting in Carnarvon on December 28 [1886], Gribble was again called upon to resign. He took the floor, stating that he would 'never cease the fight for the downtrodden natives.' Someone in the crowd heckled Gribble. 'He is no Britisher – he must be of some foreign extraction'.[82]

The strongest hostility inevitably came from the pastoralists themselves, men with political power and influence. They were joined by the conservative newspaper *The West Australian*. Gribble pursued a libel suit against newspaper editors Charles Harper and Winthrop Hackett, who had described him, on 24 August 1886, as 'one whom, without exaggeration, we might designate as a lying canting humbug'. That assertion was effectively and ironically disproved by the evidence of one Gascoyne pastoralist, and member of the Anglican church, George Bush.

> There are about 100 natives on my run; about forty of whom are in my service. The others are uncivilised natives. I have trained my 40 natives more or less...I have heard of natives out of my own (property) being run down and unlawfully taken and I believe they were chained up...I have heard that nigger hunting in the northern parts of the colony has been a profitable employment...I have sent the women off to the white men myself. The probable consequence is that the women will be used as the white man wishes.[83]

Despite this evidence and some judicial sympathy, Gribble lost his libel suit and was forced to pay legal costs. Penniless, and described by his son Ernest as a broken and desolate man, Gribble and his family left Western Australia. Later, he established the Yarrabah Mission at Cape Grafton in Queensland, where he died in 1893 at the age of forty-five. The words 'Black Fellow's Friend' were engraved on his tombstone.[84]

The only support for Gribble's efforts had come from the Perth newspaper the *Inquirer*, in an article published on 29 June 1887.

> Let the Squattocracy say the colony is cleared! But of what? Not of anything Mr. Gribble has said respecting their cruelties towards 'niggers', but cleared of a Missionary effort that would have made the colony what a vigorous Church and good Government should strive to make it.[85]

Some Europeans displayed a conscience about the ill-treatment of their fellow human beings. But were Aboriginal people part of the 'human race'? Historian Anna Haebich reminds us that most settlers were influenced by prevailing social and racial attitudes.

> *Aboriginal people were being described by anthropologists in Britain as being equivalent to the very early stages of humanity. These ideas were consolidated in the pseudo-scientific theories of social Darwinism, which said that Aboriginal people were 'at the bottom of an evolutionary ladder of humankind'. And this view also took on Darwinian ideas of survival of the fittest, suggesting that lesser peoples like the Aboriginal people, in*

> *this struggle for survival, would lose out in the face of superior groupings like the Europeans. So, when Aboriginal people started to die from disease and were being killed off and their numbers declined dramatically, people looked around and said, 'Oh well, that's just inevitable. It's part of this almost biblical process that's almost been ordained by the Bible'. And people often referred to the Bible to support the process that was going on.*[86]

Part of that process involved imprisonment. The present-day holiday resort of Rottnest had been established in 1839 as a penal institution for the transportation of Aboriginal 'trouble makers'. Closed in 1849, when resistance in the south-west had weakened, the prison was reopened in 1855 as pastoralism spread northwards. Aboriginal people were frequently taken from their own country and imprisoned on what was, for them, a cold and remote southern island.[87] Their offences? Howard Pedersen lists just one.

> *The convictions always listed 'sheep spearing'...and some two hundred Aboriginal people from those regions sent to Rottnest...and often it was the young, economically dependent people were taken away and often crushed at Rottnest. Everyone was sentenced to three years imprisonment. Many died there and others suffered there enormously. And when they returned, they found their families living in the Aboriginal camp in the proximity of the pastoral homesteads.*[88]

Gribble described the fate of those Rottnest-bound prisoners.

> These natives, most of whom had been brought down from the Peedong country, more than 300 miles, were accused of having speared cattle. I was present when, on the evidence of a very young white man, they were sentenced to two years' banishment on Rottnest Island. But the strange part of the tale is yet to be told. One of the troopers in charge told me that some of these unfortunate beings had never seen a white man until the day they were captured and chained. Now the question arises here, were they individually guilty, and who could say they were? There was no one to speak of their side of the question.[89]

These Aboriginal men sent to Rottnest were, in practice, enslaved and the conditions in which they were held, particularly inhumane when observed from a historical perspective. Infections and epidemics were common and stories of their brutal treatment caused concern among some settlers on the mainland.[90] However, Alexander Forrest, later a pivotal figure in Kimberley exploration, saw Rottnest as an 'instructional institution'.

> Natives who were taken to Rottnest were pampered too much, and when liberated, were as bad as when they were first imprisoned; but when they had to do a hard day's work, chained to a wheelbarrow, and occasionally flogged for bad conduct, they gradually recognised that it was not desirable to spear cattle or break the law in any way.[91]

Earlier explorers, like George Grey, who had travelled to the coastal areas of northern Australia, had imagined a very different future for this region. Pedersen describes Grey's vision:

> *He portrayed the Kimberley as having this tremendous economic potential. It would grow wonderful tropical fruit and a city would emerge north of where Derby is now. He thought that northern Australia would be a heavily settled area and the Kimberley would propel Western Australia into economic prosperity.*[92]

Grey, who had seen the effects of slavery in the southern United States, was also mindful of how the local people should be treated. When he set out on his exploratory expedition to the Kimberley in 1837, his preliminary instructions from the British government were clear:

> The greatest forbearance and discretion in treating with the Aborigines is strongly impressed and urged upon the travellers – it should be distinctly borne in mind that as all exploring expeditions in this country are sent out with a view to future colonization, it is of the utmost importance to make friends with the natives...**It should be remarked that their's is the right of soil, – we are the intruders.**[93]

THE END OF THE BEGINNING OR THE BEGINNING OF THE END?

While George Grey had been instructed to show 'forbearance and discretion', the reality became very different. Cathie Clement has shown that pastoral expansion inevitably brought disputes about a precious asset, water:

> *The tendency for Europeans to camp on water was a key source of conflict. In order to be able to move through a previously unexplored area, they needed to find sufficient water for a party of men and horses. It was impossible for would-be pastoralists to water a mob of horses from a small waterhole. Aboriginal people also needed to camp near water but European needs were far greater and it was common for explorers to excavate wells and waterholes, almost certainly upsetting the Aboriginal principle of looking after traditional resources.*[94]

Access to water was often at the core of conflict. When settlers camped near water, they barred Aboriginal people from what were often sacred sites. Neville Green visited some of these locations.

Access to waterholes caused conflict.

When the Aborigines approached their sacred site, the Europeans shot at them. In 1967, some of the old men took me to these sites. They showed me where the homesteads were and they told me how their uncles and grandfathers speared the newcomers and drove their horses and sheep into the mud flats, cut off the horses' tails and made hair belts out of them. Eventually the pastoralists withdrew.[95]

A temporary reprieve for traditional owners, but an early conflict involving water use in the La Grange area south of Broome, erupted in 1864. The La Grange sub-basin extends about 150 kilometres south of Broome and is predominantly the country of the Karajarri people. Their knowledge of the location, size and condition of their water sources has always been essential to their survival.[96] For the Karajarri, country is both a physical and metaphysical landscape for which they assume responsibility of care.[97] People who do not come from this country must seek permission. Karajarri man John Dudu Nangkiriny described the correct protocol to historians Fiona Skyring and Sarah Yu.

> People, strangers shouldn't come into our country. It can be dangerous and first they must ask. That's the proper way. If other people want to use things from our country, like the water or the shell, or if they want to come and get fish, they should ask the Karajarri first. And after that we can ask them for something. They might give us fish, or tucker, or other things we need.[98]

Historian Bruce Scates describes what ensued when three men from the Roebuck Bay Pastoral Company, travelling north to explore the possibility of new pastoral holdings, came onto Karajarri country without observing these protocols.

We know that Panter, the leader of the expedition, captured and interrogated an Aboriginal woman, demanding to know the whereabouts of water. We know that they went to native wells, that they dug them out, they watered their horses there, that the native wells were left dry and useless as a consequence.[99]

The Karajarri retaliated for this violation of a water source by killing the three explorers, probably because they had camped at the water source without permission or introduction from the local people. It seems from Panter's last diary entry that the Karajarri may have tried to warn the Europeans in sign and language that they were effectively trespassing, but the intruders did not understand the message.[100]

Scates describes the sequel to these killings.

> *In 1865 a search party led by Maitland Brown, a close personal friend of Panter, was sent to find the perpetrators. At La Grange, they took Aboriginal men hostage and refused them food and water until they led them to the campsite. Once they found the remains of the explorers, the Europeans opened fire and killed the hostages. Then two days later they come across an Aboriginal campsite of about seventy people and we know that at least twenty Aboriginal people were killed on that occasion.*[101]

Fifty-one years later, in 1913, a monument erected in the Esplanade Park at Fremantle commemorated only the deaths of the white men and was inscribed,

---

THIS MONUMENT WAS ERECTED BY

G.J. BROCKMAN

AS A FELLOW BUSH WANDERER'S TRIBUTE TO THE MEMORIES OF

PANTER, HARDING AND GOLDWYER

EARLIEST EXPLORERS AFTER GREY AND GREGORY OF THIS

'TERRA INCOGNITA", ATTACKED AT NIGHT BY TREACHEROUS NATIVES

WERE MURDERED AT BOOLE BOOLA, NEAR LE GRANGE BAY

ON THE 13 NOVEMBER 1864.[102]

As a historian then working at Murdoch University, Scates was aware that this inscription told only one side of the story. Following his representations, and with the support of Murdoch University staff, Fremantle City Council and the Karajarri community, a fresh inscription was placed on the reverse face of the monument. Installed in 1994, the memorial now gives both sides of the story.[103]

> THIS PLAQUE WAS ERECTED BY PEOPLE WHO FOUND
> THE MONUMENT BEFORE YOU OFFENSIVE.
>
> THE MONUMENT DESCRIBED THE EVENTS AT
> LA GRANGE FROM ONE PERSPECTIVE ONLY: THE
> VIEWPOINT OF THE WHITE 'SETTLERS'.
>
> No mention is made of the right of Aboriginal People to defend their land or of the history of provocation which led to the explorers' deaths.
>
> [...]
>
> This plaque is in memory of the Aboriginal people killed at La Grange. It also commemorates all other Aboriginal people who died during the invasion of their country.
> LEST WE FORGET MAPA JARRIYA-NYALAKU

Panter memorial, Fremantle.

In a reconciliatory speech at the unveiling of the revised inscription, Joe Roe, speaking for the Karajarri community, spoke of wanting to put this 'bloody episode' behind them:

> *Let's not keep the hatred in our hearts because that will destroy us. But I also want you to remember, not to forget about the past. So, to all non-Aboriginal and Aboriginal people, let's be in peace.*[104]

Another memorial, this time in Broome, was unveiled in 2010 on the Roebuck Bay foreshore. It commemorates the involvement of Aboriginal women who, in the early days of the pearl shell industry, were captured and sold as slaves through the 'blackbirding' trade.[105] Western Australian sculptors Joan and Charlie Smith, who created the statue of a pregnant diver, described the work performed by Aboriginal women pearl divers as 'a secret history' and hoped that their work would 'make people aware of the real stories underlying the official histories. And to make sure these sorts of things never happen again.'[106]

Pearling began near Roebourne in the 1860s and, like pastoralism, had a significant impact on the original inhabitants. By the end of the 1870s, a lucrative trade in pearl shell had been established, using Malay and Aboriginal labour. Some pastoralists also owned pearling boats and controlled the activities of young Indigenous men, women and children, pressing them into service as divers. Contemporary correspondence provides evidence of 'blackbirding'. Aboriginal divers were enslaved and taken on board the pearl luggers.[107] In 1869, Robert Sholl, government resident in the north-west, described the impact of European pearling on the local population. His report referred to the coastline from Exmouth Gulf in the Gascoyne to King Sound in the Kimberley as an area where the 'natives were made available by the traders' for the pearl shell boats.

> Were the employers of native labour all just and humane men, their presence along the coast would doubtless [be] more beneficial to the Aborigines who receive food and clothing for their services,

> but it is too much to expect that a band of adventurers who are practically not subject to control will always act justly or humanely especially when their interests are at stake.[108]

As early as 1871, the colonial government began to legislate to control the operations of the pearl shell industry. But these measures were less than effective in this frontier country[109] and pearling was not the only industry requiring labour.

Between the 1860s and the 1880s a thriving industry developed. Success, however, depended on Aboriginal men and women being forced to work as skindivers in dangerous conditions. Dying in large numbers, they were in effect slaves. Djugan and Yawuru woman Mary Theresa Torres Barker heard painful stories from her grandmother about the 'sad time' in Broome's history.

> In the early days, there was no-one to do the job and they found the women had the lung capacity to stay underwater longer – they were the best. Sometimes they used to go a little bit further and they would put the women in respirators but tie stones to their

Pearling became an important industry in the north-west.

> legs to keep them down…they were knocked around, tied on the dinghies. It was very cruel – just talking about it makes me sad.[110]

As Gribble and Carley observed, Aboriginal people, particularly women, were captured, sold and forced into diving. Some women were separated from their menfolk for weeks on end as the luggers plied the coast in search of shell. Bart Pigram, descendant of a Yawuru family with a long involvement in pearling, was a curator of a 2015 Broome exhibition, 'Lustre and Pearling in Australia'.

> Indigenous people have been trading mother of pearl long before anyone else found it in the world. But the natural wealth of Broome became a curse for the Yawuru people when it attracted the European pearling industry hungry for shell to supply to Europe for buttons, ornaments, inlays and cutlery handles. Aboriginal land was taken for towns and farming and Aboriginal people were taken for labour. But out of the exploitation grew the modern and empowered Yawuru. Aboriginal Bardi people would tell stories of people being forced to go down diving and come up. If they didn't have shell, they'd get hit with one of the oars until they came up with the shells.[111]

For Pigram, pearling in and around Broome influenced the diverse Aboriginal cultures across the region. It was not only a melting pot of international races, but also a mixing of Indigenous groups. His own connections go deep.

> I am Yawuru and also of Jabirrjabirr descent and grew up in Broome. Our old people along the northwest coast used guwan (pearl shell) long before the arrival of European settlers and have continued their traditions to this day.
>
> Since the pearlers came there has always been someone from my family working in the industry, including myself. We discovered that my great, great, great grandfather William Bryan was a blackbirder who took a Jabirrjabirr woman and had a child, who is my ancestor in the Dampier Peninsula.

> This is my heritage and part of Australia's pearling story. It is etched in the land and we should know and respect these stories, the people and where they came from.[112]

While pearling exploited coastal people in the West Kimberley, peace prevailed uneasily and only temporarily further inland. In the wake of the Panter affair, and in the face of strong and determined Aboriginal resistance, the Roebuck Bay Pastoral Company withdrew from further attempts at settlement.

However, while the Kimberley's rugged topography and fierce Indigenous opposition made it harder for would-be pastoralists to occupy and rule, they still persisted. This vast area of Western Australia was the last region where white intrusion would change the world of the First Australians. In effect, a state of war existed for the rest of the nineteenth century and beyond. As Neville Green comments,

> *Australians in the city seem to feel that Aboriginal resistance ended in Western Australia with the Battle of Pinjarra in 1834. In fact, it continued.*[113]

In 1879–80, Alexander Forrest, then a surveyor for the Western Australian government, led an expedition to the Kimberley. His task was to report on the suitability of the country for sheep and cattle.[114] Forrest informed the commissioner of Crown lands in Perth on 19 September 1879 that he had crossed country along the Fitzroy River which was 'well grassed and watered' and which had 'splendid alluvial flats, well grassed on each bank of the river for at least 20 miles'. Later, Forrest's expedition:

> crossed over a range which formed a watershed, and passed through a splendid grassy and well-watered country all the way to the boundary of the Colony (longitude 129° E.) which we crossed in latitude 16° 50´, the country being some of the finest in Australia–open grassy plains, running springs at every mile.[115]

THE END OF THE BEGINNING OR THE BEGINNING OF THE END?

The region was named, as was usual in this imperial era, for a British aristocrat, the Earl of Kimberley, secretary of state for the colonies.[116]

Forrest's enthusiastic reports stimulated immediate settlement by pastoralists. In 1881, the government gazetted the *Kimberley Land Regulations* and within twelve months more than 44 million acres had been granted to just seventy-seven new leaseholders. Settlement was boosted in 1884 by the discovery of gold at Halls Creek. Steam ships now brought thousands of diggers to the Kimberley.[117]

The East Kimberley was occupied mainly by family and investment companies which, between 1882 and 1885, drove thousands of cattle from eastern Australia into these new grazing lands. Closer to hand, Western Australian investors, some from southern pioneer farming families, were the first to stock their leases. George Julius Brockman, from the Vasse, jumped the gun by sailing into Beagle Bay before the district was officially open for settlement.[118]

In asserting proprietorial rights to the land, the newcomers were certain that their actions could be justified in the name of progress and supposed racial superiority.[119] A young Sydney man, Gordon Broughton, who tried his luck as a stockman in the Kimberley at this time, later described how the white settlers saw the occupation of this land as a reward for what it had cost them to come in the first place.

> The basic philosophy of men living in the Kimberley was that the cattlemen had battled their way into the empty land with great hardship and at high cost in lives and money; that they were here to stay and if the wild blacks got in the way – in other words speared men or killed and harassed cattle, they would relentlessly be shot down. It was as simple and brutal as that.
>
> [...] Native life was held cheap, and a freemasonry of silence among the white men, including often the bush police, helped keep it that way. In far off Perth, clerics and various 'protection societies' tried to get at the truth of native killings, sometimes

spilled by a drunken bushman on a spree to the city, but up in the north men kept their mouths shut.[120]

One or two, like pioneer pastoralist Richard Allen, acknowledged the 'extinction of native life'.

> Hundreds of men, women and even children were shot down in this period. Where once natives roamed in hundreds only 40 odd years ago, hardly any survive, and you can ride in these ranges for days and never see a sign of natives, let alone tracks.[121]

Anthropologist Bruce Shaw sees this occupation of the Kimberley as one where the lives of cattle were valued above the lives of Aboriginal people and characterised by punitive expeditions, often culminating in the shooting and gaoling of Aboriginal people who speared cattle and, in rarer cases, killed Europeans.[122]

As Chris Owen points out, pastoralists were certain that occupation meant ownership. Grazier Jackson Poulton ordered an Aboriginal group off his station and was astonished when they 'ordered me off' their land. He wrote:

> It is a hard case when a pioneer has spent his capital and years of his life in opening new country for which he pays a heavy rental to the State, to be talked to in this fashion by a horde of roving insolent savages.[123]

Nat Buchanan and his brother were some of the first pastoralists to take up leases in the south-east Kimberley (Sturt Creek, later Gordon Downs) and over the border into the Northern Territory (Wave Hill). In 1933, Nat's son, Gordon, published an account of early events including confrontation with local people. He acknowledged that the original inhabitants had been dispossessed and were 'naturally retaliatory'. Gordon also admitted that pastoral lease boundaries were protected by shooting Aboriginal people who had not been incorporated into his workforce and who were competing with the station, for the available water.[124] Buchanan summed up his view of the situation.

> They held their own inquest and inquiry. In those days there were no police within three hundred miles. Every man was his own policeman; and the letter of the law was often ignored in favour of summary justice.
>
> And though the white man far removed from the restraints of formal law, sometimes perhaps rivalled his black brother in savage reprisal, on the whole the treatment of the natives compared favourably with white methods all over the world.[125]

As in the Gascoyne, would-be station owners needed labour to run their pastoral enterprises. Few white men were willing to take up the task and, under government regulation, convict labour was not allowed north of the 26th parallel.[126] That left just the Aboriginal inhabitants of the region as a potential workforce. Legislation gave both pastoralists and police extensive powers to control and restrict the lives of these original custodians of this country. Ironically, the police were also often empowered under the *Aborigines Protection Act 1886* to act as honorary protectors of Aborigines who could undertake legal action on behalf of Aboriginal people. This legislation came about partly as a result of Gribble's exposure of the harsh treatment meted out to Gascoyne First Nations people. Protectors could be resident magistrates or justices of the peace but in the Kimberley, given the vast distances and the lack of such officials, the protective task often fell to travelling police inspectors, predictably creating a conflict of interest. The police were also required, under the 1886 *Aborigines Protection Act*, to provide rations where needed. This task involved close contact with Aboriginal people whose original food sources had dwindled under pastoral expansion.

Police were also expected to protect pastoralists from stock thefts and reprisals from displaced Aboriginal occupants. They were paid an allowance of two shillings and five pence per day for each Aboriginal person arrested as a suspect or witness in a stock spearing. It was thus profitable for police to arrest as many people as possible.[127] Mary Durack, descendant of a major pastoralist family, described the aftermath of those arrests:

> Chained together neck to neck, wrist to wrist, the long lines of prisoners, men, women and children wound their miserable way over bush tracks to receive sentence in Wyndham, Derby or Halls Creek. Their crimes were murder, cattle spearing or breaking insulators to make spearheads, and…acquittals were nil. Brief scattered entries reveal Father's growing discomfiture at the situation: 'Am disgusted at the spectacle of a party of niggers on the road with police, the chains in many instances much too short from neck to neck, chafing and pulling as they move along and all appearing half starved'. Constables…Making no secret of sending the women bush so that they may pocket the greater part of the food allowance.[128]

In dealing with pastoralists' complaints, police were drawn into a role which was more military than civil and one that persisted well into the twentieth century. It involved increasing reliance on 'native assistants', in effect 'black trackers': Aboriginal men who could skilfully follow 'stock-spearers' and any other offender against British law.

In addition, the relationship between pastoralists and police was sometimes as negative as the station owners' conflict with Aboriginal communities. This could arise from the difficulty of finding the right man for the job. As Chris Owen has noted, employment requirements for police were minimal, stating only that the candidate must be: 'under 40 years of age; able to read and write; to be free of any bodily complaint calculated to interfere with his duties, and to be generally intelligent'.[129]

It was hard to find men willing to go north. Living and working conditions included poor housing, difficult terrain, a trying climate, considerable risk to health and assignments which at times, threatened lives. All these factors would have discouraged white men from seeking work in the state's north. Above all, the vast expanse of the Kimberley, its abundant rivers and defensible mountain ranges supported strong, resourceful and defiant Aboriginal communities.

Police, in their regular patrols, could acquire different understandings of issues and sometimes their observations contradicted station owners' complaints about alleged Aboriginal offences, such as killing livestock. Inspector Lodge's 1889 annual report stated that claims of 'wholesale destruction' by the petitioners (the pastoralists) were gross exaggerations. Lodge stated that, far from facing ruin, the previous year had 'been an exceptionally good one for the settlers'. Good rain brought 'plenty of feed and water'. Moreover, sheep and cattle numbers had increased, particularly along the Fitzroy River.[130]

An earlier report from Sergeant Troy, an experienced Kimberley police officer, observed in 1886 that all losses were a result of sheep being lost in the bush and killed by wild dogs, adding that it was the 'practice of station managers to attribute all losses to the depredations of the natives'.[131]

These observations are supported by other enquiries. In his 1953 Master's thesis, 'Survey of the Kimberley Pastoral Industry from 1885 to the Present', historian Geoffrey Bolton cited reports from 1884 and 1885 by Hugh Morrison, sheep inspector at Derby, that the greatest stock losses had been due to wild dogs and poisonous plants and scab, which had spread to several flocks in previous years.[132]

Bolton first went north to the Kimberley in 1952 to undertake research for his thesis. Later, he confessed that in his youth he 'knew a fair bit about Aborigines from reading but absolutely nothing at first hand' and 'I was diffident and deplorably unaware of the value of Aboriginal informants about the past'.[133] Bolton's research and some conversations with 'white bosses' began to open his eyes. Perusing documents at Moola Bulla station, he wondered what lay behind the entry for 11 October 1946:

'William William Lamarer, Tommy King, Jacky Perris caused trouble with another Halls Creek boy for no reason and influenced others to cause trouble. Left their work and came in to station where they were duly put in chains and returned'.

'In chains'; and this was only six years before my visit, not at some remote era of the pioneering frontier.[134]

Bolton ended his 'Portrait of the Historian as a Young Learner' with these words:

> Moola Bulla had taken the crude edges off my ignorant prejudices. I returned from the Kimberley convinced of the need to free Aborigines from their legal restrictions, and had written my first letter to *The West Australian* on the subject before the end of the year. I still had a long way to go, but I had learned respect for Aboriginal capacity.[135]

In the nineteenth century, two agricultural systems had collided over land management. As Bolton noted, 'The native custom of burning off large tracts of country, while hunting, was another source of antagonism to the whites, who thought that the Aboriginals were deliberately trying to "burn them out"'.[136] The pastoralists blamed the natives for burning the grass. However, for thousands of years, Aboriginal people had managed both fire and limited supplies of water.

When 1888 turned out to be a very dry season, Constable Ritchie recorded that, 'Pools and springs not known to fail have dried up, causing a great scarcity of food and water, the result being that the sheep have become poor, many of them dying'.[137] Bolton also noted that, on some properties, sheep had been turned out of the paddocks and let run in the bush, where they offered easy temptation for the First Australians who were themselves feeling the effects of a dry season and the growing scarcity of game.[138]

In addition, towards the end of the nineteenth century:

> The price of wool, in 1886, began to decline steadily from a peak price of 12d to 9d, where it remained until 1890. As most of the West Kimberley stations were capitalised from the depressed colony of Western Australia, some owners were tempted to cut

their losses and withdraw from an enterprise in which small profits were apparently not combined with quick returns.[139]

Many pastoralists, however, were resolute and resilient. They were here to stay and determined to prevail; so were the original landholders. The story of Bunuba man, Jandamarra, typifies the clash of two irreconcilable cultures and livelihoods.

In Jandamarra's brief life, he was first a station hand and an expert shearer. It was said that, by the age of fourteen, he could shear a sheep faster than any experienced European stockman in the district.[140] Howard Pedersen describes the early life of the man who white boss and station owner William Lukin called 'Pigeon':

> *Jandamarra had been brought into pastoral life at Lennard River station as a child. His mother, a Bunuba woman, had brought him there in 1883 when he was six years old. His adolescent and early adult years were spent acquiring pastoral skills, including excellent horsemanship. His employer, William Lukin, saw him as a valuable recruit to station life.*[141]

'Pigeon' spoke English confidently. He became popular with Europeans and shared their sense of humour. However, the Bunuba, Jandamarra's own people, living in the nearby Napier Ranges, also claimed him. They had remained fiercely resistant to joining the new whitefeller way of life and the tribal elders insisted that Jandamarra undergo traditional initiation. Despite the warlike atmosphere of the time, the Bunuba were still able to culturally reclaim Jandamarra. For the pastoralists, compromises of this kind were often required to attract and retain free Aboriginal labour. As Chris Owen explains:

> Social networks and kin grouping links between 'station blacks' and 'bush blacks' were maintained. That Aboriginal people learnt to navigate between the 'two worlds' would have been lost to most pastoralists.[142]

Aged fifteen, Jandamarra was inducted into manhood. Pedersen describes this initiation as *an arduously long process which requires the endurance of enormous physical hardship complemented by an intense spiritual education. The young man is put through a rigorous physical endurance test that is demanded of an Aboriginal man supporting a future family in a harsh country.*[143]

Now influenced by his own people's fierce resistance to pastoral intrusion, Jandamarra remained in Bunuba country and became a stock-spearer. Arrested for sheep stealing in 1889, he was sentenced to gaol in Derby. On release he returned to work for William Lukin as a stockman. Jandamarra was now under pressure from both societies. Lukin was no longer certain of his loyalty and while the Bunuba respected his 'stock-spearing' skills, they were unsure of his allegiance.

> Instead of mixing in a group, he often preferred to be alone, or to be in the company of young women. He showed little respect for the important taboos that regulate Aboriginal sexual relationships. The conservative Aboriginal society judged him harshly, but despite their disapproval of the way he chose to live his life, he evaded punishment because he was odd, and dismissed as a social misfit.[144]

In their account of Jandamarra's life, Banjo Woorunmurra and Howard Pedersen argue that time in prison in Derby had interrupted an important stage of Bunuba manhood development.

> Normally a young man completing formal initiation would pass a long time in quiet reflection, often spanning several months and sometimes years, before finally coming to understand the spiritual richness of the world about him. Settlers and police had denied Jandamarra the chance to grow and merge fully into the spiritual richness of his country. He was seen by his elders as an incomplete initiate of the law that flowed from his ancestral lands.[145]

The lawmen banished him from mainstream Bunuba life.[146] To escape tribal punishment for his sexual transgressions, notably that he had exploited women who were in the wrong kinship group for him, Jandamarra now had no choice but to work with the pastoralists and formed an association with settler Bill Richardson.[147]

In 1894, Jandamarra was arrested again, this time for 'absconding from bonded service', but instead of being jailed, he was attached to the police as a black tracker.[148] In their eyes Jandamarra was highly qualified for such a position because he knew station life, the country and also the opposing Bunuba. As Chris Owen has observed, that there was:

> a strong cultural change amongst young Aboriginal men who were socialised through the colonisation period. Their highest ambition, one observer stated, was to become a police tracker wielding power over others.[149]

However, all trackers were still under police control. If trackers didn't do what their police officer told them to do, or if they accused the police of a crime, they would get "beaten up". If they did it twice, they would be shot.'[150] The police were also highly conscious of the risk of appointing the right person to become a 'black tracker' because, in Howard Pedersen's words:

> *It was generally policy that local Aboriginal people weren't recruited from the area to act against their own peoples, so the employment of Jandamarra indicated how trusting the police and settlers were of this particular character.*[151]

So, was Jandamarra trapped in his new role as a tracker? He was now an asset to white authority but still their prisoner and still distrusted by his own people.

By 1894, cattle were being brought into West Kimberley grazing areas. For the Bunuba 'stock-spearers', this was a new opportunity to obtain meat. For Jandamarra it was a test of cultural loyalty. The police, now confident that he was their man, attached him as a tracker to the white man he already knew, pastoralist and part-time policeman Bill Richardson. Their first patrol into the Napier and Oscar ranges, in Bunuba country, was, from the pastoralists' perspective, very successful.[152] Sixteen Aboriginal people were captured, chained and imprisoned at Lillimooloora station, including renowned stock-spearer and Bunuba leader Ellemarra, Jandamarra's uncle. Jandamarra pretended to arrest his kinsman.

Jandamarra was now, according to Woorunmurra and Pedersen, under intense pressure from his fellow countryman and relatives to 'honour his Bunuba obligations'.[153]

Pedersen describes a relevant conversation in 1894 at Lillimooloora homestead, where the offenders had been taken in chains.

> The prisoners conversed freely with 'Pigeon' and demanded that he release them. They goaded him because he was working with the police against his own people. He had an obligation to release them, they said, as they had waived tribal punishment for his defiance of Aboriginal law concerning his relationships with women.[154]

The team lingered on at Lillimooloora, Bill Richardson pleading sickness and a need to rest but, in reality, augmenting his income by adding extra days to his prison ration allowance.[155] He would have done better not to have delayed. It was his final repose.

Bunuba Elder, Jimmy Andrews, at the Lillimooloora station ruins. Photo by Emily Jane Smith, ABC Kimberley.

THE END OF THE BEGINNING OR THE BEGINNING OF THE END?

On 31 October 1894, Jandamarra shot Richardson as he lay in his bed, unshackled the Bunuba prisoners and headed for nearby Windjana Gorge.[156] When the stockmen and cattle arrived there, they were ambushed by Jandamarra and his former prisoners. Inevitably reprisals followed. The Bunuba were eventually overpowered. Ellemarra was wounded and later died. Jandamarra was also severely wounded, but survived, hidden and helped by Bunuba women.

Jandamarra continued to hold out against pastoral invasion but met his death three years later on 1 April 1897 at Baraa (Tunnel Creek), in a shoot-out with an equally skilled Pilbara marksman, Micki, a man who, in contrast to Jandamarra, had transformed himself successfully from rebel leader to police trooper. While Micki fired the fatal shot, his role was downplayed with the white police claiming all the credit. Jandamarra's skull, like Yagan's more than half a century earlier, was sent to England as a trophy.[157]

Jandamarra had probably been treated better by both pastoralists and police than many of his compatriots. Even after his release and recruitment to work with Richardson's police patrol, the two seemed to have worked well together.[158] However, Jandamarra's decision to kill Bill Richardson effectively marked the end of his attempt to straddle two cultures.

Significant resistance by the Bunuba effectively ended with Jandamarra's death. Before long, Leopold Downs station was set up in the heart of their own country.[159] But conflict between pastoralists and the original custodians continued well into the twentieth century.

At the same time, a new kind of white man appeared in these remote areas of northern Australia: the Christian missionary. His mission to Aboriginal people is summed up by historian Christine Choo as 'evangelisation, protection from abuse, procreation, education and training'.[160] The new arrivals puzzled the local people because they did not bring guns or mistreat women. The New Norcia Benedictines founded Drysdale Mission in 1908.

Choo describes their arrival:

> *They found people were hiding, as they did when foreigners came on to their country. But a lone woman came out in full sight of everybody. And the missionaries treated her very courteously and she was amazed. She couldn't believe that's how she was treated. And the missionaries said, 'Here's some food and take it back to your people. We'd like to meet your people.' And from the account that I've read, she was amazed (presumably expecting sexual exploitation) because one of the ways in which people encountered foreigners was to send the women ahead of them.*[161]

For Aboriginal people, connecting with outsiders was and is a carefully managed business.

> *It's important to remember that sending women ahead was a way in which Aboriginal people connected with each other as well. We might interpret this as Aboriginal people selling their wives or prostituting them when there are many layers of interpretation involved here.*[162]

The twentieth century was to bring both Catholic and Protestant missionaries to the far north of Western Australia. There were, apparently, a large number of Aboriginal people in need of Christian salvation. The Benedictines from New Norcia followed the first permanent mission, established at Beagle Bay by Trappist monks in the early 1890s, and, as Choo points out, Catholic missionaries:

> *came to countries like Australia with instructions from a number of papal encyclicals, which said 'Go out and convert people'. And it was with that in mind in the nineteenth century that Trappists and Benedictines accepted going to the furthest point in Western Australia. From that perspective they were very highly motivated and their method was to settle people and then, later on, bring the children in to educate them.*[163]

While religious orders offered some protection from the worst of the pastoralists' behaviour, their presence and influence proved, in Choo's view:

a mixed blessing. The points at which state and church met in their attempts to provide corporal and spiritual service to Aboriginal people become points of friction, juxtaposed with the potential for reconciliation and mutual support.[164]

There were Aboriginal people to whom the missionaries could minister. But how many and for how long? Increasingly, in the Kimberley, as elsewhere in Western Australia, sickness, including venereal disease, brought by white settlers, was now threatening the very survival of Australia's First Nations people. In his report for 1898–99, the newly appointed chief protector of Aborigines, Henry Prinsep, stated that in Wyndham in the far north Kimberley, 'syphilis was becoming prevalent with several deaths occurring over the last twelve months'. Reporting on the situation in the south, Prinsep reinforced the common view that Aboriginal people were a dying race: 'It is not usual to see a young native; they are nearly all remnants of the tribes, gradually dying out'.[165]

Prinsep had been appointed to the new position of chief protector in 1898 by Premier John Forrest. Forrest had grown up among Aboriginal people around Bunbury and in his early explorations had depended on them as guides. In 1883 he told the Legislative Council that:

> we owed these natives something more than repression. Anyone would imagine that the natives were our enemies instead of our best friends. Colonisation would go on with very slow strides if we had no natives to assist us.[166]

But Forrest also believed that his government was supporting a dying race.

> There is probably no race of people which has done so little to leave behind it a record of its existence as the Australian aboriginal race, and no race has been so little able to cope with civilisation. After existing in their own savage state for an immense time, an intercourse of about half a century with a civilised race has been sufficient to almost remove them from the face of the earth.[167]

Despite this widespread belief, the Aboriginal people of Western Australia were not dying out. In fact, as Prinsep acknowledged, the mixed-race population was growing.

> The intercourse between the races is leading to a considerable increase of half-castes. Many of them find their way into the Missions, but a far greater number are probably reared in native camps, without any sort of education. This is a question which should, I think, receive consideration by the Legislature. I trust during the next twelve months, to be able to report more fully on the number and composition of the half-castes, apart from that of the pure Aborigines.[168]

In the next century, the ruling white society would continue to reveal a lack of understanding and compassion in dealing with this ever-larger group of 'in between' people, many of whom clung tenaciously to their sense of being primarily Aboriginal. A long period now emerged in which many white people continued to regard anyone with Aboriginal antecedents as inferior socially and culturally. It was not, however, 'the beginning of the end' for First Nations people.

Windjana Gorge.

Chapter 5

Snapped Shut the Lawbook

You once smiled a friendly smile
Said we were kin to one another,
Thus with guile for a short while
Became to me a brother,
Then you swamped my way of gladness
Took my children from my side,
Snapped shut the lawbook, oh my sadness.
At Yirrakalas' plea denied.[1]

Poet and playwright Jack Davis snaps open the story of Australia's First Nations, as it played out across Australia in the nineteenth and twentieth centuries; a history that includes the removal of children from their parents and the 'confiscation' of traditional lands.

In the last line of this excerpt from his poem 'Aboriginal Australia – To the Others', Davis is referring to the Yirrkala petitions. In 1963 the Australian Government failed to consult the Yolngu people living in the small community of Yirrkala in Arnhem Land before it announced that 300 square kilometres of that land would be taken for mining. As traditional custodians of this land, the Yolngu wanted their voices to be heard. They submitted two bark petitions (the Yirrkala petitions) to the Commonwealth government. These documents were the first to combine bark painting with typed text in English and Gumatj languages.

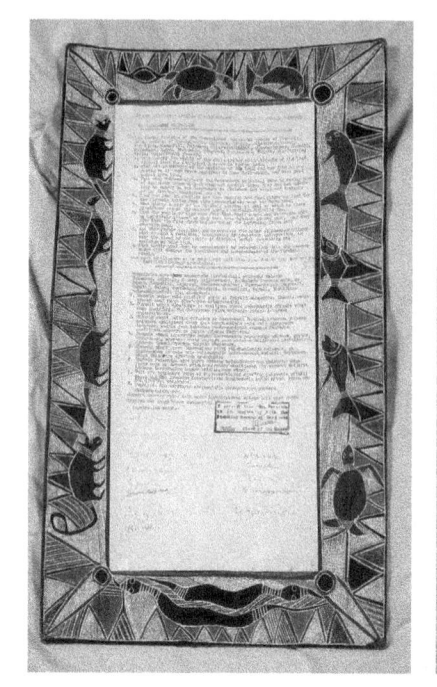

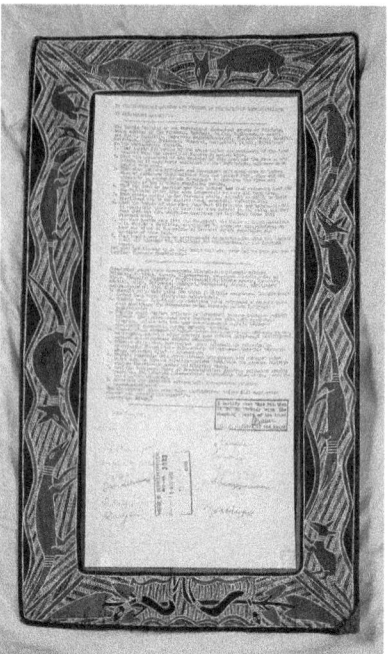

The Yirrkala Petitions, 1963. Reproduced with permission.

The Yirrkala petitions made history but did not change governmental thinking. Officially, Australia was still *terra nullius*; an empty land until the British arrived.[2] The British lawbook remained closed and impenetrable to the First Nations people.

In the final decades of the nineteenth century and well beyond, British law and numerous Australian state laws adversely affected the lives of every person of Aboriginal descent across the nation. Australia's First Nations people are not mentioned in the 1901 Australian Constitution and, until the successful 1967 referendum, they were not counted in the national population census.

State legislation relating to Aboriginal people was repressive. In Western Australia it affected every facet of their lives, and was frequently enacted in defiance of ongoing external criticism from Britain and a few local voices.

In 1886 John Gribble and David Carley had sent reports to the Colonial Office and the London-based Aborigines Protection Society about pastoralists' exploitation and enslavement of Aboriginal people in the Gascoyne region (see Chapter 4). The British government was particularly sensitive to enquiries from 'protectionists', as many of them had political influence. Such disclosures also embarrassed colonial governors and politicians, particularly because at this time Western Australia was seeking self-government within the British Empire.[3]

The then governor, Sir Frederick Napier Broome, made every effort to discredit Carley and other 'trouble makers'. Nevertheless, the government in London was sufficiently concerned to broach the idea of separating north-western Australia from the rest of the colony and retaining imperial control over the pastoral north. That suggestion soon appeared impractical, given the difficulty of administering the remote northern regions of Western Australia. Moreover, ill-treatment of the Aboriginal population was not confined to the pastoral areas, putting the local administration under considerable pressure to improve overall policies (or sometimes lack of them) as they related to First Nations peoples.[4]

In 1887, Governor Broome suggested a compromise. Authority over Aboriginal affairs would lie with the Colonial Office in London, but a Protection Board, to be established in Western Australia, would undertake local administration. Thus, initially, section 70 of the Western Australian Constitution included this provision. As expected, this compromise was highly unpopular, particularly with pastoralists, and accepted only, as Henry Reynolds comments, because 'they knew that it was an inescapable condition of the grant of responsible government'.[5]

For local politicians it was evidently humiliating to be seen by the world as not trusted to look after the country's original inhabitants. After self-government was granted in 1890, Premier John Forrest continued to complain about the Aborigines Protection Board.

> The existence of the Board is a proclamation to the world that notwithstanding the Government of Western Australia is entrusted with the entire control of ⅓ of the Australian continent and the lives of Her Majesty's white subjects, the people of this Colony are not to be trusted to do justice and distribute relief to the poor aboriginal natives.[6]

Forrest maintained his stance as a friend to the Aboriginal people but his continued failure to provide adequately for them suggests that his conduct did not always match his words. Lack of understanding of their plight became more significant after 1897 when, with predictable support from northern graziers, the Western Australian government achieved removal of the section 70 provision. The colony, which would become the State of Western Australia within four years, now assumed full control of its own affairs and over its 'native' population.

One of Forrest's first moves was to seek to replace the *Aborigines Protection Act 1886*, under which the unpopular board had been established, with new legislation: the *Aborigines Act 1897*. This statute replaced the Aborigines Protection Board with a government department, headed by a public servant enjoying the title of 'chief protector of Aborigines'. Initially, however, this position had no legal basis.[7] Forrest was also determined that the new department should stay small and cost little.[8] His priority at the time was financing the 560-kilometre Goldfields Pipeline from Mundaring in the Darling Range east of Perth to Kalgoorlie.

The new Act, which was proclaimed in 1898, anticipated an increasingly repressive regime, limiting, rather than protecting Aboriginal rights and freedoms, despite its stated purpose as 'An Act to further amend the Constitution Act of 1889 and for the better protection of the Aboriginal Race of Western Australia'.[9]

Premier Forrest wanted a public servant with a track record in establishing new government agencies. His man should have connections to important people in the colony and the imperial world, but be able to present government policies as humane and efficient. Above all, the appointee needed to be someone trusted to pursue the 'benevolent paternalism' policy which Forrest purported to support.[10]

Seen in this light, Forrest's choice is not surprising. Henry Prinsep had previously been undersecretary for the Department of Mines and had married into a pioneer south-west family, the Bussells. Like Forrest himself, Prinsep had lived alongside Aboriginal people on his estate, Prinsep Park, outside Bunbury. He had also met 'natives' camped in the hills, east of his properties. According to biographer Malcolm Allbrook, Prinsep took a keen interest in Aboriginal music and dancing and learned from George Coolbul, an employee and companion, how to throw a boomerang.[11]

Yet Prinsep had no real understanding of Aboriginal society and culture. Born in India into a prominent Calcutta-based British family, Prinsep had been educated at an English boarding school and arrived in Western Australia as a young man in 1866 to take over his father's business interests and estates. Eventually he moved to Perth and became undersecretary for mines in 1894.

Prinsep Park (rebuilt 1934), Dardanup near Bunbury.

Prinsep was a man steeped in imperial traditions and his model as an administrator might well have been the Indian Civil Service. Allbrook sees Prinsep's Australian identity as:

> framed within his conception of a global network of British men, women and children who lived in widely dispersed places but remained connected by a common sense of Britishness, a belief in the superiority and beneficence of British civilization and Empire, and thus the legitimacy of the world-wide colonial project.[12]

Historian Peter Biskup suggests that Prinsep came to his new appointment in difficult circumstances. While the public servant and the premier were friends, Forrest saw himself as 'something of an expert on Aboriginal affairs'. The stables behind his home were always open to Aboriginal acquaintances, including those with a grievance. However, his choice of Prinsep, who, Biskup argues, lacked forcefulness and knew little about Aboriginal people, enabled the premier, as the responsible minister, to make his own policy.[13]

As Allbrook asserts, Prinsep was forced to accept Forrest's policy of keeping the cost of providing material and any other support to Aboriginal people as low as possible.

> Forrest believed that governments should intervene only in the most extreme cases of mistreatment or poverty. It was his conviction that Aboriginal people were, in any case, disappearing and would have little future in the development of the State.[14]

For the new chief protector, the task was not just difficult, it was impossible. Prinsep frequently pointed out to Premier Forrest and his successors the problems inherent in heading a department with no money, no powers, a single staff member and a part-time accountant. Unsurprisingly, getting useful information from distant regions was also difficult.

At the same time, employment of the original inhabitants was declining in rural areas. There was surplus labour thanks to the Western Australian gold rush of the 1890s which had brought a large number of migrants mainly from Europe. Former miners and others who failed to make their fortunes on the goldfields, often sought other employment, and farmers generally preferred to hire white workers.

In addition, many Aboriginal people faced dire poverty when white landholders refused to provide food and relief.[15] Prinsep clashed with ministers over the level of support that these families required. At the same time his early connections to Aboriginal people around his estates in the south-west had failed to afford him an appreciation of their plight or knowledge of how to address issues resulting from loss of land and their traditional way of life. Allbrook sums up Prinsep's performance in the job of chief protector:

> Driven by 'Victorian morality', a sense of 'charity' and 'responsibility' to the underprivileged and a 'nodding acquaintance with colonial policy and practice in British India', Prinsep earned neither popularity nor respect for the way he went about his job.[16]

Prinsep might have shared the views of his father-in-law, John Garrett Bussell, who, when his own family was not threatened, believed that the colonists had a duty to dispense Christian teaching, benevolence and patronage, along with blankets, clothes and food and to raise funds for schools and orphanages.[17]

Like Archdeacon Wollaston before him, Prinsep thought that benevolence included separating 'half-caste' Aboriginal children 'from their savage life'. They should be made wards of the state, 'placed under proper care and brought up in useful knowledge'.[18] In his opinion 'half-castes' who were not subjected to 'evil influences' could be made into 'useful workmen and women'. At the same time, Prinsep lamented that most of these children lived in communities 'whose influence is towards laziness and vice; and I think it is our duty not to allow these children, whose blood is half British, to grow up as vagrants and outcasts as their mothers now are'.[19]

Prinsep took up the reins of the new Aborigines Department at a time when the number of people with both Aboriginal and white parentage was increasing. Historian Anna Haebich has concluded that, by the beginning of the twentieth century, over half the Indigenous population in the south of the state was of mixed parentage.[20] In this situation, Prinsep saw his mission as rescuing the children of 'mixed racial' unions, because 'the natural custom of their race is one of vagrancy'.[21] Widespread misunderstandings of the nature and culture of the First Nations people led him to support the introduction of legislation and policies similar to those already operating in other Australian jurisdictions; laws which would have a devastating effect on people of Aboriginal descent.

Prinsep, however, expected the future to play out differently. He was concerned about the prostitution of Aboriginal women and the spread of venereal disease, which he saw as one of the chief causes of the likely extinction of the Aboriginal race. His words, if not his assumptions, were prophetic: 'From a humanitarian point (of view) one cannot contemplate without horror the immense amount of pain and misery which lies before the unfortunate natives'.[22]

Hamstrung by lack of money and resources, Prinsep turned to his family connections to separate his charges from their 'savage life'. His wife's cousin, Edith Bussell, had set up a 'school' at Ellensbrook, the first home of Alfred and Ellen Bussell, near the future town of Margaret River. Already supportive of Dom Salvado's efforts to educate the 'native savages' in agricultural pursuits, Prinsep saw Edith's work as offering hope to Aboriginal youth. While Anna Haebich is critical of Prinsep's performance as chief protector, especially his 'niggardly handling' of the department's scarce resources, she gives him credit for supporting Aboriginal attempts to farm alongside European farmers, commenting that, unlike most of his peers, Prinsep:

> felt that there was some hope of Aborigines (particularly those with a mission-educated background) succeeding on their farms and saw this as an important way of bringing them into the wider community, despite the general pessimism, while there were still large areas of unalienated land in the south.[23]

Ellensbrook homestead.

Children sent to Ellensbrook came from all parts of Western Australia, increasing one of the problems that beset later generations of Aboriginal people: loss of contact with ancestral lands. Alienation from their traditional country was not a concern that Prinsep understood. For him, placement in a school or training institution was an ideal means of rescuing mixed-race children. It also addressed a major complaint of white settlers, the 'servant problem'. Prinsep was satisfied that children were being given the basic skills needed for future employment.

> They are taught reading and writing – indoor work for girls, sums and milking, vegetable gardening and all the small farm industries so as to become useful farm hands, both male and female, in a practical manner and such as in vogue in our country districts. The children are encouraged to bathe frequently. They spend every Sunday on the sea beach and have plenty of milk and vegetables and meat food.[24]

Some Aboriginal parents did protest at their children being taken from them. A Mr Prius wrote repeated letters to Prinsep and Bussell asking for the return of his son or stepson, 'Little Willie'. The spelling is the original.

> I have as much love for my dear wife and chuldines as you have for yours and I cannot afford to luse them so if you have any feeling atole pleas send the boy back quick as you can it did not take long for him to go but it takes a long time for him to come back and I do not think that fare you may thing because I am black I can't look after him but I am as kind to him than I am to my own. I have more love for him than I have for my own.[25]

Willie Prius was eventually sent back to his parents but neither Prinsep nor Edith Bussell sympathised with mothers or fathers who wanted their children returned to them. Initially resisting the Prius family's entreaties, Edith wrote to Prinsep:

> Little Willie is going on well and is a very jolly little fellow, a favourite all round. I suppose you have had letters from his mother as I have asking for him to be sent back to her. She must be a very silly woman. If she felt like that about him, she should not have parted with him at all.[26]

Prinsep, in his 1902 annual report, complained that 'the natural affection of the mothers...stood much in [his] way' and continued to demand legal guardianship over the children.[27] However, he had been strongly overruled by Premier Forrest when he proposed a Bill aiming to completely isolate people of Aboriginal descent from the wider community.

This draft legislation had provided for state control over where and how Aboriginal people could live, and their classification into 'full blood' or 'half-caste', thus effectively defining their social status and their education. In 1900, the draconian provisions of this Bill were too much for Forrest. Outraged at the Bill's repressive nature, he wrote, 'This would make Prisoners of the poor people in their own country', and that prohibited areas were a 'monstrous infringement on the liberty of the native. It is manufacturing offences with a vengeance.'[28] Forrest's own previous personal associations may have played a part in determining his views, and the Bill lapsed. But after his departure to federal politics in 1901, many, if not most, of the Bill's main features resurfaced in the state's now infamous '1905 Act'.

Overall, Prinsep's policies between 1898 and 1905 appear self-contradictory and inconsistent. His Christian charity and concern for the underprivileged were not apparent when he defended the punitive practice of neck-chaining Aboriginal prisoners.

> The only way to abolish the use of the chain when under confinement would be to place natives on islands far from the coast, but the objection to this is the great cost and the loss of all their services, which are now made useful to the state at the various ports, nor would the civilising influences be so possible.[29]

Following Forrest's departure and a period of inaction, Walter James became premier and also attorney general in July 1902. Allegations about the treatment and conditions of Aboriginal workers in the northern pastoral industry were now being raised in the Western Australian Parliament as well as in London.[30] James, a social reformer in other spheres of government, had some experience of pastoral life, having worked as a jackaroo in the Pilbara. He took steps to review both the *Aborigines Protection Act 1886* and the *Aborigines Act 1897*, which regulated the pay and conditions of Indigenous workers.[31]

Following outspoken criticism of the pastoralists' behaviour in the British press, in early 1904, James approached Dr Walter Roth, an Oxford-educated surgeon and Protector of Aborigines in Queensland, to head a royal commission into the conditions of Aborigines in Western Australia. Prinsep himself had suggested Roth as both men were strong supporters of racial segregation and Roth had been involved in administering Queensland legislation based on this policy.[32] Yet Roth was also known as someone who had campaigned against ill-treatment of Aboriginal people in his own state. Western Australians could not be sure of obtaining a positive report from their hand-picked commissioner.[33]

Roth was formally appointed as commissioner by the new Labour premier, Henry Daglish, in August 1904. After spending some time in Perth, reviewing written allegations of cruelty and talking to officials including Prinsep, Roth travelled north and interviewed a total of 110 'witnesses', of whom only two were Aboriginal prisoners.[34] When the Roth report was tabled in the Parliament of Western Australia in January 1905 it caused a great stir in the community. Although the commissioner refuted charges of deliberate cruelty by pastoralists, the police came in for heavy criticism, particularly for their brutality in arresting natives for cattle-stealing. There was also a focus on the Aborigines Department. Roth's questioning of Prinsep exposed the legal and economic difficulties faced by the head of that department under three different premiers. It also exposed the limitations of the chief protector's legal authority.[35]

Q.14
Roth: Have employers ever charged your Department for medicine and medical attendance?
Prinsep: Yes. A doctor here and there has sent in bills which the employer has refused to pay, stating it is the duty of the Department.

Q.15
Roth: Would the Department pay for the confinement of women under contract?
Prinsep: Legally the Department need not pay.

Q.16
Roth: Can a contract be entered into without your knowledge?
Prinsep: Yes.

Q.17
Roth: Can you prevent any Asiatic or European from being an employer under the Act (1886 Aboriginal Protection Act).
Prinsep: No I cannot.

Q.18

Roth: Can you prevent the greatest scoundrel unhung from employing an aboriginal under contract?
Prinsep: No.[36]

On the basis of these and similar questions to Prinsep, Roth concluded that:

> The Chief Protector of the Aborigines has no legal status, while his authority as head of the Department controlling the welfare and protection of the natives is a divided one and may be even ignored; indeed, so far as labour conditions of Aborigines are concerned, honorary justices are invested with greater powers.[37]

Roth's findings exposed social and financial problems in almost every area of Aboriginal employment and social recognition. He noted that in the north-west pearling industry:

> No education and no wages are stipulated for in the indenture… at Broome quite one half of the children ranging from 10 years and upwards are indentured to the pearling industry and taken out on to the boats…The Chief Protector draws special attention to the fact that he cannot prevent male children being employed on the boats…One Resident Magistrate very ably expresses the present state of affairs as follows: – 'The child is bound and can be reached by law and punished, but the person to whom the child is bound is apparently responsible to nobody'. Even the Chief Protector is obliged to admit the injustice of a system where, taking a concrete case, a child of tender years may be indentured to a mistress as a domestic up to 21 years of age, and received neither education nor payment in return for the services rendered.[38]

Roth did not say so, but the system certainly smacked of slavery. In his findings on the pastoral industry, where there was continual conflict over cattle-spearing by Aboriginal men, the commissioner was particularly critical of the fact that:

> Blacks may be arrested without instructions, authority, or information received from the pastoralist whose cattle are alleged to have been killed; the pastoralist may even object to such measures having been taken. Not knowing beforehand how many blacks he is going to arrest, the policeman only takes chains sufficient for about 15 natives; if a large number are reported guilty, he will take chains to hold from about 25 to 30...Children from 14 to 16 years of age are neck-chained.[39]

While Prinsep had accepted the economic necessity of neck chaining, Roth criticised the way the practice was carried out.

> The grave dangers attendant on the use of these iron split links, and the difficulty of opening them in cases of urgency or accident, are pointed out...the Wyndham gaoler has noticed the length of the chain joining two natives' necks to be twenty-four inches, the cruelty of which he remarked upon to the escorting police.[40]

Roth recommended that neck-chains be replaced with wrist-cuffs and that courts should impose shorter sentences on Aboriginal cattle-killers, since long imprisonment was counterproductive.[41] In the event little changed. Chaining and lengthy sentences continued to be the norm in the north-west.

In language not entirely dissimilar from views now being aired in the twenty-first century about Aboriginal imprisonment and its effectiveness, Roth also questioned the fate of those led away, 'neck-chained'.

> With regard to long sentences passed upon native prisoners, they are not considered beneficial. The blacks are far better off in their uncivilised than semi-civilised state, and are a great deal of trouble after they come out of gaol. It does not do them the least bit of good, and does not stop them from killing cattle, the same blacks being brought before the Court again and again...When blacks have been away from their native

homes so long, they seem forgotten when they return; their tribes will have very little to do with them and they often commit further crimes because in the meantime their women have been taken.[42]

Pastoralists did not emerge from the enquiry without criticism. Roth noted the absence of employment contracts and recommended the introduction of renewable biennial permits as well as the payment of a minimum monthly wage.[43] Prinsep did not support this last provision and most Aboriginal pastoral workers were to wait for well over half a century before employers were required to pay them a regular monetary wage.

However, on the plight of Aboriginal women and 'half-castes', Roth and Prinsep were very much on the same page.

> The Chief Protector has no power to enforce the protection, care and safety of unprotected Aboriginal women and children, nor to send the latter to mission stations, orphanages or reformatories. The registration of the births of either half-castes or full-bloods is a matter of difficulty even in the settled districts. Of the many hundred half-caste children – over 500 were enumerated in last year's census… – If these are left to their own devices under the present state of the law, their future will be one of vagabondism and harlotry.[44]

Both Roth and Prinsep agreed that the chief protector should have power over the care and education of Indigenous young people. In response to Roth's enquiries, Prinsep stated firmly that:

> It would be far better if the schools for native and half-caste children were immediately under the management of the Government. The instruction should be of such a nature as to bring them up as useful workers with merely such an amount of reading, writing and numbers as would be of service to them in their positions as humble labourers, the position which they cannot hope to rise from for at least two or three generations.[45]

Not surprisingly, the provisions of the legislation resulting from the Roth report were similar to those which John Forrest had objected to back in 1900.

The *Aborigines Act 1905*, which ostensibly aimed to provide for the 'better protection and care of the Aboriginal inhabitants of Western Australia',[46] effectively 'snapped shut their lawbook'. It provided a legal basis for policies under which every man, woman and child with Aboriginal heritage could come within its ambit. The last vestiges of this legislation were not swept away until well into the second half of the twentieth century.

For many Aboriginal people, the trauma it caused has still not ended. Some fifty years after the passing of the 1905 Act, Lynnette Coomer was taken from her parents and sent to a mission.

> *In my family, the young people who carried the pain, they keep asking 'Why'. I can't answer that because I've got to the stage where people call us the 'Why' people and this is where a lot of mental health issues come in; intergenerational trauma comes out where people have been incarcerated, because they are completely lost souls. But a lot of us have to be strong to pick up our weaker ones…We still have that fear of the Department.*[47]

Section 60 of the Act contained a long list of matters for which government could make regulations. These included:

> S.60(c) Providing for the care, custody, and education of the children of aborigines and half-castes.

> S.60(d) Enabling any Aboriginal or half-caste child to be sent to and detained in an aboriginal institution, industrial school, or orphanage.

Institutions included missions set up by the Catholic Church and other denominations to 'Christianise and civilise' the native people. Missionaries in the north-west argued that, where they were exposed to the worst elements of white intrusion, Aboriginal children were better off in the church's care.

Beagle Bay Church interior (photo by Amanda McInerney, supplied courtesy Kimberley Web Design).

The German Pallottines had taken over the Beagle Bay Mission from the Trappist monks at the beginning of the twentieth century. Father George Walter was superintendent of the Beagle Bay Mission in the early twentieth century. He later described his approach as a missionary.

> For Aborigines, correct mission method is to let them get used to a settled lifestyle and regular work without using force or restraining their freedom. Only love and a friendly approach can lead to success, not harshness or force. As soon as possible children can be removed from the adult camp and the nomadic ways of their parents, and be housed in dormitories on mission premises to be educated at school and in trades.[48]

While he felt strongly that Beagle Bay was a better place for his charges to be, Father Walter, nonetheless, showed a degree of sensitivity towards Aboriginal cultural practices.

> It is not the duty of a Missionary to repress a child's Aboriginal nature and for this reason the children are given as much freedom as possible to follow their customs and practices. From time to time all children are allowed to attend ordinary corrobories [sic] (under supervision) and to hold their own corrobories. Outings are utilised to make them sufficiently familiar with bush craft to survive, and one competes with another to catch snakes, lizards, kangaroos and other game, and to study animal trails.[49]

Christine Choo notes that some Catholic missionaries understood the Aboriginal need to perform important ceremonies.

> *They also understood many Aboriginal groups involved themselves with missions because there was food and safety from the pastoralists and the pearlers and that the traditional Christian practice of sanctuary was important in this situation. The missionaries did feel that they were there to reach out and give people protection and sustenance.*[50]

The Pallottine fathers realised that they also needed to reach Aboriginal women and accordingly brought nuns into the mission, women who could reach out to their local counterparts. Choo suggests the presence of female religious orders brought some benefits despite the limitations of their role.

> *In the existing hierarchy the nuns had to wash and clean and cook and run the church, in addition to looking after and educating the Aboriginal women and girls. They had a lot to do and I think the missions couldn't achieve their aims without the Sisters being there.*[51]

The policies and priorities of early twentieth-century Australia also influenced missionaries. This was especially true at Beagle Bay, close to multiracial Broome.

> *While they were blaming Asian people for taking Aboriginal women during the lay-off season in the pearling industry and using them, they were really afraid that the coloured population would increase. If you have mixed-race people of brown colour then the fear was, with the 'White Australia' bogey, that Australia would be overrun by coloured people. The*

> *Roth report of 1905 made a big thing of this issue and brought in legislation that controlled it, but passed over specific references to white people doing the same thing. It reflects the attitudes and values of the time.*[52]

As Choo also points out, the 1905 legislation facilitated the removal to the missions of mixed-race children.

> *The Act separated children from their families, institutionalised them and determined who you could and couldn't marry. It was extremely oppressive. And, while some of the primary sources indicate the missionaries at Beagle Bay were concerned about the oppression of the Aboriginal people, they, in effect, condoned the provisions of the Act which is a sad thing. The children who were removed in the north-west were of mixed white and Aboriginal parentage from the pastoral stations and they were brought up in the missions because it meant that the half-white part could be acknowledged or educated.*[53]

Rosa Bin Amat was one of those children. In 1909 she was taken to Beagle Bay Mission from Thangoo station where her father worked.

> My father wouldn't let them [take us away] but government was against every women [sic] who were native mothers, Aboriginal mothers...Our mother came with us to Broome, only far as Broome. They wouldn't let them come near us...Nothing. They wouldn't let them. They were very cruel, wouldn't let mothers go to visit their children. They wouldn't let them. Government wouldn't let them.[54]

And, at the mission, there was to be no talk or thought of the people and life they had left behind.

> We were not allowed to talk about our parents. We were not allowed to tell where's our mother and all that...A lot of others too, they all from Derby, Broome, La Grange, Wyndham, Kununurra, they all different and those children talk their own lingo...There was a lot of children too and we talk to them...not our parents what were left behind, father and mother nothing. Not allowed. Government not allowed come.[55]

The missionaries were also determined to ensure that the children under their care made appropriate marriages between those they had 'Christianised'. As Choo notes, the role of the missionaries in promoting and influencing the marriage of children in their charge was linked to the model of evangelisation they were promoting and conflicted with traditional Aboriginal practices.

> *The idea was to educate the young people so that they would become Christians and then there would be Christian marriages. They'd be part of that Christian family and the children would be educated within the system and that would be a form of evangelisation. However, the Aboriginal people had their own way of setting up marriages and there were clear rules as to who a person could marry under these arrangements. Perhaps the missionaries thought they were rescuing people from this system but it created a lot of problems in Kalumburu and other places because for Aboriginal people, the missionaries' intentions transgressed their marriage and kinship systems.*[56]

In the south-west of Western Australia, European settlement, accompanied by state legislation governing the original Australians, had already displaced much of their traditional law and customs. But the 1905 Act marked a new departure in relations between First Nations people and the newcomers. Historian Lois Tilbrook described this legislation as having:

> a singularly negative and embittering effect upon relationships between Aboriginal people and others in the south western part of Western Australia because people classified as Aboriginal were subject to severe legal and consequent social disabilities and disadvantages. People whose lifestyle was indistinguishable from that of the general society were now brought under this Act and severely limited in their freedom of choice, movement and opportunity.[57]

Many Aboriginal men and women would, like Jack Davis, feel the full force of the European 'lawbook' in their lives, particularly in childhoods spent in government institutions and missions.

State legislation now governed almost every aspect of Aboriginal life. It determined where people could live and not live, where they could work or not work, whether they could keep their children, and defined individuals in racial categories. 'Half-caste' was defined as 'the offspring of an aboriginal mother and other than an aboriginal father'.[58] Parenthood was of particular concern to the authorities as, increasingly, especially in rural and remote areas, there were mixed marriages or more casual unions. Anna Haebich explains the thinking behind this aspect of the legislation:

> *At the turn of the century ideas of race-mixing led to assumptions about all sorts of terrible consequences. Particularly it was thought that the offspring would inherit the worst of both sides, that you would be left with an intermediate race of people who fitted with neither the black mother nor the white father. So, the question was: what would be the future of these people in what was to be basically a White Australia?*[59]

The emphasis on a White Australia reflected a deliberate and determined rejection of an existing reality, as linguist and historian John Kinder points out:

> *It's easy to think that Australia become multicultural in 1972 when Prime Minister Gough Whitlam proclaimed that we were. Actually, we'd been multicultural for a very, very long time, but what happened was that, with Federation and the White Australia policy and the desire to be British to our bootstraps, we airbrushed out a lot of the earlier history of the Afghan cameleers and the Chinese market gardeners and the Chinese gold miners et cetera.*[60]

It is perhaps no surprise that this state legislation was enacted four years after the Commonwealth *Immigration Restriction Act 1901*. This Act was aimed at limiting non-British migration but it also formally ushered in the White Australia policy with all its connotations of race supremacy. Within that policy was an inference that brown and black people could not be real Australians. At the same time, beliefs about the inherent inferiority of persons of mixed-race descent were spreading.[61] The following comment appeared in a 1901 article in Australia's foremost nationalistic magazine, *The Bulletin*:

> If Australia is to be a country fit for our children and their children to live in, we MUST KEEP THE BREED PURE. The half-caste usually inherits the vices of both races and the virtues of neither. Do you want Australia to be a community of mongrels?[62]

In Western Australia, efforts to keep the breed pure were continued by Charles Gale, who succeeded Prinsep as chief protector in 1908. Gale also held the position of chief inspector of fisheries, which appears to indicate the lowly status given

White Australia Protection badge (National Museum of Australia).

by the Western Australian government to the position of chief protector of Aborigines. Gale, like Prinsep, was a strong believer in the policy of segregation. Also, like Prinsep, he had little understanding of Aboriginal culture despite or perhaps due to his previous involvement in the pastoral industry. Gale's view of parental separation was uncompromising: 'I would not hesitate for one moment to separate any half-caste from its Aboriginal mother, no matter how frantic her momentary grief might be at the time. They soon forget their offspring.'[63]

Gale, with the support of his minister, J. D. Connelly, took the first steps in implementing the segregation policies made possible by the regulatory provisions of the 1905 Act. In 1908, in response to increasing fears from the white population about the increasing incidence of venereal disease in the north, he established the infamous lock hospitals, which Prinsep had also previously argued for. Aboriginal people suspected of having a venereal disease were 'locked away' on Bernier and Dorre islands off the Gascoyne coast, described by Daisy Bates as 'tombs of the living dead'.[64] Historian Mary Anne Jebb has studied these institutions and points out that they were places without comfort or support: 'It is important to recognise that the island hospitals did not provide adequate facilities for Aboriginal patients, let alone erase the emotional traumas involved in collection, isolation and treatment'.[65]

Gale fell out with the next minister for Aborigines, Rufus Underwood, over a personality clash rather than policy differences. So, the minister replaced Gale with A. O. Neville, the man most associated with the implementation of the 1905 Act and with the extension of discriminatory provisions in 1936. For a quarter of a century, from 1915 to 1940, 'Mr Neville' controlled almost every facet of life for Western Australians with Aboriginal heritage.

Delys Fraser's mother, Alma Dunstan, born in 1932, was the daughter of an Aboriginal woman known as Minnie and a white man, Edward (Bert) Dunstan. At first the family was forced to live 'as white people' away from their Aboriginal connections but:

> When her father, Bert Dunstan, was sent away to Heathcote, due to being a demented person with a mental problem, Mum and her mother (Minnie) were unfortunately taken away to Mogumber Mission [Moore River Native Settlement]. Later in her teenage years, Mum was taken to Perth to work for the government as a domestic.
>
> I do understand my mother complaining about Mr Neville. A lot of people who would know called him the devil. She talked about the part when the Native Affairs Department was overruling the Aboriginal families and she was part of that.[66]

The cornerstone of Neville's 'separatist' policy in the south of the state was the establishment of two 'native settlements' where Aboriginal people could farm and live independently. The men could learn basic agricultural skills and the women were to be taught cooking, cleaning and sewing. In 1915, Neville opened a 'native settlement' at Carrolup near Katanning in the Great Southern region. Then, in 1917, on his recommendation, the government purchased 10,000 acres near Mogumber, on the Moore River, 130 kilometres north of Perth. This site became known as the Moore River Native Settlement. The idea was that this land would be farmed by its new inhabitants, rather in the manner of New Norcia as Pat Jacobs, Neville's biographer, makes clear.

> It is important to understand that Neville's initial aims for Carrolup and Moore River were very different from what they became. His idea was to have large independent and functioning farms, self-contained communities where Aboriginal people could learn farming skills. They could be educated and become independent. Ultimately, he didn't want them to remain dependent on government welfare.[67]

However, the soil proved unsuitable for agriculture and Neville's initial hopes for such settlements were not fulfilled.

As chief protector, Neville now had the legal right to order Aboriginal and 'half-caste' children from all over the state to be sent to either Moore River or Carrolup. As a fourteen-year-old, Jack Davis was a ward of the state:

> *And that was the law. A magistrate only had to sign a piece of paper and say 'You're going to Moore River' and people would be sent there accordingly and hundreds of people were uprooted like this and sent there. And this not only happened in the south. It happened all over Western Australia.*[68]

Carrolup was closed in 1920 when Neville lost responsibility for Aboriginal affairs in the south of the state, only to be reopened in 1939. In 1945 teachers Noel and Lily White introduced an art program there to try and boost the spirits of the children who had been removed from their families.[69] The result was a series of more than one hundred landscape paintings and drawings that have become internationally famous and have also influenced current styles of Noongar painting.[70]

Moore River remained open for the whole of Neville's tenure as chief protector. Pat Jacobs argues that, while Neville is still seen as a demonic figure in Aboriginal society, politics and the economic conditions of the time conspired against his vision for the settlement.

> *Tragically for the future of Aboriginal people in Western Australia, when Neville became Secretary for the North West, he lost control over southern affairs. From 1920 until 1926 he had no power or responsibility over Aboriginal affairs in the south of the State. Carrolup was closed and disbanded; conditions at Moore River deteriorated grossly and the place was entirely neglected. People suffered a great deal and the terrible legend of Moore River had its origins in these six years.*[71]

Born in 1922, Alice Bassett, later Alice Nannup, was one of many children sent to Moore River in the years after Neville regained responsibility for the settlement. Like many other young people, she was sent there against her parents' wishes.

Alice was the much-loved daughter of a Pilbara pastoralist and an Aboriginal mother who, in her own words, 'wanted for nothing'. But her parents parted when her mother wanted to go back to live with her own people and take Alice with her: 'They had a talk about it. I heard my father crying. He didn't want to lose me. But wherever my mother went I had to go.'[72]

Unwittingly, her mother's return to camp life attracted the attention of the authorities. They indicated that Alice, as a part-Aboriginal girl, should be taken away from her mother's community. But pastoral neighbours intervened, apparently offering Alice and three other girls in a similar situation a better alternative.

> *Well they spoke to our parents and they said they'd take us down south and educate us and then take us back home. When my father knew I was being taken down, he sold his property and came down with me, thinking he'd be with me, all the time. But he never...The Aboriginal Affairs barred him from seeing me...He went back a broken-hearted and a disappointed man, because he loved me and I loved him too.*[73]

Alice thinks that her father wrote to her but she never received any letters or heard from him again. Neither did she receive the promised education.

> *What caused me to be so bitter about it all was, when I came down south, we were under the impression that we'd go down and go to school and then go back home. But then the school closed we were shoved into the Mission, that was the end of everything. I just gave up all hope.*[74]

For young people like Alice Nannup, Moore River failed to provide anything more than a very basic education. Alice was soon taken out of school and put to work as an unpaid seamstress. The Moore River Native Settlement made clothes for the Forrest River Mission.

> *They needed girls, so they took four of us out of school took us down to the sewing room. And you know what we used to get paid every Saturday morning, chocolates, no money. Mr. Neville said one day 'As long as they can count money and write their name is all they need.' What sort of education is that?*[75]

Educational opportunity as a path to a better life was specified at Moore River, but not on offer. Several former inmates spoke about 'wanting to be somebody, like being a nurse'. Anglican Deaconess Eileen Heath, who worked at Moore River in the 1930s, recalled:

> *Only wasted promise. There was a constant turnover of teachers. I felt that a lot of the children there and a lot of the people there had so much good in them and so much could have been done if they'd been given the right opportunity.*[76]

When she was allowed to leave the settlement in her teens, Alice Nannup was barely literate. As it happened, one of her earliest jobs 'in service' was to work for the Neville household at Darlington in the Perth hills.

> *I was thrilled. I never thought about him taking me away from my home or anything like that, you know, I thought working for the Chief Protector. That's a great honour. He was very nice, very fatherly.*[77]

Finally, while working in the Neville household, Alice was able to educate herself.

> *They were great entertainers. They liked bridge — I'd have to sit up until eleven o'clock at night, waiting to serve them supper. And that's when I learned to write. I used to buy a pad and I'd sit there to test my writing. I'd copy anything I saw there because I never had an education. I was only in grade three when I left Moore River.*[78]

Jack Davis had been, in his own words, 'eager to go to Moore River' from Yarloop, where his family lived.[79] They had received a letter from Neville offering to teach Jack and his brother Harold 'farming skills' if they would go to the Moore River Native Settlement. After nine months of monotonous labour and monotonous food they were told they could go home. As Jack later wrote: 'We went there with no working skills and we left there with none, apart from root picking and palm stabbing'.[80]

Noongar leader Ken Colbung grew up at the Moore River Native Settlement in the 1930s and 1940s. Determined to find a better life, Ken joined the Australian army and later fought in the Korean War. He saw comparisons in that civil war between the situation of Koreans suffering from the conflict and that of his own people.

I saw some five thousand children displaced and starving who we tried to feed. Children were fighting for their lives. That was something that's still with me after thirty-six years and I never want to see that again and I don't think the world should ever see that again...being an Aboriginal man who at that time came from an apartheid type of situation at the Moore River Settlement I saw them as human beings in a situation like us in some ways.[81]

The 1905 Act and its successors had indeed created apartheid in Western Australia, according to Jack Davis.

The whole world screams about the apartheid laws in South Africa but we had those laws long before South Africa, to keep Aboriginal people down. These were laws such as those where you had to leave the town at six o'clock. Those laws were still in existence in the 1950s but nobody thought about changing them. So those laws to us were oppression. If you were told to get home at six o'clock and you didn't do it, you were slammed in gaol.[82]

Church at Moore River Native settlement.

Apartheid existed right from birth. Pregnant Aboriginal women were expected to give birth at the settlement and were strongly discouraged from trying to attend King Edward Memorial Hospital (KEMH), the state's main maternity hospital in Perth. Jennie Carter, who has written a history of KEMH, recalls that Adeline Corunna was one mother who managed to evade this 'whites only' policy.

> *Arthur and Adeline Corunna farmed at Mukinbudin in the Wheatbelt, but for Adeline, home was the area around the Swan River. She was therefore, prepared to go to some lengths to ensure her children were born on her own country.*[83]

Albert Corunna, himself born at KEMH, explained how the family managed to evade the native welfare officers.

> When she was ready to give birth to my sister Norma, they had to get Mum on the train to Perth. There were waiting rooms at the siding we slept there and in the middle of the night a train came through which Mum caught to Perth. Mum boarded with a white lady named Mrs Hall who had a boarding house not far from the hospital until ready to have the baby. Mrs Erickson, the postmistress at Mukinbudin helped Mum fix up the hospital bill and boarding costs and the train fare back to Mukinbudin.[84]

KEMH Matron Walsh did not approve of such subterfuges and some ten years later stated that 'native women' should not give birth at her hospital:

> There are many good reasons why nurses who are not used to natives should not be expected to handle them – those in their own hospitals are specially trained for the work.[85]

But 'their own hospital' at Moore River was not equipped to handle anything other than a simple, uncomplicated birth.[86]

According to Pat Jacobs the situation at Moore River resulted from Neville's enforced six-year absence from management of the settlement.

> When Neville returned and resumed control in 1926, he found the entire institution run down. The spirit had gone out of the place and people were resentful and hostile. Then right on top of that came the Great Depression.[87]

In 1931 Neville reported that, 'no section of the community has suffered more from the effects of the financial depression than the natives, particularly in the south-west'.[88] The following year he recorded that rations were now being issued at nearly every police station in the region. Employment prospects seem to have slowly improved and he wrote in his report for the year ended 30 June 1933:

> Permits to employ 156 'natives' in the south-west have been issued (and) forty-seven girls and boys, trainees of Moore River Settlement have been sent out to work and the demand for these youngsters is greater than the supply.[89]

Neville had intended Moore River to offer young people subject to the 1905 Act better opportunities and a chance to 'assimilate' into white society but despite his claims at finding work for young Aboriginal people, no more money was provided for the settlement and conditions continued to deteriorate. Jack Davis remembers Moore River as *'a clearing house for Aboriginal people, in the sense that they were sent just to stay there and decay in body and mind, body and soul'*.[90]

At the same time, during the Great Depression of the 1930s there were more than two thousand unemployed Aboriginal people in the south-west of the state. They had no recourse to unemployment benefits or relief work. Even those who had worked for equal pay were declared ineligible for social service benefits when their background was discovered.[91] Where relief was provided it was paid at the rate of two shillings and sixpence per person, compared with seven shillings and sixpence for white people.[92] So the practice of Aboriginal people helping each other was vital during times of unemployment. The Department of

Native Affairs was aware that this happened but opposed the practice because it was seen to militate against individual success.[93]

No one asked Aboriginal people for their views on how to cope in difficult circumstances. At the time they were simply trying to survive a situation in which they were not entitled to any of the welfare benefits available to the white population. But survive they did throughout the Great Depression of the early 1930s.

This acute downturn in the world economy followed hard on the heels of the 1929 centenary celebrations of the founding of the Swan River Colony. Former premier Sir Hal Colebatch was commissioned by the state government to write *A Story of a Hundred Years*. The book praises the achievements of the early European settlers and the problems and privations that they faced. The 'natives' are not mentioned until page 60, where the Battle of Pinjarra is portrayed as essential to white domination. Interestingly, in view of earlier denials by the white population, Colebatch does acknowledge that a large number of Bindjareb men were killed.

> Frequent troubles with the natives added to the difficulties of the outlying settlers. There were occasional lootings and murders by natives took place, particularly on the York Road and in the Murray district. In July 1834 two settlers were murdered by natives and two others severely wounded. This led to the organising of an expedition and to the so-called 'Battle of Pinjarra', in October of the same year, in which more than half the male members of the Murray River tribe were killed...The survivors of the tribe were made to understand that any further murders and depredations would lead to their complete extinction. They no longer doubted the ability and the determination of the white man to carry out the threat, and the trouble was ended.[94]

In the town of Bunbury, the centenary celebrations continued to promote the image of valiant Europeans overcoming the threat of Aboriginal violence. The authors of a history of Bunbury described a set-piece re-enactment of an Aboriginal raid on settler properties.

In glorifying the pioneering achievement by portraying the Aborigines as a virile threat to early settlement, the organisers were also implicitly drawing contrasts with the abject conditions of the twenty-seven mainly half-caste Aborigines who were officially deemed 'inside the influence of civilisation' in the Bunbury area in 1929.[95]

Two years earlier, Albany had celebrated its 'European' century with an official hoisting of the British flag. Historian Murray Arnold draws attention to a significant image.

> The photograph taken at the assembly point near the Post Office building in Stirling Terrace shows some of the participants milling around just prior to the procession moving off. Bandsmen are making last-minute adjustments to their instruments while two young Aboriginal men, identities lost in time, prepare to take their place at the procession's head. A reporter from the *Albany Advertiser* noted that hundreds of cameras were trained on these two men, as they waited, resplendent in white markings and carrying spears and shields.

Arnold also wondered:

> How many of the photographs taken that day also captured the image of what appears to be a third Aboriginal man who was standing nearby dressed in cast-off clothing, his face invisible in deep shadow.[96]

Such an image might not have concerned the settlers who were celebrating that day. Most would have been confident in the prevailing belief that the First Australians were a dying race. However, officialdom knew otherwise. Bruce McLarty, later deputy commissioner for native welfare, was well aware that by the 1930s the part-Aboriginal population was growing.

> *In the more densely settled white areas of the state, the Aboriginal population, far from dying out, was on the increase. And this increase was generated mainly not by miscegenation between white settlers and Aboriginal*

women but by propagation of the half-caste people among themselves. And there was a very rapid growth in the size of Aboriginal families.[97]

The number of people who could be identified as having some Aboriginal forebears continued to increase throughout the twentieth century. Derryce Gliddon belongs to one of those many families who can claim descent from both First Nations people and European settlers.

My Dad's father, my grandfather, Harry Phillips, was the son of a white man who came from England and Annie, a part-Aboriginal woman from the Northam area. Her father, who was also white, owned a hotel in Northam. Mum was a Fogarty. Again, my grandfather on that side had a white father. So, the background there was Irish. They were from around Paynes Find, not Perenjori. My grandmother Bridget Little was born on a station out there.[98]

It is perhaps hard now to understand why governments used legislation to respond to this increase in the population of people with some Aboriginal inheritance. First came the *Aborigines Act 1905* and later its successor, the *Native Administration Act 1936*; legislation which created what Jack Davis and Ken Colbung saw as apartheid.

A key dynamic was the overwhelming sense of white superiority, fostered, often mistakenly, by Darwinian assumptions about race and a belief that Aboriginal people were unable to match the achievements of Europeans. As far back as 1894, the colony's minister for lands had proclaimed that the idea of Aboriginal farming 'was useless and never likely to succeed as it was not in them'.[99]

But the Western Australian economy was now dominated by European-style farming and efforts by Aboriginal people to find their place in West Australian society also continued to be affected by a changing agricultural economy.

Anna Haebich describes how legislation and developments in land use permanently altered the south-west's social and physical landscape: 'Vast areas of bushland were cleared and settled and small farms of less than one thousand acres replaced the sprawling pastoral stations of the nineteenth century'.[100]

The 'vast areas' are today's Wheatbelt, where many of the early twentieth-century 'thousand acres' farms are now even bigger. But this considerable change in land use, as Haebich points out, had a significant effect on an already altered Aboriginal economy and lifestyle, both built around:

> employment on the pastoral stations and hunting and camping on the vast tracts of uncleared land in this area. They were exploited for their labour, but these adaptations also provided them with a degree of economic independence and enabled them to retain their ties with the land and certain elements of traditional Aboriginal life. With the development of the wheat belt the Aborigines were forced off the land, their existing way of life was destroyed and they were ultimately left trapped in a life of poverty in small camps on the fringes of the wheat belt towns.[101]

Despite loss of access to their traditional land, especially in the newly cleared Wheatbelt, there were still opportunities, albeit limited, for Aboriginal families to own farms themselves. Bishop Salvado's experiment at New Norcia had shown that Aboriginal people could become European-style farmers. In fact, the *Land Act 1898* had made provision for Aboriginal men and their descendants to acquire small, 200-acre properties, although in reality these were probably not viable for economic cereal production.

It also became evident that the Western Australian government had no intention of granting Aboriginal people full ownership of these blocks. At the time, as Haebich notes, the government appeared to have no clear-cut policy on the role of Aboriginal people in land development.[102] Public opinion, at official and community levels, was also discouraging. A settler in the Toodyay district told the local police in 1903 that Aboriginal farming was 'merely an excuse for harbouring large numbers of relatives on the blocks of land'.[103]

Some potential landowners made improvements to their blocks but were not able to meet the conditional purchase requirement that a proportion of native vegetation had to be cleared before the land title was issued. They were hampered by lack of capital and had to take on paid work elsewhere. Others encountered opposition from white neighbours, who deliberately drew attention to any lack of improvements made in order to gain possession of the land themselves.[104]

There were exceptions. Lois Tilbrook cites support from sympathetic white settlers in the Arthur River district. George 'Jerong' Dinah had been reported in 1906 and again in 1907 to the Lands Department for failing to improve his property. But local white settlers disagreed. One farmer, Nicholas Donnelly, wrote in support:

> Most of the farmers consider that the land should be given to Dinah and his family for all time. To my knowledge he has resided on the land on several occasions – has cut down several acres and cut and erected posts on one line of fence.[105]

The number of applications from Aboriginal men increased in the early part of the twentieth century. Generally, they applied for land in areas with which they had some long-term connection, and several succeeded as farmers, despite widespread white cynicism and racial objection.[106] Haebich draws attention to a particular case of survival against the odds. In 1907, one Aboriginal farmer, Charles Ponan, was told by the Lands Department that ownership of his block had been cancelled due to 'non-fulfilment of the labour conditions'. Ponan fought back.

> You say it has been cancelled through non-fulfilment of labour conditions. No Sir, I can prove that I had certain improvements effected here long before the 6th May last. Therefore, if I am to lose the land, I expect payment for the twenty acres which I have partly cleared there also twenty fruit trees growing well, planted over twelve months ago, also some little water holes there, as I do

not consider it fair to take it like this after all I have done. Now Sir I trust you will try to get me the land or else payment for what I have done thereon.[107]

On this occasion, the Lands Department reversed its decision. William Harris, originally from Williams, was another Aboriginal farmer who kept his farm. Harris was also an activist who protested against the legislation that affected the lives of his people. He had been educated at his father's expense at the Swan Native and Half-Caste Mission in Perth and had taken up land at Morawa.[108]

Even before the passage of the 1905 Act, Harris had made a strong plea for better understanding of his people's legal and social status. His main concern was the plight of fellow 'half-castes'. In November 1926, Harris wrote to the editor of *The Sunday Times* newspaper stating that the southern Aboriginal people were 'tired of being robbed, and shot down or run into miserable compounds' and had decided to form a union to fight for their rights as British subjects.[109]

Two years later, Harris led a deputation to Premier Philip Collier pleading strongly for the repeal of the 1905 Act which, he asserted, had done considerable damage to his people in terms of their freedom and opportunity. William's nephew, Norman Harris, recorded in a letter to a fellow Aboriginal man the questions the deputation wished to raise. They asked:

> Why shouldn't a native have land? The country belongs to him.
>
> Why can't he be allowed in a public Hotel?
>
> Why shouldn't he have a voice [sic] in the making of the Laws?
>
> Why shouldn't a native mother demand Freedom for her child?[110]

Peter Biskup describes the arrival of this unusual deputation at the seat of power.

> On the morning of 9 March 1928, a group of immaculately dressed aborigines entered the Treasury building in Perth, and a few moments

later the first aboriginal deputation to wait on a Western Australian Minister of the Crown was ushered into the Premier's office. The deputation consisted of William Harris, his brother Edward and his nephew Norman Harris, Arthur Kickett from York, Edward Jacobs from Quairading, William Morrison, a Toodyay full-blood and W. Bodney, said to be partly of West Indian negro stock.[111]

Along with other issues, the deputation complained about places like the Moore River Native Settlement, which they saw as a prison.[112] Premier Collier expressed some sympathy for their arguments but referred the delegation's concerns to A. O. Neville. The chief protector was unmoved by these arguments, insisting that he should have more, rather than less, control over the lives of part-Aboriginal people: 'Unless I am given increased powers over all part-Aborigines, the situation will become very serious and a number of coloured children will have to be treated as white'.[113]

In fact, Neville had been arguing unsuccessfully for over a decade for greater controls and he continued to do so. His long-term aim in seeking more power was not segregation but assimilation.

Anna Haebich sees the basis of Neville's thinking as:

> Influenced by ideas of biological engineering and social control emanating from the eastern states, he began to advocate the breeding out of the 'coloured race' altogether. This policy of 'biological absorption' drew inspiration from research undertaken during the 1920s, postulating common racial origins and genotypic racial characteristics for the Aboriginal and Caucasian races and from Mendelian theories of genetic inheritance.[114]

Based on this belief, at the 1937 Commonwealth Conference on Aboriginal Administration, Neville stated that the natives were suffering the effects of economic and social disadvantage, rather than from any innate racial differences, and that segregation would lead to the separate existence of a 'coloured minority'. His aim was the 'breeding out of colour, or assimilation by organised breeding'. This aim could be achieved, he thought, within three generations if 'there are no more virile full bloods alive'.[115]

This thinking was based at least partly on a set of pseudo-scientific beliefs and practices known as eugenics, which became popular early in the twentieth century. The theory was that the genetic quality of the human population could be improved by 'breeding out' genetic groups judged to be inferior, usually by the white man. It was belief in this now completely discredited theory that 'colour' could be bred out, that drove Neville's continued push to gain even more stringent powers over his charges.

Perhaps surprisingly, it was the Moseley Royal Commission into the treatment of the Aboriginal population which finally provided an opportunity for the chief protector to gain the additional powers he had long been seeking. The unlikely midwife for action which eventually led to the strengthening of the legislation was the redoubtable Mary Bennett. This would give Neville the powers he was seeking. Mary was an English woman, raised in Queensland. Bennett came back to Australia after the death of her husband and arrived in Perth in October 1930, intending to devote the rest of her life to Aboriginal welfare.[116] She taught Aboriginal children in different areas of the state and promoted the making of handicrafts. Bennett wanted to stamp out traditional Indigenous practices such as infant betrothal and polygamy, but also sought to improve the treatment of Aboriginal pastoral workers and practices which she saw as slavery.[117] She also strongly opposed both Neville's bid for new powers and the repression of Aboriginal civil liberties.[118]

Bennett published her allegations about mistreatment of the original Australians and directly blamed the state government for the condition of Aboriginal people throughout Western Australia. In June 1933 she arranged for her paper to be read at the Conference of the British Commonwealth League in London. Anna Haebich describes Bennett's attack:

> In her usual pugnacious style, she alleged that the major cause of the Aborigines' low social and economic status lay in the

'victimisation' of Aboriginal women. In their 'wild state' they suffered from the traditional practices of their men while those in touch with whites were even worse off.[119]

The state government considered that it could not allow attacks on the Aborigines Department and its policies to continue and combined with the parliamentary opposition to denounce critics of its Aboriginal policies. Opposition leader Charles Latham stated that these people were: 'Scandalmongers (who wrote) derogatory articles for personal publicity'. He also recommended the introduction of a policy of 'breeding out Aborigines in the south'.[120]

Despite potential for criticism of his department and his policies, the chief protector appeared to welcome the appointment of a wide-ranging royal commission, 'to investigate, report, and advise upon matters in relation to the condition and treatment of Aborigines'.[121] The commissioner appointed was Henry Doyle Moseley, described by historian Geoffrey Bolton as a 'decent, experienced and unimaginative stipendiary magistrate'.[122]

Moseley travelled widely, visiting pastoral stations and south-west towns. He was accompanied by a young journalist from *The West Australian*, Paul Hasluck. As a result of this journey and from earlier experiences in his school days, Hasluck was to become a life-long supporter of improved conditions for Aboriginal people.

> *Billy Boolardy and Butterballs Cox, Kanga Latham, Jack Chance and others were at primary school at the same time as I was and I think I had a foundation of great respect for them, simply because these boys could throw a boondi (sand bomb) better than I could. They could make a gidgee (short spear) better than I could — I had a great respect for them because they could do so many things better than I could.*[123]

While remaining committed throughout his later political career to the policy of assimilation, Hasluck, like Mary Bennett, was opposed to Neville's bid for increased control over the Indigenous population. He was also one of the first people to recognise publicly, as he did in *The West Australian* on 18 March 1934, that the number of people with Aboriginal heritage was actually growing: 'Perhaps we will have to adjust our views and plan a future that is not based on the expectation that sooner or later the blacks must die out'.[124]

Hasluck's visit to the Kimberley with Moseley made him aware of the problems inherent in treating Aboriginal populations as one homogeneous bloc. He was particularly interested in the status of the mixed-race populations in the north-west towns and wrote about the strict colour bar in Broome which was producing 'an annually increasing body of discontented misfits'.[125] One of his articles in *The West Australian* expressed the following views:

> Action should start from the premise that they were 'human beings with the right to lead happy and useful lives' and they must

Broome today. Home of the so-called misfits in the 1930s.
Photo by Amanda McInerney.

be admitted into the white community with the 'opportunity' to gain full citizenship without any show of contempt and with their self-respect fully restored.[126]

The 'body of misfits', otherwise known as the 'half castes of Broome', made their own submission to the Moseley Royal Commission. It was mainly put together by women who were part-Asian (Filipino, Malay or Chinese) and part-European or part-Aboriginal and involved with the pearl diving community. Their submission concluded as follows:

> Many of us own our own houses and land and many more of us could do so.
>
> We who do own our own homes pay the rates when the rate time comes along. We can read, write, sew, crochet, laundry, also make our own clothes and for other people too, also other domestic work. So that sir, on that qualification alone we think we should not be classed as natives and kept in bondage by the Act, knowing or at least hearing and reading about halfcastes of other countries of the British Empire that are not classed with their native.
>
> Again Sir, we the Half-caste population of Broome ask you to give us our Freedom and release us from the stigma of a native and make us happy subjects of this our country.[127]

In his report Moseley made special mention of the Broome situation. He found that many of the 'half-castes led decent lives' and suggested that these people should be left where they were and not be taken into settlements like Moore River or to Christian missions. However, he made no recommendation that any of them should be excluded from the provisions of the hated 1905 Act.

Fearful of the further spread of venereal disease, Moseley stated that, 'The others, in my opinion, should be kept out of town, only allowed in on permit and the greatest supervision exercised over their reserve to prevent contact with white men and of course

Asiatics'.[128] Fear of sexual and racial 'contamination' apparently justified his continuing support for the White Australia policy.

The commissioner found no evidence to support allegations of ill-treatment of Aboriginal people in the pastoral industry, although he added that he 'was not so foolish as to suggest that isolated cases of cruelty to Aborigines did not exist'. He criticised conditions at Moore River but supported the concept of such community settlements because he thought that they could, and would, provide education and training.

Moseley made a number of recommendations for administrative improvements and increased funding. But most of his beneficial suggestions were ignored and Neville's stamp, rather than Moseley's, is evident in the wording and content of the Bill introduced as a result of this inquiry.

The *Aborigines Act Amendment Act 1936*, also known as the *Native Administration Act 1936*, came into effect in April 1937. It amended the *Aborigines Act 1905*, created the Department of Native Affairs, and changed the title of 'chief protector' to 'commissioner for native affairs'. Neville favoured these administrative changes. More significantly for people subject to the legislation, it extended his powers and his role, especially as it affected children. The commissioner now became the legal guardian of all Aboriginal children younger than twenty-one years of age, 'notwithstanding that the child has a parent'. Even children who were calculated to be one-quarter Aboriginal or less were now covered by the legislation, and a definition of the term 'quadroon' was inserted into the Act.[129]

This legislation covered a large number of individuals who had one or more Aboriginal antecedents but who had previously been exempt from the 1905 Act. All persons of Aboriginal descent regardless of their lifestyle were included, with the exception of 'quadroons' over the age of twenty-one unless classed as 'native' by a magisterial order. 'Persons of less than quadroon blood' born after 31 January 1936 were also exempt from the provisions of this law. However those individuals excluded from the legislation were prohibited by law from associating with those covered by the provisions of the Act.[130]

Any sexual intercourse between 'natives' and 'non-natives' was now an offence, with a minimum penalty for cohabitation of six months. Every person classified as a 'native' under this legislation, which was not repealed until 1964, required permission from the commissioner of native welfare to marry.[131] Barladong Elder Tom Hayden summed up the situation: 'You were barred from this. You were barred from that, yet you were used for cheap labour.'[132] And if your cheap labour was not required, you could be sent straight to Moore River.

The Moore River Native Settlement continued to exist after Neville's retirement in 1940. Stanley Middleton became commissioner for native affairs six years later. He had worked for many years in Papua and disagreed with the provisions in the Act that permitted unwanted 'natives' to be carted away from anywhere in the state, and he was particularly critical of Moore River and other Aboriginal institutions as:

> *convenient dumping grounds for unwanted natives. Take Northam for example. If the Chairman of the Roads Board, as it was then, felt there were too many natives there, more than were required for their purpose, like in the off-season between harvesting and seeding, they would get the police. The police would simply round up the unwanted Aboriginal people and take them to nearby Moore River, out of sight and out of mind. In many cases these people were kept there for so long, they couldn't remember on what grounds they were originally sent there.*[133]

Noongar Wyvon Henry recalls that his relatives were taken to Moore River, from the Wheatbelt town of Brookton, in the 1950s.

> *Some of my cousins were taken away. They were sent to Moore River. They spent a few years up there. And I didn't like asking them what it was like. It was bad enough seeing them being picked up and taken – poor little things crying and that. This was in Brookton. They had a reserve there. I saw the police come and get them and the Welfare*

woman and take them. And my uncle and Auntie were staying on the Reserve. And they, the Welfare came up, said they were taking the kids, put them in the old motor they had and that was it. And I can just imagine those little ones being taken. It was just terrible to see. I try to forget about it, let it go – but it's hard. You can't. It's always in the back of my mind.[134]

Deputy Commissioner Bruce McLarty recalled that the Native Affairs Department wrestled to bridge the gulf between 'protecting' Aboriginal people and meeting the expectations of the white population. The latter expected to be safeguarded from what they saw as the nuisance and inconvenience of having unwanted Aboriginal families in their midst.

So that on one hand you had a sort of conscience-stricken effort to prove to the world that we weren't using them as slaves, that we weren't deliberately killing them off, that we were trying to make life easier for them, but at the same time, diminishing the 'nuisance' that they constituted to the white population.[135]

As former Moore River inmate Bella Yappo remembers, much of 'the nuisance' came from the distant north-west.

They used to bring a lot of people from where they lived. There were girls there from Derby...They used to bring them down for some unknown reason. I don't know why they done it from that day to this.[136]

The 'unknown reason' was that the children were often the product of relationships between white men and Aboriginal women. Some were the result of Aboriginal domestic staff being taken advantage of or raped by their white employer. The Human Rights and Equal Opportunity Commission's *Bringing Them Home* report states that:

Especially during the nineteenth and twentieth centuries, relationships between European men and Aboriginal women were often abusive and exploitative. Many children were the products of rape. The European biological fathers denied their responsibility and the authorities regarded the children with embarrassment and shame.[137]

Sometimes, however, these liaisons were based on necessity. As historian Cathie Clement sees the situation for Aboriginal women.

> *It was in their interest to form sexual relationships with European men for protection and for their sustenance. A lot of them resulted in families which were only broken up by the imposition of the 1905 Aborigines Act. I think that it must have caused an incredible amount of distress, the way the family was living as a unit.*[138]

Many Moore River inmates from these broken families came from Kimberley communities, a world away from their traditional country:

> *The Aboriginal people in the Turkey Creek (Warmun) area still talk with sorrow about the removal of aunts and uncles whose fate is still not known to them, people who disappeared perhaps via the Moore River Settlement and never ever returned to the Kimberley.*[139]

First Nations advocate Robert Riley described the disruption and dislocation of families that occurred:

> *Taking kids away from their families, of dislocating whole families from traditional areas, putting them into missions, taking kids from one side of the state to the other, or even putting brothers and sisters into the same government institution or mission and changing their names.*[140]

One effect of the redistribution of younger Aboriginal people was, as south-west born Lynette Knapp saw it, the breakdown of traditional rules governing marriage between different groups. As people, especially children, came together from separate parts of the country, they were often too young to have acquired knowledge of the kinship rules governing the community they had come from.

> *The only hierarchical systems in life are the marriage systems. So, when the government did the 1905 Act and the marriage systems the way they wanted to do it, they completely ruined those systems.*[141]

The traditional rules were strict and based on a totem structure.

> *People had totems in marriage. So, if you had a kangaroo totem, your greys [kangaroos] could marry wallaby totem people. But it had to be the old fellas that managed that so that they weren't going to marry relations to each other. You had to be different.*[142]

Language was one strong manifestation of First Nations culture. But sometimes individuals had to decide whether or not to keep traditional languages alive.

Alby and Yvonne Phillips, living in Perenjori in the northern Wheatbelt, did their best to fit in with the rest of the townspeople so as not to attract attention to their Aboriginality. As Lois Tilbrook pointed out:

> People were forced to deny their Aboriginality and their Aboriginal ties in order to avoid the Act, and to go to great lengths in attempts to prove they were justifiably outside its provisions should their appearance suggest otherwise.[143]

Alby and Yvonne's daughter Derryce Gliddon remembers that:

> *Mum could speak fluent language. Her brothers taught their children. They all knew their language till they died. It was never taught to us. It was like they wanted to block it.*[144]

Tom Hayden from Kellerberrin, recalls that dilemma:

> *I had to consider whether I was going to speak English, Wongai, Yamaji or whatever. Mum and Dad and grandparents used to speak language but they had the same problem with the Wadjelas and weren't allowed to speak our own lingo.*[145]

Within a very British Australia, English was to be spoken at all times and this requirement alone could affect schooling. Quairading man Basil Winmar recalls his father's early educational experience: 'My Dad left school when they laughed at him. He never taught us any culture or language. He could speak the language but he kept it to himself. He was very shy about it.'[146]

Basil's sister, Winnie McHenry, explains why their father quit the classroom.

> *He went into the Mission school and they asked him what a tadpole was and he said gobul-ung. The teacher said 'No! It's a tadpole'. 'No', he said, 'It's a gobul-ung'. And he got the cuts for that. And he went through the door and never came back to school.*[147]

Education, for Aboriginal people subject to the provisions of the 1905 Act, was never a right. School attendance did not become compulsory for Aboriginal children until 1948, and even then it was subject to white parents not objecting to their inclusion.[148] Much earlier, a Kellerberrin schoolmaster, J. Mack, had written to the Kellerberrin Roads Board in 1937, stating that native and half-caste children had been excluded from the Kellerberrin School and that 'something should be done for them'.[149] It was not until 1953 that the Kellerberrin School enrolled its first Noongar students, brother and sister Charlotte and Harry Winmar.[150]

While some church organisations provided education for Aboriginal children, the state Education Department argued that it was the responsibility of the Aborigines Department (after 1936 the Department of Native Affairs) to provide education for Aboriginal children. They could be, and often were, excluded from state schools. For some families who wanted schooling for their children, this was a source of great frustration but also a call to action.[151]

Back in 1917, Winnie McHenry's grandfather, John Kickett, had written letters to the government,

> *Asking for them to go to school and my auntie, Gladys, she was about 15 or 16, she rode a horse all around the Quairading area, getting up petitions for these kids to go to school.*[152]

Gladys Kickett had some success with her petition. All but two farming families in the Quairading district endorsed her request.[153] A. O. Neville, chief protector of Aborigines, who knew and respected Kickett, also supported his petition and wrote:

> It does appear to me, however, that the policy of the Education Department is to gradually exclude all half-caste children from a State School whenever an opportunity arises. You will observe that the parents of 25 out of 44 white children attending the Quairading school...are not averse to the Kickett children receiving an education there and the schoolmaster himself suggests that they might be allowed to attend.[154]

Neville's support seemingly did not assist him, but Kickett did not give up and wrote many more letters to those in authority. In August 1918, he appealed to his local member of parliament:

> Well Sir I have Five of my People in France Fighting. Since you were up here in your Election one as Been Killed which leave four. Cannot my Children have the same Privelige as Johnny Fitzgerald...
>
> Would you Be so Kind Sir see if they can goe to Dangin or the same school north of Quairading if I send them their? Sir I Cannot see why my Children could not attend here at Quairading. My People are Fighting for Our King and Country Sir. I think they should have the liberty of going to any of the State [schools].
>
> I had Fifteen Parents of whos Children are attending the State School have signed the Petition knows my Children well so they could goe to School here. But was refused By the Department. My Childrens Uncles are Fighting. Could you do some thing for the little ones.[155]

But Kickett's children remained home-schooled, as Winnie McHenry recalls:

> *They were still excluded from the school. But grandfather Kickett taught them to read and write, because they had to write out orders if they wanted anything from the town. So, reading the jam tins or the food containers, they learned from that.*[156]

Dean Collard, later a journalist and Director of Sister Kate's Home in the Perth suburb of Queens Park, did get to school, and was taught history, 'But the history that we were taught was English history. The curriculum for all children, including Aboriginal children, was English history and the early days of colonisation.'[157] The Aboriginal story was seen only through the prism of the invaders.

> *The only reference to Aboriginal history was that we were savages and hunted kangaroos. It often reinforced the idea, along with the fact that we had to live outside town, and all those other things like not having the correct school uniform, that we were second class citizens and the fact that the history books made reference to savages, who carried spears and killed white settlers.*[158]

Colonial history could also affect friendships. Dean Collard recalled being 'best friends' with a non-Aboriginal boy.

> *His father, a farmer, was quite rich. But he invited me out to his house on a weekend. And then I thought of things I didn't have, toothpaste and underpants, which none of us Aboriginal kids had. But Mum and Dad got all those things together and, on the Friday, I took a small case to school ready for the weekend.*
>
> *But my best friend then told me that I couldn't go out there, because his sister, who was a model in the city, was coming home and he had told his parents and his sister about me coming out, an Aboriginal kid. I knew my friend very well and I knew he had problems explaining that his parents couldn't accept that an Aboriginal person was coming out to the farm. That really made me feel low. I didn't ever get out there to see him or his farm.*[159]

For one Kellerberrin Aboriginal man, learning and advancement came only through work on the land.

> Cliff Humphries never went to school. Instead he grew up accompanying his father and grandfather travelling through the district seeking work. With the era of the pastoralist and the role of the shepherd ending, Noongars could now only get seasonal work as shearers or shed hands or in the clearing of land and other menial work.[160]

By the early twentieth century, many Noongars in the Wheatbelt and in the Great Southern regions of the state were adjusting to a new life, camping out in the bush and working for nearby farms or living on designated reserves on the edge of towns. They were becoming more closely tied to the white economy but seldom part of its society, as one Kojonup farmer recalled in the twenty-first century.

> *It is very difficult for the Wadjelas to understand how disadvantaged the Noongar people were, and not deliberately. It was just a thing that they didn't see…These are guys I went to school with, was quite good friends with, played sport with, but they were non-persons and that was quite an eye-opener for the white people.*[161]

Most towns had Aboriginal reserves where anyone designated as Aboriginal under the 1905 Act was required to live. This meant no running water and no electricity even when, by the 1930s, most town residents had these amenities. Charlotte Winmar-Smith described her childhood home.

Site of Badjaling reserve.

> *We had no floor in the tin humpies out in the camps. There were holes in the tin and when it rained you had it dripping everywhere. Some people had tents on the reserve, spread out on the ground with just a bag spread here and there.*[162]

Around Albany there were three Aboriginal reserves, including one at the back of Mount Melville. Lynette Knapp spent much of her childhood here.

> *Our Dad was a shearing contractor at Gnowangerup with his brothers but when that work ran out, we ended up moving down back to Albany and we ended up on the reserve. Dad was a very proud person and said he didn't like reserves. But, because he had nothing, we had to go on the reserve and the Welfare put two houses up for us. But they weren't houses, they were just tin humpies, no inside walls, you were just looking at tin. Five windows were only louvres. The tap was way outside. The ablution block was common for everybody on the reserve.*[163]

Despite material poverty, the sense of family and community was strong.

> *There was a sense that somebody would look after you. If Mum and Dad went away and if we were at school or elsewhere, they'd say 'Come up here, we'll feed you till Mum and Dad get home. Come and have a feed!' There was a kinship that you can't get these days. There was never a door locked.*[164]

Wadjela Robert Sexton thinks that his people can learn from the Noongar emphasis on family solidarity.

> *The Noongar people tell me that one of the reasons that they survived was their very strong family associations. You back up your family the whole way all the time, that's the only way you'll survive over a long period. We can learn quite a bit from that as well.*[165]

Sally Hodson has explored Aboriginal experiences of agricultural work in the Great Southern region, where Robert Sexton farms, and has found that while many families did find employment within the paid rural economy, they often worked as a family unit where women as well as men shared clearing contracts:

> An important aspect of Nyungar social relations was the obligation to share resources with close kin...People shared contract work when it was available; as one man explained, 'If you saw somebody who had no work, you'd say "well, you can come and have a hundred acres" or something like that'. Food, shelter and money were other resources shared by Nyungars...[166]

That 'hundred acres', by then part of a large farm, would have constituted a minute fraction of the original woodland 'pantry' that had supported the original Aboriginal economy. But a largely cleared and fenced landscape meant that the bush, with its once rich diversity of animal and plant life, could no longer support a traditional way of life. First Nations people now had to work for the newcomers' money. One of the main jobs was to turn forest into field for white farmers, a task that challenged their own cultural attachment to country. Tom Hayden was often distressed by the sight of cleared land.

> *You'd go out to the bush and Oh! Where's all the bush gone? You'd see people all over the places chopping trees and burning up and picking up mallee roots – it was part of a way of living then.*[167]

As Elder Fred Collard recalled, his people often:

> *had no option. We had to work to feed ourselves. But I used to think at times, those trees were talking, saying, why are you cutting me down? Later, the more I thought about it hurt because trees are very important to me. And I am part of the tree. And at night, you can look out in the moonlight and see the faces of your family who have gone on before. The trees are like living persons to me.*[168]

Basil Winmar described a day's work:

> *My uncle and I went fencing and then the farmer asked us to go and cut some posts. Well we cut 26,000 posts out on this 150-acre block.*[169]

Experience of working for farmers in the rapidly expanding Wheatbelt varied. Some showed respect for their workforce. Sally Hodson mentions a farmer described by a former employee as:

> a good man – he used to tell you what to do and then he never seen you until you came back for your cheque. When you come back he never looked whether you'd done it or not, he'd pull his little drawer out and there was all cash, notes…pay you up straight away.[170]

In the south-west, shearing was one of the main occupations for Aboriginal families. It often provided the backbone of the working year and was essential for their survival. But blackfellas were often treated differently from whitefellas. Ivan Yarran worked as a shearer in the Great Southern region. In his experience, there was little equality between the races.

> *We didn't get things that the other shearers got, like lunch and living-in and showers and things like that. I remember one day. It was lunchtime and we knocked off. We were standing outside and a guy came over with my lunch and my old man's lunch in his hand. And he says, 'You can have it here on the wood heap, if you want, but you can't eat inside'.*
>
> *So, we said, 'They're your sheep, you can shear them'. If we weren't good enough to eat at his table, we weren't good enough to shear his sheep. And he said, 'Oh, I didn't mean to say that. I didn't know it would affect you.' And he was talking to a human being and when I think about it, it seems to me, he didn't know that.*[171]

In contrast, for many Noongars, sport, especially in country towns, was the one area of life where they were often treated as equals. Neil Phillips, growing up in Perenjori, described how football could, and did, break down barriers.

> The Aboriginal guys in that town were good footballers and football was a leveller. We'd go everywhere in a truck. There was no class distinction. We were friends. If someone had a party, everyone seemed to be invited. Even when I was a kid, I didn't

think there was 'them and us.' I thought I am Neil Phillips and there's Jo Blow over there and we can both kick a football.[172]

And as Ken Colbung wrote in 1979, looking back on the past with hope about the future:

> In spite of all this, the community is looking forward. We want solidarity, because we know that if we do not have a community, if we do not stand as one people, we can be trodden into the dirt, treated as of no account.[173]

Where's all the bush gone?

Chapter 6

The Past Is Still Part of Us

> *Much that we loved is gone and had to go,*
> *But not the deep, indigenous things.*
> *The past is still so much a part of us.*
> *Still about us, still within us.*[1]

Oodgeroo Noonuccal (Kath Walker) makes a plea for Europeans to recognise the depth of Indigenous culture:

> *So Black and White may go forward together*
> *In harmony and brotherhood.*[2]

The poem's title is 'Integration – Yes'. Written in the 1970s, it is a companion piece to another poem written at the same time: 'Assimilation – No'.

> *We are different hearts and minds*
> *In a different body. Do not ask of us*
> *To be deserters, to disown our mother,*
> *To change the unchangeable,*
> *The gum cannot be trained into an oak.*[3]

By the time Oodgeroo Noonuccal wrote these pleas, the push for assimilation had begun to fade and Australia was on the way to becoming a more multicultural society. But the impacts of the earlier policy have been profound and the effects still linger for both Aboriginal and non-Aboriginal Australians. Moreover, as Anna Haebich suggests, there is no one single understanding of the meaning and application of 'assimilation':

> Even during its heyday in the 1950s, politicians, bureaucrats and academics argued over what it meant and used it to push often-conflicting agendas. Today's Indigenous Australians assert that, rather than referring to a distinct policy governing a specific slice of time, assimilation has persisted as core doctrine in policy-making over the generations from first contact to the present.[4]

Irrespective of the definition of assimilation, life for most Aboriginal people still showed little improvement in the mid-twentieth century. The Great Depression of the 1930s, triggered by the American Wall Street financial collapse in late 1929, had caused hardship to people with scant recourse even to the limited social support services available to white Australians. Perth fringe dweller Robert Bropho, born in 1930, described what happened when his father had no work.

> We'd turn back to Native Welfare or Native Department. He'd go to Perth to see Mr Neville…The Native Department was then in Murray Street, the east end of Perth. The rations would be for a fortnight. The ration order would be made out to John Wills in Wellington Street opposite the railway station. Mr Wills was also a sympathetic man to Aboriginal people then. Dad would take myself and my oldest brother, Tom, with him to get these rations. The reason why my eldest brother and I looked forward to ration day, it would be a ride to Perth in the old steam trains…We'd put all these rations into sugar bags and catch the train back to Claremont and walk through the Scots College grounds through Claremont, past Butlers Swamp (Lake Claremont) back to our camp buried away in the hills.[5]

Lake Claremont, formerly Butler's Swamp.

The Depression was swiftly followed by World War Two, which Australia entered on 3 September 1939. However, in February that year, the Commonwealth minister for the interior, John McEwen, discussing the employment of Aboriginal labour in the north, had foreshadowed one aspect of what he hoped would soon become assimilation policy.

> The final objective of the Government in its concern for native Australian people should be the raising of their status so as to enable them by rights, and by qualification to the ordinary rights of citizenship, and enable them and help them to share with us the opportunities that are available in their own native land.[6]

In a land now threatened by widespread war, that objective went on hold, as Paul Hasluck later recalled.

> *Roughly between 1940 and about 1950, there was almost total neglect of any measures for Aborigines. The effect of the war was a complete hiatus between the pre-war movement towards better measures for them*

and a complete gap with no measures at all being taken. We had other preoccupations.[7]

World War Two affected the First Nations people in unforeseen ways. In Western Australia alone, over four hundred Aboriginal men joined the armed forces, and women, regardless of background, were needed to replace former civilians now at war. Helena Clarke, from Port Hedland, volunteered for military service but came up against 'the colour bar':

> *In 1942 I went to get a job in the Armed Forces and the Air Force was the strongest and I had a brother in law in the RAAF and he was the same caste. But when I went in the lass at the doorway said 'What do you want?' I said, 'I want to join the Air Force.' She said, 'You can't. You're black.' I said, 'You're colour blind. I'm brown.'*[8]

Following that rejection, Clarke worked in a Perth florist shop, where the only colour that mattered came from the flowers. After the end of the war, she would help to found a new Aboriginal-run organisation, the Coolbaroo Club.

For many Aboriginal men, volunteering to fight for Australia offered the chance of full-time work. Some did not answer the call to arms on the grounds that, under the terms of the Commonwealth Constitution of 1901, they were not classified as Australian citizens. Others joined up along with white recruits and served overseas. For many it was their first experience of equal pay and frequently comradeship with non-Aboriginal men.

Homecoming in 1945 was less rewarding. When Jim Brennan, from the Eastern Goldfields, got his discharge from the Army, he returned to his community in Leonora where he had white friends.

> *But I couldn't walk with them to have a drink. You couldn't get a decent house to live in. Even the police were checking on you after six o'clock at night, if you got caught in the street, he'd run you in. I ended up fighting against it; I said, 'Why should I come back as a migrant. I was bred and born here.'*[9]

For state authorities the war itself presented unprecedented legal issues. As in World War One there were Aboriginal men in uniform along with white soldiers. In 1941, the secretary of the Barman and Barmaids' Union wrote to Neville's successor, Commissioner for Native Affairs F. I. Bray, about the dilemma facing the members of the union when they were asked to serve drinks to Aboriginal soldiers. If they complied, they broke the law; if they refused, the white soldiers drinking alongside their Aboriginal comrades would inevitably start a brawl. The union secretary suggested that all Aboriginal men in uniform should be exempted from this law. However, Bray rejected this proposal because in his view, 'as a body they (Aboriginal soldiers) were unsuited for that privilege'.[10]

It was not until the last year of the war that the *Natives (Citizenship Rights) Act 1944* brought a partial recognition of Aboriginal men who were serving in or had been members of the Australian armed forces. The Act gave adult Aboriginal people the right to apply for a certificate of citizenship. Application, which had to be made to a magistrate, was permitted only where a person had served in the armed forces or was deemed to be a 'fit and proper person'. At the same time, a person granted citizenship under this legislation had to meet a range of conditions, including the existing legal requirement to not associate with other Aboriginal people.[11] Once granted citizenship, a person was no longer deemed to be an Aboriginal person. In other words, it was impossible to be both Aboriginal and an Australian citizen.[12]

By 1945 servicemen were coming home from dangerous places. Women who had taken their place in essential war work were now seen as redundant. But Aboriginal men and women had glimpsed different possibilities and wanted to make wartime opportunities permanent. Post-war Australia was being pressured by the newly founded United Nations to promote universal political and social human rights. In this context, 'assimilation' into white society appeared to promise equal opportunities for First Nations people. It was intended that they should attain the same manner of living as other Australians and to live as members of a single Australian community.[13]

Paul Hasluck was a strong supporter of assimilation and one of the very few politicians who concerned himself with Aboriginal welfare in the decades after World War Two. Hasluck also acknowledged that:

> Up to the post-war years, 1950, very little was done for them. Very little except by missionaries. The governmental effort throughout Australia and the public effort was very slight.[14]

In 1951, Hasluck became the Commonwealth government's minister for territories. His remit included responsibility for the Northern Territory with its large Aboriginal population. In some ways he was ahead of his time in rejecting the status quo by which some laws applied only to Aboriginal people. Hasluck favoured the abolition of all such laws, which he considered undercut Aboriginal people's legal status as full and equal British subjects.[15] He rejected the concept of separate development which had been official policy in Western Australia since the turn of the century. For Hasluck, assimilation or absorption of Aboriginal people into mainstream Australian society was the best and only alternative to the segregation and separate development policies that had operated in the first half of the twentieth century.[16] His views were summarised in a statement issued by Commonwealth and state ministers at a conference in Darwin in 1963.

> The policy of assimilation means that all Aborigines and part-Aborigines will attain the same manner of living as other Australians and live as members of a single Australian community enjoying the same rights and privileges, accepting the same responsibilities, observing the same customs and influenced by the same beliefs, hopes and loyalties as other Australians.[17]

The statement also talks about 'meeting *their* needs' and 'protecting *them*' (emphasis added). Here lay one of the crucial mistaken assumptions underpinning the concept of assimilation. Aboriginal people were seen as passive players in a situation where white people knew best what was good for them. Hasluck himself, consciously or unconsciously, reinforced this sense of doing things *for* Aboriginal people.

> *Between 1950 and 1965 or thereabouts a great deal was done for them in all parts of Australia both by state governments and the federal governments and what was being done then was producing results. Indeed, nearly all the trophies that are claimed today of successful Aborigines are the results of an education policy in that period.*[18]

This policy was well meant but assumed that Aboriginal people were incapable of self-assistance. Interviewed in 1986, Aboriginal advocate Rob Riley still found it important to emphasise the importance of self-determination.

> *The fact that Aboriginal people themselves are involved in attempting to address the many issues and the experiences of Aboriginal people is something that no European, no matter how involved or how committed they are to Aboriginal issues, will ever have the understanding or the appreciation, simply because they have never had the experience of being an Aboriginal in Australia.*[19]

Fringe dweller Robert Bropho expressed a similar view.

> Aboriginal people and all Ministers concerned in the welfare of Aboriginal people are in a position now to solve the Aboriginal problem, only if the white man was to listen to the black man's ideas and let him make his own decisions, and let him be master of his destiny, and that destiny is land.[20]

The prospect of assimilation and the notion of 'a single Australian community' appeared problematic because there seemed no place for people with both Aboriginal and white ancestors who, in the words of a 1948 Western Australian Government report, presented a 'definite menace'.

In the South of the State there are approximately 3,500 half-castes, presenting an ever-increasing problem from day to day. They are rapidly increasing in number and promise in time to develop from a state of being a mere nuisance as at present to becoming a definite menace. They must be changed from a nomadic, idle and discontented race to a settled, industrious contented section of the community.[21]

In fact, there had been other Australian 'nomads', a decade earlier. During the Great Depression of the 1930s, many white men had become nomadic, walking the back blocks and looking for work. They too had been seen as a menace and a reproachful nuisance by various authorities.

The 1948 Bateman Survey of Native Affairs, like the 1930s Moseley report, was yet another enquiry into 'native institutions' and the 'education and welfare of natives generally'. Both reports were commissioned by the Government of Western Australia and prepared by a white magistrate.[22]

In common with Moseley, F. E. A. Bateman recommended positive changes to the regime governing the lives of Aboriginal people. He stopped short of proposing the repeal of discriminatory legislation, but this time some recommendations were implemented by the newly appointed Commissioner for Native Affairs, Stanley Middleton, who believed in a strong and benevolent approach but also in the educability of 'primitive people'.[23] Overall, the Bateman report, like others before it, failed to appreciate why Australia's First Nations people, including the population of mixed descent, still appeared to be 'an idle and discontented race'.

The original Australians, on the other hand, wanted the latecomers to fully acknowledge their distinct Aboriginal identity. Paradoxically, it was often the adversity they had experienced that spurred them to action. As playwright Jack Davis said of the Moore River experience: *'It made some of us very weak and it made some of us very strong'.*[24]

In Western Australia, as elsewhere in the nation, Aboriginal people began to set up self-help organisations, including the Aboriginal Legal Service and the Aboriginal Medical Service (now the Derbarl Yerrigan Health Service Aboriginal Corporation), both established in Perth in 1973.

More than two decades earlier, the first expression of this demand for rights and recognition of the distinctiveness of their culture had emerged in the form of the Aboriginal-run and owned Coolbaroo League and Coolbaroo Club in Perth. The league came into being in December 1946, thanks to a group of Aboriginal people from across the state. Founding members included former florist and RAAF volunteer Helena Clarke from Port Hedland, Jack and George Poland from Shark Bay, and the only non-Aboriginal, Geoff Harcus, a former soldier who had served with Aboriginal comrades. Clarke summarised their sense of grievance in a submission to the 1948 Bateman inquiry.

> We are the true Australians yet we have to fill in forms to gain citizenship rights before we actually become Australians. We do not belong to any other country – our ancestors were here before the white man.[25]

Coolbaroo is a Yamaji word for magpie – a bird of two hues – and was suggested by George Poland to sum up the club's aim. For Clarke, a black and white bird suggested a symbol of unity between white and black, but also included mixed-race people, the often belittled 'half-castes'.[26]

After World War Two, the four hundred or so Aboriginal soldiers who had joined the armed services found themselves still restricted by state laws. Former Aboriginal soldiers and civilians alike were prohibited from entering social clubs and organisations. In Perth and in most regional towns Aboriginal people were still legally required to be 'off the streets' by 6 pm. The Coolbaroo Club gave Aboriginal people access to aspects of a social life otherwise denied them and helped to build relationships. The organisation began by bringing people together for cultural and social activities, paving the way for Aboriginal-led community development. At the same time, it challenged the expectations of the white public when the club supported public protests as well as dances.[27]

From an assimilationist perspective, the club's aims were seen differently. Commissioner Middleton saw the dances, but also the political activities, as 'training grounds for uplifting Aboriginal individuals and families to the standard considered suitable for the white community'.[28] Middleton was sympathetic to the aspirations of the Coolbaroo founders. His commitment to his work as commissioner in WA came from highly personal experience.

> From earliest childhood until I left home at the age of seventeen, I heard so frequently the story of my birth and the role played by the kindly Aborigines that it requires no effort even now to recount word for word as told to me by my mother. It never failed to stir me emotionally…I often considered in those early days, if ever and how I might be able to repay in some measure the kindness of these gentle people…When I was placed in charge of the Native Affairs department in Western Australia, I perceived the opportunity to contribute something towards their welfare and took as much advantage of it as the limits of Government policy, politics, money and public attitudes would permit. I know I succeeded up to a point but wish I could have done more. I – we – owe it to them.[29]

Along with Paul Hasluck, Middleton attended social events at the Coolbaroo Club and, like Hasluck, saw political and social value in portraying the Coolbaroo Club to government as a racially unifying movement, in effect as an instrument to progress assimilation.

Historian Angela Lapham has re-evaluated Stanley Middleton's achievements as commissioner for native affairs. She suggests that he is an unappreciated figure because, in advocating for the inclusion of Aboriginal people in Australian society, he went well beyond the role of a public servant in championing their rights. Yet Lapham also points to Middleton's assumption that Aboriginal people aspired to the European way of life, and it was this conviction that led him to support the policy of removing Aboriginal children from their families so that they could be brought up within a 'white' culture. It was this policy which directly resulted in the Stolen Generations, and Lapham concludes that:

> Understanding how such contradictions occur is important for future motivations may albeit unintentionally replicate the assimilation era and governments may be tempted to renege on commitments to preserve Aboriginal culture, community and autonomy if these become costly, impracticable or incompatible with overcoming socio-economic disadvantage.[30]

Noongar woman Lynnette Coomer shares Lapham's concern, and asserts that some government actions today still replicate, if unwittingly, earlier policies under which children were removed from their Aboriginal families.

> *Grandparents who live here, where I live in Kwinana, are raising their second family, to keep the department away from actually taking their children, of disconnecting them. Aboriginal people are happier and more content when their children are housed with their own kind because, after all, we are the best people for cultural awareness and mental health awareness.*[31]

Even in the 1940s and early 1950s, Helena Clarke and her co-founders of the Coolbaroo League believed in the importance of a distinct culture and that the separate identity of people with Aboriginal heritage should be accepted and understood. In their view, First Nations people should not be regarded as 'coloured imitations of white Australians'.[32] The Coolbaroo Club became the one place where skin colour was not an issue. Elder Ben Taylor recalled its social life: *'It will always be with us. It gave us that time together, to be happy, to forget about the police and live our life, dancing.'*[33]

Coolbaroo Club dances, which were attended by families and friends, were constantly under surveillance by police, looking for Aboriginal people drinking. That alone made the club impose strict rules of its own, forbidding any member to bring alcohol onto the dance floor. The organisers also had to find venues – like a hall in East Perth just outside the area of central Perth, which Aboriginal people were not permitted to enter – and meeting places such as converted stables at the back of Trades Hall.[34]

The Coolbaroo League's efforts were not confined to Perth. A branch was set up in York, with the aim of helping younger people with evening classes in 'industrial art, elocution and deportment'.[35] By the mid-1950s, the league had established dances and social events in regional towns, including Narrogin, Katanning and Pinjarra. But in some places members still encountered hostility. Anna Haebich cites a reception in Katanning where the league secretary, Nora Shea, had booked accommodation for the dance organisers. Arriving at the hotel, they were turned away by the

Perth Trades Hall, Beaufort Street.

owner on the grounds that they were Aboriginal. Geoff Harcus recalled the ensuing argument in which the proprietor verbally abused the group, then turned on him, shouting, 'And you, you boong lover, get out of my hotel'.[36]

The Coolbaroo League continued to operate into the early 1960s. It ran a film club and in 1953 printed its own newspaper, *The Westralian Aborigine*, publishing stories that did not always come off other printing presses.[37] But perhaps its most enduring achievement was that it demonstrated to both black and white what an Aboriginal-run organisation could accomplish. The First Australians had asserted their cultural identity and distinctiveness in a way recognisable to many white people. Founders and followers of the League took up causes such as equal pay and political recognition, issues later seen as important in the 1967 referendum campaign.

In that post-war period many Aboriginal people were still subsisting in makeshift housing within the Perth Metropolitan Area. There were groups living in East Perth, Shenton Park and Daglish and also near the Fremantle cemetery off Carrington Street. Perth-based historian Denise Cook, who has researched life in these bush camps, has found limited evidence of contact with white people living close by.

> *I think a lot of people didn't know the camps were there. Some people have said to me, 'Oh we knew it was there, but we were too scared to go in there'. There was some contact but I don't think it was very much. It was a case of 'out of sight, out of mind'.*[38]

Denise became interested in these camps, partly because her own father went to school in Claremont in the 1940s and 1950s. 'He didn't know anything about the camps. I didn't know anything about the camps. How did I not know about this history?'[39]

So why did these places exist?

> *It was really difficult to rent a house. So, they built camps in bush areas because these were the only spaces they could find to live in and also because people had a traditional connection to certain places.*[40]

Corrie Bodney was one of many people Denise interviewed about bush camp life.

> We really enjoyed life in the bush, you know. We were bred and born to live in the bush, because things were just sort of free and easy, we could do what we wanted to do. You got no commitments, you know, you don't pay rent, you don't pay gas, you don't pay electricity. You don't pay for water.[41]

Despite Corrie's view of his world, this was not an easy life. People chose places where they could access building materials, so many settled near rubbish tips and locations where they could also obtain food.[42] Others benefitted from living on or near a property where a sympathetic owner would give them access to water.

Aboriginal women living in bush camps often found jobs as domestic servants but their hours of work could conflict with the 6 pm curfew within Perth's central business district. Beryl Hoffman's father had a farm near the Shenton Park camp.

> He used to say that the women used to get cajoled, made to stop back and serve up dinner, or finish off some extra work so they'd be late home for the curfew. If they were late home from curfew and they were out on the street, they used to get picked up and put into the lockups overnight.[43]

Beryl's father often came to their rescue: 'He would put some produce from the farm on the back of his truck; chicken, meat, eggs etc. and drive to the police station, and basically, bribe the police.'[44] Farm produce was exchanged for their release.

> The women would come out of the police station with their shopping bags, get underneath the tarp on the back of the truck and he would drive them to the Shenton Park camp.[45]

Camp life was the norm for many Aboriginal families. Robert Bropho lived in makeshift homes for most of his life:

living under wheat bags. And I remember my father cutting the sticks of the peppermint tree to make a shade and making stick beds, and going out and putting pepper-tree leaves down for mattresses, and going out and walking the streets, asking people for old clothes and selling drink bottles, and asking for stale bread. That's fringe-dwelling lifestyle of Aboriginal people from the mid-1930s, coming right up to now.[46]

Bropho also recalled going to see his grandmother, Clara Leyland, in Daglish.

> I can see her there walking with her from there through the high scrub to the old Shenton Park rubbish tip, digging through there, looking for bottles, copper wire…And on her way home, looking through the bush tracks to see if any green grocer loads had been dumped with fruit. We'd go over, rattle through it, get the best of apples, the best of oranges, if there's any there, bits of carrot and a bit of potatoes, clean them up have a good feed…So, in them days, a lot of bush, hardly any help and you had to walk miles.[47]

Louise Walsh (nee Bodney) spent her childhood years at the Shenton Park Bush Camp.

> The camp was made from old tins, sheets of tins, whatever they could find. Had the poles. Just chop them down. The big brothers used to build it. Mum always had a little rockery made out of sandstone…It was quite beautiful.[48]

Not a life that most white people would have appreciated, but, as Louise told Denise Cook, 'We lived life, we just didn't have electricity and all that – we just lived the best we could'.[49]

And that 'best', as Cook understood it, was that:

there were probably similarities in the sense of families camping together so that camps were a kind of extended family, rather than a whole lot of different families. And there was this whole idea of helping each other and sharing and also of culture being stronger because they were living together in that camp.[50]

For Louise Walsh's niece, Lynnette Coomer, life as a small child in the bush camps was the:

> *best life ever! I had my connections with my grandmother, 'cause we used to do a lot of things together. I loved my grandmother, 'cause we lived in the bush, we used to do a lot of bushwalking and we used to help her pick all the flowers because my grandmother used to dye them. Yeah, it's being connected to your grandmother. And if your Mum wasn't home or she had to go somewhere, grandmother was there. I had strong connection with my Mum as well.*[51]

The 'best life' was not to last, however.

> *I think it was due to the Native Welfare Department wanting to take the children away, to disconnect us from our roots from our family. The bush camp was pretty well protected but my family had moved to different places due to the Department's chasing us. I don't think I completed more than a year's education at Jolimont Primary School because I spent some time at Bibra Lake Primary School before I was institutionalised. I took a lot of memories with me to the mission.*[52]

Jolimont Primary School today.

Aged seven, Lynnette was sent to Roelands Mission, north of Bunbury.

> *Being disconnected from your family and the bush lifestyle and going to man-built homes of whatever materials and having white people, like missionaries, looking at you first thing in the morning and the last person you see at night-time. That stays with you. But the sense that I took into the mission was talking about how we used to sit around the camp fires and how we used to play in the bush, make up our own games.*[53]

Bush camp life remained a reality for some Aboriginal people many years after Lynnette was sent to Roelands but, as Cook notes:

> At some point there was more pressure for people to go into state housing when that became available. Corrie Bodney was living with his family in a camp in Eden Hill. And this bloke said 'You know you can get one of these houses', and Corrie said 'Well, I've got no money to do that and I've got no furniture'. And the guy said 'Don't worry about that, I'll help you'. Corrie talked about moving into this house in the middle of the night because they were so embarrassed that they had so little to put into it. They didn't want everybody to know.[54]

Eden Hill, Success Hill and Bennett Brook, localities north of Bassendean, were places of great significance to the local Aboriginal people and were popular camping spots. Some Noongars had legally owned land and property in these districts before the area was taken over by the State Housing Commission. These families had been protected by the Hamersley family, whose Lockridge and Pyrton properties, with their sources of good water, had been a refuge for almost one hundred years.[55] In an interview recorded for the State Library of WA in 1995, Judy Hamersley reiterated her understanding that this country was important to Aboriginal people.

There are just a series of springs all the way up to where Bennett Brook comes out of the black soil swamps some miles up near Whiteman Park. There's very good soil and very good water there. It was a very well-used, well-known camping place and the Hamersleys always accepted that this was a native camping place.

They were entitled to camp there and the only rule was if there was drinking and fighting, they'd get chucked off, otherwise they were always welcome to camp there. It was the very obvious place as far they were concerned because they were close to the river for fishing, close to good water and close to hunting in that the native animals had to drink too and they would go down to these black soil swamps.[56]

Entitled or not, some local authorities, including the then Bassendean Road Board, felt threatened by such camps and subjected them to periodic inspections and harassment. In particular, the local authority queried whether it was actually legal for Aboriginal people to be landowners, given that few

Bennett Brook at Mussel Pool, Whiteman Park.

title holders lived in conventional houses. The board therefore issued eviction orders to four Noongar landowners. It also made a submission to the Bateman Survey of Native Affairs arguing that all Aboriginal people who were not actually home or land owners should be removed from the district.[57]

In Perth's western suburbs, the last camps were demolished in the early 1960s, although people still camped at Fremantle's South Beach in the 1980s and later. Demolitions were not always sensitively handled. On one occasion, someone from the Department (of Native Welfare) wrote on the file, 'I think if this had been the camp of a non-Aboriginal person, it would have been handled differently'.[58] As Middleton wrote in his 1950 report:

> *Fifty years ago [1900] they weren't wanted in the metropolitan area and they're still not wanted now. And there only has to be a whiff of a rumour that we're thinking of settling Aboriginal people on some piece of land in the metro area and there's some huge outcry against it.*[59]

In some ways the camps did provide a place where Aboriginal people could live without fear of complaints from the white majority. Cook concludes that:

> *people have different memories as to whether the camps were a positive or negative experience. For children, it was a time of being close to family before they were taken away to missions for example, a time when things were free and easy, and it is hard to unpick how much of that is nostalgia for a childhood that seemed to hold fewer responsibilities.*
>
> *And it was obviously a different lifestyle, much closer to traditional lifestyle. Many Aboriginal people now living in the suburbs still follow traditional practices today, but they are more geographically separated. I can see that in the camps there was that sense of separateness but, at the same time, families were supporting each other.*[60]

For Lynnette Coomer, the bush camp at Shenton Park, with all its material disadvantages, was still home, while Roelands Mission was, in every sense, 'not home':

Roelands Mission today.

> With all the things they told you, not to use your language, not to do any Aboriginal things or anything like that, but bible, bible, bible. We had the bible, which was their culture.[61]

Roelands Native Mission Farm had been opened in 1938 by Albany Bell, a well-known sponsor of child welfare activities and the first president of the Native Welfare Council of WA. In 1941 Roelands became a home for 'part-Aboriginal children' under eight years old, including those classified under the *Native Administration Act 1936* as 'quadroons'. A Protestant institution, Roelands was managed by the United Aborigines Mission. By 1952, it housed seventy-eight children and included an on-site primary school.[62] Older children like Lynnette Coomer, who remained at Roelands in their teenage years, went by mission bus to Harvey High School. But Roelands did not offer family life and no adult Aboriginal people lived there.[63] Only the missionaries' children had parents.[64] For Lynnette:

> Night time was the hardest. We used to lie down and all share each other's stories. At night time, the scent of my mother would always come

> *to me. It's so different. You don't think about these things as a child, but when you're an adult all these things keep coming back.*[65]

As for many Aboriginal people who grew up in missions, Lynnette's experience of being parted from family has lasted a lifetime.

> *Being in the mission and as you grow up, there are a lot of things that keep coming back to you. You have flashbacks and you see yourself as the child there and the missionaries' children had their mums and dads with them. We didn't have ours. As a child, you don't take that on board. But I think this is part of the trauma that we go through. We don't think it affects us but it does. People think that life is OK for you but deep down, everything goes into dormant mode until you speak it out and talk about it. It doesn't keep it in. All you can do is talk and share.*[66]

Up to the 1960s, government authorities, always known to Aboriginal people as 'the Welfare', and church missionaries worked together. Their actions were based on the assumption that Aboriginal children could be helped to a 'better life' if they accepted all facets of white culture, including the Christian religion. In the south of the state, places like Roelands played an important role in this endeavour.

In the north of Western Australia there was sometimes, as Christine Choo has noted, a greater willingness among the missionaries to study traditional cultures and to invite contact with anthropologists. Benedictine Father Eugene Perez, based at Kalumburu in the Kimberley, came to appreciate the Aboriginal sense of belonging to land and the importance of recognising their need to remain connected to country.

> We need not wonder at the great attraction which the bush, and bush life has for these Aborigines, when we consider that it has no little enchantment for us. The bush is part of their aboriginal life, and often their best medicine. It would be, therefore, both cruel and imprudent to deprive them of it altogether. They need

> it now...and then in any case, if not given them, they will simply take it.[67]

Some visitors found other missionaries less in tune with the beliefs and culture of their charges. In 1963, anthropologist Robert Tonkinson spent several months at Jigalong Mission on the western edge of the Little Sandy Desert. This mission had been established by a Pentecostal denomination, the Apostolic church. Tonkinson later wrote a paper entitled 'Reflections on a failed crusade' about his time there.[68] More recently he has again reflected on working with, and learning from, the Martu people nearly sixty years ago. He observed, perhaps also in an anthropological context, the relationship between missionaries and the locals. Did they, for example, investigate the spiritual beliefs of their potential converts?

> *My feeling was that the missionaries' fundamentalism, their certainty of the one true God, closes down what one would think would be a desire to understand. The best way to understand is clearly through talking in the local language. But because these Aboriginal men had come in from the stations, they'd just about all worked on the stations, at the edge of the desert, they had some English so communication was possible.*

But was 'some English' helpful or otherwise in terms of understanding and communication?

> *For the most part there was a severe language barrier, with everybody speaking Martu Wangka as their first language and in that massive desert area, there's only one language with several mutually intelligible dialects.*[69]

Would the missionaries have learned more about the beliefs of the local people if they had learned the local language?

> *They thought that these people have no religion, were lost and totally under the control of the devil, and that approach is the antithesis of anthropology, where you're trying to elicit as much as possible about anything and everything, particularly when religion is in everything, in the landscape and their stories for that landscape. Where you don't try to*

understand that, there's a good chance that your work with them is not going to bring about a marvellous Baptism of the Holy Spirit, where they will become God's Children.

So, was this a case of misinterpretation?

It all comes back to this massive gulf of not understanding. If you go out into the desert with the notion that these people are children of the devil and lust and depravity, then how much good can you do? The idea that you can simply pray and thus achieve your goals. Nobody bought it. Very few Martu converted.[70]

Christian cultural assumptions of doctrinal superiority went with a parallel belief in confrontation. The sword has often featured as strongly as the cross, as Tonkinson notes:

European religion carries military connotations like "Crusade", triumphing over the false beliefs of "primitive people". The well-known hymn "Onward Christian Soldiers" captures that perspective.[71]

Working with Martu Wangka speakers, Tonkinson observed another theology, one not based on scripture but both practical and ecological.

If you think of their religious knowledge, some of the songlines are very relevant. They're short verses, maybe four or six, repeated and repeated. A group of twenty men would be out in the bush singing out the lines and correcting each other, listening until they got it right. 'That's him now. We've got it.'

Those songlines were so huge you had to have collective memory to store that stuff. You've got to have the right words but they've got to tell you what's going on. They might say 'Creek' or 'Big Stone'. You've got to join the dots. They're word maps of country.

In his time at Jigalong, Robert Tonkinson was initially aware of the missionaries' concern about his presence as an anthropologist. While he developed friendly relationships with several of the missionaries, he felt in some ways that these Christians had locked themselves out of helpful understanding of the people they were hoping to convert to their religion:

> *You've got deep faith in God, but then again that goes with all sorts of negatives about Aboriginal people, for example that 'their brains are smaller than ours'.*

If that were the case, he says, it would not explain their long survival.

> *It's the oldest and most enduring adaptation – and why? In dry country you move to resources when you need to. You can get out of trouble with encyclopaedic knowledge of the country, and travel at speed by night. And in an extreme climate they know what to do in hot season. You stay in the shade. You don't get up and gather a thing and you don't hunt a thing. It's the perfect adaptation.*

As he suggests:

> *This knowledge has been passed on for thousands of years. And it comes from an intimate reading of what's going on around you. You're in the desert and you get to a hole. The question is, 'Is there a lizard down the bottom of that hole?' Have you got a nice big Bungarra down there or, as with the rabbits, there are fifty exits? People lacking the desert people's knowledge wander round and very quickly say, 'No, there's nothing there' just by looking at things that we don't see, but they do.*[72]

As with the word 'savages', which derives from the Italian and Latin words for forest dwellers,[73] the term 'nomad' is often used to suggest evidence that the 'natives' were a 'primitive people', who had not learned to 'settle down' in one place like other 'civilised' human beings. Anthropologist Professor Sandy Toussaint has observed that the term 'nomadic' was coined by nineteenth- and twentieth-century scientists, missionaries and government commentators to suggest that Aboriginal Australians wandered aimlessly and lacked enduring cultural, geographic and environmental knowledge about and interconnections with particular lands, rivers and coastlines.

This misguided suggestion overlooked the great value of the laws, beliefs and practices Aboriginal women, men and children learned and handed on for countless generations through mediums such as storytelling, ritual enactments, painting. Cultural mapping and everyday activities, sometimes known publicly as the Dreaming, guided their lives and identified their Country and foreshadowed who, in future generations, would eventually succeed as custodians of those lands and waters, and all they contained. In other words, First Nations people lived anything other than aimless, nomadic lives, as the significant High Court Decision in Mabo versus The Commonwealth *clearly established in 1992.*[74]

While the Protestant missionaries at Jigalong in the 1960s might have missed opportunities, a different dialogue emerged within a decade at Balgo Mission, managed by the Pallottine Fathers. As anthropologist Peter Bindon has acknowledged:

The Pallottines have a record in Australia of having people of science among their ranks and they were very keen to do a bit of each way bargaining with Aboriginal people. It didn't always happen. It developed over the years, but they were always interested in what Aboriginal people were doing and how they were understanding things.[75]

Father Anthony Rex Peile, originally from Melbourne, worked in several missions in north-western Australia before arriving in 1973, at Balgo Mission (now the Wirrimanu community) some 200 kilometres south of Halls Creek. He undertook linguistic research and, in keeping with the Pallottines' scientific bent, set out to amass information on Aboriginal views about health and sickness. Peile's aim was to help health workers deliver appropriate medical assistance. The key, he considered, was an understanding of the culture and patterns of thought prevalent among the Kukatja people.[76]

Peile worked at Balgo for sixteen years until his death from cancer in 1989, aged fifty-eight. Peter Bindon met the dedicated missionary-priest during his own time at Balgo in the 1970s and 1980s. He cites a journalist's description of Peile as:

a burly middle-aged priest chauffeuring parties of Aboriginal grannies in a battered four-wheel drive through the mulga to look for plants, an image not easily understood or accepted by people living in the city. To them, priests belong in churches. Aboriginal Grandmothers spend their time waiting for the next welfare cheque and bush medicine belongs to a past as distant as the tribal grounds where it was practised.[77]

Priest and 'mulga chauffeur', Peile made it his business to learn about native plants both from academic study and in the field from his 'teacher' grandmothers. He saw knowledge of bush medicine as helpful in his concern for Aboriginal health in a situation where diet and living conditions had changed, following increased contact with white medicine, white food and white drink.

Father Peile was also keenly aware of the need to communicate effectively with custodians of botanical knowledge in order to both obtain that knowledge and preach the gospel. He recognised the importance of speaking the local language, in this context, Kukatja. Peter Bindon recalled that, *'Peile had a huge card index of Kukatja words and their meanings and the local people said of him, "Oh he's very good. He speaks very good Kukatja."'*[78]

So, was he more than just a conventional missionary?

> *The fact that he was very keen to preach and present Christian doctrines and rituals in their language, demonstrates that he was doing more than trying to proselytise. If he was only trying to convert people, he'd have done what many other missionaries did: make them do everything in English. He prayed and preached in Kukatja. In doing that he was ahead of his time.*[79]

The title of Peile's posthumously published treatise *Body and Soul* reveals that, while a committed Catholic missionary, he also appreciated the Kukatja awareness of spiritual life. Writing of their sense of 'spirit', Peile notes that:

> Aboriginals do not have a purely spiritual concept of their spirit beings, mythical beings or characters. They are seen as both

tangible and intangible, as material and spiritual – they are personal and social…Even though Aborigines see their spiritual beings then, as supernatural, this 'supernaturality' is not to be understood from the Judeo-Christian point of view where the supernatural is considered to be transcendent to man's human nature. Nor is it to be understood along the lines of the Greek Stoic pneuma, the all-pervading spirit in man and in the universe. Rather the Aborigine sees the spirit as something immanent, in-dwelling and pervading not only the human body, but also the universe or 'sections' within it. The spirits in people are those left in waterholes by the mythical spirits after the shaping and formation of the world. These spirits are known as 'spirit children'.[80]

Peile related this understanding of 'spirit' to the health of a person.

For the Kukatja, when any part of the body is in pain, the person's spirit is also suffering. This also points to a hazy dualism of the body and the spirit that they hold. 'The stick pierced his hand. His spirit was in pain all the time'.[81]

Peile chronicles other responses from the Balgo community that link body and spirit. Many of these relate to the conditions of life in a demanding terrain and climate:

I was tired out and exhausted, my stomach was bad, I will sit down. I came from a distance and was exhausted, my spirit was very much in pain.

and

As I have no water, my spirit has become narrow. On account of not having any water, my intestines have become narrow.[82]

Peter Bindon's own field observations, as an anthropologist at Balgo, led him to a similar understanding of 'spirit'.

I never asked Kukatja people for a definition of 'soul' in that way and it's quite hard to define these things in another culture. Spirit for them was nothing ghostlike. I think it was more an animating force. They used to say, 'A good spirit, cold and dry'. The spirit had a lot to do with breath and wind and natural animation. But the animating force was what they talked about when they were thinking about spirit. To say that 'A good spirit is cold and dry' is interesting because obviously 'hot and wet' is 'sweaty and fevered'. So, I think 'spirit' is not only the animating force of life but more directly associated with health.[83]

Bindon also recalls that the Kukatja sense of an animate world did not apply solely to humans, other animals and plants. More recently he asked an Aboriginal man how he knew what was alive and what was not. From a European perspective one could argue that:

Plants were pretty obvious. You pulled one out of the ground and it shrivelled and died and animals and people were easily seen as alive or dead. 'But what about rocks?' And he said 'Oh, rocks are alive too. They move but they move so slowly we just don't notice it.' And, coming from a geological background, of course they do move. They erode. They change shape but they do it so slowly.[84]

Rocks are alive too.

The animate world aside, how can we evaluate Father Peile's work and the approach that he took to his role as both priest and ethnobotanist? Bindon suggests that these endeavours remind us to explore the 'other' and learn in the process.

> *In articles that he'd written and what he and I talked about, they were telling him lots of things about their health and well-being. But whether they were the sorts of lessons that a European could absorb easily and benefit from is another question. Our conceptions of health and how health services are delivered are very culturally inclined.*[85]

One understanding which Bindon witnessed was an unexpected cultural acceptance by both Europeans and locals.

> *There was an open-air mass for the feast of Pentecost and the Aboriginal people had obviously been discussing Pentecost with the priest and vice versa. The Pentecost mass is one where there are references to the descent of fire from God to the apostles. And it was symbolised by these tongues of flame which stood on their foreheads. The mass started off in the usual way and, from memory, it was a mass in English.*
>
> *But when the service came to the point where the Epistle and the Gospel happen, the priest stopped and introduced the Aboriginal people. And the older men appeared, dressed very ceremonially, all painted up and with gum leaves tied to their legs. They did this little ceremony about the arrival of fire.*
>
> *People felt the power of the two stories: the business of the Apostles who were to go forth and preach the word as well as the business of the people accepting the arrival of fire which would change their lives, being able to cook food instead of eating it raw. I felt it marked an acceptance of different ideas by the two cultures.*[86]

Another very different acceptance had existed within the north-west pastoral industry. Aboriginal station workers had been largely unpaid. But the onset of World War Two changed that acceptance. It had shown some Aboriginal stockmen that there was paid work beyond the station gate. Defence construction had offered new employment opportunities. Options ranged from wharf work on the Port Hedland harbour to employment in the military camps along the northern Australian coast. While they received less money than white men, remuneration was still in stark contrast to 'station pay', as stockman Peter Coppin recalled:

> I think I was paid nothing. Nothing at all, just clothes and a bit of tucker. I was young and just liked to do work. But we were working for nothing. Some not even getting tucker. People had to feed from the river sometimes.[87]

The 1905 Roth report had recommended that Aboriginal stockmen should be paid at least a token monetary wage (50 cents per month) but this recommendation had not been implemented when the legislation was introduced into Parliament in 1905. Almost half way through the twentieth century many workers were still paid only in food and clothing for themselves and their families.[88]

When pastoralists did, at least notionally, pay money to Aboriginal employees, the workers hardly saw it. Peter Coppin's experience was of being continually in debt to the station manager.

> We paid for boots with that same money, and trousers. Got to pay for woman's dress, tobacco. We in debt all year round. Never get off the debt. That's the way they keep us there all the time. If a man wants to go away, the station manager would call the police, fetch him back because 'you owe too much in the station'.[89]

For station hands in the Pilbara the immediate problem was how to achieve wage justice. In 1942, while Australia was still at war, an organised group of Aboriginal station workers sought assistance from a white man, mineral prospector Don McLeod, who had helped an injured member of their group to get to hospital.[90]

McLeod had gone to the Pilbara to make his fortune and was initially reluctant to get involved in an industrial wage campaign.

I was drawn in insidiously and I don't know how I got caught up in it. But the more I found out about their plight, I was appalled. I realised that unless they got some help they would be destroyed by the state.[91]

McLeod's caution was based on his recognition that industrial action in wartime would be seized on by the authorities. Strikers might well be charged with treason and end up in gaol. He also became aware, as he researched the situation, that the conditions of pastoral employment dated back to nineteenth-century legislation and stipulated that a 'native' could not leave his place of employment without the permission of his employer or of the police.[92] This condition, he felt, had additional implications for any proposed walk-off by Aboriginal workers.

Given the risks of unpopular action in wartime, McLeod urged caution. He agreed to talk again with the station hands who had approached him but thought it unlikely they would reach broad agreement with other Aboriginal workers on taking joint action. But the convenors of the proposed protest surprised him by inviting him to attend an intercommunal meeting in 1942 at Skull Springs, east of Nullagine.

Skull Springs (photo by Jill Harrison).

I was guided there by three blackfellas, men of high degree who'd been giving me some sort of background as to what blackfellas' law was about. Now this meeting was like some small sort of United Nations. It took six weeks...We had sessions every morning to talk the plan through. We had twenty-three languages. We had sixteen interpreters. So, I can assure you there was a lot to say and it took a long time to say it. But after six weeks everybody was satisfied. They had the guts to do it and were stalwart enough to do it. It was the first time that organised blackfellas had come together from all over the state and beyond.[93]

A strategy was agreed.

We came away with an arrangement that if we couldn't make the authorities agree to pay their rent after forty years of not paying, then, then they would come out on strike and they'd stay on strike until they got the conditions they wanted.[94]

But the Aboriginal workers also accepted McLeod's advice to wait until the end of the war before taking action. Potential strikers had to be patient. In 1942 the Japanese armies were still undefeated. Darwin and Broome had been bombed and no one could foresee when, or how, World War Two would end.

They set a date: one year after the end of the war in Europe. The agreement remained a well-kept secret. Young activist Dorothy Hewett travelled north with aspiring lawyer Lloyd Davies six months after the strike began on 1 May 1946. She was told how the industrial action had been timed and organised for the start of the shearing season but that the 'penny did not drop' for the station owners.

Aboriginal people on the stations were given a calendar showing May the first with a big red ring around it. They kept asking the station owners when was May the first. And the station owners thought this was very peculiar. 'What do they want to know for? Oh, they must be going walkabout.' But on that particular day most of them walked off the stations.[95]

A day earlier, 30 April, shearer Sam Coppin headed for Bangalow station and put the station boss in the picture:

> *'There's your sheep. You can take them away for shearing in the morning.' Of course, they got the calendar there and they walk off in the morning. 'Tell the boss we're going away finish.' And the boss wasn't happy about it. He said, 'Who tell you fellers to pull out, walk off the station?'*
>
> *'Oh, we know, we got our calendar. We want to all go away.'*
>
> *'Well, why shouldn't you fellers tell me when you want to walk away?'*
>
> *'We don't have to! We don't have to! When we want to go away, we go away.'*[96]

As members of the Communist Party, Dorothy Hewett and Lloyd Davies were keen to report on the strike for the party's newspaper, *Morning Star*. They arrived in Port Hedland in December 1946. Posing as casual visitors, they hoped to contact Don McLeod and cover the story of the continuing strike. But McLeod was by now a fugitive and *Morning Star* was the only newspaper prepared to cover the story of the strike. The mainstream Perth press remained silent.

The authorities retaliated harshly, denying the strikers customary rations. Hewett's first impression was of 'an incredible hostility towards the Aboriginal people. It was quite outside anything I had seen before.'[97]

Wartime austerity still prevailed for everybody and Aboriginal people could obtain food only through a coupon system. Pastoralists would not provide coupons to the striking stockmen and their families. The strike dragged on. McLeod did a spell in gaol for 'entering a native camp and inciting people to leave their place of employment'.

Now camped at an area known as 'The Twelve Mile', north of Port Hedland, the Aboriginal stockmen took matters into their own hands. Believing that McLeod was in gaol for attempting to get their food coupons restored, they marched into town en masse. McLeod recalled the town's reaction.

> There were only about 150 people in Port Hedland in those days. And the storekeeper just opposite the police station thought they were after him. He deliberately sold a case of stick tobacco the day before so he could truthfully say he had no tobacco. And he thought they were going to wreak vengeance on him. So, he dived over to Dalgety's store to buy a packet of bullets for his revolver and he was going to defend his life till the last bullet. They just ignored him, went into the police station and held the police station up.[98]

McLeod was freed. But in total he was charged and tried seven times during the strike, for the offences of being within five chains (one hundred metres) of a congregation of natives and also for inciting natives to leave their 'lawful place of employment'.[99]

The principal strikers, Clancy McKenna and Dooley Bin Bin, also did time for breaking their terms of employment. But 'Blackfellas' Eureka' set a regional precedent. In 1949 Mt Edgar and Limestone stations in the Pilbara agreed to pay their Aboriginal stockmen three pounds a week and an allowance for specific skills. In the Kimberley, however, Aboriginal pastoral workers were still mainly paid in kind, and this remained the norm for another twenty years.

In 1965 the Commonwealth government's Conciliation and Arbitration Commission began to examine wage justice for all northern Aboriginal station hands and their families. This was in line with the government's pre-war resolve to create 'opportunities that are available to them in their own native land'. Australia was under international pressure to improve human rights and social justice for its First Nations people. Pat Dodson saw this undertaking as:

> the glimpse of equality, of being treated as equals, respect for the rights of Aboriginal people to their country, to their language, to their ceremony, to their social way of living.[100]

Questions about pay and conditions for Indigenous workers in northern Australia had pre-dated Don McLeod's earlier support in the 1940s for Aboriginal workers in the Pilbara. In the 1920s this had been both an industrial and a racial issue. As historian Ann McGrath pointed out, the White Australia policy was also trade union policy at that time.

> *The North Australian Workers Union very actively fought against Aboriginal people being allowed into the union. But they also put up a very big case to argue that they, themselves, should get paid higher wages because they had to supervise Aboriginal people, and that therefore the latter should not be put in their award at all.*[101]

Kimberley stockman Jacky Dan described a situation that had prevailed since the previous century.

> *We grew up in station and we bin ringing in there. And the station manager, or the station owner, we got to show him where the cattle run and how to get around but when the work starts, we were going from there and never stop – droving cattle, mustering and branding – because we were the cheap labour. Aboriginal people were the cheap labour. And, in this land, we pay the price – from all that we get nothing back.*[102]

The notion of 'pay' was hard to define. It could be described as reciprocal in a non-monetary sense. Both parties needed each other, given the scarcity of white labour in the north-west and the fact that the pastoral industry had changed the Aboriginal way of life. Many of the local inhabitants were now dependent on working for pastoralists in return for basic food and clothing. They had adapted well to the pastoral life. They proved to be skilled horsemen and their work offered an opportunity to stay 'on country'. In many situations both parties reached an accommodation between retention of culture and pastoralists' requirements. Ann McGrath suggests that Aboriginal employees had some bargaining power here.

> *Working on the cattle stations enabled them to keep looking after sites. One thing that people repeatedly said to me was, 'We held onto that place. We didn't forget that place, didn't lose that place.' That was because as part of the cattle station work, they could make sure nobody*

> was chopping down a valued tree. They could make sure the boss didn't put a dam in a sacred place. I don't think they would have said to the boss, 'That's a sacred place'. Somehow, they would have got around him and pointed out a better place for the dam. They were negotiating things which they felt were really important to their identity and their kids' future to hold onto the country. It was a retention not only of land and its ancient associations but also of the much newer world of pastoral life and work.[103]

Pastoral 'pay' of any kind varied from station to station but cash was frequently not in evidence. There might be a few pound notes paid out to stockmen if the whole station community went off to the races in the nearest town. Yet, for the most part, remuneration came via a largely welfare-based system. The pastoral owner or manager could provide new boots and clothing such as shirts and hats. Food and some accommodation were provided, while Aboriginal women who worked as cooks or household servants were similarly compensated.

In the context of isolated station life, for both pastoralists and stockmen, money was also often 'invisible'. Small towns and shops were a long way from most properties. Where station owners paid cash, they often used a compulsory savings scheme, paying money into individual accounts from which employees could draw as needed. But, as McGrath points out, there were flaws in that arrangement because station workers:

> didn't understand about book-keeping or about money being deducted out of your salary. They might work for six months and find there was none left because taking things out of the store from their account, they'd used up their cash supply.

The system also lacked transparency.

> You also don't know whether book-keepers were scrupulous, or whether they really were robbing them. A lot of money had to go into trust for the government. Aboriginal people hardly ever saw that money. It was put into savings accounts but they were not told how to access it. They had to

ask permission from a chief protector or a government man to spend their money. A woman would say, 'I would like a beautiful white dress'. And there'd be this scoffing letter back saying, 'What's the point of this woman having a white dress. It would soon get dirty and she doesn't need such an expensive dress.'[104]

In 1965, earlier defenders of the White Australia policy, the North Australian Workers Union (NAWU), now argued the case for 'equal wages' for Aboriginal pastoral workers. Its new president, Jack McGuinness, a well-respected Aboriginal leader, took the NAWU in a new direction and campaigned strongly for wage justice. However, no Aboriginal people were present at the Commonwealth Conciliation and Arbitration Commission hearings. Emeritus Professor Hal Wootten, then a young lawyer, was junior counsel assisting John Kerr QC for the pastoralists' case. Despite his brief, Wootten was personally sympathetic to the argument for Aboriginal equal pay and was conscious of their absence from the 1965 Commission hearings.

> *There was no contact with Aborigines from anybody in the case, the union advocate, the judges or anybody, they were completely outside. They weren't parties to the case, they weren't witnesses. It was all white fellows arguing about them and what ought to happen to them. In today's language it was the greatest denial of self-determination that one could imagine. But of course, people thought they were being very liberal and applying universal principles which must perforce benefit Aborigines.*[105]

However, the equal wage case hearings also overlooked a key issue for Aboriginal communities. As stockman Rex Johns succinctly put it, '*It's not the money – it's the land*'.[106]

Many pastoralists argued that replacing the longstanding welfare system with wage parity would render their stations unviable. They claimed that they were sustaining an entire community including dependants, women, children and older workers who did light jobs, such as watering vegetables. If equal wages came in, Aboriginal families would have to go out. And 'out' would mean leaving their country with all its cultural obligations and its spiritual sustenance.

The Commonwealth Conciliation and Arbitration Commission understood the pastoralists' argument but upheld the claim for equal pay on the basis that:

> The guiding principle must be to apply to Aborigines the standards which the Commission applies to all others unless there are overwhelming reasons why this should not be done…We do not flinch from the results of this decision which we consider is the only proper one to be made at this point in Australia's history. There must be one industrial law, similarly applied to all Australians, Aboriginal or not.[107]

As the pastoralists had anticipated, many Aboriginal families found themselves turned off their country and dumped into towns like Fitzroy Crossing and Halls Creek, now unemployed and directionless, despite their expertise and knowledge of station life. Historian Mary Anne Jebb, then a barmaid at Fitzroy Crossing hotel saw the effects of displacement from country.

> *What I saw was people under siege. Each night the policeman would come to the pub with his car and this awful old four-wheel drive vehicle with a cage on the back and he'd pick people up and just toss them in the back and drive off with a car full of people who were really distressed, screaming people. It was chaos, it was absolute chaos in 1976, 1977 when the big influxes were coming in. People without food, without houses, ending up in the pub. The publican would have to create all sorts of rules that suited his own situation at the pub.*[108]

The situation became so bad that one night Jebb witnessed a riot.

> *The publican found himself locked in a hotel room. The dogs that he had trained were really quite aggressive. There was a real sense of chaos and fear, particularly on the Thursday and Friday pension nights. There*

> *were hundreds and hundreds of people without anywhere to live, without houses, who camped out on the flat, were picked up by the police, taken off to the police station.*[109]

Lawyer Hal Wootten felt that the adversarial manner in which the Equal Wage Case was handled had shown an unimaginative understanding of the likely impact for Aboriginal communities.

> *It's obvious that if we interfere in this very complex situation by changing the wage rates it's going to have all sorts of consequences. These consequences should be explained to people. They should be given an opportunity to say what they want. If they're going to go off the stations the Commonwealth should provide them with a real future.*[110]

As Mary Anne Jebb was aware, some pastoralists were genuinely concerned about the future of their former employees.

> *Some of the pastoral people who I worked with in the north Kimberley were really concerned that modernisation, money and alcohol would have devastating effects on social relations. They could not see how a transition could be made from the very paternalistic semi-feudal situation to a situation of having access to towns and alcohol.*[111]

Pastoralist Peter Murray saw the Equal Wage Case as a classic failure of understanding.

> *I think the tragedy of it all was that nobody sat down – nobody thought about the repercussions – they just let it happen. And what always amazes me is that we're supposed to be a clever country, an enlightened country – and yet we allow decisions to take place without any consultation with the parties that are involved and we've got a disaster on our hands thirty years down the track.*[112]

The Commonwealth Conciliation and Arbitration Commission had made an economically and ethically just decision but their judgement failed to take account of the essential Aboriginal sense of culture and country. As a young man, Pat Dodson had worked on pastoral properties. He contrasted his experience with that of the next generation, children taken away from station life and their traditional community life to small town existence.

> There's certainly a big shift from your secure environment if you come off a cattle property, where as a young kid, you could roam around fairly freely: go to the yards, ride the horses, walk around the place fairly freely without being exploited, because at that stage, even if you were not deemed to be of great value to a non-Aboriginal person, you were of immense value to your own society. Up until the initiation period you were a young man, able to pursue a very productive and useful life, very much in tune with your country, your language, the whole tradition and values of that country.[113]

Basil Thomas remembers the mood of a people who, even in exile in Halls Creek, had spiritually never lost their country.

> They were welcome a bit but they always worried to go back to their home. It was only waiting time for them to get back home because when they were pushed off from the station, their heart was still back in the desert at Ringer Soak.[114]

Years later, several Aboriginal communities were able to return to country, thanks to buy-back finance from the Commonwealth government and supported by the newly established Kimberley Land Council.

As a result of the Equal Wage Case, the people from Ringer Soak (Yaruman) had been displaced from pastoral work and were eventually evicted from Gordon Downs station between 1978 and 1981. They were taken to Halls Creek, where they camped for several years until given government assistance to move to Kundat Djaru, their traditional land, which was made a permanent reserve in 1982. A young Aboriginal lawyer, Ribgna Green, who helped their campaign to return to country, witnessed their waiting and their return.

> The changes I saw in the people from the time when they first arrived in Halls Creek after being kicked off Gordon Downs station right through to

the time when they moved back to their country, started setting up their tents and organising their affairs which also included ceremonies. People were back in their country. So, they could sing songs again and dance dances and do things that they'd been doing for aeons of time. To see those sorts of changes was the highlight of my working career. I don't think anything will quite equal that.[115]

It was not the money. It was the land!

For some who returned to country, the opportunity to work on cattle stations was invigorating and contrasted with the enforced idleness of small-town life. Others, like the Ringer Soak mob, came back to live in a so-called outstation. An outstation was originally defined as a collection of buildings where people lived and worked some distance from the station homestead. These new 'outstations' enabled some traditional owners to stay on their own land with their kinship groups. They also offered a degree of social and cultural independence and, in many instances, removal from the temptations of alcohol.

Pat Dodson saw the growth of outstations as a reaction to being *brought in* from country to small Kimberley towns.

They arose because you had policies which brought Aboriginal people into larger communities from these more remote places. People were encouraged to live around a large settlement, often created unknowingly on a particular tribal group's country. Tribes that didn't necessarily relate or interact were forcibly removed to those places. People were being dumped off cattle stations onto the fringes of towns and left to eke out a life with no proper housing, often where there was one ablution block for forty or fifty, sixty, maybe up to two hundred people.[116]

Anthony Watson, coordinator at Jarlmadangah station, now an outstation, worked with his father, John Watson, to rebuild a pastoral property, the Aboriginal way. He described how his people had been trapped in the towns.

The town reserves were overcrowded with many different tribal groups who were expected to live together and they found it really difficult and suffered under that system with a lot of deaths, violence, abuse in those small areas. And there were no jobs available.[117]

In recent years, the remoteness, and thus the economic and social viability, of some of these outstations has raised questions about the efficient supply of goods and services. In March 2015, then prime minister Tony Abbott supported a West Australian government proposal to shut down and transfer outstation residents to larger, better resourced towns. This proposal was criticised by Aboriginal and non-Aboriginal people alike who had witnessed the dispossession resulting from the Equal Wage Case.

The prime minister's description of outstation living as a 'lifestyle choice' was seen as an unfortunate choice of words, given that it usually applies to prosperous white people able to make a 'sea' or 'tree' change. The description also ignored the fact that, for many communities, outstation living provided an opportunity to get away from problems associated with town life. Former minister for Aboriginal affairs Fred Chaney saw another major benefit of outstation living.

> *I think, though, there's another thing which is more important than, say, getting off the grog, and that's being able to access their country. They physically change. You can see the lift in their spirits. Sometimes we have to use arguments about economics and social order but the real thing for Aboriginal people is to identify with their country and remain in contact with it.*[118]

Others saw that outstation life offered First Nations people an opportunity for self-determination at a time when government policies, both Commonwealth and state, were beginning to support the aspirations of Aboriginal people for recognition of their own culture and history. Anthropologist Jon Altman outlined that policy shift.

> *The state recognised that assimilation, the centralisation of Aboriginal people into larger communities, missions and government settlements, increasingly referred to as Aboriginal townships, had been unsuccessful,*

and so there was an acceptance of the need for Aboriginal people to leave these townships and to return to live on the land that they owned.[119]

For Altman, this view was visually confirmed, flying across the Northern Territory and the Kimberley, and seeing below:

little outstation communities dotted throughout, including the coast and linking them are these bush roads. I think that some people still cling to this notion of the wilderness myth that empty landscape will somehow look after itself, but in reality, landscape needs people and outstations represent a human presence on the landscape. They're tiny hamlets but they are dotted across the landscape and they do fulfil a function.[120]

Senator Pat Dodson adds that outstations contribute to the 'wealth of the nation' in many different ways:

Not just populating the north but looking after and protecting the country, looking after the coastline...Aboriginal outstations contribute to the detection of illegal fishing and the control of the environment through fire management. They're a very important feature of national security as well as the sustainability of our northern regions. And we're talking about Indigenous people whose traditions and cultures have emanated from those particular locations. They have a depth and a richness of culture and experience and of social organisation integrated into that landscape.[121]

John Watson, former stockman and a founding member of the Kimberley Land Council, described how he worked to establish Jarlmadangah, formerly Mount Anderson pastoral station.

I set up many other communities right across the Kimberley, east and west. Two brothers were here before me, getting back cattle stations like Mount Anderson. My brother was there as manager of the cattle station. Before that, this country was sheep country. Many of us worked here.[122]

When Watson returned to the country on which his people had worked for white bosses, he found a dispirited community.

I came back here in 1986 and saw what was happening in other parts of the Kimberley. I saw people looking into rubbish bins, looking for tucker.

> *I didn't want our children looking in a rubbish bin. And it was very hard, you know, looking at what had happened. People couldn't practise their culture, living in town, they couldn't go hunting and so I said 'I have to go back home, and home is "Jarlmadangah"'. And not only for me but seventy other people.*[123]

Jon Altman identified another negative effect of town life for those displaced from their traditional land.

> *What happened at these places was that Indigenous people were encouraged to centralise, encouraged to 'sedentarise' – a terrible term, but basically a term meaning that people were encouraged to give up their traditional ways and settle down in one place.*[124]

Settling in small Kimberley towns and receiving government payments was an arrangement that Aboriginal people themselves sometimes referred to as 'sit down money'. Given cash but no work, people lost their knowledge of country, an important concern for Anthony Watson.

Jarlmadangah outstation (photo by Ben Collins, ABC Kimberley).

> We could have lost a lot of culture. In some cases, we have, because a lot of our members got taken away from their country and knowing the places, activities, all that knowledge of those areas, it was very hard for members to actually maintain and look after those countries. So, we did lose a lot and one of the things in getting back to the country is to try and gain back some of that knowledge. So, we work hard towards helping preserve and manage and maintain those cultural values.[125]

Outstation life allowed knowledge of country to be retained and regained. It also enabled the traditional owners to care for land. Watson put that important consideration into practice at Jarlmadangah.

> Fire was the best tool for regenerating and managing the country. In burning country, there is a whole lot of benefits. Birds graze in those cleared areas, new shoots come out of the ground and more seeds come out. We clean waterholes, open the waterholes for animals to come back and drink. So, fire management plays a role for plants and animals as well. There is a great deal of skill to transfer and we incorporate that into their job skills to look after country. So, it's an opportunity for young members to look after country and work in our country. They feel a great deal of ownership and being proud to do land management.[126]

Altman sees outstation life as demanding, but generating a measure of contentment.

> I think we certainly should take people's happiness, people's level of satisfaction with their way of living. Life at outstations is not necessarily easy and infrastructure is very limited. Entertainment, what we regard as the basics, television or radio, is often absent. It is a way of life which provides the most basic of services, access to water, access to a visiting teacher, visiting health care and visiting supply of foods, available only on a fortnightly cycle. People are clearly choosing that way of living in preference to living in townships or migrating to larger mainstream communities.[127]

Pat Dodson regards belonging to country as the overriding factor in a community's decision to live at an outstation.

> *It was about people's connection to that country, their sense of ceremony, their sense of place and their sense of belonging. And of course, leadership was absolutely essential as well as some decent support. In the Kimberley, for instance, once the Noonkanbah crisis abated, you had the resource agencies set up to assist people going back to country. It was a means of alleviating the social chaos created by previous policies.*[128]

The 'Noonkanbah crisis' came to a head in 1980 but factors leading up to it had been triggered by the 1965 Equal Wage Case. In 1971, the Yungngora people had walked off their traditional land at Noonkanbah station. Despite the equal wage decision, they had continued to experience poor pay and living conditions, and moved to an equally impoverished life in Fitzroy Crossing. They were not far from their own land but not on it. Five years later, in 1976, the federal government's Aboriginal Land Fund helped them to purchase Noonkanbah station for the Yungngora community. They moved back to their country, aiming to re-establish a cattle industry. The community also wanted to protect important sites on their traditional country and run Noonkanbah without interference from the negative aspects of contact with non-Aboriginal people. Yungngora man, Ivan McPhee, was a leader of the campaign to regain their country and cultural life.

> *Town life was causing a lot of problems for us. And that's the reason why we got away. We got our community to go back home and teach our kids our cultural ways, our languages and as custodians, teach them about our good life, the best life you can find.*[129]

Anthropologist Peter Bindon, then working with the Western Australian Museum to evaluate important Indigenous sites, saw the Yungngora return to country as enabling them to retain both their station work skills and their cultural practices.

> *The people on Noonkanbah felt that here they were with a unique opportunity to demonstrate that Aboriginal people could do exactly the same kinds of things that white people in that region were doing and be*

> *very successful at. They were also trying to do things that would sustain culture and yet meld that with ideals that were held as the sorts of things white people were measuring success with.*[130]

Unfortunately for the Yungngora, just as they were becoming re-established on their traditional lands, the Western Australian government instigated a plan to explore selected areas in the state's north-west for oil and gas reserves. An American exploration company, Amax, was commissioned to undertake the groundwork. Premier Charles Court was keen to strengthen and diversify Western Australia's economy.

> *You have to be part of the world scene if others need the minerals you've got, the energy you've got…It was a new concept, to unlock minerals and find some way of getting people and expertise there and of course once you get development, you get consequential development, whereby the country becomes more sophisticated, more educated, if you do it the right way and as a government we were determined to do it the right way.*[131]

The state government did not expect strong opposition to the exploration project from the newly returned Noonkanbah community. But it became an unanticipated 'consequential development'. For the Yungngora, Amax's decision to drill on their country was not 'the right way'. They feared destruction of important sites and, given their previous experience in Fitzroy Crossing, the Elders were also worried about white people bringing in sly grog. They wanted that stopped at the station gate.

Premier Court, however, was determined that oil and gas exploration should go ahead. Despite government reassurances that important places would be protected, protracted on-site discussions failed to convince the Yungngora community of any benefit from what they saw as an invasive activity. Despite widespread public protests from the Yungngora and demonstrations in Perth from non-Aboriginal supporters, an Amax convoy of drill rigs entered Noonkanbah station on 7 August 1980 with police protection. Ivan McPhee remembers that day:

We found the bulldozers coming, doing a seismic line and telling us they had permission from the state government to go ahead and drill and do what we want. And they didn't bother telling us. We were human beings living on that station and in the community. No one consulted us or had a proper talk to us to explain what they were doing. And we were trying to tell them we had a concern, why we don't want you there. Nobody understood each other.[132]

Steve Shannon, then working at Noonkanbah as technical assistant to Bindon, felt that:

Amax were coming from another culture. Most of the people were from the United States. They had no experience of Aboriginal culture. In the Kimberley if you have no knowledge of the ways of the local people, you can form opinions where you believe that everyone is in agreement.

So, you can walk away with a piece of paper that's been signed by some smiling people and go with a feeling that this is what we've all agreed upon. Whereas in many cases the people were listening and smiling and saying, 'Let's just smile and be nice to the white man and he'll go away'.[133]

A major misunderstanding arose over language. In English-derived law, properties are commonly defined as 'freehold' and 'leasehold'. Pastoral stations in Western Australia have always been leasehold. The individual or group holding the lease of that land does not have full ownership and, significantly for occupants, their terrain is open to other potential uses: hydrographic exploration, mineral exploration and mining. The leasehold tenure under which the people living on Noonkanbah held that property allowed for exploitation of what lay beneath the surface soil, rocks, pasture or woodland. To the Yungngora this distinction was meaningless. For them there was no difference between land that they walked on and what lay underneath. It was all one, as McPhee saw it:

We were telling them that we own the lot, what's on the bottom and what's on the top. That's what we thought we owned. Well they were saying, 'You only own the top of the pastoral lease'.[134]

Ownership was not 'real estate' for the Noonkanbah people. It was their country and part of their being. In their view, they were protecting a living entity. Then director of the Western Australian Museum John Bannister understood that concern.

> *There was this fear that Amax weren't only going to disturb the surface. The people said you could drive trucks over the surface and you could even remove trees and bushes without altering the nature of the land. But if you literally speared a drill right into the centre, down below, you [were] doing something awful to its vital organs. It was an 'increase place' for goannas and you would, as it were, kill the goanna if you speared its vital organs and that was a horrendous concept to them.*[135]

Central to this dispute was Umpampurru, known to non-Aboriginal people as Pea Hill, the name derived from its first naming by Europeans as P Hill, a trig point in one of the earliest Kimberley surveys.[136] As Steve Hawke and Michael Gallagher explained in their account of the Noonkanbah confrontation, 'Features like these being relatively prominent in the landscape were nearly always Dreaming Sites of importance to Aboriginal people'.[137] Moreover, the importance of Umpampurru/Pea Hill was derived from a combination of attributes, all of which can be traced back to the activities of the various Ngarranggani (ancestral beings), as Hawke and Gallagher explained.

> There was a great hero Unyupu, and the two snakes he had speared. In their great struggle they had carved out the Fitzroy River, starting from the west downstream from Noonkanbah, and passing south of Pea Hill as they travelled east and then north.[138]

As museum director, John Bannister recognised, Pea Hill was clearly of great cultural significance to the traditional owners but its importance was evidently not apparent to either government or the American drillers.

> *It wasn't so much 'There's this pile of rocks over there, or this famous place, Pea Hill'. But there was also an 'area of influence' around Pea Hill, which only the Aboriginal people knew and could describe.*[139]

MANY MAPS

The feature was important to both parties, as Peter Bindon saw it.

> *Pea Hill sticks up above the ground along the Fitzroy River. Now you can imagine, in a huge flat continent, almost anything that sticks up like that, is of significance to anybody living there. Obviously, it is of interest to geologists as an expression of something happening under the ground and its surface expression. And it is of particular interest to Aboriginal people looking at ways of navigating through the country, ways of marking off places in the countryside. It was a feature that could be referred to for all kinds of reasons.*[140]

For Amax, Pea Hill looked worth investigating.

Pea Hill (photo by Grant Boxer).

> *There was some kind of geological anomaly beneath the soil and they needed to test this. They wanted to drill a vertical hole down to it, rather than one on an angle which they could also have done. The vertical hole let them look at the various geological strata as they descended to find out what this anomaly was.*[141]

An action that John Bannister had warned was a 'horrendous concept' for the Yungngora people.

In the course of preparing his site report for the WA Museum trustees, Bindon made two visits to Pea Hill to thoroughly verify its importance and the stories attached to the site.

> *When I first got there, I was taken away by the Noonkanbah people and they gave me their perspective on the place and they told me the stories they wanted me to know about it. Out on the plain, people took me to various outcrops and they said 'Here is the evidence of this big shallow nest made by these ancestral heroes and here are the eggs that the ancestral heroes laid inside these structures in the Dreaming'. And further out we could find other pieces of limestone that related to other ancestral heroes but had obviously come from the same geological structure.*

Checking the site for a second time, Bindon realised that, uniquely in his experience:

> *I'd been able to find a cultural site more or less delineated by a geological feature. People took me to lots of different sites and showed me other outcrops and said 'You know the story. We've shown you the storyboards that tell you this story. You've seen our traditional title deeds to this place.'*[142]

Acting on Bindon's findings, the WA Museum report specified that Pea Hill and its area of influence justified protection under the *Aboriginal Heritage Act 1972*.

The state government was informed accordingly but, despite widespread growing community opposition to drilling on Noonkanbah, the WA Premier was determined to push ahead. Then minister for resources, Peter Jones, was aware of the pressure being placed:

on independent anthropologists and people who were doing anthropological work for universities and other bodies who were making public statements about sacred sites; what is a sacred site and what constitutes an 'area of influence' surrounding the site. And all of this became difficult and confusing for those on the outside, particularly in the way that it was published. So, yes, the museum had a difficult role to play and certainly the trustees were put in a difficult position. However, the government eased them out of that by making the decision for them.[143]

Drilling started on 29 August 1980 and stopped in mid-November. There was no exploitable trace of oil or gas. Station life at Noonkanbah resumed. But the dispute had highlighted a major cultural misunderstanding. Ivan McPhee summed up the experience for the Yungngora people.

I don't think we understood each other. They had their law through white man's way and we had our law in the Aboriginal way. You never forget what happened. And a lot of those old people, we lost them through what government done to us. Old people feel really bad that white man's way knocked our culture away.[144]

So does the Noonkanbah incident and others like it suggest that, in trying to impose whitefella law, we have often failed to understand or accept that Australia's First Nations have their own living Law which underpins their entire culture? As Stephen Hawke reminds us:

The greatest strength and resource of Aboriginal Australia lies in the living Law and culture ahead even of the land that draws its meaning from this source. The Law lives and gives meaning to Aboriginal life, even indirectly to those who do not follow it, and those in the cities and country towns who seem far removed from its influence.[145]

And does this landscape-based story also suggest that there are many different ways of reading a map? For Peter Bindon, 'Yes. And there are many different maps'.[146]

Almost three thousand kilometres south of Noonkanbah, Wadandi Cultural Custodian Iszaac Webb reminds us that:

> The country is alive. The country is still alive. The country sees visitors to this country, all the time whether they are Indigenous or non-Indigenous. The spirits, the djangari, they walk the country and are still there within the land and within the country.[147]

In the Great Southern region, Craig McVee, chairman of the Kojonup Aboriginal Corporation, confirms that his people also still have *'a very significant attachment to the land…Part of our tradition is you live with the land and the land will dictate to you the rights and wrongs of how you maintain it.'*[148]

For well over a century, Noongar families in the Kojonup district had not been able to care for what had been their own country. European settlers came and cleared Aboriginal hunting grounds to grow crops and raise their imported animals. Many Aboriginal families have continued to live alongside their non-Aboriginal neighbours, but not always as equals. Local farmer Robert Sexton recalls his mother asking Ted Smith, a Noongar man:

> 'Why don't you get citizenship rights?' And he says, 'Why? They'll still treat me as a blackfella.' Now Ted was probably the most dignified and articulate man you'd meet anywhere. That's how he saw it and you'd have to say he was right.[149]

Sexton is well aware of his own family's past and present reliance on the knowledge and skills of Noongar people.

> There are stories on my mother's side. Her grandparents were the first white settlers in Muradup in the 1880s. When my mother, Inez Larsen, was a very small child, perhaps four or five years of age in 1915 or 1916, she was staying or dallying with the grandparents and it got too late to go home. She was afraid to go home because the sun was setting, but an Aboriginal man, Jimmy Pardon, who lived near her grandparents, took her by the hand and led her the three miles back to their own place.

Inez's father, Henry Larsen, could speak the local language. Sexton says that this would have 'come in handy' because:

> *for the settlers, this was a strange, harsh country and without the Noongar people, the white settlers couldn't have stayed here. They didn't know where the water was. They didn't know what the seasons did. They didn't know what they could eat or what they could not eat. 'Is there water in the creeks? Have the fires been bad this year?'*[150]

The Kojonup Spring, on the outskirts of the present town, was initially important in the European settlement of the district. As Craig McVee tells it, the newcomers were shown the freshwater supply by the local Aboriginal people.[151] Local historian Barbara Hobbs relates the story from a settler perspective:

> *In February 1837 surveyor Alfred Hillman, was looking for a path from King George Sound, now Albany, through to the Swan River. The story goes that, three or so miles away from Kojonup, the party had run out of*

Kojonup Spring, water source for everyone.
Photo courtesy Kojonup Historical Precinct.

water. They met eight Aboriginal people who very kindly and generously showed them where there was water at this particular place, the spring; and Hillman was very grateful for that.[152]

While the Kojonup Spring became the white settlers' first water source, it has always been an important site for the Noongar. For the Kojonup district, an 'inclusive history' began in 1994 when the shire became involved in Landcare and local farmers began to rethink their agricultural practices. At the same time the Kojonup Spring precinct was designated an area of 'joint control and management'.[153]

Earlier, in 1988, the Australian bicentennial year, Robert Sexton, then shire president, had begun discussions with Noongar Elder Albert Michael on how to reconcile both stories about the same country. He quickly learnt a useful lesson.

As a government official no one was ever going to come into my office to talk. And I couldn't work that one out for a while until I went to Mr Michael's place and sat on his verandah and we had cake and sausages and coffee and tea – because we wanted to get onto safe ground. My office was very unsafe ground. That was where bad people lived, who took people away and fined them and imprisoned them.[154]

Albert Michael's initial response was positive but cautious: 'We will be involved but only on our own terms'.[155]

Further down the track, Sexton thought he had a 'bright idea':

'Perhaps we should return land to the Noongars?' And Mr Michael said, and this was the turning point, 'You can't give back to somebody what you never owned in the first place'. I was suitably chastened.

By the 1990s, the Noongars had created the Kojonup Aboriginal Corporation, their own community organisation. They were now happy to discuss the notion of a joint history but with one firm rule.

We'll only tell the story as we tell it alongside the European story. We've come from forty thousand years back. You've been here five minutes. But we're inextricably now bound together. So, we must tell the story together, otherwise it won't be told correctly.[156]

For Craig McVee, it was a big surprise that the white community did not understand how the Noongars lived after European settlement.

> I just thought it was part of everyday knowledge that the Noongar people lived on the local reserve, close to the rubbish tip, out of sight, out of mind, and had to be back into the reserve by dark and not allowed to leave till daylight next morning unless they were working out on a farm.[157]

Some Kojonup residents were also unaware that:

> Back in the early days of settlement, Aboriginal people were forced to break the so-called laws to continue their customs and traditions. The settlers came along, put up fences and claimed that bit of property without realising it was very important country, where people practised their customs. So, the Aboriginal people jumped the fence, were caught trespassing and, unfortunately, I don't think the government's got the gist of that yet. Breaking the law, in a sense, even though it's not the right thing to do, our people were forced to do it and, unfortunately, that's now become part of our custom.[158]

Wadjelas and Noongars now began to work together to acknowledge and chronicle an inclusive history of the Kojonup community. There were meetings and many lengthy discussions. Setting a precedent, it became a shared history and the 'bricks and mortar' outcome was The Kodja Place: A Tool for Reconciliation.

The Kodja Place is a unique gallery displaying Indigenous and settler art and tools, ancient and modern, opened in 2002 and created by volunteer effort from all sections of the local community. It is an expression of goodwill shown by two cultures determined to forge a joint history and reinforced by McVee's mural map of the geology and history of his people's land. The long Noongar custodianship of the land was acknowledged by building the gallery in the shape of a distinctive local tool, the kodj stone axe.[159]

THE PAST IS STILL PART OF US

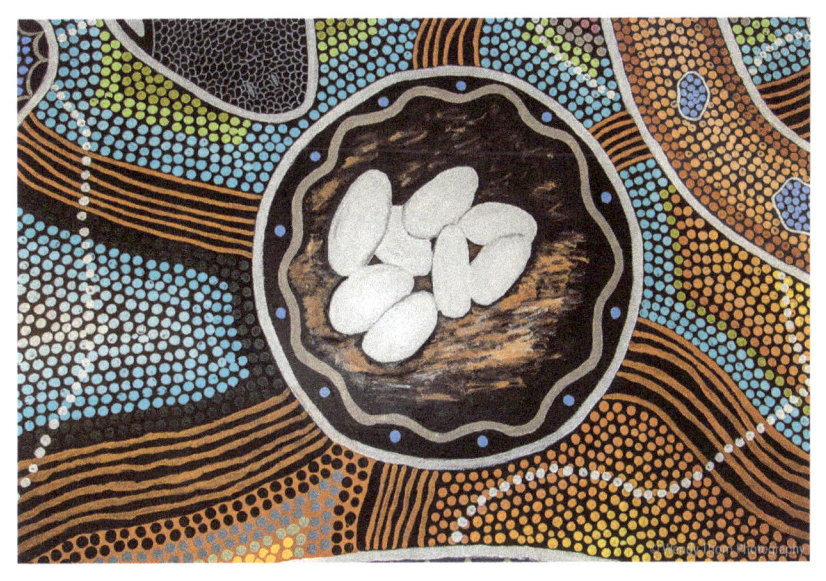

Craig McVee's map (photo by Wendy Thorn, used with permission of Craig McVee).

As McVee stated in his address at the opening, 'This complex will not be referred to as "my place", it will not be referred to as "your place" but it will definitely be referred to as "OUR PLACE".[160]

Kodja Place brought a community together and for McVee it was important that everybody now knew:

> *a lot of what was enforced upon the Noongar people through government policies. That was a good educating process. My Mum had done a lot of research on her family history and had all the documents wanting to remove all her brothers and sisters to the Carrolup settlement.*[161]

The letters that Craig's mother had obtained showed, among other things, that the community was more concerned about the risk of school closure because of loss of pupils than about the Aboriginal kids being taken away from home. For European Australians this lack of understanding:

> *really highlighted the Stolen Generation and some of the government policies which they were never aware of. And I still think that's the case*

299

today, to be honest. But I estimated right at the beginning of the project that eighty-five to ninety per cent of the Australian people didn't know of the government policies enforced upon Aboriginal people.[162]

The presence of many early Aboriginal tools had already provided a highly visible reminder of the Noongar story. As a founder member of the Kodja Place gallery, Margaret Robertson was aware of:

local farmers' collections of stone artefacts. And they became part of the story that we wanted to tell. One is a tool which farmer Terry Myers donated, once used by Noongar people to grind seeds. It has a scarifier mark running through it: an ancient implement impaled by modern machinery.[163]

Roger Bilney shares that sense of a long rural history.

I find it particularly interesting, and in fact humbling almost, to know as we move around our farm that there were people here existing quite happily in this environment in its natural state. And we find things around the farm that we treasure, indicating that there was a lot of activity going on here.[164]

Penny Young, one of the founders of Kojonup Reconciliation, came to farming in the district when it was:

a cleared agricultural landscape, and you occasionally come across something that makes you realise that it was Noongar country. For example, we were about to burn a tree on our property last year when we discovered that it had axe markings on it. That really brought us up with a halt, to think that the tree had its own history before we came here. And we don't know who those people were.[165]

As Craig McVee said, it wasn't easy:

for the local Noongar community to participate and bring a lot of the knowledge forward, because a lot of the past policies were very hurtful and shameful, and probably due to a lack of understanding from the government and from the farming community. So, finding that trust with the right group of people was something we really had to work on, and we probably really gained it three months before we were due to open Kodja Place.[166]

The Kodja Place – Our Place.

Barbara Hobbs worked closely with McVee and others to reach that trust.

> As Craig has said to us, he didn't realise that we didn't know their story, and that is vital because we didn't know some of the things that had happened to the Noongar community. When we were younger, we really didn't question what was happening. Now we're in a community where people question these things much more than they used to. That's good, but we've still got to overcome the hurts of the past, and that's a matter of continuing to listen to each other.[167]

Patsy Michael, Albert Michael's wife, gives a glimpse of how her people had lived in recent times.

> The likes of me, we were living up there, on that little hill there. All the rest were scattered up around here in this bush, up around here along the fence line, up at the little cottage. Like when the job was completed around here, they'd shift out to another paddock and they'd camp on that paddock until they burnt and cleared all that up.[168]

For farmer Geoff Thorn, re-examining history gave him an insight into how two cultures saw land that they both used.

> *I was just thinking about how we see the land, and this project has drawn out things that mostly go unsaid amongst the white community, because we just take them for granted. This process has made us think about it and put it into words, which is not something we normally do. Whereas for the Noongars, their life is expressed in relation to the land, how they are part of it.*[169]

Fellow farmer Roger Bilney sees The Kodja Place:

> *as the creation of a community. You can see over time how two communities have come together and how the sense of belonging to Kojonup now exists, and I think the documentation of that will serve to keep that community spirit going, and in time we'll look back and say 'Well, that was a community project that continued to build on a sense of belonging'.*[170]

A sense of understanding in this long story inevitably and vitally involves land, the origin of much misunderstanding between two different cultures. Iszaac Webb's map of Wadandi country conveys his sense of belonging to country within a traditional European map framework.

> *When you sing the country, and when the Elders sing, and when they tell you the stories, it's looking at it from that aerial perspective. We see the country as if we were the birds, as if we were karrak, the red-tail cockatoo, like the old people. We say they still watch the country, and that's why they fly in those flocks, especially in threes. We wongi [talk], we say: 'The old people are coming'.*[171]

For Craig McVee the Kojonup landscape changed when the new people came.

> *You get up in a plane today and you can see the way the landscape has been carved up, with straight-line fencing. I look at these paddocks and I see a fence line going straight across a waterway. For me it would be*

common sense to follow the waterway with a fence line and then carve your paddock up to match the natural geometry of those creeks and rivers. A 'map', if you visualise it from an Aboriginal perspective, follows the contours and the lines of country, whereas for a European a map is straight-line stuff.[172]

As anthropologist Peter Bindon has reminded us, '*there are many different maps*'.

Zac Webb's Wadandi map.
Photo by Undalup Association.

Afterthoughts

From conversations with the authors

Hon. Fred Chaney, former Minister for Aboriginal Affairs and Reconciliation advocate, 25 August 2018
There's been a history of miscommunication but there's also been a history of totally incompatible world views. I think the Albany case is really interesting because there was a situation of harmony and amity because the needs of the two groups were not incompatible. You had a small force of soldiers and no interference in the Aboriginal enjoyment of their country. And while I am sure there would have been communication problems, the two groups were not fundamentally at odds. That changed when people came to settle and use the land, pre-empting its use by the traditional owners. But when a demand for country and grazing for sheep and cattle takes precedence over human needs, inevitably there is conflict.

Vernice Gillies, Indigenous Albany historian, 18 November 2018

It was about greed, about having to take the land. It was certainly not about understanding in the very beginning, but it was also about people bringing their own standards and trying to project those standards onto a totally different culture. We talk about 'cultural safety' and when the first white settlers came here, there was no cultural safety. They didn't understand and because people behaved differently to the way they acted and saw things differently to the way they saw things their view was just not accepted. You will do it this way. You will do it because my way is the right way.

Robert Sexton, farmer and former Kojonup shire president, 31 May 2019

The Europeans simply stopped doing what the Noongars had been doing and that is burning the land. The Noongars burned whatever they needed to burn. Sometimes they'd burn twenty or thirty years apart and sometimes they'd burn cold. It depended on what they wanted. So, they clearly farmed the land.

Kim Scott, writer and academic, 21 June 2018

In terms of 'spirit and place' I think that an old language like Noongar or any Aboriginal language being connected to place and community for so long, holds enormous potential and I've experienced that vitality of spirit in place. Going back into my ancestral country – infamous as a taboo region because of historical death – with language, and reuniting creation stories and songs with landscape with other survivors, other descendants of the first owners, is quite magical – the sort of things that happen there. People report on how much it means to them and how they feel returning to ancestral country.

AFTERTHOUGHTS

Fred Chaney, 25 August 2018
But I think there is a single story about communication and that almost none of us speak an Aboriginal language. We expect them, who are often multilingual in lots of languages and semi lingual in English, to be the recipients of our voices.

Kim Scott, 21 June 2018
But here's still a whole lot we're not seeing – all of us who've been damaged through this shared history of ours. So, there's a whole awakening yet to come, of us as a community and what that might mean in terms of an awakening of country, to bring that to an awareness and a sharing, not a glib sharing. My belief is that, for both Aboriginal and non-Aboriginal people, both healing and their relationships are being transformed because of strengthening a connection to a pre-colonial heritage.

Robert Sexton, 31 May 2019
We have told our story and we have shown other people how to tell their story. As the Aboriginal people said, 'We need to tell our story together, so that we have one story but many voices in one story'.

Iszaac Webb, Wadandi Cultural Custodian, 6 June 2019
Definitely things are changing. People are wanting to understand that deeper connection, the connection that we all have to the country. I'm seeing a really massive change since the late '80s. It's an awareness and a shift of thinking and things are changing in a positive way. It seems it's going a bit slow but it's picked up in the last ten or fifteen years. People are wanting and really thirsting for that knowledge and that connection.

Fred Chaney, 1 February 2019
The Uluru Statement from the Heart is integral in allowing Aboriginal voices to be heard, which is essential for Australia to move forwards as a country. All they are asking for is the right to be heard on issues that affect them.

Uluru Statement from the Heart

We, gathered at the 2017 National Constitutional Convention, coming from all points of the southern sky, make this statement from the heart:

Our Aboriginal and Torres Strait Islander tribes were the first sovereign Nations of the Australian continent and its adjacent islands, and possessed it under our own laws and customs. This our ancestors did, according to the reckoning of our culture, from the Creation, according to the common law from 'time immemorial', and according to science more than 60,000 years ago.

This sovereignty is a spiritual notion: the ancestral tie between the land, or 'mother nature', and the Aboriginal and Torres Strait Islander peoples who were born therefrom, remain attached thereto, and must one day return thither to be united with our ancestors. This link is the basis of the ownership of the soil, or better, of sovereignty. It has never been ceded or extinguished, and co-exists with the sovereignty of the Crown.

How could it be otherwise? That peoples possessed a land for sixty millennia and this sacred link disappears from world history in merely the last two hundred years?

With substantive constitutional change and structural reform, we believe this ancient sovereignty can shine through as a fuller expression of Australia's nationhood.

Proportionally, we are the most incarcerated people on the planet. We are not an innately criminal people. Our children are aliened from their families at unprecedented rates. This cannot be because we have no love for them. And our youth languish in detention in obscene numbers. They should be our hope for the future.

These dimensions of our crisis tell plainly the structural nature of our problem. *This is the torment of our powerlessness.*

We seek constitutional reforms to empower our people and take *a rightful place* in our own country. When we have power over our destiny our children will flourish. They will walk in two worlds and their culture will be a gift to their country.

We call for the establishment of a First Nations Voice enshrined in the Constitution.

Makarrata is the culmination of our agenda: *the coming together after a struggle.* It captures our aspirations for a fair and truthful relationship with the people of Australia and a better future for our children based on justice and self-determination.

We seek a Makarrata Commission to supervise a process of agreement-making between governments and First Nations and truth-telling about our history.

In 1967 we were counted, in 2017 we seek to be heard. We leave base camp and start our trek across this vast country. We invite you to walk with us in a movement of the Australian people for a better future.

NOTES

Notes to Chapter 1: When Do Ships Die?

1. J. Mulvaney and N. Green, *Commandant of Solitude: The Journals of Captain Collet Barker 1828–1831*, Melbourne University Press at the Miegunyah Press, Carlton, 1992, p. 265.
2. Vernice Gillies in interview with Bill Bunbury, 18 November 2018.
3. Mulvaney and Green, *Commandant of Solitude*, p. 265.
4. Iszaac Webb in interview with the authors, 6 June 2019.
5. T. Shellam, *Shaking Hands on the Fringe: Negotiating the Aboriginal World at King George's Sound*, University of Western Australia Press, Crawley, 2009, p. 44.
6. Tiffany Shellam in interview with Bill Bunbury, 16 August 2018.
7. T. Shellam, *Meeting the Waylo: Aboriginal Encounters in the Archipelago*, UWA Publishing, Crawley, 2019, p. 45.
8. Shellam, interview, August 2018.
9. Shellam, *Shaking Hands*, p. 20.
10. Shellam, interview, August 2018.
11. Lynette Knapp in interview with the authors, 17 November 2018.
12. P. Playford, *Voyage of Discovery to Terra Australis by Willem de Vlamingh in 1696–97*, Western Australian Museum, Perth, 1998, p. 28.
13. Rottnest Island Authority, *Aboriginals on Rottnest Island*, viewed 26 November 2019, <https://www.rottnestisland.com/the-island/about-the-island/our-history/aboriginal>.
14. ibid.
15. S. Konishi and M Nugent, 'Newcomers c. 1600–1800', in A. Bashford and S. Macintyre (eds), *The Cambridge History of Australia, vol. 1 Indigenous and Colonial Australia*, Cambridge University Press, Melbourne, 2013, p. 48.
16. L. Collard and D. Palmer, 'Looking for the residents of Terra Australis: the importance of Nyungar in early European coastal exploration', in P. Veth,

P. Sutton and M. Neale (eds), *Strangers on the Shore, Early Coastal Contacts in Australia*, National Museum of Australia Press, Canberra, 2008, p. 185.
17 Konishi and Nugent, 'Newcomers', pp. 49–50.
18 Dampier quoted in K. Anderson and C. Perrin, 'The miserablest people in the world: race, humanism and the Australian Aborigine', *The Australian Journal of Anthropology*, vol. 18, no. 1, 2007, p. 19.
19 John Kinder in interview with Bill Bunbury, 5 December 2018.
20 ibid.
21 Shellam, *Shaking Hands*, pp. 15–16.
22 M. Arnold, *A Journey Travelled: Aboriginal–European Relationships at Albany and the Surrounding Region from First Contact to 1926*, UWA Publishing, Crawley, 2015, p. 49.
23 ibid., p. 90.
24 Shellam, *Shaking Hands*, p. 18.
25 Gillies, interview, November 2018.
26 Konishi and Nugent, 'Newcomers', p. 63.
27 ibid.
28 E. Duyker, *Dumond D'Urville, Explorer and Polymath*, Otago University Press, Dunedin, 2014, p. 179.
29 Louis Sainson in Dumont D'Urville, *Journal of the Voyage de la Corvette Astrolabe*, vol. 1, p. 188, quoted in N. Green, Aborigines of the Albany Region, 1821–1898, *The Bicentennial Dictionary of Western Australians*, University of Western Australia Press, Nedlands, 1989, introduction p. x.
30 Shellam, interview, August 2018.
31 ibid.
32 Shellam, Shaking Hands, p. 183.
33 Shellam, interview, August 2018.
34 Mulvaney and Green, *Commandant of Solitude*, pp. 241–42.
35 Kinder, interview, December 2018.
36 Shellam, interview, August 2018.
37 Shellam, *Shaking Hands*, p. 102.
38 Shellam, interview, August 2018.
39 N. Green, 'Mokare (1800–1831)', *Australian Dictionary of Biography*, National Centre of Biography, Australian National University, 2005, viewed 23 February 2019, <http://adb.anu.edu.au/biography/mokare-13106>.
40 Shellam, interview, August 2018.
41 I. S Nind, 'Description of the natives of King George's Sound (Swan River Colony) and adjoining country', *Journal of the Royal Geographical Society of London*, vol. 1, 1831, p. 26.
42 Neville Green in interview with Bill Bunbury, Australian Broadcasting Corporation (ABC), *Talking History*, 41, 1992.
43 ibid.
44 Shellam, interview, August 2018.

45 ibid.
46 ibid.
47 ibid.
48 Mulvaney and Green, *Commandant of Solitude*, p. 282.
49 ibid., p. 254.
50 Shellam, interview, August 2018.
51 Mulvaney and Green, *Commandant of Solitude*, p. 300.
52 Green, interview, *Talking History*.
53 Mulvaney and Green, *Commandant of Solitude*, p. 271.
54 Shellam, interview, August 2018.
55 Mulvaney and Green, *Commandant of Solitude*, p. 280.
56 Nind, 'Description of the natives', p. 34.
57 ibid., p. 40.
58 Shellam, interview, August 2018.
59 ibid.
60 ibid.
61 ibid.
62 South West Aboriginal Land and Sea Council, J. Host with C. Owen, *"It's Still in My Heart, This is My Country": The Single Noongar Claim History*, UWA Publishing, Crawley, 2009, pp. 197–98.
63 Kim Scott in interview with Bill Bunbury, 21 June 2018.
64 ibid.
65 Shellam, interview, August 2018.
66 R. Glover (coordinator), *Plantagenet, Rich and Beautiful: A History of the Shire of Plantagenet*, University of Western Australia Press, Nedlands, 1979, pp. 6–7.
67 Robert Sexton in interview with the authors, 31 May 2019.
68 J. Bird, *West of the Arthur*, West Arthur Shire Council, Darkan, 1990, pp. 13–14.
69 Mulvaney and Green, *Commandant of Solitude*, p. 403.
70 Green, interview, *Talking History*.
71 G. Chessell, *Alexander Collie, Colonial Surgeon, Naturalist and Explorer*, University of Western Australia Press, Nedlands, 2008, p. 188.
72 ibid., p. 148.
73 ibid., pp. 149–50.
74 ibid., p. 153.
75 ibid.
76 ibid., pp. 153–54.
77 ibid., p. 154.
78 G. Chessell, *Richard Spencer, Napoleonic War Naval Hero and Australian Pioneer*, University of Western Australia Press, Crawley, 2005, p. 97.
79 Arnold, *A Journey Travelled*, p. 113.
80 Chessell, *Richard Spencer*, p. 98.

81 Arnold, *A Journey Travelled*, p. 125.
82 Chessell, *Richard Spencer*, pp. 98–99.
83 Sir Richard Spencer, letter to colonial secretary, December 1833, cited in Arnold, *A Journey Travelled*, p. 124.
84 Arnold, *A Journey Travelled*, p. 126.
85 B. Goode, C. Irvine, J. Harris and M. Thomas, *Kinjarling, the Place of Rain: The City of Albany & Department of Indigenous Affairs Aboriginal Heritage Survey*, Brad Goode & Associates, Dunsborough, 2005, pp. 64–65.
86 Knapp, interview, November 2018.
87 ibid.
88 Webb, interview, June 2019.
89 Gillies, interview, November 2018.
90 ibid.
91 ibid.
92 J. H. R. Cameron (ed.), *The Millendon Memoirs: George Fletcher Moore's Western Australian Diaries and Letters, 1830–1841*, Hesperian Press, Carlisle, 2006, pp. 203–04.
93 Arnold, *A Journey Travelled*, pp. 118–19.

Notes to Chapter 2: 'A Little Bit Occupied by Natives'
1 A. Haebich, *Dancing in Shadows: Histories of Nyungar Performance*, UWA Publishing, Crawley, 2018, p. 290.
2 B. Carter, *Nyungah Land: Records of Invasion and Theft of Aboriginal Land on the Swan River, 1829–1850*, Swan Valley Nyungah Community, Guildford, 2005, introduction p. x.
3 *Perth Gazette*, 2 January 1836 quoted in A. Hunter, 'Treaties? The impact of inter-racial violence in Tasmania on proposals for negotiating agreements with Aboriginal people in Western Australia in the 1830s', *ANZ Law History e-Journal*, 2006, p. 12.
4 Carter, *Nyungah Land*, p. 9.
5 Captain Fremantle in *Diary and Letters, Sir C. H. Fremantle*, ed. Lord Cottesloe, p. 37, quoted in Carter, *Nyungah Land*, p. 9.
6 Tom Stannage in interview with Bill Bunbury, ABC Radio National, *Image & Reality: Talking History*, 29, 1990.
7 Bevan Carter in conversation with the authors, 23 August 2019.
8 P. Statham-Drew, *James Stirling: Admiral and Founding Governor of Western Australia*, University of Western Australia Press, Crawley, 2003, p. 74.
9 Account of a 'Battle Near Perth', *Western Mail*, 9 January 1914.
10 Major Irwin, *Report to Governor Stirling, 18 May 1830*, SROWA, Swan River Papers, vol. 5, pp. 120, 121.
11 *Western Mail*, 9 January 1914.
12 Irwin, *Report to Governor Stirling*.

13 *Western Mail*, 9 January 1914.
14 G. F. Moore, *Diary of Ten Years Eventful Life of an Early Settler in Western Australia; and also, A Descriptive Vocabulary of the Language of the Aborigines*, facsimile edition, University of Western Australia Press, Nedlands, 1978 [1864], p. 35.
15 ibid., pp. 79–80.
16 ibid., p. 119.
17 Statham-Drew, *James Stirling*, p. 213 (Stirling no. 12 to Goderich 2 April 1832).
18 George Grey quoted by Dave Palmer in L. Collard and D. Palmer, 'Noongar and non-Aboriginal people going along together', in S. Konishi, M. Nugent and T. Shellam (eds), *Indigenous Intermediaries: New Perspectives on Exploration Archives*, ANU, Canberra, 2015, p. 193.
19 Mrs Dorothy Winmar, cited in L. Collard and D. Palmer, in 'Looking for the residents of Terra Australis: the importance of Nyungar in early European coastal exploration', in P. Veth, P. Sutton and M. Neale (eds), *Strangers on the Shore: Early Coastal Contacts in Australia*, National Museum of Australia Press, Canberra, 2008, p. 190.
20 Lynette Knapp in interview with the authors, 17 November 2018.
21 Albert Corunna in interview with Bill Bunbury, *The Spirit of Yagan*, ABC Radio National, broadcast on *Awaye*, 29 March 2014, produced by Community Arts Network.
22 Iszaac Webb in interview with the authors, 6 June 2019.
23 A. Corunna, interview, 2014.
24 J. Hammond, *Winjan's People: The Story of the South West Australian Aborigines*, facsimile edition, Hesperian Press, Perth, 1980 [1933], p. 68.
25 Quoted in B. Bunbury, *Unfinished Business*, ABC Books, Sydney, 1998, p. 22.
26 Ted Wilkes in interview with Bill Bunbury, *The Spirit of Yagan*, ABC Radio National, broadcast on *Awaye*, 29 March 2014, produced by Community Arts Network.
27 Peter Wilkes in interview with Bill Bunbury, *The Spirit of Yagan*, ABC Radio National, broadcast on *Awaye*, 29 March 2014, produced by Community Arts Network.
28 Moore, *Diary of Ten Years Eventful Life*, p. 191.
29 Letter dated 1 November 1837 from Robert Stewart to his brother James. Battye Library, SLWA, letters of Robert Stewart to his father and brothers in Scotland, MN92, Acc. 1086A, 1835–1840 [microform]. In J. and B. Carter, *Settlement to City: A History of the Armadale District and its People*, City of Armadale, Armadale, 2011, p. 28.
30 ibid., p. 39.
31 T. Wilkes, interview, *The Spirit of Yagan*.

NOTES TO CHAPTER 2

32 L. Tilbrook, *Nyungar Tradition: Glimpses of Aborigines in South-Western Australia 1829–1914*, University of Western Australia Press, Nedlands, 1993, p. 5.
33 Moore, *Diary of Ten Years Eventful Life*, preface to a Descriptive Vocabulary, p. x.
34 ibid., p. iii.
35 ibid., p. i.
36 T. Shellam, *Shaking Hands on the Fringe: Negotiating the Aboriginal World at King George's Sound*, University of Western Australia Press, Crawley, 2009, p. 163.
37 L. Collard, G. Revell, D. Palmer and L. Leonard, *Noongar Placenames associated with the Goordandalup (Crawley Bay) Area of the Gabee Derbalor Derbal Yaragan Beloo (Swan River)*, 1999.
38 Shellam, *Shaking Hands*, pp. 165.
39 *Perth Gazette*, 26 January 1833, quoted in ibid., p. 164.
40 Irwin to Lord Viscount Goderich, 10 April 1833, *Report on the Select Committee on Aborigines*, p. 134, quoted in Shellam, *Shaking Hands*, pp. 168–73.
41 Shellam, *Shaking Hands*, p. 176.
42 Bevan Carter, personal communication to the authors, 23 August 2019.
43 J. M. R. Cameron, *The Millendon Memoirs: George Fletcher Moore's Western Australian Diaries and Letters, 1830–1841*, Hesperian Press, Carlisle, 2006, p. 233.
44 *Perth Gazette*, 25 May 1833, p. 83.
45 A. Corunna, interview, *The Spirit of Yagan*.
46 Moore, *Diary of Ten Years Eventful Life*, p. 259.
47 Gwen Corunna in interview with Bill Bunbury, *The Spirit of Yagan*, ABC Radio National, broadcast on *Awaye*, 29 March 2014, produced by Community Arts Network.
48 Moore, *Diary of Ten Years Eventful Life*, p. 206.
49 B. Reece, 'A most complete and untameable savage: Yagan', *Early Days Journal of the Royal Western Australian Historical Society*, vol. 14, part 4, 2015, p. 591.
50 ibid.
51 A. Hasluck, *Yagan: The Patriot*, 1961, quoted in ibid., pp. 593–94.
52 ibid., p. 595.
53 ibid.
54 S. Hallam, 'Aboriginal women as providers: the 1830s on the Swan', *Aboriginal History*, vol. 15, no. 1, 1991, pp. 38–53.
55 Jennie Carter in conversation with the authors, 23 August 2019.
56 L. Heal, *Jane Dodds, 1788–1844: A Swan River Colony Pioneer*, Book Production Services on behalf of L. Macalpine, Sydney, 1988, p. 47.
57 Moore, *Diary of Ten Years Eventful Life*, 'Vocabulary', p. 74.
58 Hallam, *Aboriginal History*, p. 48.

NOTES TO CHAPTER 2

59 Cameron, *The Millendon Memoirs*, p. 210.
60 Gary Wilkes in interview with Bill Bunbury, *The Spirit of Yagan*, ABC Radio National, broadcast on *Awaye*, 29 March 2014, produced by Community Arts Network.
61 I. Berryman (ed.), *Swan River Letters Volume 1*, Swan River Press, Glengarry, 2002, p. 170.
62 A. Schorer, *The Horses Came First: A History of the District of Wandering*, Shire of Wandering, Wandering, 1974.
63 Nigel Wilkes in interview with Bill Bunbury, *The Spirit of Yagan*, ABC Radio National, broadcast on *Awaye*, 29 March 2014, produced by Community Arts Network.
64 H. Reynolds, *This Whispering in our Hearts*, Allen & Unwin, St Leonards, 1998, p. 78.
65 P. Wilkes, interview, *The Spirit of Yagan*.
66 Collard and Palmer, 'Noongar and non-Aboriginal people going along together', p. 195.
67 Knapp interview, November 2018.
68 Statham-Drew, *James Stirling*, p. 211.
69 T. Wilkes, interview, *The Spirit of Yagan*.
70 Lt. Gov. Stirling to Sir George Murray, 30 January 1830 (HRA III vi, NSW, pp. 615–40) quoted in Statham-Drew, *James Stirling*, p. 156.
71 Hunter, *ANZ Law History e-Journal*, p. 4.
72 Reynolds, *This Whispering in our Hearts*, p. 26.
73 Hunter, *ANZ Law History e-Journal*, p. 11.
74 Cameron, *The Millendon Memoirs*, p. 409. Original emphasis.
75 Reported in Executive Council minutes, 13 September 1836, quoted in Hunter, *ANZ Law History e-Journal*, p. 11.
76 Carter, *Nyungah Land*, p. 11.
77 Bella Bropho in interview with Bill Bunbury, *The Spirit of Yagan*, ABC Radio National, broadcast on *Awaye*, 29 March 2014, produced by Community Arts Network.
78 Executive Council Minutes, 13 September 1836, quoted in Hunter, *ANZ Law History e-Journal*, pp. 13–14.
79 Hunter, *ANZ Law History e-Journal*, p. 14.
80 ibid.
81 Francis Armstrong, quoted by A. J. Thompson, 'The interpreter: the legacy of Francis Fraser Armstrong', BA Hons thesis, Murdoch University, 2015, p. 36.
82 Extract from a dispatch dated 23 July 1836 in *Perth Gazette*, 30 July 1836, quoted in Statham-Drew, *James Stirling*, p. 300.
83 Statham-Drew, *James Stirling*, p. 300.
84 ibid., p. 260.

85 J. S. Roe's Fieldbook no. 3, 28 October 1834, quoted in Statham-Drew, *James Stirling*, p. 265.
86 Statham-Drew, *James Stirling*, p. 267.
87 Winnie McHenry in interview with Bill Bunbury, *Noongar Voices of the Eastern Wheatbelt, Program 1: The End of the Beginning*, ABC Radio National, broadcast on *Awaye*, 29 March 2014, produced by Community Arts Network.
88 Hammond, *Winjan's People*, p. 68.
89 Bevan Carter, personal communication to the authors, 23 August 2019.
90 Jane Dodds, *Morning Herald*, 23 October 1832, quoted in Berryman, *Swan River Letters, vol. 1*, pp. 233–34.
91 N. Contos with T. A. Kearing, L. Collard and D. Palmer, *Pinjarra Massacre Site: Research and Development Project*, report for stage 1, Murray Districts Aboriginal Association, Pinjarra, 1998, pp. 38–41.
92 ibid.
93 ibid.
94 J. Stirling, no. 14 to Stanley, 1 November 1834 (rec. 28 May 1835), Colonial Office Records, London, 18/14 fr 34, quoted in Statham-Drew, *James Stirling*, pp. 264–65.
95 Jessica Warriner, 'The scars of the Pinjarra massacre still linger 185 years after one of WA's bloodiest days', *ABC News*, 26 October 2019.
96 J. M. R. Cameron and P. Barnes, *Lieutenant Bunbury's Australian Sojourn: The Letters and Journals of Lieutenant H. W. Bunbury, 21st Royal North British Fusiliers, 1834–1837*, Hesperian Press, Carlisle, 2014, pp. 247, 124.
97 ibid., p. 247.
98 ibid., p. 124.
99 ibid., p. 124, note 175.
100 ibid., p. 249.
101 ibid.
102 T. Wilkes, interview, *The Spirit of Yagan*.
103 Collard and Palmer, 'Looking for the residents', p. 184.
104 Bussell Papers, 7/5 John Bussell to his friend Wells in R. Jennings, *Busselton: Outstation on the Vasse 1830–1850*, Shire of Busselton, Busselton, 1983, p. 74.
105 Letter from Georgiana Molloy to her sister Mrs Besley, 20 November 1833, Battye Library ref. 501A: Letters of Georgiana Molloy, microfilm, quoted in Jennings, *Busselton*, p. 74.
106 E. O. G. Shann, *Cattle Chosen: The Story of the First Group Settlement in Western Australia, 1929–1841*, facsimile edition, University of Western Australia, Nedlands, 1978, p. 18 [1926].
107 John Garrett Bussell's journal for 1832, describing his expedition to the Vasse, reproduced in Shann, *Cattle Chosen*, pp. 99–100.
108 B. Gammage, *The Biggest Estate on Earth: How Aborigines Made Australia*, Allen & Unwin, Sydney, 2012, p. 17.

109 John Bussell's journal for 1832 in Shann, *Cattle Chosen*, pp. 51–52.
110 Webb interview, June 2019.
111 Marian Aveling in interview with Bill Bunbury, ABC, *Talking History*, 1992.
112 M. Allbrook, *Henry Prinsep's Empire*, ANU Press, Canberra, 2014, p. 145.
113 John Bussell's journal for 1832 in Shann, *Cattle Chosen*, p. 99.
114 Shann, pp. 92–93.
115 ibid.
116 Webb, interview, June 2019.
117 Allbrook, *Henry Prinsep's Empire*, p. 145.
118 Aveling, interview, *Talking History*, 1992.
119 Bessie Bussell in her diary for March to December 1837, Bussell Papers, 5/38:8.9 Bessie's Journal, quoted in Shann, *Cattle Chosen*, p. 104, and Jennings, *Busselton*, p. 153.
120 Bessie Bussell, diary for 30 July 1837, quoted in Shann, *Cattle Chosen*, p. 107.
121 Bessie Bussell, diary for 2 August 1837 in Shann, *Cattle Chosen*, p. 107.
122 L. Collard, *A Nyungar Interpretation of Ellensbrook and Wonnerup Homesteads*, National Trust of Australia, Australian Heritage Commission, Canberra, 1994, p. 57.
123 Bussell Papers (B.P 3/23), Lenox Bussell to John Bussell, quoted in Jennings, *Busselton*, p. 83.
124 Draft of a letter by Charles Bussell on the treatment of the Aborigines, quoted in Shann, *Cattle Chosen*, pp. 102, 173–74.
125 Lenox Bussell to Captain Molloy, Resident Magistrate, 9 July, Colonial Secretary Records, S.R. 54, 1837, quoted in Jennings, *Busselton*, p. 126.
126 ibid. in Jennings, *Busselton*, p. 125.
127 Jennings, *Busselton*, p. 144.
128 Account constructed from contemporary depositions of Cobb, a native, Elizabeth Barsay, Anne Bryan, John Dawson, Martin Welch by Alexandra Hasluck, *Portrait with Background: A Life of Georgiana Molloy*, Oxford University Press, London, 1955, pp. 216–17.
129 W. Lines, *An All Consuming Passion: Origins, Modernity and the Australian Life of Georgiana Molloy*, Allen & Unwin, St Leonards, 1994, p. 306.
130 Webb, interview, June 2019.
131 Collard, *A Nyungar Interpretation*, pp. 61–62.
132 Molloy and Bussell report to the Colonial Secretary, Vasse, 27 February 1841, Acc. no. 36, Colonial Secretary's Records, vol. 101, folio 93 (Inventory no. 46 in Collard, *A Nyungar Interpretation*).
133 Nyungar informant E (personal interview by Len Collard, 9 October 1993, at Busselton and Dunsborough) in Collard, *A Nyungar Interpretation*, p. 61.
134 ibid.
135 *Perth Gazette and Western Australian Journal*, 19 March 1841, vol. IX, no. 423 (reproduced in Collard, *A Nyungar Interpretation*, Inventory no. 47).

136 Captain Molloy to William Blaskett, 9 March 1841, Colonial Secretary Records, Battye Library, quoted in Lines, *An All Consuming Passion*, p. 307.
137 ibid.
138 W. B. Kimberly, *History of West Australia: A Narrative of her Past together with Biographies of her Leading Men*, Hesperian Press, Carlisle, 2015, p. 116 [1897].
139 ibid.
140 Nyungar informant G, interviewed by Len Collard, 10 October 1993, at Busselton and Margaret River, quoted in Collard, *A Nyungar Interpretation*, p. 61.
141 Wadjela (white man) informant K, an old-timer with long family links to the Wonnerup area, interviewed by Len Collard, 12 November 1993, at Forrest Beach, quoted in Collard, *A Nyungar Interpretation*, p. 61.
142 J. White, '"Paper talk": testimony and forgetting in South-West Western Australia', *Journal of the Association of the Study of Australian Literature*, 2017, no. 1, p. 2.

Notes to Chapter 3: A Moral Wilderness?

1 Bob Reece, 'A most singular man, Robert Lyon Milne', *Early Days: Journal of the Royal Western Australian Historical Society*, vol. 13, part 5, 2011, p. 585.
2 R. M. Lyon, Speech at public meeting at Guildford, reprinted in Lyon's Letter to the Secretary of State, 1 January 1833, quoted in H. Reynolds, *This Whispering in our Hearts*, Allen & Unwin, St Leonards, 1998, p. 73.
3 R. M. Lyon, *A Glance at the Manners and Language of the Aboriginal Inhabitants of Western Australia*, transcribed by Anita Steinberger for the Dictionary of Western Australian Aboriginal Volumes Committee, Western Australian College of Advanced Education, Perth, 1987 [1833], p. 7.
4 ibid., p. 3.
5 George Fletcher Moore, diary Tuesday 20 September 1831, in J. H. R. Cameron (ed.), *The Millendon Memoirs: George Fletcher Moore's Western Australian Diaries and Letters, 1830–1841*, Hesperian Press, Carlisle, 2006, p. 47.
6 Ray Norris in interview with Bill Bunbury, broadcast on ABC, *Encounter: The Mysteries Are Still There*, 17 November 2012.
7 Moore, diary, Monday 9 September 1833, in Cameron, *The Millendon Memoirs*, p. 276.
8 Vernice Gillies in interview with Bill Bunbury, 18 November 2018.
9 G. Bolton, H. Vose with G. Jones (ed.), *The Wollaston Journals, Vol. 1, 1840–1842*, University of Western Australia Press, Nedlands, 1991, p. 128.
10 Deborah Bird Rose, *Nourishing Terrains: Australian Aboriginal Views of Landscape and Wilderness*, Australian Heritage Commission, Canberra, 1996, p. 7.

NOTES TO CHAPTER 3

11 R. M. Lyon, *An Appeal to the World on Behalf of the Younger Branch of the Family of Shem*, 1839, quoted in Reynolds, *This Whispering*, p. 78.
12 Lyon, *Appeal*, quoted in Reynolds, *This Whispering*, p. 79.
13 Lyon, *An Appeal to the World on Behalf of the Younger Branch of the Family of Shem*, J. Spilsbury and J. M'Rachern, Sydney, 1839, p. 87.
14 L. Borowitzka, 'The reverend Dr Louis Giustiniani and Anglican conflict in the Swan River colony, 1836–1838', *Journal of Religious History*, vol. 35, no. 3, 2011, p. 352.
15 Reynolds, *This Whispering*, p. 84.
16 Borowitzka, *Journal of Religious History*, p. 359.
17 C. T. Stannage, *The People of Perth: A Social History of Western Australia's Capital City*, Perth City Council, Perth, 1979, p. 36.
18 H. M. Carey, *God's Empire: Religion and Colonialism in the British World, c.1801–1908*, Cambridge University Press, New York, 2011, p. 70.
19 Reynolds, *This Whispering*, p. 84.
20 *Swan River Guardian*, 27 April 1837, quoted in Reynolds, *This Whispering*, p. 85.
21 'Glenelg, Baron (1778–1866)', *Australian Dictionary of Biography*, National Centre of Biography, Australian National University, 1966, viewed 2 December 2018, <http://adb.anu.edu.au/biography/glenelg-baron-2101/text2651>.
22 *Swan River Guardian*, 8 June 1837, p. 16, quoted in Borowitzka, *Journal of Religious History*, p. 364.
23 Borowitzka, *Journal of Religious History*, p. 367.
24 Letter to *Perth Gazette*, 13 May 1837, quoted by Reynolds, *This Whispering*, p. 86.
25 Reynolds, *This Whispering*, pp. 88–89.
26 Borowitzka, *Journal of Religious History*, p. 362.
27 W. H. Burgess, York farmer, letter written 1 December 1837, published in *Perth Gazette*, 6 January 1838, quoted in Borowitzka, *Journal of Religious History*, p. 367.
28 *Swan River Guardian*, 8 February 1838, quoted in Borowitzka, *Journal of Religious History*, p. 369.
29 Borowitzka, *Journal of Religious History*, p. 372.
30 Aborigines Protection Society, *Report of Sub-Committee on Australia with Notes*, London, 1838, quoted in A. Hunter, *A Different Kind of 'Subject': Colonial Law in Aboriginal–European Relations in Nineteenth Century Western Australia 1829–1861*, Australian Scholarly Publishing, Melbourne, 2012, pp. 86–87.
31 Carey, *God's Empire*, p. 160.
32 Hunter, *A Different Kind of 'Subject'*, pp. 101–02.
33 Colonial secretary to government resident, 8 February 1839, Colonial Secretary Records, Acc. 49/12, no. 13, p. 117, quoted in Hunter, *A Different Kind of 'Subject'*, p. 92.

34 A. Hunter, 'John Hutt: the inconspicuous governor', *Early Days: Journal of the Royal Western Australian Historical Society*, vol. 13, part 3, 2009, p. 317–18.
35 ibid.
36 G. S. R. Kitson Clark, *The Making of Victorian England*, Methuen & Co., 1965, p. 284i, quoted in M. Arnold, *A Journey Travelled: Aboriginal–European Relations at Albany and the Surrounding Region, from First Contact to 1926*, UWA Publishing, Nedlands, 2015, p. 129.
37 Hunter, *Early Days*, p. 317.
38 A. J. Thompson, 'The interpreter: the legacy of Francis Fraser Armstrong', BA Hons thesis, Murdoch University, 2015.
39 ibid.
40 ibid.
41 R. B. Roy, 'A reappraisal of Wesleyan Methodist mission in the first half of the nineteenth century as viewed through the ministry of Rev. John Smithies (1802–1872)', PhD thesis, Edith Cowan University, 2006, p. 164.
42 ibid., p. 163.
43 M. Gourlay, *The Good Bishop: The Story of Bishop Hale*, Boolarong Press, Brisbane, 2015, p. 27.
44 Smithies quoted in W. McNair and H. Rumley, *Pioneer Aboriginal Mission: The Work of John Smithies in the Swan River Colony, 1841–1855*, University of Western Australia Press, Nedlands, 1981, p. 134.
45 ibid.
46 Tom Hayden in interview with Bill Bunbury, ABC Radio National, *Voices of the Central Eastern Wheabelt, 3: You Can hear The Ants Breathing*, broadcast on *Awaye*, April 2010, produced by Community Arts Network.
47 E. Millett, *An Australian Parsonage, or the Settler and the Savage in Western Australia*, facsimile edition with an introduction by Rica Erikson, University of Western Australia Press, Nedlands, 1980 [1872], p. 228.
48 Pat Dodson in interview with Bill Bunbury, ABC Radio National, *Encounter, Land, Culture, Religion*, broadcast 26 September 2010.
49 Gillies interview, 2018.
50 Lynette Knapp, interview with the authors, 17 November 2018.
51 Dodson, interview, *Land Culture, Religion*, 2010.
52 K. Palmer, *Noongar People, Noongar Land: The Resilience of Aboriginal culture in the South West of Western Australia*, AIATSIS Research Publications, Canberra, 2016, p. 69.
53 Millett, *An Australian Parsonage*, p. 228.
54 ibid.
55 ibid.
56 John Blacket, *Fire in the Outback: The Untold Story of the Aboriginal Revival Movement*, Albatross, Sydney, 1996, quoted in Roy, 'A reappraisal', pp. 204–05.

57 Methodist church WA, Petition for a missionary 1836, quoted in McNair and Rumley, *Pioneer Aboriginal Mission*, p. 30.
58 Izsaac Webb, in interview with the authors, 6 June 2019.
59 John Smithies, letter to authorities in London, 20 September 1841, quoted in McNair and Rumley, *Pioneer Aboriginal Mission*, pp. 62–63.
60 N. Green, 'Aborigines of the Albany Region, 1821–1898', *The Bicentennial Dictionary of Western Australians*, vol. 1, University of Western Australia Press, Nedlands, 1989, p. 81.
61 Despatch from Governor Hunt to Lord John Russell, 1 March 1842, British Parliamentary Papers, Colonies, Australia, p. 402, quoted in S. Barley, 'Out of step: the failure of the early protestant missions', in B. Reece and T. Stannage (eds), *European–Aboriginal Relations in Western Australian History*, Studies in Western Australian History VIII, University of Western Australia, Nedlands, 1984, p. 30.
62 Roy, 'A reappraisal', pp. 161–62.
63 ibid., p. 85.
64 R. Strong, 'The Reverend John Wollaston and colonial Christianity in Western Australia, 1840–1863', *Journal of Religious History*, vol. 25, no. 3, 2001, p. 267.
65 ibid, p. 268.
66 ibid, p. 266.
67 G. C. Bolton, 'Wollaston, John Ramsden (1791–1856)', *Australian Dictionary of Biography*, National Centre of Biography, Australian National University, 1967.
68 Rev. John Wollaston, *The Wollaston Journals, Vol. 1, 1840–1842*, Bolton, G.C., Vose, H., with Jones, G. (eds), University of Western Australia Press, Nedlands, p. 128.
69 Rev. John Wollaston, *Wollaston's Picton Journal (1841–1844)*, C. A. Burton (ed.), Paterson Brokensha, Perth, n.d, p. 174.
70 ibid, p.11
71 Strong, 'John Wollaston', p. 279.
72 Wollaston's, *Picton Journal*, p. 190.
73 A. O'Brien, 'Religion', in A. Bashford and S. Macintyre (eds), *The Cambridge History of Australia, Vol. 1: Indigenous and Colonial Australia*, Cambridge University Press, Melbourne, 2013, p. 414.
74 Strong, 'John Wollaston', p.283.
75 ibid, p. 280.
76 Wollaston's, *Picton Journal*, p. 82
77 Strong, 'John Wollaston', p. 280.
78 J. Groves, 'The Camfields: the comforts of civilisation in early colonial Western Australia', BA (Hons) dissertation, Edith Cowan University, 2006, p. 26.

NOTES TO CHAPTER 3

79 Rev. George King, *Notes in Connection with his Work in Western Australia, 1841–1849*, Battye Library PR 7568, quoted in ibid., p. 27.
80 ibid.
81 Archdeacon Matthew Hale, *South Australian Register*, 28 August 1850, p. 4, reproduced in Gourlay, *The Good Bishop*, pp. 25–26. Original emphasis.
82 Henry Camfield, letter to his sister, 6 June 1832, quoted in Groves, 'The Camfields', p. 23.
83 *Inquirer*, 13 September 1848, quoted in Groves, 'The Camfields', p. 32.
84 ibid.
85 Groves, 'The Camfields', p. 32.
86 Arnold, *A Journey Travelled*, pp. 136–37.
87 Patrick Taylor, settler, quoted in Arnold, *A Journey Travelled*, p. 137.
88 Knapp, interview, November 2018.
89 ibid.
90 Anne Camfield in Church of England magazine, vol. VII, no. 1, May 1868, Battye Library; and WA Legislative Council Votes and Proceedings 1871, 2nd session, 25, quoted in Groves, 'The Camfields', p. 42.
91 ibid.
92 Florence Nightingale, extract, 'Sanitary statistics of native colonial schools and hospitals', Battye Library, PR 4000, quoted in Groves, 'The Camfields', p. 50.
93 *Perth Gazette* and *West Australian Times*, 21 June 1870, p. 1, quoted in Gourlay, *The Good Bishop*, p. 55.
94 Gourlay, *The Good Bishop*, p. 56.
95 Millett, *An Australian Parsonage*, p. 131.
96 ibid., pp. 228–29.
97 ibid., p. 71.
98 ibid.
99 B. Pascoe, *Dark Emu, Black Seeds*, Magabala Books, Broome, 2014, p. 28.
100 Webb, interview, June 2019.
101 Millett, *An Australian Parsonage*, p. 74.
102 ibid., pp. 129–30.
103 ibid., p. 147.
104 ibid.
105 ibid., p. 273–74.
106 Salvado in report to the Sacred Congregation for the Propagation of the Faith, 1853, quoted in G. Russo, *Lord Abbot of the Wilderness: The Life and Times of Bishop Salvado*, Polding Press, Melbourne, 1979, pp. 132–33.
107 Abbot Bernard Rooney in conversation with Terry Quinn, chairman of the WA Catholic Social Justice Council, 'Salvado wanted an "indigenous faith"', *The Record*, 27 July 2011.
108 ibid.
109 John Kinder in interview with Bill Bunbury, 5 December 2018.
110 ibid.

111 Bishop Rosendo Salvado, 1864, in *Information Respecting the Habits and Customs of the Aboriginal Inhabitants of Western Australia*, compiled from various sources, presented to The Legislative Council by His Excellency's Command, Richard Pether, Government Printer, Perth, 1871, p. 5 (Salvado, pp. 3–10).
112 Kinder, interview, December 2018.
113 ibid.
114 *The Record*, 27 July 2011.
115 Kinder, interview, December, 2018.
116 Salvado, *Information Respecting the Habits*, p. 3.
117 T. Shellam., 'A mystery to the medical world: Florence Nightingale, Rosendo Salvado and the risk of civilisation', *History, Australia*, vol. 9, no. 1, 2012, p. 117.
118 Salvado, 'Form of return from England by Miss Nightingale', October 1860, Acc. 2953A/9, NNA, quoted in ibid., pp. 120–21.
119 Shellam, *History, Australia*, p. 121.
120 ibid., p. 124.
121 ibid., p. 125.
122 ibid., p. 126.
123 Salvado, *Information Respecting the Habits*, p. 6.
124 ibid.
125 ibid.
126 Russo, *Lord Abbot*, p. 197.
127 B. Rooney, 'An evolving concept of mission, New Norcia 1846–2006', *Australasian Catholic Record*, vol. 83, no. 3, 2006, pp. 315–16.
128 ibid.
129 Salvado, *Information Respecting the Habits*, p. 3.
130 Millett, *An Australian Parsonage*, p. 274.
131 ibid., p. 74.
132 ibid., p. 134–35.
133 Rooney, 'An evolving concept', pp. 315–16.
134 Smithies to Wesleyan Methodist Missionary Society, London, 20 September 1841, SOAS, Box 516, quoted in Roy, 'A reappraisal', p. 159.
135 Gary Wilkes, interview with Bill Bunbury, *The Spirit of Yagan*, ABC Radio, broadcast on *Awaye*, 29 March 2014, produced by Community Arts Network.

Notes to Chapter 4: The End of the Beginning or the Beginning of the End?

1 Tom Hayden in interview with Bill Bunbury, *Noongar Voices of the Central Eastern Wheatbelt, 1: The End of the Beginning*, ABC Radio National, broadcast on Awaye, April 2010, produced by Community Arts Network.

NOTES TO CHAPTER 4

2   J. Hammond, *Winjan's People: The Story of the South West Australian Aborigines*, P. Hasluck (ed.), facsimile edition, Hesperian Press, Perth, 1980 [1933], p. 13.
3   ibid.
4   ibid., p. 43.
5   G. Grey, *Journals of Two Expeditions of Discovery in the North-West and Western Australia during the Years 1837, 1838 and 1839*, vol. 2, facsimile edition, Hesperian Press, Carlisle, 1984, pp. 261–62.
6   ibid., p. 366.
7   Vernice Gillies in interview with Bill Bunbury, 18 November 2018.
8   A. Hunter, *A Different Kind of Subject: Colonial Law in Aboriginal–European Relations in Nineteenth Century Western Australia, 1829–1861*, Australian Scholarly Publishing, Melbourne, 2012, p. 17.
9   J. Purdy, *Just One Damn Thing After Another: Colonialism, Economics, The Law and Resistance in Western Australia*, Der Andere Verlag, Germany, 2010, p. 30.
10   ibid., p. 33.
11   ibid.
12   E. W. Landor, *The Bushman*, 1847, pp. 187–88, quoted in Purdy, *Just One Damn Thing*, p. 31.
13   Gillies, interview, November 2018.
14   L. Collard and I Cumming, 'Kaya Wandjoo Ngala Noongarpedia – Welcome to our Noongarpedia', *Cultural Science*, vol. 9, no. 1, 2016, p. 41.
15   *Perth Gazette*, 18 July 1838, quoted in J. Carter and B. Carter, *Settlement to City: A History of the Armadale District and its People*, City of Armadale, Armadale, 2011, p. 46.
16   J. Carter and B. Carter, *Settlement to City: A History of the Armadale District and its People*, City of Armadale, Armadale, 2011, p. 28.
17   Ashley Bell in interview with Bill Bunbury, *Sound of the Cockies*, Shire of Perenjori, Perenjori, 2015, p. 23.
18   E. Goddard and T. Stannage, 'John Forrest and the Aborigines', in B. Reece and T. Stannage (eds), *European –Aboriginal Relations in Western Australian History*, Studies in Western Australian History VIII, University of Western Australia, Nedlands, 1984, pp. 56–57.
19   ibid., p. 54.
20   L. Collard and D. Palmer, 'Noongar and non-Aboriginal people going along together (Ngulla wangkiny, ni, katitjin Noongar, nyidung koorliny, kura, yeye, boorda)', in S. Konishi, M. Nugent and T. Shellam (eds), *Indigenous Intermediaries: New Perspectives on Exploration Archives*, ANU, Canberra, 2015, p. 190.
21   ibid., p. 198.
22   O. Pustkuchen, *On the Way Through: The Story of Narrogin*, Artlook Books for the Town of Narrogin, Perth, 1981, p. 23.

23 D. S. Garden, *Northam: An Avon Valley History*, Oxford University Press, Melbourne, 1979, p. 41.
24 ibid., p. 42–43.
25 ibid., p. 48.
26 ibid.
27 ibid., pp. 48–49.
28 Pustkuchen, *On the Way Through*, p. 24.
29 H. Reynolds, *The Other Side of The Frontier: Aboriginal Resistance to the Invasion of Australia*, University of New South Wales Press, Sydney, 2006 [1982], p. 156.
30 T. Sanders, *Bunbury: Some Early History*, Roebuck Society, Canberra, 1975, p. 1.
31 ibid., p. 110.
32 ibid., p. 110.
33 Hammond, *Winjan's People*, pp. 9, 11.
34 Lynette Knapp in interview with the authors, 17 November 2018.
35 L. Tilbrook, *Nyungar Tradition: Glimpses of Aborigines in South-Western Australia 1829–1914*, University of Western Australia Press, Nedlands, 1983, p. 35.
36 M. Arnold, *A Journey Travelled: Aboriginal–European Relationships at Albany and the Surrounding Region from First Contact to 1926*, UWA Publishing, Crawley, WA, 2015, p. 162.
37 ibid.
38 Gillies, interview, November 2018.
39 Hammond, *Winjan's People*, p. 60.
40 P. Hasluck, *Oral History Interviews, 1926–1939*, State Records Office, Perth, 4553A/68.
41 ibid., 4553/70.
42 ibid., 4553/70.
43 Hammond, *Winjan's People*, p. 73.
44 Mokare's comment recorded by Captain Collet Barker in his diary 26 February 1830. J. Mulvaney and N. Green, *Commandant of Solitude: The Journals of Captain Collet Barker 1828–1831*, Melbourne University Press at the Miegunyah Press, Carlton, 1992, p. 403.
45 Ethel Hassell, *My Dusky Friends: Aboriginal Life, Customs and Legends and Glimpses of Station Life at Jarramungup in the 1880s*, C. W. Hassell, Perth, 1975, p. 9. Original emphasis.
46 Sara Meagher, Introduction to E. Hassell, *My Dusky Friends*, p. ix.
47 ibid., pp. 11–12.
48 Hassell, *My Dusky Friends*, pp. 73–74.
49 ibid., pp. 83–85.

50 Landgate, *Town names*, viewed 18 June 2019, <https://www0.landgate.wa.gov.au/maps-and-imagery/wa-geographic-names/name-history/historical-town-names#J>.
51 Collard and Palmer, 'Noongar and non-Aboriginal people', pp. 196–97.
52 R. Glover, *Plantagenet, Rich and Beautiful: A History of the Shire of Plantagenet*, Western Australia, University of Western Australia Press, Nedlands, 1979, p. 285.
53 South West Aboriginal Land and Sea Council, J. Host with C. Owen, *"It's still in my heart, this is my country": The Single Noongar Claim History*, UWA Publishing, Crawley, 2009, p. 225.
54 Knapp, interview, November 2018.
55 South West Aboriginal Land & Sea Council, '1880: Ravensthorpe massacre', *Kaartdijin Noongar – Noongar Knowledge*, viewed 8 January 2019, <https://www.noongarculture.org.au/1880/>.
56 K. Scott and H. Brown, *Kayang and Me*, Fremantle Press, Fremantle, 2013, pp. 65–67.
57 Tara de Graff, 'Memorial launch prompts reconciliation between farming and Indigenous communities in regional Western Australia', 22–25 May 2015, *ABC Country Hour*, viewed 8 January 2019, <https://www.abc.net.au/news/rural/2015-05-22/kukenarup-memorial-opened-in-ravensthorpe/6490332>.
58 M. C. Howard, 'Aboriginal society in south-western Australia', in R. M. Berndt and C. H. Berndt (eds), *Aborigines of the West: Their Past and Their Present*, University of Western Australia Press, Nedlands, 1980, p. 93.
59 Iszaac Webb in interview with the authors, 6 June 2019.
60 Howard, 'Aboriginal society', pp. 93–94.
61 A. Haebich, 'European farmers and Aboriginal farmers in south Western Australia mid 1890s–1914', in B. Reece and T. Stannage (eds), *European–Aboriginal Relations in Western Australian History*, Studies in Western Australian History VIII, University of Western Australia, Nedlands, 1984, p. 61.
62 T. Shellam, *Meeting the Waylo: Aboriginal Encounters in the Archipelago*, UWA Publishing, Crawley, 2019, p. 127.
63 Cathie Clement in interview with Bill Bunbury, ABC Radio National, *Talking History*, 85, 1993. Tiffany Shellam also describes the Hanover Bay incident in which Philip Parker King's demonstration of the clasp knife was misinterpreted by the local people as an unfriendly gesture. Shellam, *Meeting the Waylo*, p. 132.
64 Howard Pedersen in interview with Bill Bunbury, ABC Radio National, *Talking History*, 85, 1993.
65 ibid.
66 C. Owen, *Every Mother's Son is Guilty: Policing the Kimberley Frontier of WA 1882–1905*, UWA Publishing, Crawley, 2016, p. 103.

NOTES TO CHAPTER 4

67 Legislative Council, *The West Australian*, 20 November 1888, p. 3, quoted in Owen, *'Every Mother's Son'*, pp. 203–04.
68 H. Reynolds, *This Whispering in our Hearts*, Allen & Unwin, St Leonards, 1998, p. 142.
69 ibid., p. 167.
70 David Carley quoted in J. B. Gribble, *Dark Deeds in a Sunny Land*, University of Western Australia Press with the Institute of Applied Aboriginal Studies, WA College of Advanced Education, Perth, 1987 [1886], pp. 48–49.
71 Pedersen, interview, 1993.
72 S. J. Hunt, 'The Gribble affair, a study in colonial politics', in Gribble, *Dark Deeds in a Sunny Land*, 1987, p. 67.
73 ibid., p. 62.
74 Neville Green, interview with Bill Bunbury, ABC Radio National, *Talking History*, 85, 1993.
75 Reynolds, *This Whispering*, p. 163.
76 Gribble, *Dark Deeds*, 1987, pp. 47–48. (Article published in the Melbourne Daily Telegraph, 9 July 1886).
77 Gribble, *Dark Deeds*, 1987, p. 34.
78 ibid., p. 10.
79 Green, interview, 1993.
80 Reynolds, *This Whispering*, p. 151.
81 ibid., p. 150.
82 Hunt in *Dark Deeds*, p. 65.
83 *Inquirer*, 1 June 1887, quoted in Hunt, *Dark Deeds*, p. 69.
84 Hunt in *Dark Deeds*, p. 70.
85 *Inquirer*, 29 June 1887, quoted in Hunt, *Dark Deeds*, p. 70.
86 A. Haebich in interview with Bill Bunbury, ABC Radio National, *Talking History*, 85, 1993.
87 Pedersen, interview, 1993.
88 ibid.
89 Gribble, *Dark Deeds*, pp. 51–52.
90 A. Ludewig, *Wartime on Wadjemup: A Social History of the Rottnest Island Internment Camp*, UWA Publishing, Crawley, 2019, p. 41.
91 Alexander Forrest in Western Australia, Parliamentary Debates, 22 August 1895, vol. 8, p. 674, quoted in J. E. Thomas, 'Crime and society', in C. T. Stannage (ed.), *A New History of Western Australia*, University of Western Australia Press, Nedlands, 1981.
92 Pedersen, interview, 1993.
93 H. McGlashan, 'George Grey's expedition 1837–1838: first European penetration into the Kimberley interior', in C. Clement, J. Gresham and H. McGlashan (eds), *Kimberley History: People, Exploration and Development*, Kimberley Society, Perth, 2012, p. 63. Emphasis in McGlashan.
94 Clement, interview, 1993.

95 Green, interview, 1993.
96 Sarah Yu, 'Ngapa kunangkul (living water): an indigenous view of groundwater', in A. Gaynor, M. Trinca and A. Haebich (eds), *Country: Visions of Land and People in Western Australia*, Western Australian Museum, Perth, 2002, pp. 35–37.
97 F. Skyring and S. Yu, 'Strange strangers: first contact between Europeans and Karajarri people on the Kimberley coast of Western Australia', in P. Veth, P. Sutton and M. Neale (eds), *Strangers on the Shore: Early Coastal Contacts in Australia*, National Museum of Australia Press, Canberra, 2008, p. 63.
98 Dudu Nankiriny, John, Interviewed by Sarah Yu, Bidyadanga, 20 July 1999 in Strange Strangers, First Contact between Europeans and Karajarri people on the Kimberley coast of Western Australia', in P. Veth, P. Sutton and M. Neale (eds), *Strangers on the Shore: Early Coastal Contacts in Australia*, National Museum of Australia Press, Canberra, 2008, p. 63.
99 Bruce Scates in interview with Bill Bunbury, ABC Radio National, *Hindsight*, 1997.
100 Skyring and Yu, 'Strange Strangers', p. 66.
101 Scates, interview, 1997.
102 Monument Australia, *Maitland Brown Memorial (Explorers Monument)*, viewed 17 February 2020, <http://monumentaustralia.org.au/themes/people/exploration/display/60482-maitland-brown-memorial-explorers-monument>.
103 ibid.
104 Joe Roe, speech recorded by Bill Bunbury, ABC Radio National, *Hindsight*, 1997.
105 V. Mills, 'Women recognised for love and death in Broome pearling', ABC Kimberley, 29 November 2010, viewed 17 January 2019, <http://www.abc.net.au/local/stories/2010/11/29/3079734.htm?site=kimberley>.
106 ibid.
107 P. Hetherington, *Settlers, Servants and Slaves: Aboriginal and European Children in Western Australia*, University of Western Australia Press, Crawley, 2002, pp. 156–57.
108 Robert Sholl, Government Resident, Report to the Colonial Secretary, WA Colonial Secretary's Office (CSO), vol. 646, item 17, 1869, in Hetherington, *Settler, Servants and Slaves*, pp. 156–57.
109 Hetherington, *Settlers, Servants and Slaves*, p. 157.
110 Broome and the Kimberley, *Broome History and Culture*, p. 3, viewed 16 January 2019, <https://www.broomeandthekimberley.com.au/broome-history-culture/>.
111 B. Collins and H. Smale, 'Uncovering the first 20,000 years of Australia's pearling history', ABC Kimberley, 6 June 2014, viewed 17 January 2019, <http://www.abc.net.au/local/stories/2014/06/06/4020357.htm>.

NOTES TO CHAPTER 4

112 Sarah Yu, 'Searching for the in-between: developing indigenous holistic approaches to cultural heritage assessment and interpretation', *Coolabah*, nos 24 & 25, 2018, p. 171.
113 Green, interview, 1993.
114 P. Smith, 'Into the Kimberley: the invasion of the Sturt Creek Basin (Kimberley region, Western Australia) and evidence of Aboriginal resistance', *Aboriginal History*, vol. 24, 2000, p. 65.
115 *Western Australian Times*, 23 September 1879.
116 G. C. Bolton, 'Alexander Forrest's expedition of 1879 and early development of the cattle industry', in C. Clement, J. Gresham and H. McGlashan (eds), *Kimberley History: People, Exploration and Development*. Kimberley Society, Perth, 2012, p. 103.
117 Clement, interview, 1993.
118 Bolton, 'Alexander Forrest's expedition of 1879', p. 106.
119 Smith, *Aboriginal History*, p. 66.
120 Gordon Broughton, *Turn Against Home*, quoted in C. Owen, 'Every Mother's Son', p. 146.
121 Richard Allen, a Kimberley pioneer, 'Reminiscences', MSS 448A, Battye Library, quoted in Owen, 'Every Mother's Son', p. 144.
122 B. Shaw, 'On the historical emergence of race relations in the Eastern Kimberley: change?', in R. M. Berndt and C. H. Berndt (eds), *Aborigines of the West: Their Past and Their Present*, University of Western Australia Press, Nedlands, 1980, p. 263.
123 *The West Australian*, 20 April 1888, quoted in Owen, 'Every Mother's Son', p. 209.
124 Smith, *Aboriginal History*, p. 72.
125 G. Buchanan, *Packhorse and Waterhole: With the First Overlanders to the Kimberleys*, facsimile edition, Hesperian Press, Carlisle, 1997 [1933], pp. 59–60.
126 P. Smith, 'Station camps: legislation, labour relations and rations on pastoral leases in the Kimberley region, Western Australia', *Aboriginal History*, vol. 24, 2000, p. 76.
127 ibid., p. 77.
128 M. Durack, *Kings in Grass Castles*, Corgi, London, 1967 [1959], p. 370.
129 Owen, 'Every Mother's Son', p. 79.
130 ibid., pp. 214–15.
131 ibid., p. 190.
132 G. C. Bolton, 'A survey of the Kimberley pastoral industry, from 1885 to the present', MA thesis, University of Western Australia, 1953, p. 27.
133 G. C. Bolton, 'Portrait of the historian as a young learner', in D. Graham (ed.), *Being Whitefella*, Fremantle Arts Centre, Press, Fremantle, 1994, pp. 119–25.
134 ibid., p. 122.
135 ibid., p. 125.
136 Bolton, 'A survey of the Kimberley pastoral industry', p. 49.

137 ibid.
138 ibid.
139 ibid., p. 52.
140 H. Pedersen, 'Pigeon: an Australian Aboriginal rebel', in B. Reece and T. Stannage (eds), *European–Aboriginal Relations in Western Australian History*, Studies in Western Australian History VIII, University of Western Australia, Nedlands, 1984, p. 8.
141 Pedersen, interview, ABC Radio National, *Talking History*, 85, 1993.
142 Owen, *'Every Mother's Son'*, p. 282
143 Pedersen, interview, *1993*.
144 Pedersen, 'Pigeon', p. 9.
145 B. Woorunmurra and H. Pedersen, *Jandamarra and the Bunuba Resistance: A True Story*, Magabala Books, Broome, 1995, p. 95.
146 ibid., p. 99.
147 ibid.
148 Pedersen, 'Pigeon', p. 10.
149 Owen, *'Every Mother's Son'*, p. 46.
150 ibid.
151 Pedersen, interview, 1993.
152 Pedersen, 'Pigeon', p. 11.
153 Woorunmurra and Pedersen, *Jandamarra*, p. 131.
154 Pedersen, 'Pigeon', p. 11.
155 Woorunmurra and Pedersen, *Jandamarra*, pp. 131–32.
156 Pedersen, 'Pigeon', p. 11.
157 Woorunmurra and Pedersen, *Jandamarra*, p. 200.
158 Pedersen, *interview*, 1993.
159 Pedersen, 'Pigeon', p. 14.
160 C. Choo, 'Mixed blessings: Establishment of Christian missions in the Kimberley', in C. Clement, J. Gresham and H. McGlashan (eds), *Kimberley History: People, Exploration and Development*, Kimberley Society, Perth, 2012, p. 195.
161 C. Choo in interview with Bill Bunbury, 8 May 2019.
162 ibid.
163 ibid.
164 ibid.
165 H. C. Prinsep in Aborigines Department, *Report for the Financial Year ending 30th June 1899*, WA Government Printer, Perth, p. 7.
166 M. Allbrook, *Henry Prinsep's Empire*, ANU Press, Canberra, 2014, p. 238.
167 The Hon. John Forrest: Presidential Address, Australian Association for the Advancement of Science, January 1890, reprinted in M. Aveling (ed.), *Westralian Voices. Documents in West Australian Social History*, University of Western Australia Press, Nedlands, 1979, pp. 50–51.
168 Prinsep, Aborigines Department report, p. 1.

Notes to Chapter 5: Snapped Shut the Lawbook

1. Jack Davis, 'Aboriginal Australia – To the Others', poem first published in *Jagardoo: Poems from Aboriginal Australia*, Methuen of Australia, Sydney, 1977, reprinted in R. Berndt and C. Berndt (eds), *Aborigines of the West*, University of Western Australia Press, Crawley, 1979, p. 54 (lines 1–8).
2. Museum of Australian Democracy, Yirrkala Bark Petitions, 1963, *Documenting a Democracy*, viewed 31 March 2019, <https://www.foundingdocs.gov.au/item-did-104.html>.
3. H. Reynolds, *This Whispering in Our Hearts*, Allen & Unwin, St Leonards, 1998, p. 171.
4. ibid., pp. 173–74.
5. ibid., p. 174.
6. Correspondence relating to the proposed abolition of the Aborigines Protection Board, 20 April 1892, from John Forrest to Sir Alexander Onslow, Chief Justice of Western Australia, in Reynolds, *This Whispering*, p. 175.
7. Find & Connect, *Western Australia – legislation: Aborigines Act 1897 (1898–1906)*, viewed 3 October 2019, <https://www.findandconnect.gov.au/guide/wa/WE00405>.
8. M. Allbrook, *Henry Prinsep's Empire*, ANU Press, Canberra, 2014, p. 237.
9. Find & Connect, *Aborigines Act 1897 (1898–1906)*.
10. Allbrook, *Henry Prinsep's Empire*, p. 238.
11. ibid., p. 155.
12. ibid., p. 1.
13. P. Biskup, *Not Slaves, Not Citizens: The Aboriginal Problem in Western Australia, 1898–1954*, University of Queensland Press, St Lucia, 1973, p. 45.
14. Allbrook, Henry Prinsep's Empire, p. 237.
15. ibid., p. 242.
16. ibid., p. 5.
17. ibid., p. 146.
18. ibid., pp. 242–43.
19. Government of Western Australia, *Annual Report of the Aborigines Department, 1900–1901*, Perth, p. 4, quoted in Allbrook, *Henry Prinsep's Empire*, p. 242.
20. A. Haebich, *For their Own Good: Aborigines and Government in Western Australia in the South West of Western Australia 1900–1940*, University of Western Australia Press, Nedlands, 1988, p. 48.
21. Henry Prinsep in *Annual Report of the Aborigines Department, 1900–1901*, p. 4., quoted in Allbrook, *Henry Prinsep's Empire*, p. 242.
22. Allbrook, *Henry Prinsep's Empire*, p. 271.
23. A. Haebich, 'European farmers and Aboriginal farmers in south western Australia, mid 1890s–1914', in B. Reece and C. T. Stannage (eds), *Studies in Western Australian History: European–Aboriginal Relations in Western Australian History*, no. 8, 1984, p. 62.

24 Prinsep letter to Daisy Bates, quoted in Allbrook, *Henry Prinsep's Empire*, p. 244.
25 ibid., pp 244–45.
26 ibid.
27 Aborigines Department Papers 321/1902, quoted in Haebich, *For their Own Good*, pp. 67–70.
28 John Forrest quoted in Haebich, *For their Own Good*, pp. 59–60.
29 Prinsep in *Annual Report of the Aborigines Department, 1900–1901*, p. 5.
30 Haebich, For their Own Good, pp. 71–73.
31 L. Hunt, 'Sir Walter Hartwell James (1863–1943)', *Australian Dictionary of Biography*, National Centre of Biography, Australian National University, 1983, viewed 5 December 2019, <http://adb.anu.edu.au/biography/james-sir-walter-hartwell-6824>.
32 Allbrook, *Henry Prinsep's Empire*, p. 281.
33 Haebich, *For their Own Good*, p. 76.
34 Allbrook, *Henry Prinsep's Empire*, p. 278.
35 Biskup, *Not Slaves, Not Citizens*, p. 60.
36 *Report of the Royal Commission on the Condition of the Natives*, Wm Alfred Watson, Government Printer, Perth, 1905, p. 35 (Roth report).
37 ibid., p. 5.
38 ibid., pp. 8–9.
39 ibid., p. 13.
40 ibid., p. 14.
41 Biskup, *Not Slaves, Not Citizens*, p. 60.
42 Roth report, p. 20.
43 Biskup, *Not Slaves, Not Citizens*, p. 61.
44 Roth report, p. 25.
45 ibid., p. 40.
46 *Aborigines Act 1905*, Western Australia (No. 14 of 1905).
47 Lynnette Coomer in interview with the authors, 31 May 2019.
48 Father George Walter, *Australia: Land, People, Mission, 1928*, quoted in C. Choo, *Mission Girls: Aboriginal Women on Catholic Missions in the Kimberley WA, 1900–1950*, University of Western Australia Press, Crawley, 2001, p. 59.
49 ibid.
50 C. Choo in interview with Bill Bunbury, 7 May 2019.
51 ibid.
52 ibid.
53 ibid.
54 Rosa Bin Amat interviewed by Christine Choo, 10 July 1992, quoted in Choo, *Mission Girlss: Aboriginal Women on Catholic Missions in the Kimberley WA, 1900–1950*, University of Western Australia Press, Crawley, 2001, p. 149.
55 ibid., pp. 164–65.

NOTES TO CHAPTER 5

56 Choo, interview, May 2019.
57 L. Tilbrook, *Nyungar Tradition: Glimpses of Aborigines in South-Western Australia 1829–1914*, University of Western Australia Press, Nedlands, 1983, p. 5.
58 *Aborigines Act, 1905*, s.3 (d).
59 Anna Haebich in interview with Bill Bunbury, ABC Radio National, *Talking History*, 86, 1993.
60 John Kinder in interview with Bill Bunbury, 5 December 2018.
61 Haebich, For their Own Good, p. 128.
62 R. Broome, *Aboriginal Australians: Black Response to White Dominance, 1788–1980*, Allen & Unwin, Sydney, 1982, quoted in Haebich, For their Own Good, p. 128.
63 C. Gale, *Report of the Chief Protector*, 1909, quoted in M. Alroe, 'A Pygmalion complex among missionaries: the Catholic case in the Kimberley', in T. Swain and D. B. Rose (eds), *Aboriginal Australians and Christian Missions*, Australian Association for the Study of Religions, Bedford Park, 1988, p. 36.
64 M. A. Jebb, 'The lock hospitals experiment: Europeans, Aborigines and venereal disease', in B. Reece and C. T. Stannage (eds), *Studies in Western Australian History: European–Aboriginal Relations in Western Australian History*, no. 8, 1984, p. 80.
65 ibid.
66 Delys Fraser in interview with Bill Bunbury at the Back to Perenjori weekend, September 2012, and in Perenjori April 2013, quoted in Bill Bunbury and Jenny Bunbury, *Sound of the Cockies, Perenjori: 100 Years of Stories*, Shire of Perenjori, Perenjori, 2015, pp. 95–96.
67 Pat Jacobs in interview with Bill Bunbury, ABC Radio National, *Talking History*, 29, 1990.
68 Jack Davis in interview with Bill Bunbury, ABC Radio National, *Out of Sight, Out of Mind*, 1986.
69 E. Wynne, 'Rare paintings by stolen generation children to be returned to WA', *ABC Radio*, 14 May 2013, viewed 5 October 2019, <https://www.abc.net.au/local/photos/2013/05/14/3759101.htm>.
70 South West Aboriginal Land & Sea Council, 'Art', *Kaartdijin Noongar – Noongar Knowledge*, viewed 24 November 2011, <https://www.noongarculture.org.au/art/>.
71 Jacobs, interview, 1990.
72 Alice Nannup in interview with Bill Bunbury, ABC Radio National, *Out of Sight, Out of Mind*, 1986.
73 ibid.
74 ibid.
75 ibid.
76 Sister Eileen Heath in interview with Bill Bunbury, ABC Radio National, *Out of Sight, Out of Mind*, 1986.

NOTES TO CHAPTER 5

77 Nannup, interview, *Out of Sight, Out of Mind*, 1986.
78 ibid.
79 Jack Davis, *A Boy's Life*, Magabala Books, Broome, 1991, p. 116.
80 ibid., p. 134.
81 Ken Colbung in interview with Bill Bunbury, ABC Radio National, *Talking History*, 1988 (available SLWA, OH 2287).
82 Jack Davis, interview, *Out of Sight, Out of Mind*, 1986.
83 Jennie Carter, personal communication to the authors, 23 August 2019.
84 Albert Corunna, 'Statutory declaration to the Town of Bassendean', 2014, quoted in J. Carter and B. Carter, *King Eddies: A History of Western Australia's Premier Women's Hospital, 1916–2016*, King Edward Memorial Hospital Alumni, Subiaco, 2016, pp. 118–19.
85 ibid., p. 119.
86 ibid.
87 Jacobs, interview, *Talking History*, 1990.
88 Neville in *Annual Report of the Chief Protector of Aborigines, for the year ended 30th June 1932*, p. 12, quoted in South West Aboriginal Land and Sea Council, J. Host with C. Owen, *"It's Still in My Heart, This is My Country": The Single Noongar Claim History*, UWA Publishing, Crawley, 2009, pp. 170–71.
89 Neville in *Annual Report of the Chief Protector of Aborigines, for the year ended 30th June 1933*, p. 9, quoted in SWALSC, Host with Owen, "It's Still in My Heart", pp. 170–71.
90 Jack Davis, interview, *Out of Sight, Out of Mind*, 1986.
91 S. Delmege, 'A trans-generational effect of the Aborigines Act 1905 (WA): the making of the fringe dwellers in the south-west of Western Australia', *Murdoch University Electronic Journal of Law*, no. 6, 2005, p. 5.
92 ibid.
93 S. Hodson, 'Nyungars and work: Aboriginal experiences in the rural economy of the Great Southern region of Western Australia', *Aboriginal History*, vol. 17, nos 1/2, 1993, p. 78.
94 H. Colebatch, A Story of a Hundred Years, Western Australia, 1829–1929, F.W. Simpson, Government Printer, Perth, 1929, p. 60.
95 A. J. Barker and M. Laurie, *Excellent Connections: Bunbury 1836–1990*, City of Bunbury, Bunbury, 1992, p. 235.
96 M. Arnold, *A Journey Travelled: Aboriginal–European Relationships at Albany and the Surrounding Region from First Contact to 1926*, UWA Publishing, Crawley, 2015, pp. 301–02.
97 Bruce McLarty, in interview with Bill Bunbury, ABC Radio National, *Out of Sight, Out of Mind*, 1986.
98 Derryce Gliddon in interview with Bill Bunbury, Perth, August 2013, quoted in Bunbury and Bunbury, *Sound of the Cockies*, p. 96.
99 Haebich, 'European farmers and Aboriginal farmers', p. 62.
100 ibid., p. 61.

NOTES TO CHAPTER 5

101 ibid.
102 ibid.
103 ibid., p. 62.
104 ibid., p. 64.
105 Tilbrook, *Nyungar Tradition*, p. 30.
106 Haebich, 'European farmers and Aboriginal farmers', p. 62.
107 AF/157/1907, quoted in ibid., p. 65.
108 L. Tilbrook, 'Harris, William (1867–1931)', *Australian Dictionary of Biography*, National Centre of Biography, Australian National University, 1983, viewed 14 April 2019, <http://adb.anu.edu.au/biography/harris-william-6582>.
109 Biskup, *Not Slaves, Not Citizens*, p. 159.
110 ibid.
111 ibid., p. 160.
112 ibid.
113 Department of the North West (N. WT) records, 2260/1919, quoted in Biskup, *Not Slaves, Not Citizens*, p. 161.
114 Haebich, *For their Own Good*, p. 316.
115 Neville quoted in Delmege, *Murdoch University Electronic Journal of Law*, p. 6.
116 G. Bolton and H. J. Gibbney, 'Bennett, Mary Montgomerie (1881–1961)', *Australian Dictionary of Biography*, National Centre of Biography, Australian National University, 1979, viewed 6 April 2019, <http://adb.anu.edu.au/biography/bennett-mary-montgomerie-5212>.
117 Haebich, *For their Own Good*, p. 323.
118 Delmege, *Murdoch University Electronic Journal of Law*, p. 6.
119 Haebich, *For their Own Good*, p. 324.
120 ibid., p. 326.
121 ibid., pp. 327–28.
122 G. C. Bolton., 'Black and white after 1897', in C. T. Stannage (ed.), *A New History of Western Australia*, University of Western Australia Press, Nedlands, 1981, p. 147.
123 Paul Hasluck in interview with Bill Bunbury, ABC Radio National, *Talking History*, 60, 1992.
124 Hasluck in *The West Australian*, 18 March 1834, p. 18, quoted in A. Haebich, 'Paul Hasluck and the formative years', in C. T. Stannage, K. Saunders and R. Nile (eds), *Paul Hasluck and Australian History*, University of Queensland Press, St Lucia, 1998, p. 98.
125 ibid.
126 Hasluck, articles published in *The West Australian*, 21–26 June 1934, quoted in Haebich, 'Paul Hasluck', p. 99.
127 Extract from 'Submission to the Moseley Royal Commission by the half-castes of Broome', 1935, reproduced in Choo, *Mission Girls*, p. 297.

128 *Report of the Royal Commission Appointed to Investigate, Report and Advise upon Matters in Relation to the Condition and Treatment of Aborigines*, Wm Simpson, Government Printer, Perth, 1935, p. 7 (Moseley report).
129 Find & Connect, *Western Australia – Legislation: Aborigines Act Amendment Act, 1936 (1936–1964)*, viewed 6 April 2019, <https://www.findandconnect.gov.au/guide/wa/WE00411>.
130 Haebich, *For their Own Good*, p. 349.
131 ibid., pp. 348–50.
132 Tom Hayden in interview with Bill Bunbury, *Noongar Voices of the Central Eastern Wheatbelt, 1: The End of the Beginning*, ABC Radio National, broadcast on Awaye, April 2010, produced by Community Arts Network.
133 Stanley Middleton in interview with Bill Bunbury, ABC Radio National, *Out of Sight, Out of Mind*, 1986.
134 Wyvon Henry in interview with Bill Bunbury, *Noongar Voices of the Central Eastern Wheatbelt, 1: The End of the Beginning*, ABC Radio National, broadcast on Awaye, April 2010, produced by Community Arts Network.
135 Bruce McLarty, interview, *Out of Sight, Out of Mind*, 1986.
136 Bella Yappo in interview with Bill Bunbury, ABC Radio National, *Out of Sight, Out of Mind*, 1986.
137 Human Rights and Equal Opportunity Commission, *Bringing Them Home: Report of the National Inquiry into the Separation of Aboriginal and Torres Strait Islander Children from their Families*, Commonwealth of Australia, Sydney, 1997, p. 272, quoted in F. Probyn Rapsey, *Made to Matter: White Fathers, Stolen Generations*, Sydney University Press, Sydney, 2013, p. ix.
138 Cathie Clement in interview with Bill Bunbury, ABC Radio National, *Talking History*, 86, 1993.
139 ibid.
140 Robert Riley in interview with Bill Bunbury, ABC Radio National, *Anybody Could Afford Us*, 1984.
141 Lynette Knapp in interview with the authors, 17 November 2018.
142 ibid.
143 Tilbrook, *Nyungar Tradition*, p. 5.
144 Derryce Gliddon, interview, August 2013, quoted in Bunbury and Bunbury, *Sound of the Cockies*, p. 140.
145 Tom Hayden, interview, *Noongar Voices of the Central Eastern Wheatbelt*, 2010.
146 Basil Winmar in interview with Bill Bunbury, *Noongar Voices of the Central Eastern Wheatbelt, 1: The End of the Beginning*, ABC Radio National, broadcast on *Awaye*, April 2010, produced by Community Arts Network.
147 Winnie McHenry in interview with Bill Bunbury, *Noongar Voices of the Central Eastern Wheatbelt, 1: The End of the Beginning*, ABC Radio National, broadcast on *Awaye*, April 2010, produced by Community Arts Network.

148 Heritage Council of Western Australia, *Register of Heritage Places: Quairading State School & Quarters*, p. 13, viewed 7 April 2019, <http://inherit.stateheritage.wa.gov.au/Public/Content/PdfLoader.aspx?id=ccdb4f08-acf2-49db-8a9d-0602165831b9&type=assessment>.
149 ibid.
150 T. Spence, *A Man, His Dog and a Dead Kangaroo: Kellerberrin, Doodlakine and Baandee*, Shire of Kellerberrin, Kellerberrin, 2001, p. 45.
151 Heritage Council of WA, *Quairading State School*, p. 10.
152 Winnie McHenry, interview, *Noongar Voices of the Central Eastern Wheatbelt*, 2010.
153 Heritage Council of WA, *Quairading State School*, p. 10.
154 A. O. Neville to Under Secretary, 5 October 1917, quoted in ibid., p. 10.
155 John Kickett in ibid., pp. 11–12. Spelling original.
156 Winne McHenry, interview, *Noongar Voices of the Central Eastern Wheatbelt*, 2010.
157 Dean Collard in interview with Bill Bunbury, ABC Radio National, *Anybody Could Afford Us*, 1984.
158 ibid.
159 ibid.
160 Spence, *A Man, his Dog and a Dead Kangaroo*, p. 43.
161 Robert Sexton in interview with the authors, 31 May 2019.
162 Charlotte Winmar-Smith in interview with Bill Bunbury, *Noongar Voices of the Central Eastern Wheatbelt, 2: Holes in the Tin*, ABC Radio National, broadcast on *Awaye*, April 2010, produced by Community Arts Network.
163 Knapp, interview, 2018.
164 ibid.
165 Sexton, interview, May 2019.
166 Hodson, *Aboriginal History*, p. 78.
167 Hayden, interview, Noongar *Voices of the Central Eastern Wheatbelt*, 2010.
168 Fred Collard in interview with Bill Bunbury, ABC Radio National, *Hindsight: Unfinished Business*, 1996.
169 Basil Winmar, interview, *Noongar Voices of the Central Eastern Wheatbelt*, 2010.
170 Hodson, *Aboriginal History*, p. 87.
171 Ivan Yarran in interview with Bill Bunbury, ABC Radio National, *Anybody Could Afford Us*, 1984.
172 Neil Phillips in interview with Gail O'Hanlon, 1997, SLWA, OH 2853, quoted in Bunbury and Bunbury, *Sound of the Cockies*, p. 141.
173 K. Colbung, 'On being Aboriginal, a personal statement', in R. M. Berndt and C. H. Berndt (eds), *Aborigines of the West: Their Past and Their Present*, University of Western Australia Press, Nedlands, 1979, p. 104.

Notes to Chapter 6: The Past Is Still Part Of Us

1 Oodgeroo Noonuccal, 'Integration – Yes', in *My People: A Kath Walker Collection*, Jacaranda Press, Melbourne, 1970.
2 ibid.
3 Oodgeroo Noonuccal, 'Assimilation – No', in *My People: A Kath Walker Collection*, Jacaranda Press, Melbourne, 1970.
4 A. Haebich, *Spinning the Dream: Assimilation in Australia, 1950–1970*, Fremantle Press, Fremantle, 2008, p. 9.
5 R. Bropho, *Fringedweller*, Alternative Publishing Co-operative, Sydney, 1980, pp. 6–7.
6 'Statement on Aboriginal welfare and employment policy', Northern Territory Pastoral Leases Association, vol. C1A, c.1965, p. 3, quoted in G. McLaren, *Distance, Drought and Dispossession: A History of the Northern Territory Pastoral Industry*, NTU Press, Darwin, 2001, p. 163.
7 Paul Hasluck in interview with Bill Bunbury, ABC Radio National, *Talking History*, 60, 1992.
8 Helena Clarke in interview with Steve Kinnane, ABC Radio National, *The Coolbaroo Club Remembered*, 11 February 2011, produced by Community Arts Network.
9 Jim Brennan in interview with Bill Bunbury, ABC Radio National, *Anybody Could Afford Us*, 1984.
10 P. Biskup, *Not Slaves, Not Citizens: The Aboriginal Problem in Western Australia, 1898–1954*, University of Queensland Press, St Lucia, 1973, p. 206.
11 ibid., p. 207.
12 Find & Connect, *Native (Citizenship Rights) Act, 1944–71*, viewed 25 November 2011, <https://www.findandconnect.gov.au/guide/wa/WE00416>.
13 A. Haebich, *Dancing in Shadows: Histories of Nyungar Performance*, UWA Publishing, Crawley, 2018, p. 186.
14 Paul Hasluck, interview, *Talking History*, 1992.
15 W. Sanders, 'An abiding interest and constant approach: Paul Hasluck as historian, reformer and critic of Aboriginal Affairs', C. T. Stannage, K. Saunders and R. Nile (eds), *Paul Hasluck and Australian History: Civic Personality and Public Life*, University of Queensland Press, St Lucia, 1998, p. 107.
16 ibid., p. 115.
17 Quoted in P. Hasluck, *Shades of Darkness*, Melbourne University Press, Collingwood, 1988, p. 93.
18 Paul Hasluck, interview, *Talking History*, 1992.
19 Robert Riley in interview with Bill Bunbury, *Anybody Could Afford Us*, 1984.
20 Bropho, *Fringedweller*, p. 153.

NOTES TO CHAPTER 6

21 F. E. A. Bateman, *Report on Survey of Native Affairs*, W. H. Wyatt, Government Printer, Perth, 1948, p. 26.
22 ibid., p. 3.
23 G. B. Bolton, 'Black and white after 1897', in C. T. Stannage (ed.), *A New History of Western Australia*, University of Western Australia Press, Nedlands, 1981, pp. 153–54.
24 Jack Davis in interview with Bill Bunbury, ABC Radio National, *Out of Sight, Out of Mind*, 1986.
25 Quoted in Haebich, *Dancing in Shadows*, p. 188.
26 Haebich, *Spinning the Dream*, p. 284.
27 Haebich, *Dancing in Shadows*, p. 189.
28 Haebich, *Spinning the Dream*, p. 288.
29 'The life and times of S. G. Middleton', typescript held by the Middleton family, quoted in A. Lapham, 'Stanley Middleton's response to assimilation policy in his fight for Aboriginal people's equality, 1948–62', *Aboriginal History*, vol. 40, 2016, p. 27.
30 ibid., pp. 54–55.
31 Lynnette Coomer in interview with the authors, 29 May 2019.
32 A. Haebich, *Spinning the Dream*, p. 284.
33 Ben Taylor in interview with Bill Bunbury, ABC, *The Coolbaroo Club Remembered*, broadcast 22 February 2011, produced by Community Arts Network.
34 Haebich, *Spinning the Dream*, p. 286.
35 Biskup, *Not Slaves, Not Citizens*, p. 235.
36 Geoff Harcus in interview with Lauren Marsh and Steve Kinnane, quoted in Anna Haebich; *Spinning the Dream*, p. 295.
37 Haebich, Spinning the Dream, p. 296.
38 Denise Cook in interview with Bill Bunbury, 20 May 2019. (Cook's research now published as *That Was My Home: Voices from the Noongar Camps in Fremantle and the Western Suburbs*, UWA Publishing, Crawley, 2019.)
39 ibid.
40 ibid.
41 Corrie Bodney in interview with Denise Cook, for Claremont Museum, 18 and 31 January 2007, quoted in D. Cook, 'That was my home: voices from the Noongar camps in Perth's western suburbs', vol. 2, PhD thesis, Murdoch University, 2016, p. 36.
42 Cook, interview, May 2019.
43 Beryl Hoffman in interview with Denise Cook, 27 September 2012, quoted in Cook, 'That was my home', p. 213.
44 ibid.
45 ibid.
46 Robert Bropho in interview with Bill Bunbury, *Anybody Could Afford Us*, 1984.

47 Robert Bropho in interview with Denise Cook for Claremont Museum, 26 March 2007, quoted in Cook, 'That was my home', p. 232.
48 Louise Walsh (nee Bodney) in telephone conversation with Denise Cook, 23 May 2013, quoted in Cook, 'That was my home', p. 203.
49 ibid., p. 241.
50 Cook, interview, May 2019.
51 Coomer, interview, May 2019.
52 ibid.
53 ibid.
54 Cook, interview, May 2019, quoting Corrie Bodney, from oral history with Denise Cook for Claremont Museum, 31 January 2007, p. 28, and Corrie Bodney, oral history with Denise Cook, 24 February 2012.
55 J. Carter, *Bassendean: A Social History, 1829–1979*, Bassendean Town Council, Bassendean, 1986, p. 245.
56 Judy Hamersley in interview with Gail O'Hanlon, Oral Transcript OH 2635/1, p. 44, (Tape Four side B), SLWA, 1995.
57 Carter, *Bassendean*, pp. 245–46.
58 Cook, interview, May 2019.
59 Middleton quoted by Denise Cook, interview with Bill Bunbury, May 2019.
60 Cook, interview, May 2019.
61 Coomer, interview, May 2019.
62 Find & Connect, *Roelands Native Mission Farm (1938–75)*, viewed 23 May 2019, <https://www.findandconnect.gov.au/ref/wa/biogs/WE00187b.htm>.
63 ibid.
64 Coomer, interview, May 2019.
65 ibid.
66 ibid.
67 Father Eugene Perez, *The Benedictine Mission and the Aborigines 1908–1975: The History of Kalumburu Mission in North Western Australia*; Kalumburu Benedictine Mission, Wyndham, 1977, quoted in C. Choo, *Mission Girls: Aboriginal Women on Catholic Missions in the Kimberley, Western Australia, 1900–1950*, University of Western Australia Press, Crawley, p. 198.
68 R. Tonkinson, 'Reflections on a failed crusade', in T. Swain and D. B. Rose (eds), *Aboriginal Australians and Christian Missions*, Australian Association for the Study of Religions, Bedford Park, 1988.
69 Robert Tonkinson in interview with Bill Bunbury, 19 March 2019.
70 ibid.
71 ibid.
72 ibid.
73 John Kinder in interview with Bill Bunbury, 5 December 2018.
74 Professor Sandy Toussaint, personal communication to the authors, 6 June 2019.

75 Peter Bindon in interview with Bill Bunbury, 18 April 2019.
76 P. Bindon, Introduction to Anthony Rex Peile, *Body and Soul: An Aboriginal View*, P. Bindon (ed.), Hesperian Press, Carlisle, and The Pallottines in Australia, Rossmoyne, 1997, p. iv.
77 ibid.
78 Peter Bindon, interview, April 2019.
79 ibid.
80 Peile, *Body and Soul*, p. 92.
81 ibid., p. 95.
82 ibid.
83 Peter Bindon, interview, April 2019.
84 ibid.
85 ibid.
86 ibid.
87 Peter Coppin in interview with Bill Bunbury, ABC Radio National, *Hindsight: Blackfellas Eureka*, broadcast 16 July 1995.
88 Biskup, *Not Slaves, Not Citizens*, pp. 61–62.
89 Peter Coppin, interview, *Blackfellas Eureka*, 1995.
90 Don McLeod in interview with Bill Bunbury, *Hindsight: Blackfellas Eureka*.
91 ibid.
92 Biskup, *Not Slaves, Not Citizens*, pp. 61–63.
93 Don McLeod, interview, *Blackfellas Eureka*, 1995.
94 ibid.
95 Dorothy Hewett in interview with Bill Bunbury, *Hindsight: Blackfellas Eureka*.
96 Sam Coppin in interview with Bill Bunbury, *Hindsight: Blackfellas Eureka*.
97 Dorothy Hewett, interview, *Blackfellas Eureka*, 1995.
98 Don McLeod, interview, *Blackfellas Eureka*,1995.
99 Sarah Stephen, 'Pilbara: Australia's longest strike', Green Weekly, 3 May 2006, no. 666, viewed 27 February 2020, <https://www.greenleft.org.au/content/pilbara-australias-longest-strike>.
100 Pat Dodson in interview with Bill Bunbury, ABC Radio National, *Hindsight: It's Not the Money – It's the Land*, broadcast December 2000.
101 Ann McGrath in interview with Bill Bunbury, *Hindsight: It's Not the Money – It's the Land*.
102 Jacky Dan in interview with Bill Bunbury, *Hindsight: It's Not the Money – It's the Land*.
103 Ann McGrath, interview, *It's Not the Money – It's the Land*, 2000.
104 ibid.
105 Hal Wootten in interview with Bill Bunbury, *Hindsight: It's Not the Money – It's the Land*.
106 Rex Johns in interview with Bill Bunbury, *Hindsight: It's Not the Money – It's the Land*.

NOTES TO CHAPTER 6

107 Commonwealth Conciliation and Arbitration Commission, quoted in Waltzing Matilda, *Cattle Industry Case 1966*, Fair Work Commission, 10 January 2017, viewed 13 March 2020, <https://www.fwc.gov.au/waltzing-matilda-and-the-sunshine-harvester-factory/historical-material/cattle-industry-case-1966>.
108 Mary Anne Jebb in interview with Bill Bunbury, *Hindsight: It's Not the Money – It's the Land*.
109 ibid.
110 Wootten, interview, *It's Not the Money – It's the Land*, 2000.
111 Jebb, interview, *It's Not the Money – It's the Land*, 2000.
112 Peter Murray in interview with Bill Bunbury, *Hindsight: It's Not the Money – It's the Land*.
113 Pat Dodson, interview, *It's Not the Money – It's the Land*, 2000.
114 Basil Thomas in interview with Bill Bunbury, *Hindsight: It's Not the Money – It's the Land*.
115 Ribgna Green in interview with Bill Bunbury, *Hindsight: It's Not the Money – It's the Land*.
116 Pat Dodson in interview with Bill Bunbury, ABC Radio National, *Hindsight: Outstations*, broadcast 20 August 2006.
117 Anthony Watson in interview with Bill Bunbury, *Hindsight: Outstations*, 2006.
118 Fred Chaney in interview with Bill Bunbury, 25 August 2018.
119 Jon Altman in interview with Bill Bunbury, *Hindsight: Outstations*, 2006.
120 ibid.
121 Dodson, interview, *Outstations*, 2006.
122 John Watson in interview with Bill Bunbury, *Hindsight: Outstations*, 2006.
123 ibid.
124 Altman, interview, *Outstations*, 2006.
125 Anthony Watson, interview, *Outstations*, 2006.
126 ibid.
127 Altman, interview, *Outstations*, 2006.
128 Dodson, interview, *Outstations*, 2006.
129 Ivan McPhee in interview with Bill Bunbury, ABC Radio National, *Hindsight: Noonkanbah 25 Years On*, broadcast 1 May 2005.
130 Peter Bindon in interview with Bill Bunbury, *Hindsight: Noonkanbah 25 Years On*.
131 Sir Charles Court in interview with Bill Bunbury, *Hindsight: Noonkanbah 25 Years On*, 2005.
132 McPhee, interview, *Hindsight: Noonkanbah 25 Years On*, 2005.
133 Steve Shannon in interview with Bill Bunbury, *Hindsight: Noonkanbah 25 Years On*, 2005.
134 McPhee, interview, *Hindsight: Noonkanbah 25 Years On*, 2005.

NOTES TO CHAPTER 6

135 John Bannister in interview with Bill Bunbury, *Hindsight: Noonkanbah 25 Years On*, 2005.
136 S. Hawke and M. Gallagher, *Noonkanbah: Whose Land, Whose Law*, Fremantle Arts Centre Press, Fremantle 1989, p. 120.
137 ibid., p. 96.
138 ibid., p. 120.
139 Bannister, interview, *Hindsight: Noonkanbah 25 Years On*, 2005.
140 Bindon, interview, *Hindsight: Noonkanbah 25 Years On*, 2005.
141 ibid.
142 ibid.
143 Peter Jones in interview with Bill Bunbury, *Hindsight: Noonkanbah 25 Years On*, 2005.
144 McPhee, interview, *Hindsight: Noonkanbah 25 Years On*, 2005.
145 Hawke and Gallagher, *Noonkanbah*, p. 326.
146 Bindon, interview, 2005.
147 Iszaac Webb in interview with the authors, 6 June 2019.
148 Craig McVee in interview with Bill Bunbury, ABC Radio National, *Encounter: Kojonup – Place of Healing*, broadcast 14 September 2003.
149 Robert Sexton in interview with the authors, 31 May 2019.
150 ibid.
151 Craig McVee, interview, *Kojonup – Place of Healing*, 2003. 14 September 2003.
152 Barbara Hobbs, in interview with Bill Bunbury, *Encounter: Kojonup – Place of Healing*, 2003.
153 Robert Sexton, 'The Kodja Place story', manuscript provided to the authors, May 2019.
154 Sexton, interview, May 2019.
155 ibid.
156 ibid.
157 Craig McVee in interview with Bill Bunbury, 7 June 2019.
158 ibid.
159 Robert Sexton, 'Kodja Place opening ceremony 29th September 2002', viewed 3 June 2019, <http://kodjaplace.com.au/wp-content/uploads/Speech_by_Chair_Kodja_Place_Advisory_Cmte_KP_Opening-29Sept2002.pdf>.
160 Craig McVee, 'Kodja Place opening ceremony 29th September 2002', viewed 3 June 2019, <http://kodjaplace.com.au/wp-content/uploads/Speech_by_Chair_Kojonup_Aboriginal_Corporation_KP-Opening-29Sept2002.pdf>.
161 McVee, interview, 7 June 2019.
162 ibid.
163 Margaret Robertson in interview with the authors, 31 May 2019.
164 Roger Bilney in interview with Bill Bunbury, Kojonup – Place of Healing, 2003.

165 Penny Young in interview with Bill Bunbury, *Kojonup – Place of Healing*, 2003.
166 McVee, interview, *Kojonup – Place of Healing*, 2003.
167 Barbara Hobbs, interview, *Kojonup – Place of Healing*, 2003.
168 Patsy Michael in interview with Bill Bunbury, *Kojonup – Place of Healing*, 2003.
169 Geoff Thorn in interview with Bill Bunbury, *Kojonup – Place of Healing*, 2003.
170 Bilney, interview, *Kojonup – Place of Healing*, 2003.
171 Webb, interview, 6 June 2019.
172 McVee, interview, 7 June 2019.

PEOPLE MENTIONED IN TEXT
INTERVIEWED BY BILL BUNBURY 1983-2019

Jon Altman★
Marian Aveling★
Ashley Bell
John Bannister★
Roger Bilney★
Peter Bindon★
Jim Brennan★
Bella Bropho#
Robert Bropho★
Jennie Carter
Hon. Fred Chaney AO
Christine Choo
Helena Clarke#
Cathie Clement★
Ken Colbung AM★
Dean Collard★
Fred Collard★
Denise Cook
Lynnette Coomer
Peter Coppin★
Sam Coppin★
Albert Corunna#
Gwen Corunna#
Sir Charles Court★
Jacky Dan★
Jack Davis AM★
Pat Dodson★
Delys Fraser
Vernice Gillies
Derryce Gliddon

Neville Green★
Ribgna Green★
Anna Haebich★
Sir Paul Hasluck★
Tom Hayden#
Sister Eileen Heath★
Wyvon Henry#
Dorothy Hewett★
Barbara Hobbs★
Pat Jacobs★
Mary Anne Jebb★
Rex Johns★
Peter Jones★
John Kinder
Lynette Knapp
Ann McGrath★
Winnie McHenry#
Bruce McLarty★
Don McLeod★
Ivan McPhee★
Craig McVee★
Patsy Michael★
Stanley Middleton★
Peter Murray★
Alice Nannup★
Ray Norris★
Howard Pedersen★
Robert Riley★
Margaret Robertson
Bruce Scates★

Kim Scott
Robert Sexton
Steve Shannon★
Tiffany Shellam
Tom Stannage AM★
Ben Taylor#
Basil Thomas★
Phil Thomson★
Geoff Thorn★
Robert Tonkinson
Antony Watson★
John Watson★
Iszaac (Zac) Webb
Gary Wilkes#
Nigel Wilkes#
Peter Wilkes#
Ted Wilkes AO#
Basil Winmar#
Charlotte Winmar-Smith#
Hal Wootten AC★
Bella Yappo★
Ivan Yarran★
Penny Young★

★ for ABC Radio
for Community Arts
Network, broadcast on
ABC Radio National/RN

BIBLIOGRAPHY

Archival sources
State Records Office of Western Australia
Hasluck, P., *Oral History Interviews, 1926–1939*, Perth, SROWA, 4553A/68.
Irwin, F., *Report to Governor Stirling, 18 May 1830*, SROWA, Swan River Papers, vol. 5.
State Library of Western Australia
Neville, A. O. 'Relations between settlers and aborigines in Western Australia', typescript, no date (viewed in SLWA: 994.1004 NEV).
O'Hanlon, G., Interview with Mary Julia (Judy) Hamersley, Transcript, OH2635, SLWA, 1995.
O'Hanlon, G., Interview with Neil Phillips, Transcript, OH2853, SLWA, 1997.

Books, journal articles and speeches
Allbrook, M., *Henry Prinsep's Empire*, ANU Press, Canberra, 2014.
Alroe, M., 'A Pygmalion complex among missionaries: the Catholic case in the Kimberley', in T. Swain and D. B. Rose (eds), *Aboriginal Australians and Christian Missions*, Australian Association for the Study of Religions, Bedford Park, 1988, pp. 30–44.
Anderson, K. and Perrin, C., 'The miserablest people in the world: race, humanism and the Australian Aborigine', *The Australian Journal of Anthropology*, vol. 18, no. 1, 2007, pp. 18–39.
Archer, A. *Ravensthorpe Then and Now*, 3rd edn, Ravensthorpe Historical Society, Ravensthorpe, 2008.
Arnold, M., *A Journey Travelled: Aboriginal–European Relationships at Albany and the Surrounding Region from First Contact to 1926*, UWA Publishing, Crawley, 2015.
Aveling, M. (ed.), *Westralian Voices: Documents in Western Australian Social History*, University of Western Australia Press, Nedlands, 1979.

BIBLIOGRAPHY

Banivanua Mar, T. and Edmonds, P., 'Indigenous and settler relations', in A. Bashford and S. Macintyre (eds), *The Cambridge History of Australia, Vol. 1: Indigenous and Colonial Australia*, Cambridge University Press, Melbourne, 2013.

Barker, A. J. and Laurie, M., *Excellent Connections: Bunbury 1836–1990*, City of Bunbury, Bunbury, 1992.

Barley, Sheila, 'Out of step: the failure of the early Protestant missions', in B. Reece and C. T. Stannage (eds), *Studies in Western Australian History: European–Aboriginal Relations in Western Australian History*, no. 8, 1984, pp. 26–31.

Bashford, A. and Macintyre, S. (eds), *The Cambridge History of Australia, Vol. 1: Indigenous and Colonial Australia*, Cambridge University Press, Melbourne, 2013.

Berndt, R. M. and Berndt, C. H. (eds), *Aborigines of the West: Their Past and Their Present*, University of Western Australia Press, Nedlands, 1979.

Berndt, R. M. and Berndt, C. H., 'Body and soul, more than an episode,' in T. Swain and D. B. Rose (eds), *Aboriginal Australians and Christian Missions*, Australian Association for the Study of Religions, Bedford Park, 1988, pp. 45–59.

Berryman, I. (ed.), *Swan River Letters, vol. 1*, Swan River Press, Glengarry, 2002.

Bindon, P. and Chadwick, R., *A Noongar Wordlist*, Western Australian Museum, Welshpool, 1992.

Bird, J., *West of the Arthur*, West Arthur Shire Council, Darkan, 1990.

Biskup, P., *Not Slaves, Not Citizens: The Aboriginal Problem in Western Australia, 1898–1954*, University of Queensland Press, St Lucia, 1973.

Bolton, G. C., 'Wollaston, John Ramsden (1791–1856)', *Australian Dictionary of Biography*, National Centre of Biography, Australian National University, 1967, viewed 9 November 2018, <http://adb.anu.edu.au/biography/wollaston-john-ramsden-2011>.

Bolton, G. C., 'Black and white after 1897', in C. T. Stannage (ed.), *A New History of Western Australia*, University of Western Australia Press, Nedlands, 1981, pp. 125–78.

Bolton, G. C., 'Portrait of the historian as a young learner', in D. Graham (ed.), *Being Whitefella*, Fremantle Arts Centre Press, Fremantle, 1994, pp. 119–25.

Bolton, G. C., *Land of Vision and Mirage: Western Australia since 1826*, UWA Publishing, Crawley, 2008.

Bolton, G. C. 'Alexander Forrest's expedition of 1879 and the early development of the cattle industry', in C. Clement, J. Gresham and H. McGlashan (eds), *Kimberley History: People, Exploration and Development*, Kimberley Society, Perth, 2012, pp. 101–12.

Bolton, G. C. and Gibbney, H. J., 'Bennett, Mary Montgomerie (1881–1961)', *Australian Dictionary of Biography,* National Centre of Biography, Australian

National University, 1979, viewed 6 April 2019, <http://adb.anu.edu.au/biography/bennett-mary-montgomerie-5212>.

Borowitzka, L., 'The reverend Dr Louis Giustiniani and Anglican conflict in the Swan River colony, 1836–1838', *Journal of Religious History*, vol. 35, no. 3, 2011, pp. 352–72.

Braid, E. and Forbes, E., *From Afar a People Drifted: The Story of Koorda, a Wheatbelt Settlement*, E. Forbes, Peppermint Grove, 1997.

Broome, R., *Aboriginal Australians: A History since 1788*, 4th edn, Allen & Unwin, Crows Nest, 2009.

Broomhall, F. H., *A History of Mount Marshall from Earliest Times to 1942*, Shire of Mount Marshall, Bencubbin, 1983.

Bropho, R., *Fringedweller*, Alternative Publishing Co-operative, Sydney, 1980.

Buchanan, G., *Packhorse and Waterhole: With the First Overlanders to the Kimberleys*, facsimile edition, Hesperian Press, Carlisle, 1997. (First published 1933.)

Buchanan, J., Collard, L., Cumming, I., Palmer, D., Scott, K. and Hartley, J., The influence of Nyungar knowledge, *Cultural Science Journal*, vol. 9, no. 1, 2016, pp. 37–53.

Bunbury, B., *Unfinished Business*, ABC Books, Sydney, 1998.

Bunbury, B. and Bunbury, J., *Sound of the Cockies, Perenjori: 100 Years of Stories*, Shire of Perenjori, Perenjori, 2015.

Burton, Canon A., *Wollaston's Picton Journal (1841–1844)*, Paterson Brokensha, Perth, n.d.

Burton Jackson, J. L., *Not an Idle Man: A Biography of John Septimus Roe*, M. B. Roe, West Swan, Western Australia, 1982.

Cameron, J. H. R. (ed.), *The Millendon Memoirs: George Fletcher Moore's Western Australian Diaries and Letters, 1830–1841*, Hesperian Press, Carlisle, 2006.

Cameron, J. H. R. and Barnes, P. (eds), *Lieutenant Bunbury's Australian Sojourn: The Letters and Journals of Lieutenant H. W. Bunbury, 21st Royal North British Fusiliers, 1834–1837*, Hesperian Press, Carlisle, 2014.

Carey, H. M., *God's Empire: Religion and Colonialism in the British World, c. 1801–1908*, Cambridge University Press, New York, 2011.

Carter, B., *Nyungah Land: Records of Invasion and Theft of Aboriginal Land on the Swan River, 1829–1850*, Swan Valley Nyungah Community, Guildford, 2005.

Carter, J. and Carter, B., *King Eddies: A History of Western Australia's Premier Women's Hospital, 1916–2016*, King Edward Memorial Hospital Alumni, Subiaco, 2016.

Carter, J., *Bassendean: A Social History, 1879–1979*, Bassendean Town Council, Bassendean, 1986.

Carter, J. and Carter, B., *Settlement to City: A History of the Armadale District and its People*, City of Armadale, Armadale, 2011.

Chase, D., *Just a Horse Ride Away: A History of Capel and its People*, Shire of Capel, Capel, c. 1995.

BIBLIOGRAPHY

Chate, A. H., 'Moore, George Fletcher (1798–1886)', *Australian Dictionary of Biography*, National Centre of Biography, Australian National University, 1967, viewed 24 September 2018, <http://adb.anu.edu.au/biography/moore-george-fletcher-2474>.

Chessell, G., *Richard Spencer: Napoleonic War hero and Australian Pioneer*, University of Western Australia Press, Crawley, 2005.

Chessell, G., *Alexander Collie: Colonial Surgeon, Naturalist and Explorer*, University of Western Australia Press, Nedlands, 2008.

Choo, C., *Mission Girls: Aboriginal Women on Catholic Missions in the Kimberley, Western Australia, 1900–1950*, University of Western Australia Press, Crawley, 2001.

Choo, C. 'Mixed blessings: establishment of Christian missions in the Kimberley', in C. Clement, J. Gresham and H. McGlashan (eds), *Kimberley History: People, Exploration and Development*, Kimberley Society, Perth, 2012.

Clement, C., Gresham, J. and McGlashan, H. (eds), *Kimberley History: People, Exploration and Development*, Kimberley Society, Perth, 2012.

Cockman, D. and Cockman, M. (compilers), *The Story of Wanneroo*, Shire of Wanneroo, Wanneroo, 1979.

Cohen, B. C., 'Collie, Alexander (1793–1835)', *Australian Dictionary of Biography*, National Centre of Biography, Australian National University, 1966, viewed 21 January 2018, <http://adb.anu.edu.au/biography/collie-alexander-1911/text2267>.

Colbung, K., 'On being Aboriginal, a personal statement', in R. M. Berndt and C. H. Berndt (eds), *Aborigines of the West: Their Past and Their Present*, University of Western Australia Press, Nedlands, 1979.

Colebatch, H., *A Story of a Hundred Years, Western Australia, 1829–1929*, F. W. Simpson, Government Printer, Perth, 1929.

Collard, L., A *Nyungar Interpretation of Ellensbrook and Wonnerup Homesteads*, National Trust of Australia, Australian Heritage Commission, Canberra, 1994.

Collard, L. and Cumming, I., 'Kaya Wandjoo Ngala Noongarpedia – Welcome to our Noongarpedia', *Cultural Science*, vol. 9, no. 1, 2016.

Collard, L. and Palmer, D., 'Looking for the residents of Terra Australis: the importance of Nyungar in early European coastal exploration', in P. Veth, P. Sutton and M. Neale (eds), *Strangers on the Shore: Early Coastal Contacts in Australia*, National Museum of Australia Press, Canberra, 2008, pp. 181–97.

Collard, L. and Palmer, D., 'Noongar and non-Aboriginal people going along together (Ngulla wangkiny, ni, katitjin Noongar, nyidung koorliny, kura, yeye, boorda)', in S. Konishi, M. Nugent and T. Shellam (eds), *Indigenous Intermediaries: New Perspectives on Exploration Archives*, ANU, Canberra, 2015.

Collard, L., Bracknell, C. and Palmer, D., 'Nyungar of southwestern Australia and Flinders: a dialogue using Nyungar intelligence to better understand coastal exploration', *ab-Original*, vol. 1, no. 1, 2017, pp. 1–16.

BIBLIOGRAPHY

Collard, L., Revell, G., Palmer, D. and Leonard, L., *Noongar Placenames associated with the Goordandalup (Crawley Bay) Area of the Gabee Derbalor Derbal Yaragan Beloo (Swan River)*, 1999.

Contos, N. with Kearing, T. A., Collard, L. and Palmer, D., *Pinjarra Massacre Site: Research and Development Project*, report for stage 1, Murray Districts Aboriginal Association, Pinjarra, 1998.

Cook, D., *That Was My Home: Voices from the Noongar Camps in Fremantle and the Western Suburbs*, UWA Publishing, Crawley, 2019.

Cottesloe, Lord (ed.), *Diary and Letters of Admiral Sir C.H. Fremantle, G.C.B. Relating to the Founding of the Colony of Western Australia, 1829*, Fremantle Arts Centre Press, Fremantle, 1979. (First published 1928.)

Coy, N., *The Serpentine: A History of the Shire of Serpentine–Jarrahdale,* Shire of Serpentine–Jarrahdale, Mundijong, 1984.

Crawford, I. M., 'Aboriginal cultures in Western Australia', in C. T. Stannage (ed.), *A New History of Western Australia*, University of Western Australia Press, Nedlands, 1981.

Crawford, P. and Crawford, I. M., *Contested Country: A History of the Northcliffe Area, Western Australia*, University of Western Australia Press, Crawley, 2003.

Cresswell, G., *The Light of Leeuwin*, Augusta Margaret River Shire History Group, Margaret River, 2003.

Davis, J., *Jagardoo: Poems from Aboriginal Australia*, Methuen of Australia, Sydney, 1977.

Davis, J., 'The first 150 years', in R. M. Berndt and C. H. Berndt (eds), *Aborigines of the West: Their Past and Their Present*, University of Western Australia Press, Nedlands, 1979.

Davis, J., *A Boy's Life,* Magabala Books, Broome, 1991.

De Garis, B. K., *Portraits of the South West: Aborigines, Women and the Environment*, University of WA Press, Nedlands, 1993.

Delmege, S., 'A trans-generational effect of the Aborigines Act 1905 (WA): the making of the fringe dwellers in the south-west of Western Australia', *Murdoch University Electronic Journal of Law*, no. 6, 2005, pp. 1–14.

Durack, M., *Kings in Grass Castles*, Corgi, London, 1967. (First published 1959.)

Durack, M., *The Rock and the Sand*, Corgi, London, 1979. (First published 1969).

Duyker, E., *Dumont d'Urville, Explorer and Polymath*, Otago University Press, Dunedin, 2014.

Fox, C. (ed.), *Studies in Western Australian History: Historical Refractions*, no. 14, 1993.

Gammage, B., *The Biggest Estate on Earth: How Aborigines Made Australia*, Allen & Unwin, Sydney, 2012.

Garden, D. S., *Albany: A Panorama of the Sound from 1827,* Thomas Nelson, West Melbourne, 1977.

Garden, D. S., *Northam: An Avon Valley History*, Oxford University Press, Melbourne, 1979.

BIBLIOGRAPHY

Gaynor, A., Trinca, M. and Haebich, A. (eds), *Country: Visions of Land and People in Western Australia*, Western Australian Museum, Perth, 2002.

Glover, R., *Plantagenet, Rich and Beautiful: A History of the Shire of Plantagenet, Western Australia*, University of Western Australia Press, Nedlands, 1979.

Goddard, E. and Stannage, T., 'John Forrest and the Aborigines', in B. Reece and C. T. Stannage (eds), *Studies in Western Australian History: European–Aboriginal Relations in Western Australian History*, no. 8, 1984, pp. 52–57.

Goode, B., Irvine, C., Harris, J. and Thomas, M., *Kinjarling, the Place of Rain: The City of Albany & Department of Indigenous Affairs Aboriginal Heritage Survey*, Brad Goode & Associates, Dunsborough, 2005.

Gourlay, M., *The Good Bishop: The Story of Bishop Hale*, Boolarong Press, Brisbane, 2015.

Graham, D. (ed.), *Being Whitefella*, Fremantle Arts Centre Press, Fremantle, 1994.

Greble, W., *A Bold Yeomanry: Social Change in a Wheatbelt District, Kulin, 1848–1970*, Creative Research in association with Kulin Shire Council, Perth, 1979.

Green, N. (ed.), *Nyungar – the People: Aboriginal Customs in the Southwest of Australia*, Creative Research in association with Mt Lawley College, Perth, 1979.

Green, N., *Broken Spears: Aboriginals and Europeans in the Southwest of Western Australia*, Focus Education Services, Perth, 1984.

Green, N., 'The cry for justice and equality', in T. Swain and D. B. Rose (eds), *Aboriginal Australians and Christian Missions*, Australian Association for the Study of Religions, Bedford Park, 1988, pp. 1–10.

Green, N., 'Aborigines of the Albany region, 1821–1898', *The Bicentennial Dictionary of Western Australians*, vol. 1, University of Western Australia Press, Nedlands, 1989.

Green, N., 'Mokare (1800–1831)', *Australian Dictionary of Biography*, National Centre of Biography, Australian National University, 2005, viewed 23 February 2019, <http://adb.anu.edu.au/biography/mokare-13106>.

Grey, G., *Journals of Two Expeditions of Discovery in the North-West and Western Australia during the Years 1837, 1838 and 1839*, 2 vols, facsimile edition, Hesperian Press, Carlisle, 1983–84.

Grey G., *Journals of Two Expeditions of Discovery in the North-West and Western Australia*, Dodo Press, London, 2005. (First published in 1841.)

Gribble, J. B., *Dark Deeds in a Sunny Land*, University of Western Australia Press with the Institute of Applied Aboriginal Studies, WA College of Advanced Education, Perth, 1987. (First published 1886.)

Haebich, A., 'European farmers and Aboriginal farmers in south western Australia, mid 1890s–1914', in B. Reece and C. T. Stannage (eds), *Studies in Western Australian History: European–Aboriginal Relations in Western Australian History*, no. 8, 1984, pp. 59–67.

BIBLIOGRAPHY

Haebich, A., *For their Own Good, Aborigines and Government in Western Australia in the South West of Western Australia 1900–1940*, University of Western Australia Press, Nedlands, 1988.

Haebich, A., 'Paul Hasluck and the formative years', in C. T. Stannage, K. Saunders and R. Nile (eds), *Paul Hasluck and Australian History: Civic Personality and Public Life*, University of Queensland Press, St Lucia, 1998.

Haebich, A., *Spinning the Dream: Assimilation in Australia, 1950–1970*, Fremantle Press, Fremantle, 2008.

Haebich, A., *Dancing in Shadows: Histories of Nyungar Performance*, UWA Publishing, Crawley, 2018.

Hallam, S., 'Aboriginal women as providers: the 1830s on the Swan', *Aboriginal History*, vol. 15, no. 1, 1991.

Hammond, J. E., *Winjan's People: The Story of the South-West Australian Aborigines*, P. Hasluck (ed.), facsimile edition, Hesperian Press, Perth, 1980. (First published 1933.)

Hasluck, A., *Portrait with Background: A Life of Georgiana Molloy*, Oxford University Press, London, 1955.

Hasluck, P., *Black Australians: A Survey of Native Policy in Western Australia, 1929–1897*, Melbourne University Press, Melbourne, 1970. (First published 1942.)

Hasluck, P., *Shades of Darkness*, Melbourne University Press, Melbourne, 1988.

Hassell, E., *My Dusky Friends: Aboriginal Life, Customs and Legends and Glimpses of Station Life at Jarramungup in the 1880s*, C. W. Hassell, Perth, 1975.

Hawke, S. and Gallagher, M., *Noonkanbah, Whose Land, Whose Law*, Fremantle Arts Centre Press, Fremantle, 1989.

Haydon, P. R., *Westward to the Sea: Reminiscences and History of the Carnamah District, 1861–1987*, Carnamah Historical Society, Carnamah, 1988.

Heal, L., *Jane Dodds, 1788–1844: A Swan River Colony Pioneer*, Book Production Services on behalf of L. Macalpine, Sydney, 1988.

Hetherington, P., *Settlers, Servants and Slaves: Aboriginal and European Children in Western Australia*, University of Western Australia Press, Crawley, 2002.

Hodson, S., 'Nyungars and work: Aboriginal experiences in the rural economy of the Great Southern region of Western Australia', *Aboriginal History*, vol. 17, nos 1/2, 1993, pp. 73–92.

Howard, M. C., 'Aboriginal society in south-western Australia', in R. M. Berndt and C. H. Berndt (eds), *Aborigines of the West: Their Past and Their Present*, University of Western Australia Press, Nedlands, 1980.

Hunt, S. J., 'The Gribble affair, a study in colonial politics', in Gribble, *Dark Deeds in a Sunny Land*, University of Western Australia Press with the Institute of Applied Aboriginal Studies, WA College of Advanced Education, Perth, 1987.

Hunt, L., 'Sir Walter Hartwell James (1863–1943)', *Australian Dictionary of Biography*, National Centre of Biography, Australian National

University, 1983, viewed 5 December 2019, <http://adb.anu.edu.au/biography/james-sir-walter-hartwell-6824>.

Hunter, A., 'Treaties? The impact of inter-racial violence in Tasmania on proposals for negotiating agreements with Aboriginal people in Western Australia in the 1830s', *ANZ Law History e-Journal*, 2006, viewed 28 October 2018, <http://classic.austlii.edu.au/au/journals/ANZLawHisteJl/2006/10.pdf>.

Hunter, A., 'John Hutt: the inconspicuous governor', *Early Days: Journal of the Royal Historical Society of WA*, vol. 13, part 3, 2009, pp. 309–21.

Hunter, A., *A Different Kind of 'Subject': Colonial Law in Aboriginal–European Relations in Nineteenth Century Western Australia 1829–1861*, Australian Scholarly Publishing, Melbourne, 2012.

Jacobs, P., *Mister Neville*, Fremantle Arts Centre Press, Fremantle, 1990.

Jebb, M. A., 'The lock hospitals experiment: Europeans, Aborigines and venereal disease', in B. Reece and C. T. Stannage (eds), *Studies in Western Australian History: European–Aboriginal Relations in Western Australian History*, no. 8, 1984, pp. 68–87.

Jennings, R., *Busselton: Outstation on the Vasse 1830–1850*, Shire of Busselton, Busselton, 1983.

Jennings, R., *Busselton, A Place to Remember, 1850–1914*, Shire of Busselton, Busselton, 1999.

Kimberly, W. S., *History of West Australia: A Narrative of her Past together with Biographies of her Leading Men*, Hesperian Press, Carlisle, 2015. (First published 1897.)

Kinnane, S., 'Recurring visions of Australindia', in A. Gaynor, M. Trinca and A. Haebich (eds), *Country: Visions of Land and People in Western Australia*, Western Australian Museum, Perth, 2002, pp. 21–31.

Konishi, S., *The Aboriginal Male in the Enlightenment World*, Pickering and Chatto, London, 2012.

Konishi, S. and Nugent, M., 'Newcomers c.1600–1800', in A. Bashford and S. Macintyre (eds), *The Cambridge History of Australia, Vol. 1: Indigenous and Colonial Australia*, Cambridge University Press, Melbourne, 2013.

Konishi, S., Nugent, M. and Shellam, T. (eds), *Indigenous Intermediaries: New Perspectives on Exploration Archives*, ANU Press, Canberra, 2015.

Lange, S., *Pingelly: Our People and Progress*, Pingelly Tourist and Town, Beautification Committee, Pingelly, 1981.

Lapham, A., 'Stanley Middleton's response to assimilation policy in his fight for Aboriginal people's equality, 1948–1962', *Aboriginal History*, vol. 40, 2016.

Le Souef, S., 'The Aborigines of King George's Sound at the time of early European contact: an ethnohistorical study of social organisation and territoriality', in B. K. De Garis (ed.), *Portraits of the South West: Aborigines, Women and the Environment*, University of WA Press, Nedlands, 1993.

Lines, W., *An All Consuming Passion: Origins, Modernity and the Australian Life of Georgiana Molloy*, Allen & Unwin, St Leonards, 1994.

BIBLIOGRAPHY

Ludewig, A., *War Time on Wadjemup: A Social History of the Rottnest Island Internment Camp,* UWA Publishing, Crawley, 2019.

Lyon, R. M., *A Glance at the Manners and Language of the Aboriginal Inhabitants of Western Australia,* Western Australian College of Advanced Education, Perth, 1987. (First published 1833.)

Lyon, R. M., *An Appeal to the World on Behalf of the Younger Branch of the Family of Shem,* J. Spilsbury and J. M'Rachern, Sydney, 1839.

McGlashan, H., 'George Grey's expedition 1837–1838: first European penetration into the Kimberley interior', in C. Clement, J. Gresham and H. McGlashan (eds), *Kimberley History: People, Exploration and Development,* Kimberley Society, Perth, 2012, pp. 61–70.

McLaren, G., *Distance, Drought and Dispossession: A History of the Northern Territory Pastoral Industry,* NTU Press, Darwin, 2001.

McNair, W. and Rumley, H., *Pioneer Aboriginal Mission: The Work of John Smithies in the Swan River Colony, 1841–1855,* University of Western Australia, Nedlands, 1981.

McVee, C., 'Kodja Place opening ceremony 29th September 2002', viewed 3 June 2019, <http://kodjaplace.com.au/wp-content/uploads/Speech_by_Chair_Kojonup_Aboriginal_Corporation_KP-Opening-29Sept2002.pdf>.

Millett, E., *An Australian Parsonage, or the Settler and the Savage in Western Australia,* facsimile edition with an introduction by Rica Erikson, University of Western Australia Press, Nedlands, 1980. (First published 1872.)

Moore, G. Fletcher, *Diary of Ten Years Eventful Life of an Early Settler in Western Australia; and also, A Descriptive Vocabulary of the Language of the Aborigines,* facsimile edition, University of Western Australia Press, Nedlands, 1978. (First published 1864).

Mulvaney, J. and Green, N., *Commandant of Solitude: The Journals of Captain Collet Barker 1828–1831,* Melbourne University Press at the Miegunyah Press, Carlton, 1992.

Neville, A. O, *Australia's Coloured Minority: Its Place in the Community,* Currawong Publishing Company, Sydney, 1948.

Nind, S., 'Description of the natives of King George's Sound (Swan River Colony) and adjoining country', *The Journal of the Royal Geographical Society,* vol. 1, 1831, pp. 21–51.

Noonuccal, Oodgeroo, *My People: A Kath Walker Collection,* Jacaranda Press, Melbourne, 1970.

O'Brien, A., 'Religion', in A. Bashford and S. Macintyre (eds), *The Cambridge History of Australia, Vol. 1: Indigenous and Colonial Australia,* Cambridge University Press, Melbourne, 2013.

Owen, C., *'Every Mother's Son Is Guilty…': Policing the Kimberley Frontier of WA 1882–1905,* UWA Publishing, Crawley, 2016.

Palmer, K., *Noongar People, Noongar Land: The Resilience of Aboriginal culture in the South West of Western Australia,* AIATSIS Research Publications,

BIBLIOGRAPHY

Canberra, 2016, viewed 9 March 2019, <https://aiatsis.gov.au/sites/default/files/products/monograph/noongar-people-noongar-land_2.pdf>.

Pascoe, B., *Dark Emu, Black Seeds,* Magabala Books, Broome, 2014.

Pedersen, H., 'Pigeon: an Australian Aboriginal rebel', in B. Reece and C. T. Stannage (eds), *Studies in Western Australian History: European–Aboriginal Relations in Western Australian History,* no. 8, 1984, pp. 7–15.

Peile, A. R., *Body and Soul: An Aboriginal View,* P. Bindon (ed.), Hesperian Press, Carlisle, and The Pallottines in Australia, Rossmoyne, 1997.

Perez, Father Eugene, *The Benedictine Mission and the Aborigines 1908–1975: The History of Kalumburu Mission in North Western Australia,* Kalumburu Benedictine Mission, Wyndham, 1977.

Playford, P., *Voyage of Discovery to Terra Australis by Willem de Vlamingh in 1696–97,* Western Australian Museum, Perth, 1998.

Pope, B., 'Aboriginal messages and mail carriers in south western Australia in the early and mid-nineteenth century', in B. K. De Garis (ed.), *Portraits of the South West: Aborigines, Women and the Environment,* University of WA Press, Nedlands, 1993, pp. 57–77.

Popham, D., *First Stage South: A History of the Armadale-Kelmscott District,* Town of Armadale, Armadale, 1980.

Probyn-Rapsey, F., *Made to Matter: White Fathers, Stolen Generations,* Sydney University Press, Sydney, 2013.

Purdy, J., *Just One Damned Thing After Another: Colonialism, Economics, The Law and Resistance in Western Australia,* Der Andere Verlag, Germany, 2010.

Pustkuchen, O., *The Way Through: The Story of Narrogin,* Artlook Books for the Town of Narrogin, Perth, 1981.

Reece, B., 'Eating and drinking at early Swan River Colony', *Early Days: Journal of the WA Royal Historical Society,* vol. 13, part 4, 2010, pp. 462–77.

Reece, B., 'A most singular man, Robert Lyon Milne', *Early Days: Journal of the WA Royal Historical Society,* vol. 13, part 5, 2011, pp. 358–368.

Reece, B., 'A most complete and untameable savage: Yagan', *Early Days: Journal of the WA Royal Historical Society,* vol. 14, part 4, 2015, pp. 591–616.

Reece, B. and Stannage, T. (eds), *Studies in Western Australian History: European–Aboriginal Relations in Western Australian History,* no. 8, 1984.

Reynolds, H., *The Other Side of the Frontier: Aboriginal Resistance to the Invasion of Australia,* University of New South Wales Press, Sydney, 2006. (First published 1982.)

Reynolds, H., *This Whispering in our Hearts,* Allen & Unwin, St Leonards, 1998.

Rice, J. C., *Wyalkatchem: A History of the District,* Wyalkatchem Shire Council, Wyalkatchem, 1993.

Rooney, B., 'An evolving concept of mission, New Norcia 1846–2006', *Australasian Catholic Record,* vol. 83, no. 3, 2006, pp. 309–19.

Rose, D. Bird, *Nourishing Terrains: Australian Aboriginal Views of Landscape and Wilderness,* Australian Heritage Commission, Canberra, 1996.

BIBLIOGRAPHY

Russo, G., *Lord Abbot of the Wilderness: The Life and Times of Bishop Salvado*, Polding Press, Melbourne, 1979.

Salvado, Bishop R., 'Letter from his lordship, Rosendo, bishop of Port Victoria to the hon colonial secretary, New Norcia, 19 February 1864', in *Information Respecting the Aboriginal Natives of Western Australia*, Western Australia, 1971, viewed 1 October 2018, <https://aiatsis.gov.au/sites/default/files/catalogue_resources/92972.pdf>.

Sanders, T., *Bunbury: Some Early History*, Roebuck Society, Canberra, 1975.

Sanders, W., 'An abiding interest and constant approach: Paul Hasluck as historian, reformer and critic of Aboriginal Affairs', C. T. Stannage, K. Saunders and R. Nile (eds), *Paul Hasluck and Australian History: Civic Personality and Public Life*, University of Queensland Press, St Lucia, 1998.

Schorer, A., *The Horses Came First: A History of the District of Wandering*, Shire of Wandering, Wandering, 1974.

Scott, K., *That Deadman Dance*, Picador, Sydney, 2010.

Scott, K. and Brown, H., *Kayang and Me,* Fremantle Press, Fremantle, 2013.

Sexton, R., 'Kodja Place opening ceremony 29th September 2002', viewed 3 June 2019, <http://kodjaplace.com.au/wp-content/uploads/Speech_by_Chair_Kodja_Place_Advisory_Cmte_KP_Opening-29Sept2002.pdf>.

Shann, E., *Cattle Chosen: The Story of the First Group Settlement in Western Australia, 1929–1841*, facsimile edition, University of Western Australia, Nedlands, 1978. (First published 1926.)

Shaw, B., 'On the historical emergence of race relations in the Eastern Kimberley: change?', in R. M. Berndt and C. H. Berndt (eds), *Aborigines of the West: Their Past and Their Present*, University of Western Australia Press, Nedlands, 1980, pp. 261–272.

Shellam, T., *Shaking Hands on the Fringe: Negotiating the Aboriginal World at King George's Sound,* University of Western Australia Press, Crawley, 2009.

Shellam, T., 'A mystery to the medical world: Florence Nightingale, Rosendo Salvado and the risk of civilisation', *History, Australia*, vol. 9, no. 1, 2012.

Shellam, T, 'Miago and the great northern men: Indigenous histories from in-between', in R. Standfield (ed.), *Indigenous Mobilities: Across and Beyond the Antipodes,* ANU Press, Canberra, 2018, viewed 6 September 2018, <http://press-files.anu.edu.au/downloads/press/n4260/pdf/ch08.pdf>.

Shellam, T., *Meeting the Waylo: Aboriginal Encounters in the Archipelago*, UWA Publishing, Crawley, 2019.

Skyring, F., and Yu, S., 'Strange strangers: first contact between Europeans and Karajarri people on the Kimberley coast of Western Australia', in P. Veth, P. Sutton and M. Neale (eds), *Strangers on the Shore: Early Coastal Contacts in Australia*, National Museum of Australia, Canberra, 2008, pp. 60–73.

Slee, J. and Shaw, B., *Calamunda: A Home in the Forest*, Shire of Kalamunda, Kalamunda, 1979.

Smith, P. A., 'Into the Kimberley: the invasion of the Sturt Creek Basin (Kimberley region, Western Australia) and evidence of Aboriginal resistance', *Aboriginal History*, vol. 24, 2000, pp. 62–74.

Smith, P. A., 'Station camps: legislation, labour relations and rations on pastoral leases in the Kimberley region, Western Australia', *Aboriginal History*, vol. 24, 2000, pp. 75–97.

South West Aboriginal Land and Sea Council, Host, J with Owen, C., *"It's Still in My Heart, This is My Country": The Single Noongar Claim History*, UWA Publishing, Crawley, 2009.

Spence, T., *A Man, His Dog and a Dead Kangaroo: Kellerberrin, Doodlakine and Baandee*, Shire of Kellerberrin, Kellerberrin, 2001.

Standfield, R. (ed.), *Indigenous Mobilities: Across and Beyond the Antipodes*, ANU Press, Canberra, 2018.

Stannage, C. T., *The People of Perth: A Social History of Western Australia's Capital City*, Perth City Council, Perth, 1979.

Stannage, C. T. (ed.), *A New History of Western Australia*, University of Western Australia Press, Nedlands, 1981.

Stannage, C. T, Saunders, K. and Nile, R. (eds), *Paul Hasluck and Australian History*, University of Queensland Press, St Lucia, 1998.

Statham-Drew, P., *James Stirling: Admiral and Founding Governor of Western Australia*, University of Western Australia Press, Crawley, 2003.

Stocker, L., Collard, L. and Rooney, A., 'Aboriginal world views and colonisation: implications for coastal sustainability', *Local Environment: The International Journal of Justice and Sustainability*, vol. 21, no. 7, 2016, pp. 1–39.

Strong, R., 'The Reverend John Wollaston and colonial Christianity in Western Australia, 1840–1863', *Journal of Religious History*, vol. 25, no. 3, 2001, pp. 261–85.

Swain, T., and Rose, D. B. (eds), *Aboriginal Australians and Christian Missions*, Australian Association for the Study of Religions, Bedford Park, 1988.

Thomas, J. E., 'Crime and society', in C. T. Stannage (ed.), *A New History of Western Australia*, University of Western Australia Press, Nedlands, 1981.

Tilbrook, L., *Nyungar Tradition: Glimpses of Aborigines in South-Western Australia 1829–1914*, University of Western Australia Press, Nedlands, 1983, viewed 16 March 2020, <https://aiatsis.gov.au/sites/default/files/catalogue_resources/m0022954.pdf>.

Tilbrook, L., 'Harris, William (1867–1931)', *Australian Dictionary of Biography*, National Centre of Biography, Australian National University, 1983, viewed 14 April 2019, <http://adb.anu.edu.au/biography/harris-william-6582>.

Timperley, J., *Beyond the Fence*, Kukerin History Group, Kukerin, 1996.

Tonkinson, R., 'Reflections on a failed crusade', in T. Swain and D. B. Rose (eds), *Aboriginal Australians and Christian Missions*, Australian Association for the Study of Religions, Bedford Park, 1988, pp. 60–73.

BIBLIOGRAPHY

Undalup Association Inc., *Wadandi Boodja Kaaditjin,* presented by the Wadandi Cultural Custodians, Cultural Awareness Training Booklet, Busselton, n. d.

Veth, P. and O'Connor, S., 'The past 50,000 years: an archaeological view', in A. Bashford and S. Macintyre (eds), *The Cambridge History of Australia, Vol. 1: Indigenous and Colonial Australia,* Cambridge University Press, Melbourne, 2013.

Veth, P., Sutton, P. and Neale, M., *Strangers on the Shore: Early Coastal Contacts in Australia,* National Museum of Australia, Canberra, 2008.

White, J., '"Paper talk": testimony and forgetting in south-west Western Australia', *Journal of the Association of the Study of Australian Literature,* 2017, no. 1.

Willis, P., 'Riders in the chariot: Aboriginal conversion to Christianity at Kununurra', in T. Swain and D. B. Rose (eds), *Aboriginal Australians and Christian Missions,* Australian Association for the Study of Religions, Bedford Park, 1988.

Wollaston, J. R., *The Wollaston Journals, Vol. 1, 1840–1842,* G. C. Bolton, H. Vose with G. Jones (eds), University of Western Australia Press, Nedlands, 1991.

Woorunmurra, B. and Pedersen, H., *Jandamarra and the Bunuba Resistance: A True Story,* Magabala Books, Broome, 1995.

Yu, S., 'Ngapa kunangkul (living water): an indigenous view of groundwater', in A. Gaynor, M. Trinca and A. Haebich (eds), *Country: Visions of Land and People in Western Australia,* Western Australian Museum, Perth, 2002, pp. 32–55.

Yu, S. 'Searching for the in-between: developing indigenous holistic approaches to cultural heritage assessment and interpretation', *Coolabah,* nos 24 & 25, 2018, viewed 16 March 2020, <https://doi.org/10.1344/co201824&25168-182>.

Government reports

Aborigines Department, *Report for the Financial Year ending 30th June 1899,* WA Government Printer, Perth, viewed 16 March 2020, <http://nla.gov.au/nla.obj-55058106>.

Information Respecting the Habits and Customs of the Aboriginal Inhabitants of Western Australia, compiled from various sources, presented to The Legislative Council by His Excellency's Command, Richard Pether, Government Printer, Perth, 1871.

Report of the Royal Commission on the Condition of the Natives, Wm Alfred Watson, Government Printer, Perth, 1905 (Roth report).

Report of the Royal Commission Appointed to Investigate, Report and Advise upon Matters in Relation to the Condition and Treatment of Aborigines, Wm Simpson, Government Printer, Perth, 1935 (Moseley report).

Report on Survey of Native Affairs, W. H. Wyatt, Government Printer, Perth, 1948 (Bateman report).

News articles

Collins, B. and Smale, H., 'Uncovering the first 20,000 years of Australia's pearling history', *ABC Kimberley*, 6 June 2014, viewed 17 January 2019, <http://www.abc.net.au/local/stories/2014/06/06/4020357.htm>.

de Graff, T., 'Memorial launch prompts reconciliation between farming and Indigenous communities in regional Western Australia', 22–25 May 2015, *ABC Country Hour*, viewed 8 January 2019, <https://www.abc.net.au/news/rural/2015-05-22/kukenarup-memorial-opened-in-ravensthorpe/6490332>.

Mills, V., 'Women recognised for love and death in Broome pearling', *ABC Kimberley*, 29 November 2010, viewed 17 January 2019, <http://www.abc.net.au/local/stories/2010/11/29/3079734.htm?site=kimberley>.

Rooney, B., in conversation with Terry Quinn, 'Salvado wanted an "indigenous faith"', *The Record*, 27 July 2011, viewed 3 February 2020, <https://therecord.com.au/news/local/salvado-wanted-an-indigenous-faith/>.

Stephen, S., 'Pilbara: Australia's longest strike', *Green Weekly*, 3 May 2006, no. 666, viewed 27 February 2020, <https://www.greenleft.org.au/content/pilbara-australias-longest-strike>.

Warriner, Jessica, 'The scars of the Pinjarra massacre still linger 185 years after one of WA's bloodiest days', *ABC News*, 26 October 2019

Wynne, E., 'Rare paintings by stolen generation children to be returned to WA', *ABC Radio*, 14 May 2013, viewed 5 October 2019, <https://www.abc.net.au/local/photos/2013/05/14/3759101.htm>.

Unpublished material and theses

Bolton, G. C., 'A survey of the Kimberley pastoral industry, from 1885 to the present', MA thesis, University of Western Australia, 1953.

Cook, D., 'That was my home: voices from the Noongar camps in Perth's western suburbs', vol. 2, PhD thesis, Murdoch University, 2016.

Groves, J., 'The Camfields: the comforts of civilisation in early colonial Western Australia', BA (Hons) dissertation, Edith Cowan University, 2006, viewed 8 March 2019, <https://ro.ecu.edu.au/cgi/viewcontent.cgi?article=2266&context=theses_hons>.

'The life and times of S. G. Middleton', typescript held by the Middleton family.

Roy, R. B., 'A reappraisal of Wesleyan Methodist mission in the first half of the nineteenth century as viewed through the ministry of Rev. John Smithies (1802–1872)', PhD thesis, Edith Cowan University, 2006, viewed 12 March 2020, <https://ro.ecu.edu.au/theses/96>.

Sexton R., *The Kodja Place Story*, manuscript provided to the authors, May 2019.

Suckling, A. J., 'The history of Northampton district', Teachers Higher Certificate Thesis, Claremont, n. d.

Thompson, A. J., 'The interpreter: the legacy of Francis Fraser Armstrong', BA Hons thesis, Murdoch University, 2015, viewed 12 October 2018, <http://www.warpedtime.com.au/encyclopedia/wp-content/uploads/2016/10/The-Interpreter-PRINT.pdf>.

Web pages

Broome and the Kimberley, *Broome History and Culture*, viewed 16 January 2019, <https://www.broomeandthekimberley.com.au/broome-history-culture/>.

Find & Connect, *Native (Citizenship Rights) Act, 1944–71*, viewed 25 November 2011, <https://www.findandconnect.gov.au/guide/wa/WE00416>.

Find & Connect, *Roelands Native Mission Farm (1938–75)*, viewed 23 May 2019, <https://www.findandconnect.gov.au/ref/wa/biogs/WE00187b.htm>.

Find & Connect, *Western Australia – legislation: Aborigines Act 1897 (1898–1906)*, viewed 3 October 2019, <https://www.findandconnect.gov.au/guide/wa/WE00405>.

Find & Connect, *Western Australia – legislation: Aborigines Act Amendment Act, 1936 (1936–1964)*, viewed 6 April 2019, <https://www.findandconnect.gov.au/guide/wa/WE00411>.

Heritage Council of Western Australia, *Register of Heritage Places: Quairading State School & Quarters*, p. 13, viewed 7 April 2019, <http://inherit.stateheritage.wa.gov.au/Public/Content/PdfLoader.aspx?id=ccdb4f08-acf2-49db-8a9d-0602165831b9&type=assessment>.

Landgate, *Town names*, viewed 18 June 2019, <https://www0.landgate.wa.gov.au/maps-and-imagery/wa-geographic-names/name-history/historical-town-names#J>.

Monument Australia, *Maitland Brown Memorial (Explorers Monument)*, viewed 17 February 2020, <http://monumentaustralia.org.au/themes/people/exploration/display/60482-maitland-brown-memorial-explorers-monument>.

Museum of Australian Democracy, Yirrkala Bark Petitions, 1963, *Documenting a Democracy*, viewed 31 March 2019, <https://www.foundingdocs.gov.au/item-did-104.html>.

South West Aboriginal Land & Sea Council, *Kaartdijin Noongar – Noongar Knowledge*, <www.noongarculture.org.au>.

Waltzing Matilda, *Cattle Industry Case 1966*, Fair Work Commission, 10 January 2017, viewed 13 March 2020, <https://www.fwc.gov.au/waltzing-matilda-and-the-sunshine-harvester-factory/historical-material/cattle-industry-case-1966>.

ABC Radio National documentaries
Anybody Could Afford Us, 1984
Out of Sight, Out of Mind, 1986
Talking History, Ken Colbung
Talking History 29, 1990
Talking History 41, 1992
Talking History 60, 1992
Talking History, The Bussells, 1992
Talking History 85, 1993
Talking History 86, 1993
'It's Not the Money, It's the Land', *Hindsight*, 2000
'Black Fellas Eureka', *Hindsight*, 1995
'Unfinished Business', *Hindsight*, 1996
'Panter Memorial', *Hindsight*, 1997
'Kojonup Place of Healing', *Encounter*, 2003
'Noonkanbah 25 years on', *Hindsight*, 2005
'Outstations', *Hindsight*, 2006
'Noongar Voices of the Central Eastern Wheatbelt', *Awaye!*, 2010, produced by Community Arts Network (CAN)
'Land, Culture, Religion', *Encounter*, 2010
The Coolbaroo Club Remembered, 2011, produced by CAN
'The Mysteries are still there', *Encounter*, 2012
'The Spirit of Yagan', *Awaye!*, 2014, produced by CAN

Unpublished interviews by the authors
Peter Bindon, 18 April 2019
Hon Fred Chaney, 25 August 2018
Christine Choo, 7 May 2019
Denise Cook, 20 May 2019
Lynnette Coomer, 29 May 2019
Vernice Gillies, 18 November 2018
John Kinder, 5 December 2018
Lynette Knapp, 17 November 2018
Craig McVee, 7 June 2019
Margaret Robertson, 31 May 2019
Kim Scott, 21 June 2018
Robert Sexton, 31 May 2019
Tiffany Shellam, 16 August 2018
Robert Tonkinson, 19 March 2019
Iszaac Webb, 6 June 2019

PHOTOGRAPHIC CREDITS

All photographs by Bill Bunbury except for:

Chapter 1

p. 2   *Looking out from Mount Clarence*, Bob Symons, ACE Camera Club, Albany

p. 5   *Waterway created by the Wagyl*, Bob Symons, ACE Camera Club, Albany

p. 14   *Michaelmas Island*, Bob Symons, ACE Camera Club, Albany

p. 34   *Albany, Land and Sea*, Bob Symons, ACE Camera Club Albany

Chapter 2

p. 79   *Cattle Chosen Bussell Homestead* – Bill Bunbury photograph of drawing by Stan Dilkes

Chapter 4

p. 137   *Menang country (Albany)* Bob Symons, ACE Camera Club Albany

p. 146   *Albany convict gaol, (now museum)* Bob Symons, ACE Camera Club, Albany

p. 156   *Remembering Kukeranup*, Ravensthorpe Historical Society.

p. 184   *Bunuba Elder, Jimmy Andrews at the Lillimooloora station ruins*, Emily Jane Smith, ABC Kimberley.

Chapter 5

p. 190   *Yirrkala petitions* – Will Stubbs, reproduced by courtesy Speaker of the House of Representatives, Commonwealth Parliament of Australia

p. 205   *Beagle Bay Church Interior* Amanda McInerney *Broome and the Kimberley* Kimberley Web Design

PHOTOGRAPH CREDITS

p. 210 *White Australia Protection Badge* George Serras, National Museum of Australia.

p. 228 *Broome today. Home of the so-called Misfits in the 1930s* - Amanda McInerney *Broome and the Kimberley* Kimberley Web Design.

Chapter 6

p. 273 *Skull Springs* Jill Harrison
http://www.lifeimagesbyjill.blogspot.com.au

p. 286 *Jarlmadangah outstation* Ben Collins, ABC Kimberley

p. 292 *Pea Hill* Grant Boxer

p. 296 *Kojonup Spring,* Kojonup Historical Precinct, Shire of Kojonup

p. 299 *Craig McVee's map,* Wendy Thorn with permission from Craig McVee

p. 303 *Zac Webb's Wadandi map* Rachelle Cousins, Undalup Association, Busselton

Cover insert map: Courtesy State Records Office: Cons4567 110/6

INDEX

Abbott, Tony 284
ABC (Australian Broadcasting Corporation) vii, ix, 155, 184, 286, 347, 364
Aboriginal Heritage Act 1972 293–4
Aboriginal Land Fund 288
Aboriginal Legal Service 251
Aborigines Act 1897 192, 199
Aborigines Act 1905 199, 204–238, 272
   see also Native Administration Act 1936
Aborigines Act Amendment Act 1936, see Native Administration Act 1936
Aborigines Department 195, 200–1, 204, 211, 227, 235
   see also Native Affairs/Welfare Department
Aborigines Protection Act 1886 177, 192, 199–200
Aborigines Protection Board 191–2
Aborigines Protection Society (UK) 100, 162, 191
Aboriginal reserves 229–32, 238–9, 282–4, 298
agriculture
   Aboriginal 25, 33, 48, 121–2
   European viii, 27–8, 47–8, 75–7, 81, 103–4, 120–2, 127–33, 139–40, 221–2, 295
   see also farming skills; fire-stick farming; land title; pastoralism
Albany 1–4, 8–34, 37–8, 42, 50, 89, 109, 116–20, 137, 140, 146–50, 158, 220, 239, 296, 305–6
   Michaelmas Island 14–15

Strawberry Hill 28–30
   see also Menang people and country
alcohol 116, 246–7, 254, 268, 281–3, 289
Allen, Richard 176
Altman, Jon 284–7
Amax 289–93
Americans 15, 86, 112, 116–17, 166, 244
   see also Amax
animals
   introduced 39, 42, 46–48, 55, 58, 68, 72, 77, 82–3, 138, 149–52, 159, 165, 168, 175–6, 179–81, 183, 295, 305
   native 6, 31–32, 46, 48, 55, 58–59, 68, 72–75, 81–2, 87, 116, 179, 260, 287, 291
Annesfield 118–20
Armstrong, Francis 36, 53, 62–65, 72, 102–03
Arnhem Land 93, 189
artefacts, Aboriginal 12, 21, 54, 185, 298–300
Ashworth, Ralph 147–9
Asians 5, 171, 200, 206, 209, 229–30
assimilation policy 103, 143–5, 218, 225–7, 243–9, 252–3, 284
Augusta (Talanup) 73–89
Australian armed forces 215, 246–7, 251–2, 271–2
Aveling, Marian 78–80
Avon Valley 71, 140, 146

Balgo (Wirrimanu) 267–9
Bannister, John 291–3
Bannister, Thomas 25

INDEX

Bangalow station 275
Bardi people 173
Barker, Collet 1–5, 16–28, 30, 33, 149
Barker, Mary Theresa Torres 172–3
Barladong people xi, 105–07, 120–22, 135, 234
   see also Hayden, Tom
Bassett, Alice, see Nannup, Alice
Bateman Survey of Native Affairs 250–1, 261
Bates, Daisy 106, 211
Battle of Perth 39–40, 65
Battle of Pinjarra, see Pinjarra: massacre
Baudin, Nicolas 9–10
Beagle Bay 175, 186, 205–7
Beeliar country 46, 52
   see also Midgegooroo; Yagan
belief systems, Aboriginal viii, 3–4, 20–23, 42–44, 60, 91–96, 105–09, 112, 122–6, 144, 150, 264–71, 277–8, 295, 306
Bell, Albany 262
Bell, Ashley 140
Benedictines 124–33, 137, 146, 185–6
Benillo 48
Bennett, Mary 226–7
Bilney, Roger 300–2
Bin Amat, Rosa 207
Bin Bin, Dooley 276
Bindjareb people 35, 65–70, 83, 219
   see also McHenry, Winnie; Pinjarra: massacre
Bindjareb Pinjarra 35
Bindon, Peter 267–71, 288–294, 303
birds 6, 57, 74, 94–95, 251, 302
'blackbirding', see pearling
Blackwood River 73, 76, 86
Blechynden, Mrs 148
Bodney, Corrie 256, 259
Bodney, Louise, see Walsh, Louise
Bodney, W. 225
Bolton, Geoffrey 111, 179–80, 227
boomerangs 94–95, 193
Bray, F. I. 247
Brennan, Jim 246
British
   Empire 14, 97–98, 100–02, 113, 119, 191, 194, 229
   explorers 2, 5–15, 24–25, 37, 42–44, 51, 54, 119, 128, 136–7, 158, 166–9, 296–7, 334n63

   government 62, 101, 166, 191
   law 14–15, 18, 33, 48, 64, 96–102, 136–9, 190, 208, 248
   'superiority' 27–30, 38–39, 49, 61, 79, 84, 86, 91, 94–95, 101–02, 112–13, 143, 164–5, 175, 187–8, 195, 249, 263–5, 306
   see also Colonial Office; colonial secretary
British Commonwealth League 226
Brockman, George Julius 169, 175
Broome 105, 171–3, 201, 206–7, 228–9, 274
Broome, Lady 162
Broome, Sir Frederick Napier 191
Bropho, Bella 63–64
Bropho, Robert 244, 249, 256–7
Broughton, Gordon 175–6
Brown, Hazel 154–5
Buchanan family 176–7
Bulletin, The 210
Bunbury 87–88, 111, 140, 144, 187, 193, 219–20, 259
Bunbury, H. W. 70–72
Bunuba country and people 181–85
burning regimes, see fire-stick farming
bush, descriptions of 24–25, 105, 240
bush camps 244, 255–62
   Claremont 244–5, 255
   Daglish 255–7
   Eden Hill 259
   Fremantle 255, 261
   Jolimont 255, 258
   Shenton Park 255–7, 261
   Success Hill 67–68, 259–60
bush medicine 267–8
Bussell family 73, 76–85, 193, 196–8
Bussell, John Garrett 75–85, 195
Busselton (Undalup) xi–xii, 74, 82–4

Camfield, Anne and Henry 114–20
Canning River 50, 58, 60, 77
Cape Leeuwin 73
Capel River (Mollakup) 85–7
Carley, David 160–1, 173, 191
Carnac Island 50
Carnarvon 147, 160–3
Carrolup Native Settlement 146, 154–5, 212–13, 299
Carter, Bevan and Jennie 36, 38, 140, 217
centenary celebrations 219–20
Chadd, Lance 54

INDEX

Chaney, Fred 284, 305–8
Chapman family 83
chief protector of Aborigines 187–8, 192–6, 200–3, 210–15, 225–7, 230, 235, 279
   see also Gale, Charles; Neville, A. O.; Prinsep, Henry
Choo, Christine 185–7, 206–8, 263
church and state relationship 97, 164, 187, 263
Church Missionary Society 98–100
churches 92
   Anglican 78, 95–7, 100, 107, 111–15, 118–20, 160–4, 215
   Apostolic (Pentecostal) 264, 271
   Catholic 98, 102, 106, 124–25, 186, 204–6, 268
   Protestant 98, 102, 107–09, 117–18, 124, 186, 262, 267
   Wesleyan (Methodist) 102–15, 123, 133–4
   see also Benedictines; Evangelism; missions; Pallottines
citizenship rights 229, 245–7, 251, 295
Clark, William Nairn 98
   see also Swan River Guardian
Clarke, Helena 246, 251–3
   see also Coolbaroo Club and League
Clement, Cathie 158, 167, 233
clothing 11, 21, 29, 61, 103, 120, 133, 135, 157, 171, 195, 214, 220, 229, 257, 272, 277–8
Cocanarup, see Kukenarup massacre
Colbung, Ken 215–16, 221, 242
Collard, Dean 237
Collard, Fred 240
Collard, Len 6–7, 59–60, 81–2, 85–86, 139–42, 153
Collie, Alexander 26–29
Collier, Philip 224–5
Colonial Office (UK) 62, 65–66, 69–70, 138, 190–1
colonial secretary (UK) 30, 42, 85, 98
commissioners, native affairs/welfare 230–1
   see also Bray, F. I.; McLarty, Bruce; Middleton, Stanley
Commonwealth Conciliation and Arbitration Commission 279–81
   see also Equal Wage Case
Commonwealth conferences 225, 248
Communist Party 275

Community Arts Network vii, ix, xi
Constitution Act 1889 192
   see also *Aborigines Act 1897*
convicts 13, 26, 98, 110, 133, 142, 146, 149, 160, 177
Cook, Denise 255–61
   see also bush camps
Coolbaroo Club and League 246, 251–75
Coolbul, George 193
Coomer, Lynnette 204, 253, 258–63
Coppin, Peter 272
Coppin, Sam 275
Corunna, Albert, and family 44, 53, 217
Court, Charles 289, 293

Daglish, Henry 200
Dale, Ensign Robert 40, 51, 54
Daliak 148
Dampier, William 7–8
Dan, Jacky 276
Darwin (NT) 248, 274
Darwin, Charles 119
Darwinism 125, 164–5, 221
Davies, Lloyd 274–5
Davis, Jack, and family 189, 208, 212–221, 250
Davis, John Okey 60–61
Dawson, Elijah 85
Derbarl Yerrigan Health Service 47, 251
Derby 166, 178–9, 182, 207, 232
Dinah, George 'Jerong' 223
Dineen, Dennis 14–15
disease 26–27, 118, 127–29, 132, 147, 154–6, 165, 187, 267–8
   measles 132, 147–8
   venereal 117, 147, 187, 196, 211, 229
displacement 31, 99, 120, 134, 136–8, 145–7, 154, 177, 197, 232–3, 280–6
Dodds, Jane 55–56, 68
Dodson, Patrick 105–06, 276, 281–8
Domjum 52
Dreaming, the, and Creation 3–4, 23–24, 126, 267, 291–3, 308
   see also belief systems, Aboriginal; Wagyl
Drysdale Mission 185
Dumont D'Urville, Jules 11
Dunn family 154
Dunstan, Minnie, and family 211–12
Durack, Mary 178
Dutch East India Company 5

INDEX

education of Aboriginal children 102–03, 109–10, 114–20, 131–2, 196–8, 201, 203–8, 212–15, 224, 230, 234–7, 249–50, 258, 262, 299
see also Moore River Native Settlement; Smithies, John
Egan, William or Thomas 146
Ellemarra 184–5
Ellensbrook 196–8
employment, Aboriginal 30–31, 79–80, 119, 130–33, 139–44, 149–51, 158–60, 177, 181, 194–7, 200–1, 218–19, 237–42, 246, 256, 271–3, 279, 283
see also pastoral 'pay'; slavery
Enlightenment, Age of 9, 15–16, 97
equal pay 218, 246, 255, 279–84, 288
Equal Wage Case 279–84, 288
see also pastoral 'pay'
eugenics 225–6
Evangelism 95–102, 110–18, 134, 185, 208
Exeter Hall Movement 97, 101
explorers and guides, Aboriginal 9, 139–42, 187
explorers, European 5–13, 140–42, 174–5
see also British: explorers

farmers 222–41, 256, 295–302, 306
farming skills 196–7, 212, 215
see also New Norcia mission
fences 31–32, 44–45, 58, 62, 77, 138–9, 240, 298, 302–3
fire-stick farming 24, 31–32, 46, 76, 81–2, 142–3, 180, 285–7, 306
fish traps 10, 57, 76
Flinders Bay, Augusta 73–74
Flinders, Matthew 9
Flying Foam massacre 161
Fogarty family 221
food 19, 26, 33, 197, 256–7, 271–2, 277–80, 287
competition for and shortages 55–57, 80–82, 112, 115–17, 159, 177, 195, 275, 285–6
traditional Aboriginal foods 9, 21, 33, 55–57, 72–75, 99, 136–8, 240
see also agriculture; rations
Forrest, Alexander 140–1, 159, 166, 174–5
Forrest, John 140–1, 187, 191–4, 198–9, 204
Forrest River Mission 214

Foundation Day 110
Fraser, Delys 211–12
Fremantle 50, 52, 169–70, 255, 261
Fremantle, Captain 37
friendship 1, 11, 16, 19–21, 27–28, 67, 148–50, 166, 237–8, 241–2, 246–7, 251, 305
fringe dwellers, see bush camps

Gale, Charles 210–11
Garden Island 38, 64
Gascoyne region 157–64, 171–2, 177, 211
Shark Bay 251
Gayware 84–86
Geographe Bay 10, 76
Geraldton 161
Gillies, Vernice 1, 10, 31–33, 94, 105, 137–9, 147, 306
Giustiniani, Louis 97–101, 114
Glenelg, Lord 98–101
see also colonial secretary
Gliddon, Derryce 221, 234
gold rush 177, 194–5
Goldfields Pipeline 192
Gordon Downs station 176, 282
government
colonial 159, 172, 191–2
federal 189, 245, 248–9, 276, 282–8
WA 191–2, 248–51, 284, 289–94, 300
see also British: government; Parliament; Swan River Colony
Great Depression 218–19, 244, 250
Great Southern region 148, 212, 238–41, 295
Boyerine 148
Jerramungup 150–3
Katanning 212, 254
Kendenup 150
Mount Barker 24, 153
Muradup 295
Stirling Ranges 31–32
see also Albany; Kojonup
Green, Neville 16–17, 20, 26, 161–2, 167–8, 174
Green, Ribgna 282–3
Grey, George 42, 44, 119, 128, 136–7, 166–9
Gribble, Ernest 162–4
Gribble, John 160–5, 173, 177, 191
Guildford 55–56, 103, 120
Gyallipert 50–51

370

INDEX

Hackett, Winthrop 163
Haebich, Anna 164–5, 195–6, 209, 221–7, 244, 254
Hale, Matthew 115, 120
Hall family 47
Hamersley, Judy 259–60
Hammond, Jesse 45, 67, 106, 135–6, 142, 145–9, 156–7
Hanover Bay 158
Harcus, Geoff 251, 255
Harper, Charles 163
Harris, William, and family 224–5
Hasluck, Paul 147–8, 227–8, 245–52
Hassell, Ethel (nee Clifton) 106, 150–3
Hawke, Steve 291–4
Hayden, Tom 105–06, 135, 231, 234, 240
Heath, Eileen 215
Henry, Wyvon 231–2
Hester, Thomas 58
Hewett, Dorothy 274–5
Hillman, Alfred 296–7
Hobbs, Barbara 296–7, 301
Hoffman, Beryl 256
Host, John 23, 153–4
human rights 247, 276
  see also citizenship rights
Human Rights and Equal Opportunity Commission 232
Humphries, Cliff 237
Hutt, John 101–01, 109–10

Immigration Restriction Act 1901 (Cwth) 209
  see also White Australia policy
imprisonment 64, 98–99, 116, 176, 182–4, 202–4, 216, 225, 273–6, 297, 309
  see also neck-chaining; police; Rottnest Island
Inquirer, The 116, 161, 164
Irwin, Frederick 33, 39–40, 51–52, 62

Jabirrjabirr people 173
Jacobs, Edward 225
Jacobs, Pat 212–13, 217–18
James, Walter 199
Jandamarra 181–5
Jarlmadangah outstation 283–7
Jebb, Mary Anne 211, 280–1
Jigalong Mission 263–7
Johns, Rex 279
Jones, Peter 293–4

Kalgoorlie 192
Karajarri people 168–71
Keates, James and William 53
Kelso, Geoff 35
Kerr, John 279
Kickett, Arthur 225
Kickett, Gladys 235–6
Kickett, John 235–6
Kimberley 105, 131, 157, 166, 171–80, 187, 228, 233, 276–7, 281–91
  East 175–7
  Fitzroy Crossing 280–1, 288–9
  Fitzroy River 174–5, 179, 291–2
  Halls Creek 175, 178–9, 280–2
  Kalumburu 208, 263
  Kununurra 207
  La Grange 168–70, 207
  Ringer Soak (Yaruman) 282–3
  Roebuck Bay 171
  Tunnel Creek 185
  Turkey Creek (Warmun) 233
  West 159, 174, 180, 183
  Wyndham 178, 187, 202, 207
  see also Noonkanbah
Kimberley Land Council 282, 285
Kinder, John 7–8, 13–14, 125–27, 209
King Edward Memorial Hospital 217
King, George 114–15
King George Sound, *see* Albany
King, Phillip Parker 12, 15, 158, 328n63
King, Tommy 179
Knapp, Lynette 4, 31, 43, 60, 106, 117, 146, 154, 233, 239
Kojonup 24, 238, 295–303
  Kodja Place 298–302
Kojonup Aboriginal Corporation 295
Korean War 215–16
Kukatja people and language 267–70
Kukenarup massacre 154–6

Lamarer, William William 179
land
  access 63–64, 137, 140
  clearing 44, 75–76, 105, 117, 157, 222–3, 237–40, 295, 300–1
  conceptions of 23–24, 36–38, 42, 48, 53, 59–64, 95–96, 104–06, 113, 121, 139, 143–4, 240, 263–7, 277–82, 290–5, 302–3, 306–9
  return to Aboriginal people 282–88, 297

371

INDEX

title 147, 222–4, 259–61
  see also agriculture; fences; pastoral: encroachment on Aboriginal land
Land Act 1898 222
Landcare 297
Landor, E. W. 138–9
Lands Department 223–24
landscape 31, 76–77, 89, 170, 218, 270–71, 291, 300, 307–09
language use 12–16, 36, 41, 46–50, 76, 88, 92, 101, 104, 109, 134, 135, 140–2, 145–7, 153, 169, 189–90, 207, 234–5, 251, 262–8, 274, 290, 296, 306–7
  Noongar/English vocabularies 16, 49, 56
Larsen, Henry and Inez 295–6
Latham, Charles 227
Layman, George 79, 84–9
Lennard River station 181
Leonora 246
Leopold Downs station 186
Leyland, Clara 257
Lillimooloora station 184–5
Limestone station 276
lock hospitals 211
Lockyer, Edmund 5, 11, 13–18
Lukin, William 181–2
Lyon, Robert Menli 48–50, 59, 62–63, 91–93, 96–98

Mabo decision 267
McEwen, John 245
McGrath, Ann 277–8
McGuinness, Jack 279
McHenry, Winnie 67–68, 235–6
McKenna, Clancy 276
McLarty, Bruce 220–1, 232
McLeod, Don 272–6
McPhee, Ivan 288–90, 294
McVee, Craig 295–303
Maitland Brown 169
Mandurah 47, 153
Manyat 50–51
maps viii, 1–2, 9, 265–7, 302–3
Martu people 264–6
Melbourne 24, 161, 267
Menang people and country 1–4, 8–34, 43, 50–52, 60, 94, 105–06, 116–17, 137–9, 146–9, 154, 238–9, 306
Michael, Albert and Patsy 297, 301
Micki 185
  see also Jandamarra

Middleton, Stanley 231, 250–3, 261
Midgegooroo 46–53
Migeo/Miago/Migo 3, 47
Millett, Janet 105–08, 120–24, 132–33
Milne, Robert, see Lyon, Robert Menli
mining 139, 189, 193, 272, 289–294
  see also gold rush
missionaries 95–134, 185–7, 204–8, 248, 259, 262–8
  see also Gribble, John
missions 97, 102–134, 164, 185–8, 203–8, 214, 224, 229, 233–5, 259–67
  see also Carrolup Native Settlement; Moore River Native Settlement
Mitchell, William 114–15
Mogumber, see Moore River Native Settlement
Mokare 1–3, 11, 16–28, 33, 116, 149
Molloy family 73
Molloy, John 83–88
Molloy, Georgiana 75
Mollydobin 47
Moola Bulla station 179–80
Moore, George Fletcher 33, 41–42, 46–57, 62–63, 92–94
Moore River Native Settlement (Mogumber) 212–18, 225, 229–33, 250
Morley, John 33
Morning Star 275
Morrison, Hugh 179
Morrison, William 225
Moseley Royal Commission 226–30
Mount Anderson station 285
Mount Clarence (Corndarup) 1–2
Mount Edgar station 276
Mount Manypeaks 22
Mount Melville (Kardarup) 1, 28, 239
Mount Singleton (Ninghan, Kundawa) 140–1
multiculturalism 209, 244
Murchison region 160–1
Murray, George 61
Murray, Peter 281
Murray Districts Aboriginal Association 68
Murray River 35–36, 57, 66, 77, 83, 219
Murray River (SA) 26

Nakinah 20–21, 27
Nangkiriny, John Dudu 168
Nannup, Alice 213–14
Napier Ranges 181–3

INDEX

Napoleonic wars 17, 28, 35–37
'native', use of term 12–14, 266
Native Administration Act 1936 211, 221, 230, 262
Native Affairs/Welfare Department 204, 212, 218–19, 230–32, 235–36, 244, 252–53, 258, 261
  see also Aborigines Department
Native Police 48
  see also police: native assistants
Native Welfare Council of WA 262
Natives (Citizenship Rights) Act 1944 247
neck-chaining 160–1, 164–5, 178–80, 184, 199, 202
Neville, A. O. 211–231, 235–6, 244
New Holland 5–9, 13
New Norcia mission 124–33, 135, 146, 185–6, 212, 222
Nightingale, Florence 119, 128–9
Nind, Isaac Scott 16, 21
Nisbett, Hugh 65–66
Noongar people and country 3, 6–7, 10, 23, 36–43, 48, 62–63, 97, 106–7, 122–3, 126–7, 133, 135, 138–42, 145–6, 153–5, 213–15, 231, 235–42, 253, 259–61, 295–302, 306
  see also Barladong; Bindjareb; Menang; Wadandi; Whadjuk
Noonkanbah 288–294
Noonuccal, Oodgeroo 243–4
Norris, Ray 93
Northern Territory 176, 248, 285

oil and gas exploration 289–294
outstations 283–9
  see also Noonkanbah

painting the body 16, 41, 271
Pallottines 205–8, 267–71
Panter, Frederick 168–70
Panter memorial 169–71
Papua, *see* Middleton, Stanley
Parliament
  federal 141
  WA 38, 140–1, 159, 187, 199–200, 227
Parry, Henry 162
pastoral
  encroachment on Aboriginal land 28–29, 32, 36–38, 47, 55–58, 72–73, 77, 116, 138, 145–6, 157, 165–7, 174–7, 185, 221–2, 277–8, 282, 285

industry 24–25, 28, 141–2, 150, 157–9, 180–1, 230, 237
leases 116, 159, 175–6, 290
'pay' 199, 203, 271–82
stations 150, 159, 176, 180, 184–5, 207, 227, 275–6, 282–7, 290
  see also outstations
pastoralists 156, 159, 162–3, 171, 175–86, 191–2, 199–203, 206, 213–14, 277–81
  see also Buchanan family; Forrest, Alexander; Forrest, John
Pea Hill (Unpampurru) 291–4
pearling 159, 171–4, 201, 206–7, 229
Pedersen, Howard 158–9, 165–6, 181–4
Peel, Thomas 65–68
Peile, Anthony Rex 267–71
Perenjori (Mid-West) 234, 241
Perez, Eugene 263
Perris, Jackie 179–80
Perth 6, 54–55, 67, 73, 104, 114–16, 120, 133, 161–3, 175, 193, 200, 212, 217, 224–6, 244, 251, 254–5
  curfew 251, 254–6
  see also Battle of Perth; bush camps; Fremantle; Swan River Colony; Wanneroo district
Perth Gazette 50–53, 65, 72, 86, 98–99, 140
Pettigrew, Thomas 54
Phillips, Alby and Yvonne 234
Phillips, Derryce, *see* Gliddon, Derryce
Phillips, Harry 221
Phillips, Neil 241–2
phrenology 54
Pigeon, *see* Jandamarra
Pigram, Bart 173–4
Pilbara 157, 161, 272–6
  Cossack 160
  Nickol Bay 161
  Roebourne 171
  Skull Springs, Nullagine 273–4
  see also Port Hedland
Pilbara strike 272–6
Pinjarra 70, 254
  massacre 35, 65–70, 83, 98, 174, 219
Poland, George 251
Poland, Jack 251
police 48, 65, 84, 159–60, 175–85, 200–2, 218, 231–2, 246, 253–6, 272–3, 276, 280–1, 289
  native assistants 178, 183–5
Ponan, Charles 223–4

373

INDEX

Pope Gregory XVI 125
population
    Aboriginal 46, 132, 147, 156–7, 187, 190, 228
    of mixed parentage 117, 146, 154–6, 188, 195–6, 203, 206–13, 220–1, 228–33, 249–51, 262
    see also Aborigines Act 1905; removal of Aboriginal children; settlers
Port Hedland 246, 272, 275–6
Port Jackson (Sydney) 9, 12–13, 24
Port Phillip (Melbourne) 24
Poulton, Jackson 176
press, Perth 39–41, 50–53, 65, 72, 86, 98–100, 116, 140, 147, 161–4, 180, 224, 227–9, 275
Prinsep, Henry 187–8, 193–203, 210–11
property 36, 63, 77, 101, 123, 130–3, 175, 290
    held in common 59
    private 48, 57–59, 64, 72, 101, 259
    see also land: conceptions of
'protectors' of Aborigines 27, 100, 177, 199
    see also chief protector of Aborigines
protocols, Aboriginal visiting 37, 44, 126, 137, 168–9

Queensland 164, 199, 226

racism 125, 130, 141, 162–5, 175–6, 196, 199, 209–10, 221–6, 237–8, 241, 246, 253–5
    see also Aborigines Act 1905; British: 'superiority'; White Australia policy
rations 79, 82, 177, 184, 218, 244, 275–6
Ravensthorpe 154–6
    see also Kukenarup massacre
reconciliation 155, 171, 187, 299–302, 305
referendum (1967) 190, 255, 309
removal of Aboriginal children 114, 118–19, 189, 195–8, 204–14, 230–3, 253, 299–300, 309
reserves, *see* Aboriginal reserves
resistance, Aboriginal 96, 114, 121, 143, 157, 165, 174
    see also Battle of Perth; Jandamarra; Yagan
Richardson, Bill 183–5
Riley, Robert 233, 249
Robertson, Margaret 300
Roe, Joe 171
Roe, John Septimus 66

Roebuck Bay Pastoral Company 168–9, 174
Roelands Native Mission Farm 259–63
Roth Commission 199–207
Rottnest Island (Wadjemup) 6, 64, 77, 85, 114, 161, 165–6

sacred sites 167–8, 278, 294
    see also belief systems, Aboriginal
Salvado, Rosendo 124–32, 196, 222
Sanders family 144–5
'savages', use of term 7–9, 13
Scates, Bruce 168–9
Scott, Kim 23, 154–6
sealers 9, 14–15, 116–17, 150, 156
segregation 198–9, 211–12, 225, 248
self-determination 259, 279, 284, 309
serpent, *see* Wagyl
Serra, Joseph Benedict 124–6
settlers
    character of 61, 133
    gender imbalance of 146, 157
    land aspirations of 37–38, 58, 77–80, 98–100, 111
    numbers of 39
Sexton, Robert 24–25, 239, 295–7, 306–7
Shannon, Steve 290
shearing 127, 180–1, 237–41, 274–5
sheep, *see* animals: introduced; pastoral: industry; shearing; wool price
Shellam, Tiffany 3–4, 9, 12–24, 51, 129, 328n63
ships
    Menang interpretation of 1–4
    sightings of 37, 43–45, 67, 74
Sholl, Robert 171
Single Noongar Claim 153
slavery 97–98, 159–74, 181, 201, 226, 232
Slavery Abolition Act 1833 (UK) 97
Smith, Joan and Charlie 171
Smith, Ted 295
Smithies, John 103–13, 123, 133–4
social support services 218–19, 244, 279
South Africa 216
South America 38
South Australia 26, 115
Southern Ocean 11, 73
South West Aboriginal Land and Sea Council 153
Spain 131
    see also Benedictines; Salvado, Rosendo

INDEX

spears 10, 12, 21–22, 69, 227
spearing
    retaliatory 15, 18, 48
    stock 39, 46, 77, 159, 165, 177–9, 182–4, 201–2
    see also violence
Spencer, Richard, and family 28–30
Stannage, Tom 37–38, 45, 97
state housing 259
Stewart, James, John and Robert 47
Stirling, James 26–28, 35–42, 51, 61–73, 79, 83, 99–101, 140
Stokes, John Lort 3
Stolen Generations, see removal of Aboriginal children
stratification, social 61, 77–8, 100, 110, 119, 125, 133–4, 198, 237
    see also Aborigines Act 1905
Sturt Creek station 176
Sunday Times, The 224
swamps 4–5, 41, 55, 73, 244–5, 260
Swan River (Derbarl Yerrigan) 6, 37–41, 45–46, 49, 52, 56, 73, 217, 296
Swan River Colony 18, 25–26, 33, 35–75, 91–101, 109–10, 115, 119–20, 130–31, 138–9, 219
    Armadale district 47
    Bull Creek 52
    Lake Monger (Galup) 50–51
    mail service 140
    Mount Eliza (Kings Park) 39, 43, 102–03
Swan River Guardian 98–100
Swan Valley 142
Sydney 9, 12–13, 24–26, 175

Taragon 20–21
Tasmanians, original 10, 117
    see also sealers
Taylor, Ben 253
terra nullius 14, 190
Thangoo station 207
Thomas, Basil 282
Thomson, Phil 45–46
Thorn, Geoff 302
Tonkinson, Robert 264–6
Torres, Fulgentius 131–32
Toussaint, Sandy 266–7
trade unions 277–9
trading encounters 4, 12, 21–22, 173
Trappist monks 186

treaty proposal 62–65, 101
Turner family 73

Uluru Statement from the Heart 308–9
United Aborigines Mission 262
United Nations 247

Vancouver, George 2, 8–9
Vasse district 74, 76–89, 112
Velvick, John and Tom 52
Victoria (state) 160
violence 284
    between settlers and locals 14–15, 18, 26, 48–52, 65–68, 71–72, 81, 99–101, 154–61, 164, 170–6, 185
    British view of Indigenous 15–19, 29–30, 33, 48, 96
    rape 117, 154–9, 232
    see also Battle of Perth; Flying Foam massacre; Jandamarra; Kukenarup massacre; Layman, George; Pinjarra: massacre
Vlamingh, Captain William de 6

Wadandi people and country 74–89, 295–303
    see also Gayware; Webb, Iszaac
Wadjemup, see Rottnest Island
Wagyl 4–5
Wakefield, Joseph 5, 18
Walker, Kath, see Noonuccal, Oodgeroo
Walsh, Louise 257
Walter, George 205–6
Wanneroo district 103–04, 115
Waste Lands Act 1846 (UK) 138
water
    access to 33, 44, 58, 62, 76, 79, 133, 139, 142, 167–70, 174–80, 238, 256, 259–60, 269, 287, 296–7
    words for 12
waterholes 4, 44, 81, 167, 223, 269, 287
waterways 4–5, 23, 302–3
Watson, Anthony 283–7
Watson, John 283–6
Webb, Iszaac (Zac) 3, 31, 44, 77, 84–5, 108–09, 122, 157, 295, 302–3, 307
Weld, Frederick Aloysius 130–1
Wesleyan missions, see Hale, Matthew; Smithies, John
West Australian, The 147, 163, 180, 227–8
Western Australian Missionary Society 97

375

INDEX

Western Australian Museum 288, 291–4
Western Mail 39–41
Westralian Aborigine, The 255
Whadjuk people 50–51, 59, 104
   see also Benillo; Bropho family; Colbung, Ken; Collard family; Corunna, Albert; Domjum; Midgegooroo; Migeo; Mollydobin; Wilkes family; Winmar family; Yagan; Yellalonga
whalers 9, 87, 112, 116–17, 150, 156
Wheatbelt 105, 222, 238, 241
   Arthur River 223
   Brookton 231–2
   Kellerberrin 234–7
   Mukinbudin 217
   Narrogin 142–3, 254
   Northam 142–3, 221, 231
   Quairading 225, 234–6
   Toodyay 142, 222–5
   Victoria Plains 156
   Wandering district 59
   see also Barladong people; Perenjori (Mid-West)
White Australia policy 206–10, 230, 277–9
White, Noel and Lily 213
Whitlam, Gough 209
Wilkes, Gary 57, 134
Wilkes, Nigel 59
Wilkes, Peter 46, 59
Wilkes, Ted 46–48, 61, 72–73
Wills people (Aboriginal group) 18–22, 30

Wilson, Thomas Braidwood 24
Windich, Tommy 143
Windjana Gorge 185, 188
Winmar, Basil 234–5, 240
Winmar, Dorothy 43
Winmar, Harry 235
Winmar-Smith, Charlotte 235, 238–9
Wirrimanu community 267
Wittenoom, John 97
Wollaston, John 95–97, 110–19
Wonnerup 79, 84–6
wool price 180–1
Woorunmurra, Banjo 182–84
Wootten, Hal 279–81
World War One 247
World War Two 245–8, 251, 271–75

Yagan 46–47, 50–55, 185
Yamaji people and language 140, 147, 234, 251
Yappo, Bella 232
Yarloop 215
Yarrabah Mission (Qld) 164
Yarran, Ivan 241
Yawuru country and people 105, 172–3
Yellalonga 51
Yirrkala petitions 189–90
Yolngu people 93, 189–90
York (Barladong) 72, 98–99, 104–05, 108, 113, 120–23, 138, 142, 147–48, 225, 254
Young, Penny 300
Yungngora community 288–94

Printed in Australia
AUHW011122021222
372031AU00012B/12